Compassionate Child-Rearing

An In-Depth Approach to Optimal Parenting

Compassionate Child-Rearing

An In-Depth Approach to Optimal Parenting

Robert W. Firestone, Ph.D.

The Glendon Association
Los Angeles, California

Foreword by
R. D. Laing

 INSIGHT BOOKS

Plenum Press • New York and London

Library of Congress Cataloging-in-Publication Data

Firestone, Robert.
    Compassionate child-rearing : an in-depth approach to optimal
  parenting / Robert W. Firestone ; foreword by R.D. Laing.
        p.   cm.
    Includes bibliographical references.
    ISBN 0-306-43356-7
    1. Child rearing. 2. Family psychotherapy. 3. Parent and child.
  4. Parents--Psychology. 5. Parenting--Psychological aspects.
  I. Title.
    [DNLM: 1. Child Rearing. 2. Family Therapy. 3. Parent-Child
  Relations. 4. Parents--psychology.   WS 105.5.F2 F523c]
  HQ769.F43 1990
  649'.1--dc20
  DNLM/DLC
  for Library of Congress   89-26835
                                                                 CIP

HQ
769
. F43
1990

copy 1

© 1990 Plenum Press, New York
A Division of Plenum Publishing Corporation
233 Spring Street, New York, N.Y. 10013

An Insight Book

Printed in the United States of America

A Tribute to R. D. Laing

I met R. D. Laing face to face for the first time this summer, a chance meeting in Austria; perhaps it was magic. Before that we were familiar only through our writings and viewing each other as we appeared in documentary films. I found a friend, the hours passed quickly, and I sailed on.

Later I received a call: "I read your book, it is a strong book, an important book, but it needs some work on literary style. I fear that without these stylistic changes it will fall on even more deaf ears."

My response, "Join me for a sail. Come to Portofino or Nice and we'll talk."

He agreed and we worked on the book straight through many days and nights. There was a sense of urgency in the work. We shared ideas of all varieties, and came to know and love each other. When he first arrived I noted his frailty and ill health, yet days of sun, and the companionship of other friends and loved ones, seemed to help. A light came back into his eyes. He was truly happy at sea. He swam, he socialized, he embraced his children, and he made new friends. In St. Tropez, six days after coming aboard, he died suddenly. And I cried for the loss.

Let me tell you what I know of this man. He was a hurt man, angry in the best sense; strong and stubborn, with an uncanny brilliance. He cared deeply and passionately about people, human rights, and psychological justice. He was uncompromising in his honesty. Tortured by what he saw, there was not much that he didn't see. He was very pained by all that was phony, perverse, and cruel. He remained finely tuned to all that was contradictory and paradoxical, exhibiting a wonderful insight and humor about existential issues.

Lastly, he had enormous love and tender feelings for the plight of children. When commenting on Bettelheim's contribution to psychology at the Evolution of Psychotherapy Conference in Phoenix in 1985, tears filled his eyes as he suggested that Bettelheim deserved the Nobel Prize for his work with disturbed children.

Ronnie was a truly compassionate man. He brought his compassion to our work on this book and there are no words that can do justice to the gratitude I feel.

Robert W. Firestone

Foreword

Suffer the little children to come unto me. Unless you become as little children, you cannot enter the Kingdom of Heaven.

Do we believe it? This is not a plea for regression.

This is not a suggestion that we should spend time with our children, for their sakes.

It is, as I understand it, not a threat, but a warning. We can never be fully human unless we suffer, that is, unless we carry along with us, unless we "bear" the little child in ourselves, to come along with us, all the way with us.

Over one hundred years ago, a fellow Scotsman, Calvinist theologian and mathematician McLellan, came out with the extraordinary proposition that "it" all began with killing children, especially little girls. This had the unintended consequence of creating a scarcity of women, and that led to a phase of matriarchal communism. The balance tipped again to patriarchal possession of women, who became little more than cattle, used by men to breed more men. McLellan's student Robertson Smith, another Scotsman, took up the theme and wrote a book called "The Religion of the Semites," in which he envisaged infanticide, the killing of children, and the eating of children, as the dark totemic pole right at the dead center of the Mesopotamian origins of Western social organization.

Engels hated the book. The American anthropologist Morgan greatly admired it, and Sigmund Freud used it as his take-off point for "Totem and Taboo" wherein he imagined the band of brothers who forestall their father's eating them, by eating their fathers first.

It is not difficult now for us to see these nineteenth century historical anthropological mythologies as projections from the present to the past.

In this book, Firestone has no hesitation, on the basis of his thirty years of clinical experience with parents and children and "normal" adults, in characterizing a great deal of parental so-called "love," as parental hate and hunger. He documents here ways in which parents kill and eat their children, not physically, but psychologically. The living ghosts of these dead devoured children grow up to become *normal* adults and are now, in our generation, continuing to pass on this living death to their offspring. As he says, "unfortunately."

Unfortunately, his message is going to fall on many dulled and deadened ears and many blinded eyes will not be opened.

Firestone is not a preacher. He is a clinician through and through. But maybe he should take a chance on preaching what he practices. He calls it compassion. It is also called love.

A strange idea of love in this post-Freudian era, where Jacques Lacan has many backers when he quips that to love is to get what you don't need from someone who has not got it, etc.

They are wrong. It is a lie that you need love to love. Love needs us to resurrect it from the cave of our hearts.

This is a desperately sad book. But it is not despairing. It is based on case study after case study, which Firestone claims are "typical." Everyone would like to believe they are not and he is wrong. So would he. But the only way to prove he is wrong—not by argument, statistics, or counter-instances, as far as we are concerned—is to show he is.... Let us hope and pray that if he is not wrong yet, he will be proved to be by the next generation of loved and loving parents and children.

There is an issue that runs through this whole book. It is the shift from what Freud called the "Psychopathology of Everyday Life" to what Fromm called "The Pathology of Normalcy." The shift is seen in Freud. Up until "The Future of Illusion," Freud conceived a normal person intruded upon by psychopathological features, even in everyday life. These intrusions are seen as aberrations from a norm. Normal persons reach the promised land of opportunity if they can pass through the oral, anal, phallic, urinary stages to get to mature genitality. Those who don't, fall by the wayside—neurotics, psychopaths, perverts, and psychotics. However traces of these aberrations are acted out, even in the everyday life of "normal" people, they also carry psychopathological features which stem from the failure to work through completely these earlier stages of development. By the time he comes to "Future of Illusion," Freud sees the *norm* of society as itself an aberration, as itself an alienation from these possibilities of humanity which are most desirable, worthwhile, and, as the humanists like to say most: "human." And then in "Civilization and Its Discontents," he says that he doesn't even believe that ordinary, simple, human love between human beings is any longer possible.

This book crosses back and forth over that line between the psychopathology of what you might say is "everyday life" and in many places what is regarded as the norm of everyday life.

Who is Firestone talking to? To those whose idea of "maturity" has nothing to do with his. "Mature" individuals now have canceled dry eyes. They do not need to avoid eye contact with infants. They don't have need to defend their psychophobic psyches. They have nothing to defend. The war is over, you can disarm, the fortress is empty.... Yet ghosts still fight for their lives.

Diaphobia: The fear of being affected, of being directly influenced by the other.

Babies, and infants, before they have become normalized (dulled and deadened, etc.) have to be defended against. They are tiny foci who emit signals genetically programmed to elicit reciprocity from adults. The schizoid, narcissistic, autistic, paranoid adult who is diaphobic is terrified of spontaneous reciprocity. The baby's genetic programmed devices to evoke responses which are cultured out of the normal adult pose a paranoid danger therefore to the normal adult.

However, the normal adult may still be "soft." The smiles, eyes, the outstretched arms of the still healthy baby "demand." Their genetically programmed evocative qualities, programmed to elicit happy, effortless, complimentary, returning, reciprocal responses in the adult, are experienced by the normal schizoid, narcissistic, autistic, paranoid parent as assaultive, demanding, draining.

The normal adult has had his/her genetic own responses either completely cultured out, *or*, has learned at least to be suspicious, very, very ashamed, or guilty of them. He/she senses those of the baby as a threat, a danger, a manipulation, a demand, a pull, a tug, a *drain*, a trap. If the normalized adult gives into them, he/she will invite catastrophe. One has to resist them.

For example, it is necessary to avoid the eye contact. That eye "contact" is more than mere "contact." "Contact" is just the opening of the *vertical* barrier, the letting down of the barrier.

The one-way screen is a one-way mirror.

Me →|←— it, becomes me ⇌|→ another me.

Those outstretched arms open up a well of loneliness. The resistance to being drawn into the sphere of *horizontal* reciprocal influence out of the stable isolation across the *vertical* dividing line, the *invisible wall*, brings up *gushes* of "bad" feelings—physical feelings, horrible feelings, feelings one has never felt before. But in these feelings, mixed up in them at once physical smells new and stale of ghosts of awakened sensations in oneself, are evoked, by that dead *me*, that me that was me, I see in the baby.

I feel *responsible*. This sense of responsibility is a cruel ironical play on the sense of the word "responsibility," which means, literally, response-ability. My response-ability, my ability to respond, benignly, neither assaultively nor demandingly, has been cultured out of me.

I live, I am vulnerable. But to the normalized autistic paranoid "I," my softness is a dangerous softness. I am soft. I can weaken. But I am thrown into an awfully confused state. The greatest threat to the paranoia of normalcy is love. Both the threat of being loved, and the threat of loving.

I can't distinguish me from the baby. I see my feelings in his-her-your/its eyes. I tell myself that that baby is not-yet a you, a him, or a her, much less another me. It is just an it. But I "know" emotionally that is not true. This is another paranoid *danger*. I am in danger of seeing *it* as a him, or as a her. The baby is still appealing to me with the language of the heart, the language I have learned to forget, and to mistrust with all my "heart." I can go in different directions. I can hate the baby for making me feel bad. I can envy the baby for still being human. I can feel bad/guilty/for feeling bad. I can feel a terrible burden of responsibility because I feel incapable to respond spontaneously.

I feel I *ought* to respond, but I feel I ought *not* to respond. Two feelings demand, forbid, and cancel, each other. I forget. I feel nothing. I *feel*—nothing. Finally I do *not* feel—anything.

The less I feel response-ability, the more I feel this hateful, envious, piteous, guilty mix or mush of responsibility.

> Last night I dreamed a dreary dream.
> Beyond the Isle of Skye
> I saw a dead man win a fight
> and that dead man was I.

The sort of thing described here is not coming from the typical neurotic, not coming from typically psychotics, typically. It comes out of observations of and self-descriptions by typically normal people typically. Firestone is forced to the conclusion that not only are many "normal" patients bogged down in psychopathology destructive to themselves and to those closest to them, especially their children, he has to conclude that what is now "*normality*" is pathology.

Pathology has, or has almost, taken over, and has become the norm, the standard that sets the tone for the society he lives in. This is a social document which testifies to what Eric Fromm, Karen Horney and others after them, characterized as the *pathology of normalcy*.

This book documents the epidemic proportions to which Wilhelm Reich's endemic "Emotional Plague" has expanded. Maybe a plague of love will break out. Why not? Are we so immune to the virus of compassion?

R. D. Laing

The integration and organization of this Foreword were interrupted by the untimely death of R.D. Laing on August 23, 1989, in St. Tropez, France.

R.W.F.

Preface

This book is addressed to people who, out of a deep concern for children, want to better understand parents' limitations in giving their children the most they have to offer. The emotional life of parents, indeed of all adults, depends to a considerable extent upon the sensitivity, care, and feeling that they experienced when they were growing up. Unfortunately, in the process of being mishandled and misunderstood as children, we suffer trauma that causes us pain and even terror. We spend the rest of our lives defending ourselves from feeling this pain, concomitantly limiting ourselves as sensitive, feeling people. In becoming closed to our deepest feelings, we necessarily damage those persons closest to us, especially our children.

To understand the basic problem involved in raising children, we need to understand the fundamental ambivalence with which we view life, other people, and ourselves. All of us have strong desires to live and fulfill our potential on the one hand, while at the same time, we have self-destructive tendencies that compel us to limit our lives. These self-limiting propensities generally exist on an unconscious level. Parents exhibit the same mixed feelings and attitudes toward their children; they have strong desires to nurture their children and help them fulfill their potential, and, on the other hand, they often limit their children, stifle their excitement, and cut off their emotional responses in order to protect their own defenses.

No technique or method set forth in traditional child-rearing books can have a long-lasting or profound effect on the ways parents treat children, because any attempt to play out roles that are "proper" or "constructive" inadvertently causes more damage. The child is confused by parents whose actions contradict their words or whose words and actions contradict their underlying attitudes and feelings. Children intuitively sense the real motivation of their parents, and their sense of reality is distorted by duplicitous communications.

Furthermore, children tend to idealize or protect their parents at their own expense. Patients in therapy often feel guilty about exposing the truth of what happened to them in their families because they feel sensitive about hurting others and being disloyal for revealing family secrets. In addition, they are fearful of recriminations from their parents for exposing the "real people" behind the facades. In my clinical experience, I have encountered considerable guilt and resistance to my discoveries about the true conditions within most families. However, coming face to face with painful issues in one's development can lead to a deeper understanding and break the chain of damage that links the generations, despite the inclination to rationalize and defend one's family.

As we explore the basic conflict that characterizes all human experience and as we uncover the ambivalence that all of us manifest to varying degrees toward our children, parents will encounter material that is threatening to their accustomed ways of thinking. However, they can come to understand the basic source of the problems inherent in their own self-protective defenses. Through a growing awareness of important issues in child-rearing, they can learn to cope more effectively with core issues that previously demoralized them and made them mindlessly critical of themselves. Learning about and understanding the contents of this book can help parents and educators to reach into their own experience and find the lost child in themselves.

As a father of eight children, I have come to recognize that there are no easy solutions, no short cuts to "good parenting practices." As a psychotherapist, I have learned that there are methods that parents can utilize to develop understanding and compassion for themselves and feeling for what happened to them as children. Parents are enabled to achieve better relationships with their children through the recovery of feelings for themselves and their lives.

For the past 30 years, I have been deeply involved in tracing the roots of the emotional problems of my patients and devoted to studying the problem of resistance in psychotherapy—the fundamental resistance to a "better life" and the fear of change. This book is an out-growth of that study. The material is based on empirical data gathered during these years of investigation, observation, and participation with people in a variety of therapeutic settings and psychosocial milieus.

This work focuses on parental interactions and the psychological and emotional issues in child development. However, it does not deny or minimize other powerful influences on the psyche of the child. Biological tendencies, inherited temperamental differences, and physiological predispositions combine with personal environmental influences to form unique and complex phenomena (Chess & Thomas, 1987). There is no single cause of specific symptoms or mental aber-rations. All psychological functions are multidetermined. In some cases, somatic aspects clearly outweigh environmental components in the etiology of ego weakness, maladjustment, and psychological dis-turbance. However, in most cases, the impact of psychological ele-ments on the child's development in all probability exceeds the influence of innate predispositions. Maladaptive attitudes and beha-vior of adult patients appear to be overdetermined by interactions in the family.

Moreover, the view that environmental influences play a central role in the mental life of children and in their subsequent mental ad-justment as adults, as well as being true, is optimistic. Remedial action and preventive measures can be taken in relation to many of the psychological factors that cause human misery. By contrast, it is dif-ficult, if not impossible, to alter hereditary patterns that originate in a biological substrate. Thus, it is our fundamental responsibility to give full weight to those causative agents within the family structure that are within our power to change.

My associates and I have observed that, without exception, all our patients and volunteer subjects suffered a certain amount of trau-ma during their developing years. In other words, despite the best intentions of their parents, unconscious malevolent forces were at work, hurting these children at a time when they were most vulner-able to hurt. Our efforts have been continuously devoted to trying to understand the sources of this incidental damage and to developing a psychotherapy and a social milieu that could minimize the hurt and repair the damage from the hurt. It is to these subjects, volunteers, patients, parents, and to our own families that this book is dedicated: To Parents: The Lost Children.

NOTES ON THE ORGANIZATION OF THE BOOK

Part I of the book sets forth our theory of parental ambivalence and its origins, and it provides insights necessary for parents and professionals to change their attitudes and behavior constructively. Part II offers guidelines for child-rearing, derived from this general theory. For parents to have full use of these guidelines, they need to develop a more compassionate view of themselves, through understanding the sources of their difficulties in relating to their children. Part III describes therapeutic interventions undertaken in an effort to prevent the perpetuation of the mistreatment of children and includes references to the work of others as well as to my own.

Robert W. Firestone

Acknowledgments

The author would like to express his appreciation to Joyce Catlett, associate and collaborative writer, for her incredible effort and intellectual contribution to this work. We thoroughly shared this project from inception to completion.

I thank Barry Langberg, Jo Barrington, Tamsen Firestone, Frank Tobe, Susan Short, and Bob Feinberg for their comments during the editing phase. I am very grateful to Jerome Nathan, Lisa Firestone, and Jina Carvalho, who researched relevant material in the literature, and also to Anne Baker who organized and helped complete the final drafts. She was ably assisted by Catherine Cagan, Eileen Tobe, Ana Blix, Leticia Lopez, Louise Firestone, Gretchen Stein, and Richard Tubis.

I would like to thank each person who contributed his/her experiences to this volume thereby opening a window to the core dynamics affecting patterns of child-rearing. I feel privileged to have been able to share their lives.

In addition, I want to thank The Glendon Association, a group of associates and friends who have been staunch supporters of my work. They have expended considerable time and effort to disseminate my theoretical ideas, and completely financed the films that express the concepts visually. I want to thank all of the people who participated in those films for the honest expression of their struggles and their willingness to share their emotional reactions.

I want to personally acknowledge Geoff Parr, who organized, edited, and directed the films, for his sensitive handling of the psychological issues he documented.

Last, and most importantly, I want to express my gratitude to R. D. Laing for his help in critically evaluating the current work, improving the mode of expression, his integrity and unwavering courage in exposing the "psychopathology of normalcy" in his work, and, more recently, for his friendship.

The author gratefully acknowledges permission to reprint excerpts from the following:

"Family Psychotherapy with Schizophrenia in the Hospital and in Private Practice," by Murray Bowen, in *Intensive Family Therapy: Theoretical and Practical Aspects*, edited by Ivan Boszormenyi-Nagy, M.D., and James L. Framo, Ph.D. Copyright 1965 by Hoeber Medical Division, Harper & Row, Publishers, Inc. Reprinted by permission of Ivan Boszormenyi-Nagy, M.D.

The Prince of Tides, by Pat Conroy. Copyright 1986 by Pat Conroy. Reprinted by permission of Houghton Mifflin Company.

The Motherhood Report: How Women Feel about Being Mothers, by Louis Genevie, Ph.D., and Eva Margolies. Copyright 1987 by Dr. Louis Genevie and Eva Margolies. Reprinted by permission of Macmillan Publishing Company.

Family Therapy in Clinical Practice, by Murray Bowen, M.D. Copyright 1985, 1983, 1978 by Jason Aronson, Inc. Reprinted by permission of Ivan Boszormenyi-Nagy, M.D., and James L. Framo, Ph.D.

The Mother, Anxiety, and Death: The Catastrophic Death Complex, By Joseph C. Rheingold, M.D., Ph.D. Copyright 1967 Little, Brown and Company (Inc.). Reprinted by permission of Little, Brown and Company, Inc.

The Politics of Experience, by R. D. Laing. Copyright 1967 by R. D. Laing. Reprinted by permission of Penguin Books, Ltd.

The Death of the Family, by David Cooper. Copyright 1970 by David Cooper. Reprinted by permission of Pantheon Books, a Division of Random House, Inc.

The Fear of Being a Woman: A Theory of Maternal Destructiveness, by Joseph C. Rheingold, M.D., Ph.D. Copyright 1964 by Grune & Stratton, Inc. Reprinted by permission of Grune & Stratton, Inc.

Schizoid Phenomena Object-Relations and the Self, by Harry Guntrip. Copyright Harry Guntrip. Reprinted by permission of International Universities Press, Inc.

The Politics of the Family and Other Essays, by R. D. Laing. Copyright 1969, 1971 by The R. D. Laing Trust. Reprinted by permission of Pantheon Books, a Division of Random House, Inc.

"Punishment Vs. Discipline," by Bruno Bettelheim. Copyright 1985 by The Atlantic Monthly Company. Reprinted by permission of The Atlantic Monthly Company.

Somewhere a Child Is Crying: Maltreatment—Causes and Prevention (Revised Edition), by Vincent J. Fontana, M.D. Copyright 1973, 1976, 1983 by Vincent J. Fontana. With permission of Macmillan Publishing Co.

Mary Barnes: Two Accounts of a Journey Through Madness, by Mary Barnes and Joseph Berke. Copyright 1971 by Mary Barnes and Joseph Berke. Reprinted by permission of Mary Barnes and Joseph Berke.

Family Therapy for Suicidal People, by Joseph Richman, Ph.D. Copyright 1986 by Springer Publishing Company, Inc. Reprinted by permission of Springer Publishing Company, Inc.

My Mother/My Self: The Daughter's Search for Identity, by Nancy Friday. Copyright 1977 by Nancy Friday. Reprinted by permission of Delacorte Press.

Psychotherapy: A Basic Text, by Robert Langs, M.D. Copyright 1982 by Jason Aronson, Inc. Reprinted by permission of Jason Aronson, Inc.

"Limitations of Marriage and Family Therapy," by Robert A. Harper. Copyright 1981 by The Journal of the Institute for Rational Living. Reprinted by permission of The Institute for Rational/Emotive Therapy.

The Prophet, by Kahlil Gibran by permission of Alfred A. Knopf, Inc. Copyright 1923 by Kahlil Gibran; Renewal Copyright 1951 by Administrators C.T.A. of Kahlil Gibran Estate, and Mary G. Gibran.

Home Is Where We Start From: Essays by a Psychoanalyst, by D. W. Winnicott. Copyright the Estate of D. W. Winnicott, 1986. Reprinted by permission of W. W. Norton & Company, Inc.

A Good Enough Parent: A Book on Child-Rearing, by Bruno Bettelheim. Copyright 1987 by Bruno Bettelheim. Reprinted by permission of Alfred A. Knopf, Inc.

The Shoemaker: The Anatomy of a Psychotic, by Flora Rheta Schreiber. Copyright Flora Rheta Schreiber, 1983. Reprinted by permission of Simon and Schuster.

"The Influence of Family Studies on the Treatment of Schizophrenia," by Theodore Lidz, M.D., in *Progress in Group and Family Therapy*, edited by Clifford J. Sager, M.D., and Helen Singer Kaplan, M.D., Ph.D. Copyright 1972 by Brunner/Mazel, Inc. Reprinted by permission of Clifford J. Sager, M.D.

The Nature of the Child, by Jerome Kagan. Copyright 1984 by Basic Books, Inc. Reprinted by permission of Basic Books, Inc.

"Interview: R. D. Laing," by Anthony Liversidge. Copyright 1988 by Omni Publications International Ltd. Reprinted by permission of Omni Publications International, Ltd.

NOTE TO READERS

The names, places, and other identifying facts contained herein have been fictionalized, and no similarity to any persons, living or dead, is intended. In the excerpts from videotaped material, many names were not fictionalized, as several individuals specifically requested that their names remain unchanged.

Because of the awkwardness inherent in constructing sentences so as to avoid sexist language, the author has chosen to use the generic "he" at those times when "one," "they," or "he/she" would have been cumbersome.

Contents

Compassionate
Child-Rearing

PART I

GENERAL THEORY

CHAPTER 1

Overview

Only if we become sensitive to the fine and subtle ways in which a child may suffer humiliation can we hope to develop the respect for him that a child needs from the very first day of his life onward, if he is to develop emotionally.

Alice Miller (1979/1981), *Prisoners of Childhood* (p. 76)

This is a true story about how young people are damaged, inadvertently, by those who consciously wish them the best—their parents. I am writing about every person whose life has been fractured by the perpetuation of the myths of family and society. We can think of human experience as a series of feelings that flow through us; sensations, perceptions, and thoughts impact on our unique personal attributes and predispositions, leading to an individual style of coping with environmental conditions. If any aspect of our experience is damaged—if, for example, we repress feeling for ourselves and others—we lose much of what is most alive and human. Parents who have themselves suffered emotional deprivation and rejection, and who have shut down on themselves, cannot but pass on this damage to their offspring. This form of destruction is the daily fare of most children, despite their parents' good intentions and efforts to love and nurture them.

In this book, I will show how parents' fundamental ambivalence toward their children—both their desire to love and nurture them on the one hand, and on the other, their unconscious hatred of and resentment toward them—profoundly affects the child's development. It is *not* my premise that parents have no love for their children or that they merely imagine that they do. Quite the contrary: in my experience, most mothers and fathers love their children and are fond of them, and wish them the best. My concern has always been with understanding why, despite the love and fondness parents have for their children, they so often behave in ways that are not sensitive, loving, or even friendly. Why, despite their wishes to instill a sense of independence and self-reliance in their offspring, do parents demand conformity and submission? And why, despite their desire to foster spontaneity and vitality in their children, do they actually create deadness and dullness in them?

PARENTAL AMBIVALENCE TOWARD CHILDREN

My observations of family interactions, as well as my clinical findings, indicate a core ambivalence in parental reactions. Parents' feelings toward their children are *both* benevolent and malevolent. These conflicting attitudes coexist within all of us. Many mothers and fathers honestly *believe* that they love their children even when an outside observer would view their parenting patterns as indifferent, neglectful, or even abusive. They mistake an imaginary connection and anxious attachment to their children, which is a *destructive dependency* or *fantasy bond*,[1] for genuine love, affection, and regard for the child's well-being. To be effective, any child-rearing approach must take into account the fundamental ambivalence of parents and its sources. However, negative, hostile feelings toward children are generally unacceptable socially. Parents show strong resistance to recognizing such negative and hostile feelings. They tend to deny aggression toward their children, whether it be covert or overt.

Covert Aggression in Parental Reactions

Understandably, parents have considerable resistance to recognizing how divided they are and how aggressive and hostile they may be toward their children as well. This resistance parallels strong conflicting attitudes they have toward themselves. In both cases, they unconsciously fear that if they become aware of these negative feelings, they will be more likely to act on them. They anticipate terrible consequences from acknowledging these "unacceptable" emotional responses. They are afraid that they will become more guilty or even *more* punishing to their children if they openly admit their hostility.

On the contrary, I have discovered that this recognition actually has positive effects. Far from feeling more guilty, parents generally have benefited from sharing these reactions with other parents who expose similar feelings. Catharsis not only *reduces* their guilt but also helps them to gain control over acting out hostility in family interactions. I believe that it is necessary, even vital, to uncover these unconscious feelings of resentment and hostility toward children, because only then can parents master and overcome these tendencies.

Behaviors in Children That Arouse Parental Aggression

Although many parents feel guilty about their anger toward children and make every effort to maintain control over hateful, punishing thoughts and feelings, certain characteristics and behaviors in the child can trigger intense feelings of rage and angry outbursts. Incompetence, messiness, whining, crying, helplessness, or a look of vulnerability in a child frequently bring out punishing rebukes from parents. In these instances, generally the child is seen to be at fault and is perceived to be the *cause* of his parents' anger and irritability. If parents act on their anger toward the child, they will attempt to justify their actions, claiming it was the child who was "out of line" or was "driving them crazy." Once this pattern is established, the child may well become annoying and is no longer the "innocent, pure" child he once was. He tends to display passive-aggressive behavior in relating to his parents, thereby preserving an image of the "bad child" formed during earlier stages in his development.

Even when parents refrain from blaming or attacking the child and attempt to do the "right" thing, their children intuitively sense their underlying tenseness and irritability and become confused by their attempts to disguise this underlying anger. To compound the problem, many child-rearing books teach parents to "act" proper roles and say the "right" words in relating to their children, thereby contributing to a subtle form of damage—a distortion of the child's reality—that can be even more insidious than outright rejection or anger (E. J. Anthony, 1972; Bateson, Jackson, Haley, & Weakland,

1956/1972; Satir, 1983; Watzlawick, Beavin, & Jackson, 1967; Wynne, 1970/1972).

Manifestations of Love and Hostility in Family Interactions

Very often, parental behavior contradicts any generally acceptable definition of love. Consequently, we must consider the observable actions of parents when attempting to present criteria for loving responses to children. Our criteria include genuine expressions of warmth—a smile or a friendly look that communicates empathy and good humor; physical affection; respectful, considerate treatment; tenderness; sensitivity to children's wants and needs; companionship; and a willingness to be a real person with the child rather than simply act the role of "mother" or "father." Much of what we see around us does not fit these criteria. When we observe family interactions in everyday situations, we see parents behave in ways that are largely detrimental to their offspring. These abuses range in intensity from minor irritability and disrespect to sadism and brutality. For example, we witness scenes like this:

> As she prepared to leave the plane, my associate watched as a couple roughly woke up their four-year-old girl, yelling at her to "Get up *now*! Or we're going to leave you here!" In the rush of people leaving the plane, the little girl awoke in a panic and burst into tears; the terrified expression on her face showed that she believed her parents' threat of abandonment.*

Apparently, these parents were more sensitive to their fellow passengers' than to their daughter's feelings—a not uncommon practice. Parents often speak *for* their children in a way that is insensitive and disrespectful, acting as though the child were mindless, mute, or invisible. The child in that situation feels like a nonperson. Some people even believe that children, and especially infants, have no feelings. Children suffer from being overly defined and categorized. They are classified as "the smart one," "the angry one," or "the sensitive one" in a way that restricts their personal identity or conception of themselves.

---

*This scene was observed by an associate on a recent plane trip.

Frequently, children are teased unmercifully, despite their protests, by parents who are aware of their sensitive areas. For example, a woman recalled that when she was 5 years old, her father took great delight in bursting balloons close to her face just so he could hear her scream. All of us have seen parents reacting with annoyance, literally dragging children through shopping centers, while loudly reprimanding them for lagging behind.

These incidents are not unusual. Manifestations of disturbed parenting can affect every aspect of child-rearing. A baby may be handled roughly in being dressed or bathed; he may be fed insensitively—the food may be literally shoveled into his mouth by an indifferent mother preoccupied with other concerns. Older children may be spoken to with nastiness, sarcasm, and ridiculed by fathers and mothers who are unaware of their tone of voice or their choice of words. Many of these behaviors, verbal and nonverbal, exist on the periphery of parents' consciousness. Consequently, parents themselves do not have a true picture of their child's experience in the family. In each of these interactions, behaviors that clearly contradict generally acceptable definitions of love are being expressed by people who believe they love their children.

Of course, parents vary in their responses to their children and express *both* aspects of conflicting attitudes toward them. Sometimes they are warm and affectionate; at other times, they can be cruel or unfeeling. Children, however, tend to be especially sensitive to painful experiences as compared with positive ones and form their defenses at these times of undue stress. Further, when parents are inconsistent or erratic in their responses, children learn to expect punishment in the midst of, or immediately following, pleasurable events and tend to withdraw *before* they can be hurt. This expectation of hurt, rejection, or punishment persists into adulthood, influencing our responses in interpersonal relations. As a result, we frequently avoid closeness and intimacy because we anticipate future rejection, loss, or other negative consequences.

Misconceptions about Parental Love

One explanation for the discrepancy between parental feelings and behaviors is related to the mistaken notions that many men and women have about love. Almost everyone takes for granted that parents, especially mothers, have an innate ability to love their

children, and to form positive attachments. Unfortunately, this is not
the case. Many parents confuse intense feelings of need and anxious
attachment with feelings of genuine affection and inadvertently take
from their children, rather than give to them.

Very often, parents assume that their inner thoughts and feelings
about loving their children are comparable with outward expressions
of warmth and tenderness and think that their children can read their
minds and somehow know that they are loved. These mothers and
fathers imagine that they care deeply, while in fact they may have
very few personal interactions with their children. It is surprising how
infrequently parents make meaningful contact with their young
children. Questioning, lecturing, and nagging one's children are attempts at dutiful parenting, but they do not necessarily constitute
meaningful personal communications. Genuine contact can be said to
occur only when a parent expresses feelings honestly as a real person—a rare event in our modern society. In fact, a survey (Szalai,
1972) found that the average parent spends only 5.4 minutes per day
talking with his child.

Effects of Childhood Experiences on the Adult Personality

The long-lasting effects of the painful experiences we all endured
as children can be seen in later interactions within the family. Why
do so many parents need to play on the guilt of their adult children
in order to persuade them to call or visit? Why are so many family
reunions marred by disharmony and disillusionment? What really
happened between the time the infant gazed with innocent love and
trust into mother's eyes, and the time this now grown child looks at
his parents with suspicion or discomfort and fear? What transpired
in the intervening years to erase the bright smile from the face of the
toddler who once leaped joyfully into his father's arms?

In the following pages, I will develop a theoretical structure to
explain how incidental abuses to children lead eventually to psychological ills and emotional distress. This exploration challenges illusions
and exposes hidden aspects of our personalities we wish to conceal.
However, this painful undertaking can be very rewarding for personal
growth and development. Parents and professionals alike can utilize
the narratives and case histories of the individuals described here,
who questioned their accustomed ways of thinking, revealed the truth

of their experience, and developed an openness in relation to the basic issues involved in child-rearing.

REFERENCE POPULATION

The findings that support my thesis on child-rearing were derived from three principal sources: (1) historical data gathered from adult patients, ranging from hospitalized schizophrenic patients to neurotic and "normal" clients in an office setting; (2) the sincere revelations of parents in individual and group psychotherapy about their reactions to their children; and (3) individuals in an experimental social milieu who were motivated by a deep, abiding interest in psychology and a special interest in their own development. This unusual psychological laboratory began some 15 years ago, formed out of a small group of professional associates and long-standing friends, and it has expanded to include over 100 persons. These people meet in small and large group settings to explore important aspects of their personal lives. They have devoted themselves to minimizing or eliminating toxic influences in their important personal interactions, and were particularly focused on their couple and family relationships. This social milieu is perhaps unique and it is the most important source of our hypotheses.[2]

Clinical Findings from Parents' Discussion Group

Early in our observations of family interactions, we noted a recurring phenomenon indicating an intolerance on the part of many parents for sustained, close, personal contact with their children. As we listened to the accounts of these parents, we began to conjecture that their difficulties were in some way related to a defensive, self-protective need to deaden their children psychologically, emotionally, cognitively, and somatically. Parents report that when they see their children looking at them with love, this makes them feel uneasy and discomforted, particularly when their children express love.

One striking example of this disturbance is evidenced by Susan, a mother active in our parents' group since its inception. Her irritability and impatience with children in general and her problems in relating to her own children had long been a source of deep concern.

SUSAN: The last time I talked about feeling uncomfortable with children, I had the thought that I don't like to look at children's faces, at their eyes, especially my own children. I don't know why—I don't know what I'm afraid I would see. The second I started to say something right now, I started to feel sad.

DR. F.: If you picture yourself looking at your children, what do you see? What do you feel?

SUSAN: I know it makes me so pained. I don't know what I see because I don't really look at them most of the time.

DR. F.: What do you imagine you are going to see if you picture looking at them now?

SUSAN: If I picture Tamara [Susan's 3-year-old daughter], I think I would see myself. I don't know why that is so hard, but I know that I don't want to see her.

DR. F.: Somehow you see yourself.

SUSAN: But not happy, not a happy self. (*sad*)

It was clear to others in the meeting that Susan's relationship with her daughter caused her pain. Several people identified with the feelings she described. Marilyn, another participant in the group, indicated that for the most part she had avoided having close personal interactions with her son when he was a baby because she had not wanted to be aware of his helplessness and vulnerability.

MARILYN: I felt mostly sad, because he was so vulnerable; you can't avoid seeing it, and you might see it in yourself—and you don't want to.

SUSAN: I think that's what I feel. I see children's vulnerability and then I get angry. I'm afraid of taking advantage of that vulnerability in a child, and then it makes me angry. My *own* feelings get stirred up. I feel really embarrassed by these feelings.

Such parents don't want these primitive longings to be stirred up. In a later group meeting, Susan recognized that she warded off direct eye contact and close moments with her children to avoid painful realizations about her own mother's coldness and indifference. For the first time, Marilyn understood why she distanced herself from her young son; more personal relating aroused feelings of sadness and anxiety in her and brought back feelings of helplessness she had experienced as a child.

In closing off aspects of their personalities to protect themselves and to avoid feelings of pain and vulnerability, parents like Susan and Marilyn must dull these same emotional responses in their children. They cannot avoid but teach their children their own defenses and self-protective life-styles, both implicitly and by direct instruction. Many parents stifle their children's natural spontaneity and enthusiasm by such statements as "Don't make a fool of yourself." "Why get so excited?" "Don't wear your emotions on your sleeve." Parents caution children about feeling *too* good about themselves, saying: "Don't be so proud or conceited." They warn adolescents not to get too attached to persons or things to "protect" them against rejection and loss. The methods of transmitting parental defenses to children are extensive and extremely effective in perpetuating self-limiting life-styles from one generation to the next.

ORIGINS OF PARENTAL HOSTILITY:
THE UNIVERSALITY OF CHILDHOOD TRAUMA

There are three major reasons why parents unconsciously resent their children, limit their development, and cause them pain. (1) Children threaten the parents' defense system by reawakening painful feelings from the past; (2) parents unknowingly project or extend critical, negative feelings and attitudes they have toward themselves onto their children; (3) the negative traits and behaviors internalized by parents when *they* were children now intrude into their ongoing behavior in interactions with their offspring.

Threats to Parents' Defense Systems

Parental defenses are threatened by live, spontaneous children. Their innocence reminds the parents of the hurts in their childhoods. The child threatens to reactivate these past hurts. In this situation, parents direct their hostility toward the child. The child is usually expendable, whereas the defense system of the parent is preserved.

All of us have been caused pain in growing up, and to the extent that we have insulated ourselves from this emotional distress and our feelings of sadness, we have become removed and alienated from our "child selves," from parts of ourselves that are vital and alive. We spend the rest of our lives protecting and defending ourselves against reexperiencing these painful feelings.

In our clinical work over a 4-year period (1973-1976) with patients and normal subjects in an intense feeling release therapy, we found that, without exception, *every* individual expressed deep, primitive feelings of sadness, desperation, and rage associated with traumatic events in childhood. Once one is defended against these feelings, one continually manipulates the environment so that this repressed pain does not surface, that is, one attempts to avoid any experience that reminds one of the emptiness and fears one suffered as a child (Janov, 1970).

To some extent, all parents are inward and defensive because of the frustrations they encountered in *their* early lives. Children threaten their parents' defense systems in various ways; for example, a mother who is somewhat quiet or reserved and in control of her feelings is disturbed by her child's natural enthusiasm, liveliness, and movement. These behaviors may intrude on her cutoff state and disturb her "tranquility." Spontaneous action, freedom, and the lack of shame typical of young children arouse feelings of tension, embarrassment, and guilt in both mothers and fathers, who then feel compelled to control and limit their children. Many acts of cruelty and sadism are justified in the name of this socialization process. A child's directness, honest communication, and open expression of feeling impinge on the fantasy bond (the imaginary connection with the mother) and the dishonesty within the family. The child soon learns to swallow or suppress perceptions and to protect the defenses and illusions within the family unit.

Responsibility for a life other than their own overwhelms such parents. They feel incompetent or somewhat immature and find it difficult to cope with life themselves. People who feel as if their resources barely keep them alive and secure feel frightened and inadequate when they imagine they must supply love and affection to another person. The pressure of this added dependency load is very threatening.

A child's helplessness and vulnerability remind everyone of their own weakness and vulnerability. Those parents who find these traits unacceptable in themselves see these traits as unacceptable in their children. In addition, there is evidence that parents experience considerable discomfort where their child passes through stages of development that were particularly traumatic for the parents themselves. During this transition, parents can become unusually insensitive, indifferent, or punitive to the youngster.

Paradoxically, a large part of the damage that parents inflict on their children stems from strong *benevolent, protective* feelings that they have toward them. In attempting to spare their children the trauma of inevitable separations and to help them avoid vulnerability to death anxiety, they often deceive their children and teach them attitudes and defenses that later limit their lives and fix them at a level of development below their potential. Parents do this largely because they experience unconscious guilt for bringing children into the world, where they will be faced with uncertainty, anxiety, and the inevitability of dying. They unwittingly choose to destroy their children's humanness and sensibilities rather than expose them to the painful realities surrounding an awareness of aloneness, separation, and death.

Most people justify and rationalize their psychological defenses in the sense that they believe these defenses have no effect on others; however, these defenses *do* have an adverse effect on their loved ones, particularly on their children. When people sense that their defenses and destructive habit patterns are damaging to a young person, they generally feel guilt and remorse, but these guilt reactions only serve to compound the problem.

Negative Attitudes toward Self Extended to the Child

Professionals recognize that in most cases of physical child abuse, the abusing parent was once the abused child, that is, that there is a compulsion to repeat patterns of abuse in succeeding generations (Elmer, 1975; Freedman, 1975; Garbarino, 1976; Oliver & Cox, 1973; Oliver & Taylor, 1971; Silver, Dublin, & Lourie, 1969; Sroufe & Ward, 1980). Physical child abuse, however tragic and reprehensible, represents only one aspect of human experience. More extensive damage may be inflicted on the emerging personality of a child by incidents of emotional and mental abuses, and the harmful effects are frequently more long-lasting (Garbarino, Guttmann, & Seeley, 1986; Miller, 1980/1984). The determining factors in both forms of child abuse are the same; to the extent that parents have repressed or forgotten the mistreatment they suffered in interactions with *their* parents, they tend to act out compulsively the mistreatment in some form on their own children.

In later investigations (1976 to the present), we uncovered more evidence to support our conclusions about childhood trauma; that is, that the painful experiences that children suffer turn them against themselves and lead to a divided self (Firestone, 1988). We discovered that virtually all of our subjects suffered from critical, derisive thought patterns and covert aggression toward themselves, which they had incorporated or assimilated from their parents' negative attitudes toward them. This destructive thought process or "voice" came to the foreground in specialized therapy sessions that were termed *voice therapy*.[3] The patients *themselves* connected their negative thought patterns to parental prohibitions and frustrating experiences within the family. Later, in further investigations of child-rearing practices, it became obvious to us that parents extend their self-critical thoughts and self-attacks to their children. They tend to *project* their self-hatred and negative voices onto their children and are overly critical of these projected qualities and traits in the youngsters. This process often leads to harsh or rejecting treatment that seriously undermines the self-esteem of their offspring.

In the process of projection (Bowen, 1978; Zilboorg, 1931, 1932), the child is basically used as a waste receptacle or dumping ground; the parents disown weaknesses and unpleasant characteristics in themselves and perceive them instead in the child. In one case, a mother with a rigid, prudish view about sex disowned any sexual feelings in herself and constantly worried about her daughter's emerging sexuality. Fearing the girl would become promiscuous when she reached adolescence, she intruded into her daughter's privacy, opening letters from her boyfriend and searching her belongings and schoolwork for clues indicating misconduct. Later, when she attended college, the girl fulfilled her mother's predictions by becoming casually involved with many men and by deceiving her parents about her sexual activities.

As a result of parental projections, many children become imprisoned for life in a narrow, restrictive labeling system that formed their identity within the family. As adults, they feel guilty to move away from these definitions, even though they may be negative or degrading.

The process of projecting undesirable parental traits onto a child is prevalent throughout family life (Kerr & Bowen, 1988). The dynamics have been clearly described by Murray Bowen (1965):

> There are three main steps in each episode in the projection process.... The first is a *feeling-thinking* step. It begins with a *feeling* in the mother which merges into *thinking* about defects in the child. The second is the *examining-labeling* step in which she searches for and diagnoses a defect in the child that best fits her feeling state.... The third step is the *treating* step in which she acts toward and treats the child as though her diagnosis is accurate....

The projection is fed by the mother's anxiety. When the cause for her anxiety is located outside of the mother, the anxiety subsides. For the child, accepting the projection as a reality is a small price to pay for a calmer mother. Now the child *is* a little more inadequate. Each time he accepts another projection, he adds to his increasing state of functional inadequacy. (p. 225)

Kerr and Bowen (1988) go on to conclude that

those actions [of being inadequate or incompetent] are used by mother to justify her image of the child. The mother is not malicious; she is just anxious. She is as much a prisoner of the situation as the child. (p. 201)

As noted above, parents' negative attitudes toward themselves also predispose or generate self-limiting and self-destructive behaviors in their children. These negative behavioral patterns and character traits often appear to be compulsive repetitions of the parents' behaviors.

Identification and Incorporation of Parental Behaviors

Under conditions of extreme stress, children assimilate or incorporate the negative, punitive traits of their parents; that is, when they are the most anxious and threatened, they no longer identify with themselves (as children who are weak and powerless), but align themselves with the powerful parent, who at the time resents the weak child. In other words, the child takes on, as his own, the traits that he dislikes or hates in his parents.

Because the process of incorporation or assimilation is so powerful under conditions of anxiety and stress, people sometimes display behaviors and personality traits that appear totally "out of character." Indeed, the internal caricature of the parent—the parent at his worst—endures within the personality of the child over his entire lifetime and can emerge almost intact on occasions that are similar to the situations in which the original trauma occurred. For example, a mother described punishing her young son for getting his new shoes wet. She found herself suddenly hitting him on his bare legs again and again. Later, with remorse, she said, "I felt as if someone were standing behind me and telling me to punish him, that he *should* be punished, and that what I did was a good thing. I didn't feel at all like myself at the time." At a later session, she connected this incident to the mistreatment and cruel punishment she recalled suffering throughout her childhood at the hands of *her* parents.

Nowhere is this intrusion of an alien point of view more apparent than in those situations where parents feel compelled to force their child to submit his will to theirs. They feel duty bound to assert their supremacy and to socialize the child. In addition, there is a belief, supported by society, that children "belong" to their parents and that their children's behavior reflects on them; therefore, the children must be made to conform. Mothers and fathers are frequently very caustic and derisive in these angry confrontations, manifesting fierce, punishing attitudes. Their punitive overreactions are characterized by "parental role-playing" behavior as contrasted with mature actions and communications. Their words have a condescending tone and their speech contains self-righteous "shoulds," "musts," and other commands assimilated from *their* parents' speech patterns.

To summarize, all children suffer trauma and rejection to varying degrees in the developmental process, and, as described earlier, they incorporate an internal parent represented by a destructive, self-critical thought process or negative voice. They carry this abusive voice with them through life, restricting, limiting, and punishing themselves, and eventually acting out similar abuses on their children. These abuses, in turn, are internalized as punitive, self-critical voices by *their* children, thus perpetuating the cycle (Firestone, 1988).

Parents not only damage their children but also unknowingly prevent the healing process, that is, they do not allow their offspring to recover from the trauma. By not permitting them to express their painful reactions, to cry or scream out, or to talk about their feelings, parents perpetuate the damage. Children then suppress their feeling reactions to stresses within the family. However, feelings cannot be isolated or cut off selectively. In warding off painful emotions, both adults and children limit their capacity to respond to positive circumstances and dull themselves to life experience.

CONCLUSION

Today's parents are attempting to raise healthy, potentially productive individuals in a confused age of alienation. The death of feeling in our society has increased anxiety and led to considerable stress, making genuine personal relationships progressively more difficult

(Berke, 1988; Lasch, 1979, 1984). With the changes in traditional family life, these symptoms have come more to the surface in the form of increased divorce rates and a partial breakdown of family and church. The erosion of this traditional structure has been incorrectly considered by many to be the principal *cause* rather than the *effect* of emotional distress and neurosis.

The true sources of the difficulty, however, are deeply rooted in the individual defensive process, which manifests itself in the formation of destructive couple and family bonds and their extension into the institutions of society at large. Environmental factors, such as parental ambivalence, duplicity, role-playing in the family, false ties and the illusion of connection between family members, and the myth of unconditional parental love, have a devastating effect on the minds and feelings of young people. Finally, it is vital for us to remember that children are not our possessions; they are not ours in the proprietary sense of the word; rather they belong to themselves and have the right to an independent existence.

NOTES

1. It is important to differentiate the specific use of the word *bond* (or *fantasy bond*) from its usual meaning in psychological and popular literature. It is not meant to describe "bonding" in a positive sense nor does it refer to a relationship that is personified by loyalty, devotion, and genuine love (Firestone, 1984). Our usage relates to addictive or destructive ties or fantasized connections that restrict experience and damage relationships. The concept of the fantasy bond is elucidated in *The Fantasy Bond: Structure of Psychological Defenses* (Firestone, 1985).

2. Most of the case histories and clinical examples used as illustrative material throughout the book have been excerpted from videotapes of the parent discussion groups described in the next section. Clinical material dealing with parent-child relations, voice therapy, couple therapy, and child and adolescent development have been excerpted from videotapes of other group meetings and interviews. Much of this material has been incorporated into the documentaries listed in Appendix A.

3. *Voice Therapy: A Psychotherapeutic Approach to Self-Destructive Behavior* (Firestone, 1988) describes the concept of the "voice" and the procedures developed to elicit and identify the contents of negative thought processes, bringing them more into the patient's consciousness.

CHAPTER 2

The Fantasy Bond in Couple and Family Relationships

> I do not know...when my mother and father began their long, dispiriting war against each other. Most of their skirmishes were like games of rin-golevio, with the souls of their children serving as the ruined captured flags in their campaigns of attrition. Neither considered the potential damage when struggling over something as fragile and unformed as a child's life.... As with many parents, their love proved to be the most lethal thing about them.
>
> Pat Conroy (1986), *The Prince of Tides* (p. 3)

In observing and studying the symptom patterns and limitations of our adult patients, we became aware that the origins of these disturbances are deeply embedded in childhood experiences. But where did these experiences begin? What are the core dynamics? The emotional climate into which a child is born is largely determined by the nature of the relationship that has already evolved between the parents, based on their own defense systems. By the time the child is born, there are often important negative influences operating within the couple. To better understand the specific dimensions of the couple's interaction that have the most profound and destructive impact on the child, it is important to understand the concept of the fantasy bond.

The *fantasy bond* refers to an *imaginary* connection or *fantasy* of love and closeness that gradually replaces the genuine love and affection usually present at the beginning of a couple's relationship. The more a couple form this imagined tie and become involved in role-playing, the more this has a detrimental effect on their children. Therefore, it is essential to trace the process of bond formation in typical couple interactions and describe its effect on the emerging family.

Most people are accustomed to think of *bonds* as close, loving attachments of enduring devotion and loyalty, or to think of such in terms of the positive "bonding" between mother and infant. However, we are using the term *bond*, or *fantasy bond*, to connote a limitation of personal freedom, a form of bondage, an unhealthy dependency on another. The fantasy bond, though an attempt to answer a very human need for safety and security, fosters an illusion of connection and oneness, which has a devastating effect on individuals, their relationships, and their children.

SYMPTOMS OF THE FANTASY BOND IN COUPLES

People generally have strong feelings of love, attraction, tenderness, and respect toward their loved ones at the beginning of a relationship. Yet there is a gradual deterioration over time, as most men and women sacrifice real friendship and caring for a possessive, intrusive attitude. In their misguided attempts to nail down their relationship and to establish lasting security, they destroy the essence and vitality of their love.

Men and women tend to fall in love during a period in their lives when they are expanding their worlds, are open to new experiences, and are striving to break old dependency ties with their families. In this period, they usually feel relatively independent, vital, and centered in themselves. Often a strong attraction exists between them initially. They are excited about getting to know each other and have strong feelings of friendship. However, the condition of "being in love" is volatile and unstable. Fear of loss or abandonment, dread of being rejected, the poignancy and sadness evoked by the positive emotions of tenderness and love themselves, eventually become intolerable, particularly for those men and women who suffered from lack of love and affectionate contacts in childhood. Most people, I believe, are intolerant, on a deep level, of being loved, admired, and personally prized for their unique qualities. They retreat from being close and gradually, almost imperceptibly, manipulate, dull, and deaden the feelings of the other to protect themselves. In a real, and not imaginary sense, they ward each other off while, at the same time, they strengthen the fantasy of closeness and connectedness.

Part of the fantasy bond, or addictive attachment and dependency, is present even during the early stages of the relationship. People seek compensatory qualities in their partners. A person who is aggressive looks for someone who is somewhat passive. A spontaneous, lively person is attracted to someone who is rigid, quiet, or retiring. To compensate for their weaknesses and inadequacies, the partners become paradoxically more weak and inadequate, self-hating, and more needy and dependent. Perversely enough, the very qualities that initially attracted them are frequently the ones they later criticize and resent (Sager & Hunt, 1979; Willi, 1975/1982).

As a couple's relationship unfolds, signs of the fantasy bond become more apparent. People who at the beginning of their relationship spent hours in conversation begin to lose interest in talking and in listening. Spontaneity and playfulness gradually disappear, and there is a decrease in the amount of direct eye contact between the partners. People who once gazed lovingly at each other now avert their glance. This particular sign of diminished relating indicates an increasingly impersonal style of interaction.

The couple's conversation becomes dishonest and misleading. They speak across each other, for each other, and interrupt and intrude while talking as a unit or in stylized "we's" instead of "I's" and "you's." Eventually, their communication degenerates into bickering, picking at each other, arguing, aggressive, disrespectful exchanges, or communication simply ceases. Germaine Greer (1970/1971) has graphically described the typical married couple's conversation:

> She belittles him, half-knowingly disputes his difficult decisions, taunts him with his own fears of failure, until he stops telling her anything. Her questions about his "day at the office" become a formality. She does not listen to his answers any more than he heeds her description of her dreary day. Eventually the discussion stops altogether. (p. 285)

A Decline in Sexual Attraction

The adoption of a routinized, mechanical style of lovemaking, as well as a reduction in the level of sexual attraction, are significant signs that a damaging bond has been formed.[1] This decline is *not* the result of familiarity, as many people assume. When partners are temporarily separated or when they develop more independence, they frequently recover their original feelings of attraction. In the discussion groups referred to in Chapter 1, many couples have talked openly about their diminished feelings of sexual attraction. In the following excerpt from a session of a couples' group, Jeanne, married for 6 years, describes changes that occurred in the sexual relationship with her husband:

JEANNE: At first, just before we were married and we would make love, I felt so free, and I would just go with the feeling. Then, after that, when we were married, I remember holding back. I remember, especially if we'd had a really nice time, then the next day I thought, "Now, okay, now don't get carried away. Slow down."

RUFUS: I remember the times when you would say to me that you thought that it was too much. I would want to make love with you because I was attracted to you, and you would even say, "Well, we just made love last night." It's the kind of thing that I felt frustrated about, and a lot of the fights that we used to have at that time I know were because of that.

Another group member in the same group reveals a similar pattern. In this case, Don describes losing a sense of his own sexual identity in his marriage to Lorraine:

DON (*talking to Lorraine*): I was very naturally attracted to you and fell in love with you very easily. I had a strong sense of myself in the relationship originally. I really knew what I wanted, and I really pursued you. At some point, the feelings switched over, and I started almost living through you and gave up any sense of what I wanted in my life. I started to feel like I needed you to show me who I was, or what I wanted, even sexually.

LORRAINE: When you're like that, it's very difficult for me to be with you, because I feel like defending myself against you. And then it becomes painful because I don't feel attracted to you. It's a painful state. (*sad*)

Although these couples initially had difficulty communicating honestly, the process of speaking frankly in the group about these symptoms of deterioration tended to improve their relationships, leading to a gradual emergence of renewed sexual interest and attraction.

Progressive Withholding of Qualities Valued by One's Partner

Men and women who have been damaged in early family relationships attempt to control the amount of love and satisfaction they receive from their spouse by giving up or withholding personal qualities prized by the partner. In holding back traits and actions that are lovable and that would elicit tender responses, they are, in effect, manipulating each other into a relationship that they both *can* tolerate, rather than preserving one in which they are especially loved and chosen. Many men and women give up caring about their appearance or put on excess weight. They hold back the excitement and communication they initially enjoyed with their mates. Both members of the couple gradually lose the pleasure they took in each other's company. And, they begin to withhold their sexual responses.

In this example, Edie, married for 14 years, describes the first few months of her relationship with her husband:

EDIE (*talking to husband*): When we decided to live together, I remember radically changing my looks. Prior to that, I had worked hard on being slender, because it meant a lot to me. But once I started to live with you, I immediately put that weight back on, and I became much less interested in sex. It seems that there have been key times when I remember changing. When we got married, I remember sort of deadening out after that. I don't recall having much feeling about anything in my life then.

Substitution of Obligation for Choice

As each partner begins to withhold the desirable qualities in him or herself that attracted the other, he or she tends to experience feelings of guilt, resentment, and remorse. Consequently, both come to act out of a sense of obligation and responsibility instead of a genuine desire to be together. As couples get to know each other, they frequently make more and more demands on each other. They search for signs of safety and security and ask for reassurances of love and preference. In trying to find more security by extracting or demanding promises of loyalty and devotion from the partner, they actually destroy all that is most precious and special about the relationship.

Most people have been taught early in life that they belong to their families in a proprietary sense, so they tend to have little sense of "belonging" to themselves. They are blackmailed through guilt. Both members of a couple learn that they can restrict the lives of their mates and get them to conform. This blackmail of another subverts any genuine feelings that may have existed or still exist. People cannot imprison one another without damaging their relationship in the process, and without loss of dignity and self-respect.

Howard talks about his motive for wanting to be married and contrasts it with the present state of his relationship with his wife:

HOWARD (*talking to his wife*): My original feeling of getting married was that I wanted it to be a statement of our friendship, but it's really turned into the thing that killed our friendship. I know one of the main things that we had before is that we respected each other's independence. But then I started to give up certain things I was interested in, and I know also that I started to restrict you. I started to expect you to be home at a certain time, to be there waiting. Little things like that really add up and take their toll.

Mutual Self-Deception

Men and women who form destructive ties are usually unable to accept the fact that they have lost their feeling for each other and have become alienated. They are deeply ashamed that they no longer feel as attracted or as interested as they were. Unable to live with this truth, they try to cover up their lack of emotional involvement with a *fantasy* of enduring love. They begin to substitute *form*, that is, routine, role-determined behavior, for the *substance* of the relationship—the genuine love, respect, and affection.

This illusion of love is enhanced by a capacity for self-deception. Many couples who form a fantasy bond use external symbols—anniversaries and other family occasions, etc.—to support a false sense of togetherness and an *imagination* of being close, while they act in ways that contrast with any recognizable definition of love. R. D. Laing's (1961/1971) graphic description of the manner in which couples conspire to protect their pretense of love illustrates our strong propensity toward mutual *self-deception* and role-playing.

> Two people in relation may confirm each other or genuinely complement each other. Still, to disclose oneself to the other is hard without confidence in oneself and trust in the other.

> Desire for confirmation from each is present in both, but each is caught between trust and mistrust, confidence and despair, and *both settle for counterfeit acts of confirmation on the basis of pretence* [italics added]. To do so *both* must play the game of collusion. (pp. 108-109)

Idealization of the Partner

In my experience, couples who come for marital therapy typically display behaviors that are disrespectful, sarcastic, indifferent, or even abusive, while they claim to love each other. Couples I have seen together for conjoint therapy sessions are often hypercritical of each other's traits, and blame their mates for deficiencies in the relationship.

Their disappointment and their critical views of each other stem partly from their tendency to idealize their spouse as they idealized their family in the past.

Many husbands and wives build each other up in their own minds in order to gain a sense of security. Each partner gets angry and resentful whenever his mate fails to live up to these high expectations. They become critical since they are disillusioned with the weaknesses and foibles in their partner which they were not aware of at the beginning of the relationship.

Loss of Independence and a Sense of Separate Identity

Perhaps the most significant indication that such a fantasy bond has been formed is when one or both partners give up vital areas of interest and functioning, their own unique point of view and opinions, in effect, their individuality, to become one-half of a couple. The attempt to merge oneself with another to find security in an illusion of safety leads to an insidious and progressive loss of identity in each. The individuals involved learn to rely more and more on repetitive, habitual contact, with less and less personal feeling. They find life increasingly hollow and empty as they give up more aspects of their personalities. Further, this propensity to surrender one's independence and individuality is supported by the conventional belief in the myth of enduring love. The belief in the myth prevents people from becoming aware of, or understanding, the basic source of trouble in their relationships by supporting their *imagination* of connection and oneness, when real closeness is actually deteriorating. One partner becomes frightened by being loved and especially chosen by the loved one and reverts to childish or dependent behavior.

The following in-depth interview with Jeanne and Rufus documents Jeanne's progressive retreat from the relationship as she gave up her independence and individuality. She dates this change from the time she had the realization that Rufus genuinely loved her:

JEANNE: I swear, I even remember the day. I remember when he told me that he really loved me and I knew it. It was like a panic, I felt a panic, like a responsibility for another person—"don't do that to me!"

So then I felt like I was going to be a responsibility to *him* instead of him being a responsibility to me. I got so dependent in ways that—I knew I was more competent in certain areas than Rufus, we had even talked about it. Then all of a sudden, it's like I was weaker, and then I would ask him for help.

RUFUS: I know I didn't want to be a parent in the relationship. I didn't want to help her get out of anything. I just wanted the relationship to be equal. I liked it when she was putting in as much energy as I was.

DR. F.: Did you actually feel childish?

JEANNE: Oh, yeah, I started to ask him how did I look—I didn't know how I felt anymore. I didn't know how I looked; I was asking him if I was okay sexually—I mean, I didn't even know anymore.

Jeanne goes on to examine the reasons why she assumed a dependent role in relating to Rufus:

DR. F.: Why would recognizing that he loved you bring out feelings like that?

JEANNE: The only thing I can think of is that I had never felt love like that before. I felt like he really knew me, and I felt like he liked me for the same reasons I liked me. And I had never felt like that before. Something about his sweet face. I don't remember anybody looking at me with a really sweet face like that, ever. And at first it made me happy, and then it made me just—I wanted to cover up.

DR. F.: Did it feel painful in some way?

JEANNE: Yeah, but then it made me angry. I wouldn't stay with the pain long. I would begin to say nasty, mean things that I knew would hurt him. I would hear myself saying these things and I couldn't believe it—but it took the look off his face. (sad)

DR. F.: You say that no one looked at you like that before. How was it in your family? What was it like?

JEANNE: My parents were so rigid with themselves. There was no affection, physical affection, in my family at all. There was no hugging. I never remember sitting on my dad's lap. It's not that they were mean people, but it was just very rigid. It was never out of control, you know, joy, happiness or anything. There was never any shouting. It was just very contained.

Over the course of the interview, Jeanne gained insight into the reasons she found it difficult to accept Rufus's love and into the underlying dynamics of her retreat from adult functioning and an independent point of view. It became apparent that Jeanne had learned to control her emotional and affectionate responses in her family and that she had transferred this habitual withholding pattern, or lack of response, to her relationship with Rufus *after* she became frightened of the closeness and love he offered.

Most of us are unaware of our strong propensity to surrender our individuality for an illusion of togetherness and eternal love. The fantasy bond manifests in most relationships, and is present to some extent in all marriages. A number of family therapists have investigated this problem, among them Murray Bowen (1961, 1978), Jurg Willi (1975/1982), R. D. Laing (1969/1972), Mark Karpel (1976), Wexler and Steidl (1978), and Boszormenyi-Nagy and Spark (1973/1984). This process of forming destructive bonds greatly reduces the chance of achieving a successful marriage and has a devastating effect on our children.

DEVELOPMENTAL ASPECTS OF THE FANTASY BOND

The fantasy bond, or imaginary connection, between persons is formed under stress in an attempt to cope with the pain of emotional and physical deprivation in early life. The most primitive aspect of the bond is the infant's fantasy or image of being merged with the mother's body, most particularly the breast (Firestone, 1984). The original bond with the mother is later extended to the father and to the family at large. The fantasy process, along with self-nourishing habits such as thumb-sucking and, later, masturbation, is used by children to alleviate the emotional pain of rejection and the fear of separation and aloneness. This self-parenting process persists into adult life and may come to be preferred to real relationships as a source of comfort.

LOVE-FOOD: A NECESSARY INGREDIENT FOR EMOTIONAL DEVELOPMENT

To provide her infant with proper emotional sustenance, a mother or parental figure must be able to feed and care for her child without arousing undue anxiety in the child. To succeed on this level, she must be sensitive to the child's needs. In addition, in the process of socialization, she must be capable of offering her child control and direction. I have called the product of this ability on the part of the primary caretaker *love-food*. This implies both the capacity *and* the desire to provide for the need-gratification of the infant. A child's basic needs for love, control, and direction can hardly be met by basically immature, needy, dependent, hostile parents.

When parents are inadequate and immature, that is, when they do not provide sufficient love-food, the infant experiences separation anxiety and lack of love as a threat of annihilation (Winnicott, 1958) and draws upon its imagination for relief from emotional pain and anxiety.

The fantasy bond is effective as a core defense because our capacity for imagination provides partial gratification of needs and reduces tension arising from physical or emotional deprivation. We compensate for the pain and anxiety aroused by adverse conditions in early life by progressively choosing fantasy gratification and self-nourishing behaviors as a substitute for satisfaction from other persons. This process acts very much like an addiction, offering temporary relief followed by increased hunger, desperation, and maladaptation.

DESTRUCTIVE EFFECTS OF THE FANTASY BOND ON CHILD DEVELOPMENT

> When he was born I knew that motherhood was created by someone who had to have a word for it.... He [Anse] had a word, too. Love, he called it.... I knew that that word was like the others: just a shape to fill a lack. (Addie Burden talks about motherhood in William Faulkner's [1930/1987] *As I Lay Dying* [pp. 157-158].)

The destructiveness of the bond within the family lies in its dual function of protecting the physical lives of children and nurturing their bodies, while it also functions to dull or deaden all but socially role-determined feelings and to distort their perceptions of reality.

Imagine a child born to two people who for years have been deeply involved in a mutual delusion of closeness and love, a pact of self-deception, an exclusive, and false, "special" relationship in which each tells the other that he or she is preferred over all others. Imagine a child born to a couple in which each partner has allowed the slow erosion of their love to occur without admitting the transformation; in which each partner has been diminished in his or her uniqueness, vitality, and sense of self by the destructive workings of their bond.

Parents in such a bond have very little energy to offer love or to care for others, especially for their children. To compound this lack of emotional sustenance, the family situation is complicated by the rules, regulations, and obligations that are part of the family's role-playing. Even when two people have strong potential for genuine caring, they often lose it within the traditional family structure. Many of us maintain an idealized, romanticized picture of childhood, whereas in actuality there were few close and happy times. In some sense, the lives of most children are nightmarish and painful, due partly to the situation they find themselves in and partly to their help-lessness and vulnerability to pain.

One symptom of bondage in a couple is the unpleasant atmos-phere created by the incessant arguments and disputes the partners engage in, generally to the exclusion of others. Even adults feel un-comfortable in the company of a bickering, warring couple. The small child, however, is tortured and torn apart by his or her parents' fights and arguments. Many children live in cringing anticipation of hostility and explosiveness that can erupt at any moment. These outbursts only temporarily dispel the paralyzing routine tension of the home. In other families, the underlying tension and hostility persist without clearly surfacing, and there is no relief, only anticipatory fear.

Children feel excluded not only by the obvious negative aspects of a bond, but by its ostensibly positive aspects. They are, and they feel, left out of long conversations that take place between their parents behind the closed bedroom door. The secretiveness of parents' sexual relationships and contradictory patterns of interaction between them are confusing to the naive child, however intelligent. In addition, children are forced to see their parents as fallen heroes during their parents' never-ending childish, irrational moments.

In the light of all of this, many of us fail to recognize that *none* of us has had the idyllic childhood we see portrayed in the media. Several years ago, a TV documentary (Gilbert, 1973) was produced featuring a "typical" American family. This family turned out to be filled with psychopathology and with serious disturbances evident in many of its members.

Genuine closeness, love, and intimacy, combined with indepen-dence and strength of family members, can and does foster personal growth. Most often, this support is absent. The child born to a couple who have cut off feeling for each other, but who pretend still to be close is starved for affection and emotional gratification. The illusion of love is not satisfying for an infant whose parents no longer love or like themselves or each other. The infant's predicament when faced with overwhelming anxiety, fears of annihilation, and physical and emotional pain demands defenses as a necessity for psychological, and perhaps even physical, survival. The child whose basic needs for love-food are not met not only resorts to fantasy but also tries to take care of and to parent him or herself.

Case Study

The formation and long-lasting effects of this self-protective process on the child's developing personality are illustrated in the following case history.

Kathy was approximately 18 months old when her mother, responding to pressures from relatives, suddenly decided it was time to take her off the bottle and feed her from a cup. The first night she was denied the bottle, Kathy screamed all night. After listening to her daughter's cries the entire night, the mother returned to her crib and offered her the bottle. Kathy threw it on the floor and began to suck her thumb. She never took to the bottle again. In refusing gratification from outside, she substituted thumb-sucking and later other forms of self-nourishment. This incident—what seemed like a normal step in the weaning process—was a key event in Kathy's deprived existence and acted to solidify already well-formed defenses.

Family History. Kathy had been born to an emotionally immature couple, where neither partner was capable of offering nurturance or guidance to their two daughters. Kathy's parents, David and Joanne, were narcissistic and emotionally deprived individuals. Each had experienced much trauma during *their* early years.

The most glaring and puzzling characteristic of this couple's relationship, however, was the fairy-tale quality of their family life that had persisted uninterrupted until Joanne, no longer able to ignore the alarming symptoms her daughters were beginning to exhibit, sought professional help. Indeed, David and Joanne had been admired as the "ideal couple" by their circle of friends. Gradually, this front broke down as Joanne became seriously concerned about her children. Against the wishes of her husband, she finally took the youngsters for evaluation at a child guidance clinic.

Symptoms and Analysis. In the initial interview, both children cried excessively, and the younger daughter, aged 2½, threw repeated tantrums and could not be soothed by her mother. Kathy, who was almost 4, was quite pale and listless, with dark circles under her eyes. She displayed signs of impoverished affect and symptoms of depression. Her mother reported that Kathy spent long hours in front of the television set and when diverted to other activities would show very little interest. Sometimes she would simply fall asleep on the floor, in the midst of play, if left alone in a room for several minutes.

In seeking help, Kathy's mother had disrupted the couple's fantasy of the perfect family and had destroyed their pact of noncommunication and mutual protection. By including their children in their life of pretense and role-playing, this couple had inadvertently damaged their older daughter's spirit and vitality, which gave rise to serious psychological disturbance. The younger daughter's rage against her surroundings was evident in her tantrums and was, in some sense, a healthier response to the parental environment.

My subsequent involvement with Kathy and her parents, who later divorced, revealed other factors impinging on this particular child that were different from the factors affecting her younger sibling. According to Joanne, Kathy was her "fantasy child," a beautiful plaything whom she visualized as carrying forward into her adult life all the beauty, the superior intelligence, and the exceptional talents that Joanne felt had been unacknowledged in her by her own parents. Although neglected in many respects, Kathy was enrolled in a progressive nursery school where her mind would be "stimulated" by the advanced program.

It became obvious that Kathy's mother had extreme dependency needs and strong feelings of emotional hunger, which had their sources in her own childhood and which she now focused on Kathy. The combination of abject rejection and intrusive proprietary interest shown by this mother had a draining effect on the youngster, causing her to give up basic wants and needs at an early age, perhaps even prior to the incident with the bottle. The incident served to crystallize in Kathy's mind her parents' long-term neglect and hostility, as well as the disregard of her needs as an infant.

Following her parents' divorce when she was 5, Kathy was raised by another couple, close friends of the family. As of this writing, her progress has been observed over a period of 13 years.

In the following discussion, we will examine the ongoing effects of Kathy's pseudoindependent stance on her personality. Her illusion of total self-sufficiency consisted of the strong belief that she could feed herself, that she needed no one outside herself to give her love or to satisfy her needs, an illusion symbolized by her defiant rejection of the bottle.

The Fantasy Bond as an Addiction

When one suffers considerable frustration in one's development, one tends to rely on internal gratification and self-parenting. As was evident in Kathy's case, the original fantasy of connection leads to a posture of pseudoindependence in the developing child: "I don't need anyone; I can take care of myself." The fantasy bond staves off painful feelings of emotional starvation and emptiness and hence can become functionally autonomous. It can persist for long periods after the deprivation has ceased. Indeed, the internal gratification one achieves through fantasy eventually comes to be preferred over real satisfactions from others.

This preference was clearly demonstrated as Kathy entered adolescence. When she was 15 years old, Kathy developed a serious eating disorder, consisting of compulsive overeating and purging, and at times gained up to 10 pounds within a 2-day period. Whenever she began to show signs of more mature functioning and started forming more consistent relationships, she defended herself against her feelings and sense of vulnerability by engaging in compulsive eating. This was a central theme in her life. She found it difficult to sustain long-term friendships and maintained a peculiar indifference or blankness in relation to planning her future or even toward activities typically enjoyed by adolescents.

Kathy showed several signs of improvement during the years she spent with her foster parents. Nonetheless, when she reached adolescence and tried to develop an adult orientation to school, to peer relationships, and to career possibilities, she began to show signs of regression to a more oral level. In spite of the emotional sustenance and affection she received from her new family, the damage she had sustained in her early life led to a fixation at this level of development, and these patterns were strongly resistant to change.

Even during the more quiescent period of her life from age 5 through 11, Kathy continued to maintain a certain aloofness toward her foster parents. She reacted defensively to her new surroundings and continued to unconsciously imitate patterns of dishonesty and deceit of her biological parents. Lying and stealing were an important part of Kathy's pattern. When confronted, she would persist in lying until the truth could no longer be denied. Sometimes she actually repressed the incidents, successfully lying even to herself about stealing.

As noted previously, when she was a teenager, Kathy entered a phase of self-abuse with laxatives to try to control her weight, a self-destructive posture of serious proportions. In the following excerpt from a group therapy session, Kathy, at age 17, reveals aspects of the underlying pain that drove her to engage in addictive habit patterns symptomatic of her need to "feed" herself.

KATHY: Over the past months I've started to think about myself more and more that I'm bad and that I make people feel bad. I feel like I don't deserve anything myself and I hurt other people, so I should just leave.

THERAPIST: When you start to overeat and start to put on weight, you act as though you're a bad person. How did you connect it to being bad? You hate yourself over this, but why do you think you're a terrible person for it?

KATHY: I know that I feel happy when I'm losing weight. It gives me a sense of myself in a way, but when I'm overeating, I feel bad.

I know that I've always felt bad or there would be things that I did that I knew were bad for me, but instead of just thinking that they make me feel bad or they make me feel unhappy, I think I'm bad for doing them, and then I don't talk about them or I lie about them.

THERAPIST: It seems that first you do something to isolate yourself, something negative or self-destructive like overeating, then you hate yourself for it and then you go further into more destructive behavior. It's a cycle.

KATHY: It doesn't happen overnight. It's been happening my whole life. I've felt bad my whole life. I've always felt that I'm bad. I just know people hate me.

THERAPIST: But where did it come from? How did you get a feeling that you're bad?

KATHY: I don't remember specific things, but I do remember feeling hated, or feeling just a coldness or like it didn't matter that I was there, like I was like a doll or something. I mean, I wasn't a person.

    My mother just wanted a doll, and anything that I needed she hated me for. So I feel like she just hated me because I had needs. She would have rather had a doll that she could just dress and carry around with her and show off to people, that would make her proud and that wouldn't need anything.

THERAPIST: Did you start to feel bad for wanting things?

KATHY: Yeah, I didn't want anything, and whenever I did want something, I felt like I was mean. And I still feel that way.

Later in the session, Kathy recognized that several of the other teenagers had similar feelings about themselves, and they also saw themselves as "bad." She began to identify with their struggle to change their negative view of themselves and, in so doing, developed more compassion for herself and her own struggle to overcome her problems.

KATHY: When I look at myself from the point of view that I'm *not* bad, when I think of myself like that, I feel sad, like saying, "Why did you hate me? I didn't do anything. I don't hate you." And I feel like I don't hate them now, even though I feel like they hate me.

    I don't feel like anything's changed, but I don't hate them. I mean, I don't feel vindictive or like they owe me anything, and I feel like—(*sad, crying*)—"What kind of person hates a baby for being alive?" I feel like that's why *I* was hated, but I feel like it's not my fault.

THERAPIST: I hope you get used to looking at yourself from that point of view.

During this crucial period, Kathy slowly and painstakingly shifted her reliance from the addictive pattern of feeding herself, manifested in her eating disorder, to accepting help and support from others. Signs of progress were seen when she broke her habit of first cheating on her diet and then lying about it. She was encouraged to call whenever she felt the impulse to break her diet. For a time, she phoned several times a day. During this transition, Kathy reported feelings of resentment and guilt about letting people into her life.

However, as the months passed and despite several setbacks, Kathy gradually gave up her dependence on secretive eating to gratify herself and began to depend on other people for support, affection, and validation of herself as a person. Kathy still finds it somewhat difficult to handle affection and admiration from others. She tends to interpret people's positive feelings for her as a sign that they *want* something from her, as her mother did, and she quickly withdraws.

However, understanding and working through the basis for her retreat has enabled her to gradually increase her tolerance for warmth and affection from others.

Repetition of One's Early Family Circumstances in Present-Day Associations

In my clinical work, I have found that the more rejected the child, the more desperately he or she clings to the mother and forms a fantasy bond with her. In this sense, the rejected child cannot leave home, cannot develop an independent life, and transfers this abnormal dependency to other people in new associations (G. Blanck & R. Blanck, 1974; Jacobson, 1964; L. J. Kaplan, 1978; Mahler, Pine, & Bergman, 1975). Consequently, he or she avoids or rejects any experience or person that is not a *repetition* of the early experience. This is the primary reason Kathy was unable for so many years to accept the more constructive environment offered her by her foster parents. This adolescent girl was bound to her natural parents, especially to her mother, by invisible ties of guilt and by her own compelling need to maintain the illusion of parenting herself.

In Kathy's mind, no new set of parents, no amount of warmth or affection, could induce her to "accept the bottle" again. She stubbornly refused to take a chance again after her early experiences with oral deprivation, rejection, and the dreadful feelings of annihilation and disintegration. On one level, she found it necessary to continue to engage in the behaviors she originally used to preserve her integrity and some sense of self by not subjecting herself to potential rejection. In Kathy's eyes, at a deep unconscious level, this was a matter of physical and psychological survival. On a defensive level, she felt that she *must* prove that her new circumstances were as rejecting and as exploitive as the original situation. She was destined, in this sense, to repeat her past rather than develop new ways to cope with her environment.

As in Kathy's case, most of us try to re-create the original conditions in our families. We can do this through three major modes of defense mechanisms: *selection, distortion,* and *provocation* (Firestone, 1985). (1) There is tendency to *select* and marry a person similar to a parent or family member because this is the person to whom one's defenses are appropriate. (2) Perceptions of new significant persons are *distorted* in a direction that corresponds more closely to the members of the original family. (3) If these defensive maneuvers fail to protect us, we tend to behave in ways that *provoke* similar parental reactions in our loved ones.[2]

This latter pattern was the primary defense utilized by Kathy with her foster parents. Beginning with a refusal to keep her room neat, a pattern that brought out nagging, parental, angry reactions from her foster mother, Kathy progressed to acts of delinquency in her bid for negative attention, rejection, and punishment. She needed to prove that she was bad and that others would reject her as her parents had. In the therapy group described above, she gained insight into this habitual reliving of her earlier life.

Progressive and Regressive Polarizaton in Destructive Couple Bonds

Kathy's parents were involved in certain modes of interaction that typify couples who have formed a destructive bond. Whenever one person in a marital relationship habitually responds to the other from a childish, immature posture or from a parental, controlling posture, the relationship inevitably deteriorates into a destructive bond (Firestone, 1987a). By regressing to childish modes of relating, one person can manipulate another into taking care of him. In this way, he or she is able to preserve the imagined security of the original fantasy bond with his or her parents. Some marriages demonstrate role reversals in certain areas of functioning. However, it is rare for *both* parties to relate from an *adult mode.*

External manifestations of the fantasy bond are observable in couple interactions that lend support to an illusion of belonging to another person. Paradoxically, while imagining this connection, people become increasingly divided and alienated from themselves. Most people externalize the self-parenting process through acting out either this "good parent" or "bad child" image with new attachments. In describing this "unconscious interplay of partners," Jurg Willi (1975/1982) writes:

> A person playing a regressive [childish] role despises his progressive partner because being dependent makes him feel weak. He delegates ego-functions such as control, leadership, decision-making and initiative because he is not willing to take responsibility. Indeed, rather than perform these progressive functions himself, he undermines all his partner's

progressive efforts. However, he despises himself for it, because he knows
that he is continually dependent on the partner. (pp. 148-149)

Hellmuth Kaiser, one of the first clinicians to write about a
"delusion of fusion," a concept similar to that of the fantasy bond,
also comments on this polarity:

As his adult intellect does not allow him to maintain an illusion of unity
he [the patient] does something which is a compromise between fusion
and mature relationship: Namely, he behaves *either submissively or
domineeringly* [italics added]. (Cited in Fierman, 1965, p. xix)

People who become involved in long-term relationships tend
either to defer to the other person or to act out a critical, parental
role.

Kathy was born into this type of parental-childish role-playing
with her parents. She learned at an early age to imitate her parents'
style of interacting with each other from parent/child modes. Her
mother had played the helpless child, and her father had assumed a
parental posture of pseudostrength. Because of her father's false
power and authoritarian stance, Kathy learned to associate strength
with meanness. With her foster parents and later with her therapist,
Kathy, like her mother, acted out the child aspect of this polarization.
She attempted to pull excessive caretaking responses from her new
parents and indulged in negative, attention-getting behavior that
nevertheless gave her a sense of security. Actually, her provoking behavior ultimately threatened the relationship with her foster parents.
At one point, her foster parents had nearly reached the limits of their
tolerance of her self-abuse and destructive acting out.

Kathy has now begun to regain some feeling for herself and an
understanding of the ways in which she was damaged. As she has
become more successful in controlling her destructive eating patterns,
her interest in other people and her curiosity about the world, qualities
previously submerged in her personality, have begun to surface.

DAMAGING COMPLICATIONS OF THE FANTASY
BOND ON THE EMERGING FAMILY

To the extent that parents are involved in a fantasy bond and
are deceiving themselves about the nature of their relationship and
about their inward, defended life-style, personal communications be-

tween parents and children will be duplicitous and manipulative. Parental dishonesty and the pretense of closeness perhaps have the most damaging effects on the child's developing sense of reality. To the degree that parents are defended and have substituted a bond for genuine relating, children incorporate their parents' illusions and patterns of self-deception. They learn to distort their own perceptions and deny the reality that their parents are hostile, distant, inward, and self-protective.

Psychologists have commented on the distortions present in many families and have described how they are passed on to the children. Ivan Boszormenyi-Nagy and Geraldine Spark (1973/1984) have written that

> the child's conflicts are directly connected with the interlocked, collusively unconscious, or denied processes which disrupt and interfere with growth of all the family members.... There is a conscious and unconscious *compliance to avoid exposure of the basis of unmet reciprocity* [needs] *between all family members* [italics added]. (p. 251)

In our clinical experience, we have observed the compelling need that couples have to reach a consensus on most issues and find agreement with respect to world view, political allegiance, religious beliefs, and child-rearing philosophy. For example, many people recall a parent telling them, "Your *father and I* (or your mother and I) think you should do thus and so." These individuals report they never knew either parent's separate point of view, opinion, or personal reaction to anything. When parents present this type of united front to the world and to their children, the children find it impossible to voice their perceptions, particularly if they contradict parental belief systems.

The bond within the couple leads to the curtailment of freedom of speech, because certain topics are forbidden. Any communication or conversation that threatens to disrupt the bond or interrupt the illusion of enduring love between parents and family members is not permitted. When personal communication is so restricted, a toxic environment is created for the developing child that fosters hostility and resentment. The child must not show this pain or unhappiness, because this would betray the destructiveness of the family. Perceptions and emotional responses that disrupt the illusion of closeness are suppressed. This, in turn, increases the child's tendency to become inward, secretive, and cynical.

One patient, B.L., who grew up in a household where his parents alternated between violent arguments held in the privacy of their bedroom and long weeks of a silent "truce" nevertheless tended to idealize his parents on some level. In turn, as a young man, he tended to isolate himself and his girlfriend in long, complicated discussions about their relationship. Once, in a moment of clarity, he was able to capture the essence of his parents' bond in a succinct statement, which he applied to himself and to couple relationships in general:

B.L.: Couples choose secret conversations, which are deadly to each person, over being open, honest, and *not* secretive. Their children then are forced to make that same choice, between the secrecy of the bond and real life. The bond in the family implicitly requires secrecy. In a sense, the child dies in the bond rather than choosing the openness of the world.

We have observed that the idealization of parents extends to each family member, who, in turn, believes that his family is superior to other families, that each member must subscribe to family beliefs and to the family's point of view, and that it is wrong to deviate from family tradition. Therefore, free speech and honest perceptions are controlled in typical family life. In this sense, many family constellations take on the dimensions of an oppressive dictatorship that is very hurtful, both to members and outsiders.

CONCLUSION

Unless manifestations of the bond are identified and consistently challenged by parents, their style of relating and pretense of love have a profound detrimental effect on the child born into their union. Initially, parents are virtually the child's whole world. The vulnerable child is born into the unhealthy climate of his or her parents' bond and develops defenses that serve to limit later adjustment. The extent of psychological impairment manifest in the child will depend to a substantial degree on the strength of the fantasy bond in the family and the particular vulnerability and sensitivity of the individual child.

On the other hand, a child who grows up in an atmosphere created by loving and mutually independent parents, who do not subordinate themselves one to the other, has a much better chance of developing his or her full potential. By understanding the dynamics of the fantasy bond and by identifying the symptoms of deterioration within their relationship, parents can begin to disrupt this disruptive destructive tie and halt the perpetuation of the neurotic process into the next generation.

NOTES

1. This decline in sexual activity and attraction is not a symptom that occurs in *all* couples; some couples report increased satisfaction with their sexual relationship as it matures (H. S. Kaplan, 1979; Weigert, 1970).
2. The concept of "projective identification," first described by Melanie Klein (1946) and elaborated by Tansey and Burke (1985), Grotstein (1981), and Ogden (1982), has certain properties in common with the defensive modes of relating that characterize the fantasy bond.

CHAPTER 3

The Core Conflict in Parents:
Hunger versus Love

People are torn between feeling and experiencing their lives and leading a self-protective life-style, cut off from feeling and emotional involvement. The resolution of this conflict has serious implications for child-rearing. Parents exist in a state of conflict between the active pursuit of their goals in the real world, and inward, self-protective defense systems characterized by reliance on fantasy gratification and manifestations of self-nourishing behavior.[1] The more one is damaged in one's early life experiences, the less likely one is to be willing to undertake the risks necessary for self-actualization. Suspicion and distrust in interpersonal relationships, combined with compensatory bond formation, progressively interfere with reality testing and one's ability to cope with real-life situations. The more a person relies on fantasy for satisfaction, the more debilitated he or she becomes in pursuing goals. This, in turn, leads to more frustration and a downward spiral of increasing maladjustment (Firestone, 1985).

All people must choose between self-assertion and dependence, seeking independent fulfillment of their potential or clinging desperately to others and retaining their original identity within the family. Many refrain from taking a chance on adventure, uncertainty, and the possibility of intimate relationships and, instead, repeatedly act out destructive, self-limiting routines that are "safe," familiar, and emotionally deadening.

Aspects of this conflict frequently can be detected in an individual's fantasies or dreams. For example, an associate, who was very assertive and active, revealed that he often had fantasies indicating strong desires to be dependent and taken care of by others. He reported taking a certain amount of satisfaction in imagining that he was ill or hurt. Although his hypochondria was very unpleasant, on a deeper level his fantasies of hospitalization and medical care, where all his needs were attended to, had a certain appeal. This man was particularly open in recognizing and facing his dependency feelings rather than attempting to deny their existence, as is more common. Most people are very ashamed of "childish" propensities in themselves. Thus, they attempt to cover up or overcompensate by becoming authoritarian or parental in their responses or by utilizing other forms of a facade. Basically they repress the unpleasant or socially unacceptable part of the assertion-dependence conflict.

An important dimension of this core conflict involves positive attitudes toward oneself that lead to self-affirmation and approbation versus negative attitudes that influence self-critical and self-destructive behavior. All people are divided within themselves in the sense that they have feelings of warm self-regard as well as feelings of self-hatred and self-depreciation. As they turn inward toward fantasy gratification and become involved in self-nourishing behaviors, they tend to become increasingly self-hating and guilty. Conversely, when they honestly pursue their interests in the real world, they feel a sense of dignity and self-respect. The more an individual comes to rely on fantasy gratification to the exclusion of real relating, the more childlike and dependent he or she becomes. Thus, each dimension of the core conflict is inextricably tied to the others. How a person resolves each aspect of the conflict affects the decision-making process at any moment in time.

THE EFFECTS OF THE CORE CONFLICT ON CHILD-REARING

The resolution of this core conflict has a profound effect on each person's attitudes and overall functioning as a parent and as a role model. The more parents retreat from valuing themselves and minimize or avoid personal relationships, the greater the impairment of parental functions, regardless of their stated commitment or concern for their children. Self-hating adults cannot offer love and physical affection to a child; they cannot relate personally with empathy for a child's needs, nor can they provide the necessary strength and protection to make a child feel secure. Moreover, they are unable to provide sensitive discipline and appropriate socialization of the child while retaining respect and true regard for the child's individuality.

Much as parents indicate positive and negative feelings toward *themselves*, they exhibit both tender, nurturing impulses *and* covert aggressive feelings toward their children. The fact that parents want to nurture their children does not invalidate the hostility they feel toward them. Conversely, the fact that they have destructive feelings toward their children does not negate their love or concern for them. Everyone expresses *both* tendencies in *all* their close relationships. These conflicting responses have far-reaching significance to the development of our children.

This extension of life-style and self-attitudes of the parents has an enormous impact on child development. People who are withdrawn and self-protective are handicapped in adjusting to the responsibilities of parenthood. They tend to pass on their own self-protective style of dealing with life, as they act neglectfully and behave overprotectively. A more self-reliant, outward person relates appropriately to the child's level of maturation and inspires independence and self-direction in his or her children.

Children are incredibly sensitive to their parents' feelings and attitudes toward themselves and react accordingly. Children feel comfortable in an atmosphere in which parents manifest positive regard for themselves, and are able to relax and find security. However, if parents possess strong feelings of inferiority and are predominantly self-critical or self-hating, the child senses an implicit threat to his or her own security and tends to have anticipatory fears of actually losing the parents.

Parental attitudes toward children are a by-product of parents' fundamental conflicts and ambivalence toward themselves. Only through developing compassion toward themselves, and insight into this core conflict, can parents provide the necessary requirements for their children's emotional development. By the same token, to the extent that they fail to recognize this core ambivalence about their own lives and toward their children, they will cause unnecessary damage to their offspring. Suggestions for improving parent-child relations that fail to take into account this basic truth about people can have no lasting effect on parents or children. No parenting technique can be effective in the hands of individuals who are compulsively acting out patterns that express the negative side of this conflict. Paradoxically, any positive approach to child-rearing must include a thorough awareness of covert aggression and its sources.

EMOTIONAL HUNGER—A NEGATIVE MANIFESTATION OF THE CORE CONFLICT IN CHILD-REARING

[First mother]: "I felt angry and intruded upon. That feeling lasted for months. His loud wails...just set me off. I really didn't want to be around him and wished someone would just take him away. I thought to myself, 'You idiot, why did you have this little thing in the first place?'" (p. 131)

[Second mother]: "I breast-fed my child for the first six months, and the closeness was fantastic. I felt merged and meshed with my little one, a feeling that compared to nothing else." (p. 133) (Genevie & Margolies, 1987)

One main reason many parents cause painful and unnecessary damage to their children is that they themselves are often emotionally hungry and immature. This immaturity seriously interferes with a sustained positive relationship, and this is especially evident within the family. When parents are childlike, they frequently are desperate for a connection or a bond with their child. In acting on their desperation and desire to be taken care of themselves, they tend to make parents out of their own children (Parker, 1983).

Individuals who have strong dependency needs left over from childhood have a damaging rather than a nurturing effect on their child's development. Many parents confuse these intense feelings of need and anxious attachment with feelings of genuine love and affection. They fail to make a distinction between emotional hunger, which is a strong *need* caused by deprivation in the parent's own childhood, and feelings of genuine love and concern.

Feelings of emotional hunger are experienced as deep internal sensations, ranging in intensity from a dull ache, to a sharp painful feeling, to general agony. A number of participants in our parenting groups have graphically described their experience of this state of emotional hunger and how they learned to distinguish it from genuine affection. These parents have become progressively more aware of the difference between their strong need to fulfill themselves by living through their children and their desire to give *to* their children.

To illustrate, in one group session, Mrs. R., a mother of two children, recalled feeling that she was desperately searching for emotional satisfaction in her contact with her older son when he was an infant. Here she contrasts her internal state with her outward behavior at the time, which, in retrospect, she now has recognized as being indifferent and even rejecting:

MRS. R.: I felt wrapped up with him, and yet I was a very neglectful mother in other ways, even though I felt strong, intense hungry feelings toward him. If he hugged me I was full. It was fulfilling; I couldn't get him close enough. When I hugged him, I almost could squeeze him back inside myself. It was like a desperate, devouring feeling toward him.

I saw him for what I needed. These words are strong, like what I *needed* from him or with him. I didn't have a feeling for a human being who was there, but I had a feeling for the need and the compulsion toward him.

Parental Behaviors Motivated by Emotional Hunger

Emotional hunger is a powerful feeling. When acted upon, it is both exploitive and damaging to others, especially to children. Often a parent seeks physical contact with his or her child in an attempt to relieve this ache, longing, or agony, as the mother described above had done with her infant son. This type of physical "affection" drains rather than nourishes the emotional resources of the child. It is a form of *taking from* rather than *giving to* the child.

Living through One's Child

A common manifestation of emotional hunger is "feeding on," or living vicariously through, one's child's accomplishments. In one group discussion, Marilyn spoke of feelings of inferiority that drove her to try to enhance her self-image through her son:

MARILYN: He was really everything I ever wanted, from the moment he was born. I remember that I wrote a poem expressing my feelings of wanting. I wanted something that would be all mine. All my frustrations, all my hunger, everything I missed in my childhood, in my life, I wanted to get from him.

My esteem about myself was so low that I was afraid that he would reflect the way that I felt about myself, about people, about life. So he had to be dressed really well. His hair was combed in a way that there was no flaw in it.

I knew that I wanted him to fulfill everything I missed in my life. And it's sad to say this, because at the same time, I thought I was a good mother.

Children Taking Care of Parents—"Parentification"

Parents who have been emotionally deprived to varying degrees while *they* were growing up still have unfulfilled needs for love, comfort, affection, and respect. Many of these men and women turn to their children for reassurances that they are loved and respected.

Mrs. G. felt overwhelmed by the responsibility of raising two small daughters. She recalled how she tried to elicit sympathy and affection from her children whenever she was upset:

MRS. G.: There were many times when I wasn't feeling good myself. A lot of times it would come after I would be explosive with them or I would blow up—not that they were doing anything terrible—but it was just my own mood. Then I would want them to hold me and tell me things were going to be okay, by just holding me and telling me that they still loved me.

Parents use children to soothe their fears and relieve feelings of anxiety. Clare, a successful businesswoman and mother of three children, revealed that she had allowed her daughter to sleep with her from the time the girl was born until she was 5 years old. In a parents' group, she talked about the effect this pattern had on her daughter:

CLARE: I've always had a hard time sleeping by myself at night. When my first daughter was born—you know how a baby cries at night—it's a normal thing. But in pretending to take care of her, I would take her into bed with me. I would sleep with her and keep her with me all night and hold her really close, thinking that I was really loving her and taking care of her. But it soothed me and put me to sleep.

  She grew up feeling like she had to take care of me. When my other two children were born, she took over my role and I went to work. I got a divorce and she took over the role of the mother. I'd come home from work, and this little 6-year-old would pat my face and say "Well, how did you do at work, how are you feeling?" Today she says that she feels like she was never a child.

Anxious Overconcern

Nervous overconcern is another symptom of emotional hunger. Several researchers and clinicians (Minuchin, Rosman, & Baker, 1978) found that psychosomatic illnesses are common in families where parents show an exaggerated degree of fear and concern for each other's health and welfare. Within these families, members are hypersensitive to signs of distress.... The children in turn, particularly the psychosomatically ill child, feel great responsibility for protecting the family. For the sick child, the experience of being able to protect the family by using the symptoms may be a major reinforcement for the illness. (p. 31)

Generally, psychologists agree that many dysfunctional families are "held together" through the process of designating one family member, usually a child, as the "sick one," the "bad one" ("scapegoating"), or the "mentally ill one." By focusing negative attention on a particular child, the family is able to maintain a semblance of stability and continue to function as a cohesive unit. On another level, the "sick" child is aware that he serves this function and that, by remaining ill, he is, in effect, saving his family from dissolution.

Mrs. B., the mother of a 6-week-old infant, gradually became aware of fundamental changes in her interactions with her son that appeared to depend upon her emotional state. She noticed that when she became anxious and self-hating, she concentrated all her attention on her baby and was preoccupied with his physical health and well-being to the exclusion of her husband and friends.

MRS. B.: One difference I notice is that when I'm just relaxed that I have a lot of contact with a lot of people, no matter where he [the baby] is. If I'm holding him, or if someone else is holding him, the rest of my life goes on. I'm aware of all kinds of things that are happening around me.

When I'm in the other frame of mind, I'm very focused on him. I'm aware of who's holding him, how they're holding him, if he's fussy. If I'm holding him, I'm looking at him all the time, even if he's asleep.

Mrs. B. focused on the slightest sign of discomfort or illness in her infant. Later, when she recalled her mother's morbid preoccupation with detecting symptoms of physical illness in herself and her siblings, she came to understand the basis of her hypochondriacal attitude toward both herself and her child. Only with this insight was she able to relax her agitated preoccupation with her son.

Focus on Appearances

Immature parents often become overly concerned with their children's appearance, rather than with their well-being. In describing her feelings, one overly anxious mother stated: "I was more concerned with how he looked than how he really felt." In another case, a patient, whose mother had required him to perform for friends and relatives when he was a child, now finds himself worried about his own daughter's demeanor, behavior, and personality traits. He reported looking at his daughter very critically. "If she isn't looking exactly right, then I feel terrible. I think it's some kind of reflection on me, and I'd better fix it up." Other parents neglect certain areas of their children's lives while intruding insensitively on others. They make concerted efforts to "improve" their children's posture, appearance, dress, athletic or intellectual ability, while at the same time showing indifference to their feelings and opinions.

Overprotection

Parents often have difficulty reconciling a real desire to protect a child from injury with an overawareness of the child's movements, which tends to inhibit and restrict the child's development of independence. These parents unduly restrict their children not because of concern for their safety but because of their emotional hunger, their need to have their child close at hand, and their fears of his or her independence. It is important for the development of independence in the child to allow as much freedom of movement as is consistent with safety.

Parental overprotection is a major dimension of faulty child-rearing and is clearly an outgrowth of emotional hunger and parents' unresolved dependency needs. Murray Bowen (1978) considers "undifferentiated" parents to have grown up "as dependent appendages of their parents, following which they seek other equally dependent relationships" (p. 367). Bowen's studies on parental overprotection show that some forms of oversolicitousness are linked to "the family projection process":

> The process begins with anxiety in the mother. The child responds anxiously to mother, which she misperceives as a problem in the child. The anxious parental effort goes into sympathetic, solicitous, overprotective energy, which is directed more by the mother's anxiety than the reality needs of the child. It establishes a pattern of infantilizing the child, who gradually becomes more impaired and more demanding. (p. 381)

In his book, *Parental Overprotection*, Gordon Parker (1983) also suggests that

> in any attempt to consider the nature and determinants of maternal overprotection some consideration must be given to the mother's incapacity to allow a child's progressive detachment.... Difficulty...may occur if the

infant is oversaturated with the mother or if the mother is intrusive or smothering. (p. 82)

Levy (1943) categorized four separate manifestations of overprotection: excessive contact, infantilization, prevention of independent behavior, and lack or excess of maternal control.

Both fathers and mothers can become overprotective of their offspring. Mr. K. described how he overidentified with his son whenever the youngster was in pain. In making every effort to soothe the boy, he was actually attempting to shut off painful feelings in himself. This overly solicitous treatment, however, was also based on Mr. K.'s desire to spare his child the kind of suffering he had experienced in his own childhood.

MR. K.: When I hear a child cry, it doesn't typically bother me, but when I hear Michael's crying, it's excruciating. I feel like he's in such pain, even if it's a minor thing that's happening. And I think that I'm the only one who can make him feel better.

 I even project what he's going to feel in the future, like he's going to go through such pain when he gets to be a teenager. I know I'm projecting what went on with me, and that it's a gloomy way of looking at things, but my contact with him always has this element to it. He *has* to pick it up. I'll make eye contact with him, and I see a switch. He changes his mood to go along with that feeling I project onto him.

There appear to be two primary motives underlying overprotective tendencies in parents: a benevolent, although misplaced, desire to spare the child pain, as in Mr. K.'s case; and disguised hostility or aggression toward the child. Hostile, self-hating parents try to disown their resentment by reacting to their children overprotectively. At the same time, they become oversolicitous toward their child because they overidentify with his pain.

Exclusion of One Parent

In many family constellations, one parent tends to form an exclusive relationship with the child, which pushes the other parent into the periphery. In most of these cases, it is the mother who forms this close tie, by reason of her availability to the infant, and becomes the most significant figure in the life of her children. But then she turns this close tie into an *exclusive* tie and thereby excludes and minimizes the importance of her husband as father.

In some instances, after becoming a mother, a woman finds less satisfaction in the sexual relationship with her husband and turns to her child for fulfillment and gratification of her need for closeness and affection. Many women find it difficult to combine motherhood and sexuality. Children of such women may come to be used as replacements for their husbands. When this condition exists, the child will feel an inordinate sense of pressure that has a detrimental effect as his sexuality emerges.

FEARS UNDERLYING PARENTS' IMMATURE OR OVERPROTECTIVE RESPONSES

Parenthood symbolizes the end of childhood, and, to many, this signifies separation from parental support systems and the assumption of a role for which they are not emotionally equipped (LeMasters, 1957/1963). This separation anxiety experienced by the parents, together with the needy demands of the infant, arouses strong resentment toward the child. In working with new parents, we have found that many had idealized fantasies of what life would be like after their baby arrived. But reality quickly intruded as the parents faced the responsibilities of 24-hour care of their infant. Reactions to having such fantasies disrupted are varied. Many parents express disappointment, anxiety, resentment, disillusionment, and feelings of being burdened by the care of a new baby (Brody, 1956; Deutsch, 1945; Genevie & Margolies, 1987).

We also found that the infant is often perceived as an intrusion by his or her parents because he or she makes them aware of their responsibilities for another person. Many people find it difficult to take this significant step into adulthood and feel insecure and self-doubting.

A young woman, Janice, contrasts her feelings about being a mother with her former sense of freedom in taking care of other children:

JANICE: When I became the "parent," and I was responsible, I know that I felt differently than before, when I could always give them back. *Then* they weren't an intrusion into me. Now I feel that being the ultimate responsibility really does cut into my being childish, or my deciding that I want to think about myself or my own problems. It even gets down to practical things like sleep. If they feel sick during the night and I have to get up and walk with one of them, that's an intrusion into a time when I have my life set up to sleep.

Other parents who had been deprived or neglected as children find they had trouble offering security and guidance to their own children, particularly during times of stress. Recalling the feelings of insecurity she had experienced while raising her son, Helen connects her fears about being a parent to her own parents' immaturity:

HELEN: When Paul was small, as long as things were running smoothly and there were no ups and downs, I more or less provided for his needs, but if anything happened which disturbed the routine, not even a crisis, but simply changing schools or joining a club, then my whole mood changed. My anxiety became so intense that I didn't know how to deal with it, and I became like a child myself.

I also remember when I was a child and didn't have any mature person around me for guidance. Sometimes my anxiety was aroused to the point that I didn't even know my name; I couldn't think clearly at all. When I had to go to a new school, I felt totally lost.

Immature parents often perceive their child as getting the care and attention that they desire for themselves, and they have strong angry reactions. The childlike, undeveloped parent will actually respond to the child as a competitor for affection and love (Zilboorg, 1932). In some cases, new mothers and fathers show significant signs of jealousy toward the needy infant because the baby requires the undivided attention of their partner.

MANIFESTATIONS OF LOVE AS DISTINGUISHED FROM EMOTIONAL HUNGER

I would define *parental love* as behavior that enhances the well-being of children and would exclude those operations that are destructive to the child's sense of self. A loving attitude reflects all that is nurturing and supportive of the unique personality development of the child. Conversely, it would be a gross distortion to define as *loving* those responses that are detrimental to psychological growth.

In contrast to emotional hunger, which we have seen has a profound destructive effect on the developing child, genuine love sustains and nurtures. Outward manifestations of love—the observable operations of love—can be seen in parents who establish real emotional contact with their children. They make frequent eye contact, display spontaneous, nonclinging physical affection, and take evident pleasure in the child's company.

These parents generally refrain from forming the type of relationship with their children that excludes others. They are sensitive to the fact that love is *not* an emotion that exists in limited quantities and are generous in giving and receiving love in all their important relationships. They are aware of their ambivalence toward their children, and they avoid making pronouncements of unconditional, enduring love, which are usually misleading.

The difference between loving responses and those determined by emotional hunger can be distinguished by an objective observer, but it is difficult for parents themselves to make the distinction. Three factors are valuable in ascertaining the difference: (1) the internal feeling state of the parent, (2) the actual behavior of the parent in relating to the child, and (3) the observable effect of the parent's emotional state and behavior on the child's demeanor and behavior (Greenspan, 1981).

A parent who is capable of giving love typically has a positive self-image (Partridge, 1988) and maintains a sense of compassion for the child and for himself, yet remains separate and aware of the boundaries between them. Such a parent acts respectfully toward the child, and is not abusive or overprotective. The tone and style of communication is natural and easy and indicates a real understanding of the individuality of the child. The loved child actually *looks* loved. He is lively and displays independence appropriate to his age level. He is genuinely centered in himself. The child subjected to emotional hunger is desperate, dependent, and emotionally volatile. An onlooker can observe these important differential effects on children and can often trace them to the specific feeling states of the parents.

In the following sequence from a parenting group, the participants describe how they experience both emotional states—the one of being nurturing and loving and the other of being desperate for a connection with their child. Barry, the father of a 5-year-old girl, talks about his increasing awareness of the contrast in these feeling states:

BARRY: If I'm feeling good and not focused on Marie, then I feel relaxed and also I don't expect anything from her. I don't want anything back. I may be affectionate to her, or I may just look at her or watch her play.

In that other state, I really want a specific response from her, and I want it to be almost in the format that *I* want it. It's something I want out of her, not something that I'm giving to her. And there's also a feeling of tension in being with her.

DR. F.: It's the difference between giving and getting.

BARRY: Yeah, a big difference in that state. Also I know that the feeling of hunger blocks the feeling of love; they don't seem to coexist. If I'm feeling hungry toward her, I don't feel the loving feelings. I realize that the desperation blocks it—it's a different approach to her entirely.

DR. F.: How does it affect her?

BARRY: I think it creates tremendous tension in her, so that she loses her own self and whatever she's doing and she's now looking—to me—to satisfy the hunger.

CATHERINE (mother of two children): Sometimes I feel a joyous feeling or a warmth towards Jenny. She's a very free moving girl, and at a party the other night, she came over to me and I had that feeling of just loving to see her. I thought she was pretty. She got up on my lap, I hugged her and kissed her and then she left. I mean, that was a free-flowing exchange. She went off and folk-danced and I went on about my life.

DR. F.: That is one characteristic of a loving situation—people move in and out of it freely. You don't get that clinging or desperation or holding on to. That is one of the distinguishing characteristics between hunger and love. When children feel comfortable and happy, they move back and forth toward the mother and away from her, and the mother is much the same.

Catherine goes on to make a clear distinction between the feelings she just described and those she experiences when she feels drawn to forming an exclusive connection with her daughter.

CATHERINE: At other times, I feel as if I can help her out in a way that nobody else can. And I'm the only person. It's like we're the only two people in the world, and there are no other people around.

TAM (mother of four): I've noticed that kind of relationship between a mother and a child where I see that intensity and that focus and that type of interest in the child. The child's mother says, "Don't you think he's cold?" And I put myself down that I'm being neglectful because I lack that intense concern.

  I've seen a lot of fathers who put themselves down with their children like that. They think that mothers have these natural maternal feelings that are just part of them genetically and that *they* don't have them. And they don't even realize that something destructive is happening.

Effects of Parental Emotional Hunger on the Child

Immature, overly dependent parents exert a strong pull on their offspring that drains them of their emotional resources. Children feel the pull of this implicit demand by the parents to be taken care of and try to respond to it. Premature efforts by children to fill an "adult" role and offer caretaking responses to parents eventually give rise to psychological or physical symptoms in many children.

Clinging or Avoidant Behavior

Children raised by emotionally hungry or immature parents develop a reciprocal hunger toward their parents. This is frequently seen in the child who clings desperately to the mother and who is afraid to venture out on his or her own. Other children resist being held or cuddled by their parents and stiffen their bodies when they are picked up. These children are often responding to the parent's underlying desperation. Children who avoid or pull away from contact with this type of parent are acting appropriately under the circumstances. Their avoidance is understandable in the face of a parent's devouring need to fulfill herself or himself through the child.

Elsie Broussard (1984), a researcher in child development, has filmed infants reacting adversely to overly nervous or anxious mothers by arching their backs and violently pushing themselves away from their mothers' bodies. Other clinicians have observed patterns of parent-child interactions that are similar to those noted by the author and his associates. Child psychiatrists John Bowlby (1973) and Mary Ainsworth (Ainsworth, Blehar, Waters, & Wall, 1978) have described two unhealthy patterns of attachment that fit the above descriptions of infant behavior. The patterns of anxious/resistant and anxious/avoidant attachment delineated by these clinicians show characteristics that contrast sharply with patterns of secure attachment (Ainsworth, 1982). They found that babies who were anxiously and resistantly attached to their mothers cried more, were less responsive in face-to-face contact, and expressed anger more frequently in reunions with the mother following brief separations than were infants who were securely attached. The mothers were observed to be nervous and tentative and delayed in their responses to their infants' crying. They appeared also to react inconsistently to other behavioral cues in their babies.

Other infants evaluated as anxiously and avoidantly attached to their mothers displayed *less* positive behavior than securely attached babies when picked up and put down. They were less likely to mold their bodies to their mother's body, indicating a general restlessness and inability to relax.

We have observed one distinguishable characteristic of the "clinging" child in his/her appearance and demeanor when being held by his/her parent. There is an all-too-evident spaced-out look similar to a person on drugs. This is *not* the expression one expects to find on a baby's face who is secure. The unhappy, forlorn, pinched expressions on the faces of these children reflect a state of regression, not a happy sense of being the center of mother's attention. Their obvious discontentment and agitation, alternating with a state of stupor, are signs of rejection and emotional deprivation. They are desperately in need of reassurance, love, and approval.

Here, Janice (mentioned earlier), goes on to describe this type of behavior in her children and associates it with an overall feeling of apathy and her withholding state:

JANICE: When I'm not interested in my own life, I notice they become very clingy. I think without knowing it, I'm very clingy to them, and I know it creates a hunger in them, and I know that they are absolutely not satisfied. The more contact I have with them, the hungrier they get. It gets so that they're literally hanging on me or wanting me to hold them. And they're not babies any more; they're getting older and more independent in other ways.

Excessive "Stranger" Anxiety and Separation Anxiety

Studies have shown that infants between the ages of 6 months and 2 years react somewhat fearfully to strangers (Ainsworth, *et al.*, 1978; Bowlby, 1973; Main, Kaplan, & Cassidy, 1985). This type of behavior is partly the result of the child's growing awareness that he and mother are not one, as well as fears of loss triggered by separation experiences. However, the child cared for by immature, emotionally hungry parents tends to exhibit an intensity of fear that is greatly exaggerated in these situations. Being left with a baby-sitter or at a day-care center can be a traumatic experience for the child who is anxiously attached to his/her parent. A secure child, on the other hand, whose parents have little need to hold on to him/her for their own security, has a milder reaction to the same situation.

In one parenting discussion about the effects of parents' desperation toward their children, Marsha described her 3-year-old daughter's behavior at nursery school:

MARSHA: She clings to me and gets very desperate. I can't walk in and out of a room just like anybody else would. It's a big thing. When I leave she falls apart or she'll beg me to stay, practically beg me, like she's desperate, like her life depends on my staying there.

In the same group meeting, Louise revealed similar observations of her 2-year-old son. She has recently become aware of the contrast between her son's independence and initiative when she observes him from a distance, and his deterioration to a whimpering baby whenever she appears on the scene as well as when she leaves. From these observations, Louise gained insight into the subtle signals she was giving him that he was incompetent and helpless:

LOUISE: When he's with me, he clings to me. He'll hang onto my skirt. Yet when I see him from a distance, he's a pretty independent person. I see how he moves freely, and I love to see him that way when I'm not in direct contact with him. So I know that he's not himself when he's clinging to me and acting extremely babyish. He falls apart and doesn't look good. I don't like how he looks when he's in that state.

Symptoms in Older Children and Adults

Children tend to develop a strong sense of insecurity when they are being raised by immature parents. Sometimes these feelings of uncertainty and self-doubt are repressed, and the developing child assumes a pseudoindependent, tough exterior to compensate for the underlying panic and fear. In a family meeting, Wendy, who at 16 typically displays a self-assured, sophisticated facade, talks about recurring nightmares she remembers having when she was younger:

WENDY: I always had nightmares, really bad dreams of terrible disasters, and I had to take care of everybody, like I was this super-hero and I had to save everybody. But it was every night, I had those same dreams. Also I had another dream, that I got lost and fell in a manhole and couldn't find my way back home. I would alternate those two nightmares.

   (*Talking to her mother*): I know I felt like you weren't going to take care of me. I felt like I had to take care of you.

Feelings of Being Suffocated, Drained, and Depleted

A child caressed b a hungry, needy parent does not feel loved and secure. Such a child becomes refractory to physical touch and feels trapped by close relationships later in life. Many adult patients who report feeling drained of their initiative and energy as children by their parents' insecurity continue to feel drained of their energy by partners, regardless of the real situation.

In these individuals, the residual effects of parental hunger on the adult's personality are frequently expressed as a fear of success, severe anxiety, or passive-aggressive tendencies. As children, they were made to believe that they were too helpless to cope with the world on their own. At the same time, they felt compelled to try to make their parents happy: in some cases, to relieve the distress of a seriously depressed parent. Some children become withholding out of a fear of being depleted because their parents are *overinvested* in their achievements and feed off, "swallow up," their accomplishments.

In the following sequence from a parenting discussion, Norma, 28, talks about her difficulties in maintaining close, enduring relationships because of recurring anxiety states and phobic reactions. She begins by describing her mother's need to be taken care of and how it affected her:

NORMA: I've been trying to think about my mother's desperation towards me and how it really affected me, how it manifested itself in me. One thing I thought about is that she specifically related something to me, because she was always miserable and I felt like she needed my attention a hundred percent of the time, all the time; particularly if she felt bad, she needed me.

And I feel like that's what was in her hunger towards me, that she really made me feel like I kept her alive and that she kept me alive and without her I would not exist—that I cannot exist or I don't have the resources to be a full human being.

I know that even in my life now that's the anxiety I go through when I begin to feel good. If I feel strong, that's the feeling I get.

That's the lie between the parent and the child, that the parent transmits. The kid is not free any more. They aren't free to go on, to live their own life as if they're an entity in themselves.

DR. F.: They feel like they don't belong to themselves.

NORMA: Exactly, and if I see anything with a child now, a small child, where I feel that going on, I feel such rage, you know, I feel so bad for the child. (*sad and angry*) I feel so angry when I see a woman being protective toward a child in that way to make them feel that they cannot exist. I mean, I feel like screaming. I feel like saying: "Stay away from the child, let him be, let him feel strong and good by himself."

At a later session, Norma related a conversation she had initiated with her father in an effort to learn more about her childhood. Her father revealed that he had always felt rejected *by her* and described how, at 6 months, she had cried and screamed, pushing him away whenever he had tried to pick her up. This new information confirmed Norma's insights concerning the strong connection her mother had established with her very early in her life—a destructive tie that had completely excluded her father.

Others recalled feeling smothered in the "affectionate" embrace of their mothers. One young man, Donald, whose mother was overly demonstrative during his formative years, spoke of her style of affection in a recent group meeting:

> DONALD: Just listening to people talk about these feelings or just hearing the subject being addressed made me feel something about the way my mother was toward me—just the intense focus on me, but it was so confusing. First there would be that intensity of the focus on me and how great I was and I felt like I had to perform, and then there would be a total rejection.
>
> But I think that when Mrs. R. (the mother who reported having felt "desperate, devouring feelings" toward her infant son) was talking more than anything, I could identify that feeling of being smothered. I remember my mother's affection. She would wrap around me so that I couldn't breathe.

As a father, Donald now had difficulty relating closely to his family. He tended to push away his children's affection, because he was embarrassed and uncomfortable with their enthusiasm. Their attention revived claustrophobic feelings from his childhood, causing him to distrust and limit their positive responses.

CONCLUSION

Parents in conflict within themselves have mistaken notions about the nature of love, as well as misconceptions about the helplessness of children. In the first instance, as described throughout this chapter, parents often confuse feelings of emotional hunger with genuine concern for their children. In the second instance, many parents tend to have an exaggerated notion of the helplessness of children based on a projection of their own fears and feelings of inadequacy. Their overprotectiveness fosters unnecessary fear and dependency in their children. Because of a sense of their own helplessness, they fail to appreciate the real capabilities of their children at different developmental stages. In attempting to protect their children from feeling fear and sadness, they inadvertently inhibit their growth and development.

There are exceptions (Tronick, Cohn, & Shea, 1986), but the concept of emotional hunger has not been sufficiently investigated in the psychological literature. Yet it is one of the principal factors affecting child-rearing practices. The immaturity of many parents expressed as their need to fulfill themselves through their children has powerful negative effects on a child's development and subsequent adjustment.

By recognizing important manifestations of this core conflict within themselves, many parents in our groups have changed responses to their offspring that were based on incorrect assumptions, and have significantly improved the quality of their family relationships. Finally, from our studies of family interactions, we have begun to question the quality of the maternal-infant bond or attachment formed in the early hours and days of an infant's life. As students of human behavior, we feel it is incumbent on us and on developmental psychologists to clarify the extent to which this bond or attachment may be based on emotional hunger and the needs of immature parents for a *connection* to the child rather than on genuine concern and love for the child.

NOTES

1. In his essay "On Narcissism: An Introduction," Freud (1914/1957) postulated a basic conflict between the energies of the sexual drive, that is, the libido, which are directed toward preserving the species, and the ego-instincts, which are directed toward preserving the self. In the same essay, Freud also described the individual's compensatory reliance on fantasy gratification versus seeking satisfaction in the real world—a theme that is central to my own conceptualization of man's basic conflict.

   In *Civilization and Its Discontents*, Freud (1930/1961) developed his conceptualizations concerning the death instinct (Thanatos) operating in opposition to the life instinct (Eros).

   My approach is a departure from classical drive theory and is more closely aligned with the approaches of Sullivan, Fairbairn, Balint, and Sandler, in that it represents an interplay between the classical drive/structure model of Freud and the relational/structure model of the object relation theorists. (See *Object Relations in Psychoanalytic Theory* [Greenberg & Mitchell, 1983] for a complete discussion of theoretical models of neopsychoanalytic thought.)

   In my conceptualization of neurosis, I suggest that emotional deprivation creates ego deficits and disturbances in early object relations during the pre-Oedipal phase. Compensatory defenses (the fantasy bond and secondary defenses) lead, in turn, to the core conflict wherein man is torn between actively seeking gratification in the external world and relying on fantasy and self-nourishing habit patterns for gratification.

   In formulating early faulty object relations as the basis of later inappropriate and self-defeating resolutions to internal conflicts, my theoretical approach advances neopsychoanalytic theory by giving primacy to a relational/structure model. At the same time, it accounts for powerful conflicting drives toward self-actualization on the one hand, and dependent, self-parenting, and self-destructive machinations on the other.

CHAPTER 4

Parental Defenses and How They Are Transmitted

Man is inherently capable of cooperation, and there will be less unnatural behavior [war, genocide, racial persecution, human exploitation, and crimes of violence] when the transmission of destructiveness from mother to daughter [and from parent to child] is meliorated.
Joseph C. Rheingold (1967), *The Mother, Anxiety, and Death* (p. 209)

Psychological defenses erected by children to protect themselves against painful feelings can eventually become more damaging than the original trauma. Reactions that once were appropriate for the child, who was at the mercy of his or her environment, are no longer appropriate for an active adult who can, to a large extent, affect his/her world. Yet, the fear of change leads people to preserve these self-protective patterns long after the original traumatic events have passed.

It is important to note that defenses are instituted early in life in an attempt to cope with emotional deprivation and separation anxiety. Most people experience some degree of pain in their childhood that leads them to develop defenses. Later, these patterns crystallize in relation to the anxiety of death, the ultimate separation. A complete awareness of our personal death, or of the end of our existence as we know it, fills us with terror if we look at it without our customary defenses. In this sense, psychological defenses become a matter of life and death, in that they reduce or dispel our anxiety and dread of death.

It is logical, then, that parents would feel both a need and an obligation to instruct their children in the basic ways *they* have learned to cope. In addition, most parents are unaware that they are reverting to inappropriate responses with respect to their present circumstances. They simply attempt to pass on what they know. Although most parents remain largely unconscious of the fact that their defenses operate to the detriment of their child, parental defenses have a profound influence on the developing child's position and attitudes toward life. These so-called survival techniques are passed on to the child not only directly through instruction, reward, and punishment, they are transmitted also indirectly through nonverbal cues and the process of imitation.

THE INHERENT DESTRUCTIVENESS
OF DEFENSES

Most parents manipulate the emotional climate in the home to maintain a certain distance from each other and from their children, a distance and control with which they are comfortable. This alienation interferes with genuine empathic contact and is injurious to the child.

In his book, *The Politics of Experience*, R. D. Laing (1967) focused his attention on the fact that people's defenses not only detract from their own life experience, but they also harm other individuals:

> These "defenses" are action on oneself. But "defenses" are not only intrapersonal, they are *transpersonal*. I act not only on myself, I can act upon you. (pp. 35-36)

Laing's view of defense patterns is congenial to my own approach. I contend that human beings cannot be "innocently" defended, because by protecting themselves against being vulnerable to pain and sadness, they necessarily fracture the experience of others and distort their sense of reality.

The defended individual is basically unwilling to take a chance again on external gratification, fearing disappointment and rejection from the interpersonal environment. People's self-protective armor supports a basic distrust that keeps them from investing fully in their personal lives. This defensive trend causes harm in all interpersonal relationships but is particularly destructive in child-rearing.

MAJOR DEFENSE PATTERNS

The Suppression of Feeling Responses

Adults who grew up in a hurtful home situation gradually disengage from that part of the self that was in pain. In doing so, they remove themselves from feelings of compassion for themselves and for others. As parents, they move in and out of feeling for their children. When they retreat to a more detached, inward state, they are blocked from responding sensitively. Furthermore, many parents become depersonalized to varying degrees and no longer identify closely with their lives. Instead, they develop facades or masks, and their children are starved for real contact. These mothers and fathers interact impersonally with family members, responding primarily with role-determined, conventionally acceptable feelings. Feelings of anger, sadness, competitiveness, and jealousy are unacceptable. Therefore, they suppress their emotions, already turned against the self, and experience self-hatred and guilt.

Eventually, existing in an unfeeling state becomes a comfortable way of life. In fact, many parents have revealed that until traumatic events, that is, work failure, loss of status, or divorce, created a major disruption in their lives, they felt reasonably content, cut off from feeling.

A number of other defense patterns function to dull or suppress feelings of pain and anxiety, including addictive and compulsive habits.

Addiction to Substances as Painkillers

In denying oneself satisfaction from personal relationships, one comes to rely on self-nourishing habits as a substitute. Parents who become involved in addictive habits, such as excessive drug use, alcoholism, or a cycle of overeating and dieting, are trying to numb primal pain from the past, as well as reacting to present-day stress and frustration. Those who make excessive use of addictive substances come to exist in a dazed, dulled state for extended periods of time, thereby prohibiting constructive relating to their children. It has been well documented that children of alcoholic parents "learn" through imitation to adopt a life-style of addiction when *they* become adults and find it very difficult to break their addictive habits (Black, 1981; Wegscheider, 1981).

Addiction to Routines or Compulsive Work Habits

Any routine, repetitive activity, or ritual can be used to reduce one's sensitivity to painful emotions. Routines offer a false sense of permanence because of their repetitive nature, yet they have the effect of deadening oneself as a feeling person. Compulsive athletics, shopping, TV watching, card playing, and so forth, can be very detrimental to couple and family relations. A large number of family disputes are precipitated by these compulsive habits.

Many parents become workaholics, using work that would otherwise be constructive to cut off feelings and retreat from personal life. It is ironic that the man who devotes himself to making a living by working long hours "for the sake of his children" ends up hurting himself, his children, and alienating his family irreparably. The wage earner returns home in the evening, anticipating gratitude, warmth, and personal contact with his family, but is often disappointed. His habitual use of work to cut off feeling has left him in a state of tension that has alienated him from the people closest to him.

Withholding

Withholding is a major defense that protects the self-parenting process from intrusion by limiting an individual's emotional transactions both in giving to, and in taking from, the interpersonal environment. Withholding is a holding back of *positive* qualities and emotional responses. It entails both passive-aggressive elements and more fundamental components of self-denial. Very often, a child learns to inhibit feelingful responses, such as affection or enthusiasm, that are not tolerated because they pose a threat to his parents. This policy persists into adult life, with or without conscious awareness. Although basically directed against oneself as self-denial or self-limitation, withholding incidentally hurts one's close associates and family members.

A child of withholding parents displays an exaggerated hunger and desperation for love. Harry Stack Sullivan (1953) pointed out that the child who is hurt by rejection develops a malevolent, hostile, untrusting attitude toward people that becomes a basic character defense. Sullivan's observations validate our point of view on the origins of defensive patterns of withholding. When parents covertly or overtly reject their child, he/she, in turn, learns *not* to trust other persons and progressively holds back from significant others as an adult.

The defense of withholding also includes the inhibition or holding back of sexual responses, a defense that is unconscious and automatic in many cases. Men and women who have retreated from fulfilling themselves in an adult manner in their sexual relating manifest other signs of immaturity. The hostility, tension, and confusion in the home when one or both partners withhold sexually have very destructive effects on the psychological climate.

Isolation and Solitary Activities

Isolation can be used for creative work, planning, and relaxation, but time alone is often utilized by people for indulging in self-nourishing habits, for engaging in self-hating ruminations, or for unrealistic fantasizing. Many parents we worked with grew up in homes where they experienced an absence of tension *only* when they were alone. They learned to cherish their private time and found it absolutely necessary for replenishing themselves after abrasive contact with their parents and siblings. As adults, they still felt a strong need to retreat to a private sanctuary and maintain an inward posture. A parent's exaggerated need to be alone, quiet, and insulated conflicts with the child's need for ongoing personal companionship and genuine sharing of activities. When true relating is absent, the child feels hurt and rejected and has a sense of not being seen. Eventually, the isolated child responds to his parents' inwardness by adopting a similar defensive posture.

Self-Depreciating Attitudes and Self-Hatred

An important part of the structure of such defenses involves maintaining an image of one's parents as "good" and an image of oneself as bad. These attitudes serve to maintain one's bond with one's family and offer a kind of security, even after one becomes an adult. On a deep level many parents still believe they are unlovable or unworthy of being loved, and they project these feelings of self-depreciation onto their children.

Child-rearing experts (Branden, 1969/1971; Earls, Beardslee, & Garrison, 1987; Ricks, 1985) agree that a parent's feeling of positive self-regard is a major factor which contributes to the child's developing a healthy self-esteem. When parents hate themselves, consciously or unconsciously, they pass on their lack of self-regard to their offspring. Either they reject the child as they reject themselves, or they see their own negative qualities in the child and punish him for them.

Vanity as a Defense Mechanism—Compensation for Feelings of Inferiority

Vanity is a fantasized positive image of the self that originates when people utilize false praise and flattery to make up for the absence of genuine emotional responses of affection and real appreciation and acknowledgment. Vanity as such represents an individual's attempt to cover up, to defend against, deep-seated feelings of inadequacy. This compensatory image serves still another function. Its powerful survival connotation acts as a defense against death anxiety. In imagining oneself as "special," unusually talented, beautiful, or exceptionally brilliant, one does not feel subject to death, as are "ordinary" people. In that sense, vanity and fantasies of "greatness" are associated with omnipotence.

Feelings of exaggerated self-importance and superiority are self-feeding mechanisms whereby one nourishes oneself with an image of being superior, or special, and establishes a feeling of pseudo-independence and invulnerability. When a person has a strong stake in feeling omnipotent, blows to vanity generate pain and hatred (Sullivan, 1940). Moreover, when vanity is threatened, the person is thrown back into a state of feeling worthless and unlovable.

How Parents' Defenses Interfere with Sustaining Close Personal Relationships

There are several reasons why parents are unable to maintain consistent loving relationships with their children: (1) children arouse painful primal feelings in parents; (2) parents are themselves intolerant of accepting love; (3) there is social pressure to offer unconditional love to children; and (4) many children become unlikable.

1. *Children arouse painful primal feelings.* As noted earlier, one of the most significant findings gathered in our clinical practice and from parents in our discussion groups is the phenomenon of parents' remaining insensitive to their children in the areas where they, the parents, are most defended. We have observed that, in general, a parent unconsciously avoids close personal contact with the child or becomes punishing when the child is going through a specific phase in his development where the parent was hurt and forced to construct defenses. Many people have revealed that they become distant from their child during these periods, because contact with the child reminds them of painful events from specific periods in their own childhoods. They report that positive interactions and tender, sensitive moments with the child arouse deep, "primal" emotions they have been avoiding for years.

In the following transcribed segment of a parents' group, Mr. W., the father of two children, explores his reactions to his 6-year-old daughter. As he talks, he begins to realize that his daughter is experiencing the same pain and distress that he suffered in interactions with his own father. He recognizes that he is constantly defending himself against feeling this pain by avoiding close contact with the child. Furthermore, the time sequences coincide; this man was approximately 6 years old when his mother began to develop signs of chronic mental illness, and he turned more to his father for support.

MR. W.: I remember that when my father would come home from work, I would be thrilled to see him. I would run and jump into his arms and hug him. Sometimes he would be happy to see me, but mostly he would seem angry or would seem to ignore me.

I remember especially Sunday mornings. I would wake up, and my father would be sitting in the living room, reading his newspaper. I would ask him to play with me or take me to the park or play catch, but he would be angry at me disturbing him from reading his newspaper. I remember trying to stifle that feeling of enthusiasm or that feeling of loving him—(*sad*)—just struggling to get that feeling under control, because I thought there was something wrong with it.

Today I feel that same thing going on with my daughter. She rushes up to me just like that, but I try to squelch her. I know that I'm having the same effect on her that *he* had on me, but I almost can't help it.

By recognizing the similarities between the treatment he received from his father and his own responses to his daughter, Mr. W. was able to begin to make positive changes in his relationship with her. Several months later, he speaks again about this subject:

MR. W.: I feel a definite change in the way I relate to my daughter since I began talking about the relationship. I'm better able to carry on an ordinary conversation with her, to talk to her about myself, just as I would to any other person.

I think the most important thing that has happened is that when I find myself wanting to discourage her affection, I have an awareness that stops me in my tracks and makes me turn it around, so that I'm not pushing her away. I'm able to accept her affection in a way that *does* make me sad at times, but I feel happy being able to give her something that I was never able to have as a child.

2. *Parents are intolerant of accepting love.* Parents who have grown up with an image of themselves as unlovable are often resistant to having close, tender moments with their children and having their child look at them with love. It is painful and anxiety-provoking to feel loved as an adult when there was very little love and affection in one's own childhood. It is difficult to change one's identity as unlovable.

Parents may initially feel affection for their baby and yet begin to hold back their positive responses as the baby grows older. Some mothers and fathers simply cannot tolerate their baby's budding recognition of them. They find it too painful to feel the trusting, loving looks and smiles their baby gives them during the first few months of life.

One young mother who had grown up with deep feelings of being unlovable began to reject her baby as soon as it started to respond to her with smiles and expressions of pleasure. She avoided direct eye contact with her daughter and gave up breast-feeding. Her rationalization was that her baby was "more comfortable" bottle-fed. She began holding back her expressions of affection when her infant was 2 months old and was able to recognize and to respond to familiar faces. However, it was not until months later that she noticed the child's unhappiness and distress and was able to trace the change in her own feelings to this significant phase in her daughter's development. She realized that she had found it too painful to allow her baby to react to her with obvious love and recognition and that she had distanced herself unconsciously from the child.

Being loved and valued by their children induces in many parents a poignant, painful sadness they find difficult to endure. Many pull away from their child soon after close contact.

When parents cannot bear to feel their children loving them, they respond negatively to them. Books on child-rearing do not give this phenomenon the importance it deserves. Most people and many clinicians assume that parents are gratified and thrilled to see their baby's first smiles of happy recognition. Generally, this is true on a conscious level. However, these same expressions arouse painful feelings of sadness in parents who have spent their lives warding off intimacy and positive interactions. *The unwillingness of defended parents to allow repressed emotions to reemerge during tender moments with their children is a major reason those parents find it difficult to sustain loving, affectionate relationships with their children.*

3. *Social pressure is related to the myth of unconditional love.* The myth of unconditional love has become a fundamental part of our morality and leads to guilt reactions in parents who have a limited ability to sustain loving interactions with their offspring. The fact that parents are *supposed* to love their children, all the time, unconditionally, creates a lot of pressure in most parents. It is quite unusual to encounter parents who have no personal limitations and who are capable of loving a child to such a degree. It serves no constructive purpose for parents to conceal their limitations or weaknesses from themselves and their children. An honest acceptance of inadequacies enables parents and children to cope with reality without additional defensive pressure.

The myth or fantasy of love within the couple extends to the family and can develop into a conspiracy to deny negative feelings and to cover up pain. It is well to be cautious of the words *love* and *I love you.* If parents would examine their motives honestly, they might discover that they say these words most often *not* when they really feel *for* their children, but rather when they feel the need for reassurance *from* them. For this reason, many children grow up resentful, hostile, and suspicious about "love" and about the obligations it implies.

If the naive conception or illusion of unconditional parental love were withdrawn from the child-rearing situation, it would be better for all concerned. Honest, unloving fathers and mothers inflict far less damage on their children than role-playing, "loving" parents. The alienated or rejecting parent, of course, causes the child pain. However, a dishonestly accepting/rejecting parent not only causes the child emotional distress but also compounds the hurt by distorting the child's sense of reality.

4. *Many children become unlikable.* Another reason parents find it difficult to sustain affectionate responses toward their offspring is that hurt children often develop unpleasant, undesirable personality traits;

they become unlikable. Damage to children early in life tends to have negative effects on their character, making them difficult to like and love. Many rejected children become needy, desperate, hostile, unattractive, difficult to be with, and inspire further rejection by parents and other people as well.

Defenses and bad habits are formed very early in life. A cycle of rejection is set in motion. By the time children are 2 or 3 years old, they no longer are the naive, innocent, pure creatures they once were. They learn early in life to withhold their capabilities, to act out passive or active aggression, whine, complain, and embarrass and manipulate their parents through "learned helplessness." Contrary to popular opinion, children are not just "going through a phase" when they act out these regressive behaviors or are "bad" or unpleasant. Unless interrupted, the obnoxious habits children form at an early age will persist and develop into more sophisticated negative behavior patterns and deep character defenses when they are adults.

In addition to adopting many of their parents' positive traits, children take on their parents' self-protective maneuvers and negative characteristics as their own through the process of imitation. Many fathers and mothers, observing traits developing in their offspring that they dislike within themselves, find the youngster increasingly unappealing and unpleasant to be with. Parents' efforts to correct bad habits in their children often fail because they do not deal with the underlying causes of these negative manifestations.

HOW DEFENSES ARE TRANSMITTED

Parents' defenses are transmitted through direct teaching and through unconscious modeling or imitation. The latter is by far the more important and has more extensive effects, because children have a strong need to model themselves after parental figures.

Direct Methods of Transmission

One of the first lessons one is taught in the course of one's family conditioning is that one is not enough to exist in the world on one's own. One is *instructed* [italics added] in great detail to disown one's own self and to live agglutinatively, so that one glues bits of other people onto oneself.... This is alienation, in the sense of a passive submission to invasion by others, originally the family others. (Cooper, 1970/1971, p. 9)

There are two principal methods of explicit training or teaching utilized by parents in the socialization process: (1) verbal instruction and (2) differential rewards and punishments.

Verbal Instruction

Parents teach their children the information necessary to "get along in the world" and train them in the behaviors acceptable in our culture. They instruct children in the particular belief systems held by the family in order to transmit the values and idiosyncratic points of view that they believe to be appropriate and functional. Mothers and fathers anticipate that this formal mode of instruction will function as a preventive measure and that their children will adopt their beliefs and values, which in most instances are permeated with the parents' defensive strategies. In addition, in many instances, this training takes the form of lecturing, nagging, or even attacking the child. Children may receive severe tongue lashings when they fail to live up to parental expectations. They internalize the harsh tone that usually accompanies these punitive, sometimes humiliating, "object lessons," when parents reiterate their warnings and prohibitions.

The emotional attitudes implicit in the training program are assimilated and internalized by the child and form the core of subsequent self-attacks and recriminations. The content of verbal training and the parents' underlying feelings are both important in the child's development.

Differential Rewards and Punishments

Parents react positively to behavior that they approve of and negatively to reactions of the child that are not in harmony with their ideas, value systems, or basic defenses. They attempt to control the child's behavior and teach him eventually to discipline himself accordingly. Although behavior modification is not totally a conscious process on the part of parents, their system of rewards and punishments shapes the child's character and personality for better or worse.

The effectiveness of positive and negative reinforcement in learning has been validated by numerous research findings (Bandura, 1969; Bandura & Walters, 1963; Skinner, 1938, 1953). Child-rearing experts emphasize that *threats* of punishment are less effective than actual punishment, primarily because parents generally fail to back up their threats with action. But in some instances, punishment can even result in an *increase* in the undesirable response. This occurs when parents feel guilty about excessive or harsh punishment and attempt to "make amends by being overly solicitous or offering special treatment after punishment" (Bellack & Hersen, 1977, p. 196).

Both tangible rewards and verbal approval are used by parents as inducements for desirable behavior. A combination of reward and some form of negative consequence or disapproval for misconduct, *if applied consistently*, is usually an effective means to socialize children. However, its application requires the categorization of children's behavior as either "good" or "bad." Unfortunately, all of these methods—lectures, object lessons, and a system of reward and punishment—are also used by parents to teach children defensive behaviors that act to perpetuate the parents' defense systems.

Indirect Methods of Transmission

Assimilation of the Mother's Anxiety through Touch and Other Nonverbal Cues

Recent studies indicate that infants are exceptionally sensitive to their immediate surroundings soon after birth (and perhaps even before) (Macfarlane, 1977; Stratton, 1982). They tend to react with their entire being to stimulation, especially to touch. Recent research in infant development has been directed toward studying aspects of the mother's feeling state that appear to be transmitted to her infant through this sense of touch (Stern, 1985).

Much as the young deer stiffens in fear at the moment its mother is startled by a sound in the forest, so does the infant respond totally to nonverbal cues from the mother (Hinde, 1974). Indeed, it is impossible for a fearful, nervous mother to hide her anxiety from her baby. He/she will pick up or assimilate *her* emotional state and automatically take it on as his/her own, eventually experiencing the sensation of fear as if it had originated within him/her. This primitive form of implicit learning sets the stage for more complex forms of imitation (Clyman, Emde, Kempe, & Harmon, 1986; Massie, Bronstein, Afterman, & Campbell, 1988; Spitz, 1950; Stern, 1985; Stewart, 1953; Tronick *et al.*, 1986).

Physical touch, facial expression, and other cues in the mother transmit differential affective states to babies from birth. Rheingold (1964) contends that even in the first months of life, "some inarticulable impress of her [the mother] becomes incorporated in what is to be deep body-memory" (p. 30).

> [The infant] receives his information through direct body contact, empathy, and the emergent special senses....
>
> In the long period of their [mother and infant] relatedness by direct body contact, does he receive the jarring physical impact of an unconsciously hostile, anxiously tense, or overefficient mother?...
>
> So far as known sensory channels are concerned, I am impressed by the extraordinary informativeness of physical contact, not only in infancy but throughout life. Not even the mother's facial expression, her tone of voice, and her muscle tonus and movements, all of which are sensitive indicators, approach in telltaleness what is conveyed to the child when his mother touches him. In my experience one of the most telling insights into the mother's attitudes is the patient's recall of how he felt when the mother performed the ordinary duties of child care and even when embracing him with apparent affection. The hand, it would seem, betrays the mother. (pp. 30-31)

Our findings and observations are similar to those reported by Rheingold. The process of defending oneself starts earlier than many people recognize. Very young babies can learn to be impersonal, to look beyond or through another person, to turn their heads away, to avert their gaze. Babies and infants sense parents' unwillingness to make real contact, because of the discomfort and anxiety aroused. They learn very soon to adjust their own responses accordingly.

Imitation

The process of imitation has been shown to be more powerful than direct learning (Baer & Sherman, 1964; Baer, Peterson, & Sherman, 1967; Bandura, 1969, 1971; Bandura & Walters, 1963). Even newborn infants have the ability to imitate the actions of a *model* (the person performing the behavior to be imitated).

One reason why imitation is so powerful and has such long-lasting effects is because it often takes place on an unconscious level. Specialists in child development have found that children readily imitate the behaviors and communications of a model under a wide range of conditions. Most children learn quickly through imitating the actions of individuals whom they admire and who offer them rewards for accurate imitations. This form of learning is incidental. Young children acquire the model's character traits, mannerisms, and habitual styles of responding to the world, all without being aware that they are assimilating these patterns. The process of imitation is primarily responsible for the child's taking on both the positive and *negative* parental traits, as well as their defensive responses to the world.

Learning under Traumatic Conditions

Incorporation and Introjection of Negative Parental Characteristics under Stress

Research has demonstrated that imitation may occur *more readily under punitive conditions or trauma*; that is, when parents are acting on aggressive impulses and hostile feelings (Bandura, 1986). Even when a parent is congenial and accepts the child most of the time, the child is powerfully affected at those less frequent times when that same parent becomes harsh and punitive. In other words, children become sensitized to the worst side of the parent.

A father of my acquaintance, who was generally easygoing and generous with his three children, nevertheless was at times very impatient with the incompetence and lack of coordination of his 5-year-old son. One day he became increasingly annoyed with the boy's lack of success in learning to ride his new 2-wheeled bicycle. He suddenly began yelling loudly at the youngster, locked the bike in the garage, and refused to allow the boy to ride it for a week. Although expressions of anger by this father were atypical, they had a profound effect on the boy's development. These negative interactions were the experiences that the son recalled in later life and that remained in the foreground of his perception of his father. As an adult, he showed the same intolerance for incompetence and awkwardness in his own children that had characterized his father's attitude when defensive and angry.

Identification with the Aggressor

When parents become excessively angry or explosive and the child's anxiety is aroused, the child tries to avoid the full experience of distress. In a desperate attempt to relieve his or her fear, he or she ceases to identify with the self as a weak, hurting child, and identifies with the powerful, punishing parent. This shift in identification affords a measure of relief to the child, who no longer feels inadequate or helpless, but has assumed the identity of the aggressor—the angry parent—and now imitates that parent's punitive posture and behavior.

The process of identification with the aggressor was first described by Anna Freud (1946), and the concept was employed by Bettelheim (1943/1979) to explain the behavior of prisoners in concentration camps who imitated the sadistic, cruel behavior of SS guards. (See also Sandler, 1985, and Steele & Pollock, 1974.) In a similar fashion, children take on negative traits of their parents and, through the process of identification, they introject or incorporate their parents' hostile, critical attitudes *toward themselves*. In aligning themselves with the parent in this way, they become at once the weak, bad child and the strong, good parent—the helpless victim and the severe, punitive critic. This process acts to reduce the anxiety and insecurity felt by children under extreme conditions of stress, and the fantasy bond or connection with parental figures is maintained and supports an illusion of safety and self-sufficiency. The parents' rage is internalized by the child during these traumatic episodes and is indelibly stamped on his psyche, to be unleashed much later on himself and on succeeding generations.

This phenomenon of identification with the aggressive or attacking adult is sometimes observed in play therapy sessions, when an abused child takes the role of the authoritarian, punitive parent in symbolic play with dolls or other objects. These children repeatedly act out forms of abusive behavior (with considerable emotional release) they experienced within the family—a direct link to the later parental abuse of their children.

Case Study Illustrating Transmission of Defenses

The following is an intergenerational study of three men—a grandfather, a father, and a son—each of whom lived and acted upon a somewhat paranoid orientation toward life. Each family member pursued an isolated, tight, defended pattern of existence. Defensive withholding patterns characterized by omnipotence and superiority, contrasted with self-critical and self-punitive attitudes, played a significant role in their unhappiness and maladjustment.

Interview material with second- and third-generation family members (Wally and Danny) revealed the means, both direct and implicit, of transmitting these patterns. These deeply entrenched character defenses were very resistant to change and extremely difficult to challenge in psychotherapy.

Wally reported that his father, a lonely, deeply cynical man with perfectionistic standards, had often warned him about personal relationships, especially with women. Statements such as "Women are impossible to predict; you never can trust them," were spoken, and similar attitudes were implied. Wally's relationship with his mother, and later with his stepmother, confirmed his father's impression. These women were cold, unfeeling, and manipulative. His father's basic prejudices toward women acted as a self-fulfilling prophecy. Over the years, Wally became progressively more distrustful of women's moods and learned to be wary and guarded in his relationships with them. His attitude was not only molded by his father's point of view but was also reinforced by his own hurt and frustration with his mother and stepmother. In that sense, these attitudes were overdetermined, which is often the case.

Wally spent many years in therapy overcoming his distorted, paranoid views of women. His marriage ended in divorce when his son Danny was 5 years old. Later, he participated in our parenting groups in an effort to understand and work through his confused feelings about himself and Danny. At the same time, Danny became involved in one of the adolescent discussion groups.

The following excerpts of interviews were taken from discussion groups in which Wally and Danny took part. It is interesting to trace the basic theme of isolation and withholding in their lives and to note the repetition of these defensive patterns over the span of three generations.

The Tendency toward Isolation

As noted earlier, a defensive life-style of inwardness and pseudo-independence is transmitted not only by direct verbal instruction, by teaching attitudes of cynicism and distrust, but, more importantly, through the process of unconscious imitation. In this session, Wally comes to the realization that his self-imposed isolation was, in reality, an imitation of his father's life as a social isolate.

WALLY: I've recently started to think, am I really a person who is a loner? Am I really a person who doesn't get along with people, who's very uncomfortable with people?

I remember in college, I did that to a "T." I mean, I never was with people, but I was also very uncomfortable and very self-conscious that I was alone. And then I got into trouble psychologically and I started seeing a psychologist, and I turned that around immediately. I started to be with people, and I started to enjoy them. So it suddenly struck me, I had been just trying to be like my father, who had almost no friends. I thought that was the way to be.

My father was always by himself. Completely. He was always isolated. He couldn't get along with people, so I was copying him. I was just a goddamn copy. What a waste of time! So maybe I'm not that kind of person, a loner. Maybe I'm not a loner. (*tears and sadness*)

In the young people's discussion group, Danny describes a pattern very similar to that of his father, underscoring the point that Wally's defensive ways of living had been effectively transmitted to him.

DANNY: Sometimes I've *got* to get by myself. It's just like a sigh of relief or something—but when I'm sitting there, I'm kind of hateful toward other people, like I'll think angry things about other people. I feel like I have the goods on everybody and criticize them a lot in my mind when I'm alone.

It's like I'll overreact to things and get really hateful. Then if I see the person later on, I feel guilty for feeling so angry at them. I tell myself, "God, you're so mean—you're a real jerk."

Both Wally and his son tended to alienate friends by judgmental, overly critical evaluations. The picky, cynical thoughts they had about people limited their associations. In the period following his insight and emotional catharsis regarding his pattern of defensive isolation, Wally was gradually able to relate more closely to friends and to family members.

Patterns of Withholding and Perfectionism

The defense of withholding affection and approval was an important dynamic in this family. These deep-seated patterns were transmitted at an unconscious level. As a child, Wally had attempted to defend himself against his father's covert rejection by becoming guarded and distant himself. It appeared that he had incorporated his father's attitudes of superiority and perfectionism as well. As a parent, Wally held back verbal approval and genuine acknowledgment from his son Danny and, instead, pressured him to perform at unrealistically high levels. Danny internalized this pressure on a subliminal level as a negative thought process. Whenever minor incidents or imperfections upset the youngster, this obsessive thought pattern was activated, and Danny became depressed and irritable.

In a parents' group, Wally talks about his dawning recognition of the type of hostile withholding that characterized his interactions with Danny ever since he was a young child:

WALLY: Before Danny was old enough to be competent, I would have a huge rage at something he couldn't do. I would try to teach him and I would get immediately very angry and I would quit, and punish him. I'd lash out at him. I don't even know how he was able to learn from me after that. That was pretty consistent throughout his whole childhood.

In this instance, Wally's self-disclosure offers an insight into the source of Danny's depression and sense of failure. Danny's response to Wally's impatience had been to withdraw and to hold back his performance out of a deep fear of provoking angry responses and stern disapproval. Later in the same group, Wally reveals his reluctance to show approval or affection to his son in their present-day interactions:

WALLY: Just recently I've noticed that when I'm with Danny, he's a lot more friendly to me than I am to him. I just ignore a lot of what he says. I realize that my father must have done that a lot with me.

I love to watch Danny play baseball. It's like at a distance I can enjoy something he's doing, but I will not enjoy it directly. I love to watch him handle the boat, but I don't let him know. I've never told him. I would never say "You did well," or "You did very well."

Many parents, like Wally, hold back praise and approval because they fear the child will be "spoiled." Children, in turn, *learn* to withhold their abilities and talents in the absence of positive acknowledgment from their parents. Here Danny reveals the ongoing effects of his father's "lesson."

DANNY: I thought about the way I'm hard on myself and how I put so much pressure on myself. Even in elementary school, I was so afraid to get bad grades. I mean, I was petrified to get in trouble and I got straight A's, but it was like even if I got a B, it was such a huge thing. It's like I was nothing.

If I'm playing baseball and I make an error, it's like I just tear into myself. I think I'm such an idiot, I mean, I just sit there and call myself an idiot a hundred times; it's like I'm screaming at myself inside my head.

Both Danny and Wally expected and demanded perfection in themselves and others. They withheld approval and positive responses in their personal relationships. This defensive posture covered over the rejection and underlying hostility that was manifested in their childhood experiences. By blaming themselves and finding fault with their own performances, both Wally and Danny protected an idealized image of their fathers, to their own detriment. They maintained self-protective behavior patterns that effectively tied them to a negative identity formed early in childhood. In this way, they preserved their bond with their family.

Prescriptions and sanctions for behaviors that support an illusion of connection or a destructive bond with one's parent are transmitted on a subliminal level from one generation to the next (Bowen, 1978). Most parents believe that because they brought a child into the world, they have an inherent proprietary right that takes precedence over the child's rights. They impose their own standards, beliefs, and value systems, although these may be distorted and inappropriate, and teach their own coping mechanisms although they may be crippling and maladaptive. It is natural for parents to educate and socialize their children according to their own values and principles. Yet, when parents are rigid, hostile, or overly defended, the family takes on the quality of a dictatorship wherein powerful forces operate to control other family members, fit them into a mold, "brainwash" them with a particular philosophy of life, and manipulate them through guilt and a sense of obligation. It is within this exclusive, restrictive family constellation that many children are "processed." Consequently, most children are unable to feel that they are their own persons, and that they have an inherent right to their own points of view as separate human beings.

CONCLUSION

People form defenses at a time in their lives when they are faced with pain and anguish. Later, they learn to avoid and ward off other persons who respond warmly to them. They become wary and distrustful and attempt to control events that might impinge on them and hurt them again. Once they retreat, people have a strong tendency to preserve their defense system and keep it intact at any expense—

and the expense can be great. Most people give up significant parts of their lives in order to live in an "empty fortress." We need to be especially sensitive to the child's needs and his remarkable and unique nature so as not to create an emotional climate that inspires a self-destructive posture. Ideally, we want to make it possible for children to be free and open in their approach to life and to the exigencies of fate.

The Concept of the "Voice" and the Cycle of Child Abuse

Our life is what our thoughts make it.

Marcus Aurelius, *Meditations*

Unconsciously...people inflict punishments on themselves to which an inner court has sentenced them. A hidden authority within the ego takes over the judgment originally expected of the parents.

Theodor Reik (1941), *Masochism in Modern Man* (p. 10)

THE CONCEPT OF THE VOICE

The "voice" may be defined as critical, self-parenting patterns of thought that reflect the language of the defensive process and are the result of internalizing or incorporating negative parental attitudes, feelings, and thoughts. Thus, the negative conception of self effectively ties them to their identity within the family and perpetuates the fantasy bond. Our definition of the voice excludes those cognitive processes involved in creative thinking, planning, and realistic self-appraisal, as well as fantasies and daydreams.

Our studies have convinced us that the "voice" is the unconscious or partly conscious mechanism primarily responsible for the transmission of negative parental traits, behaviors, and patterns of defense from one generation to the next. Its power lies in the fact that most people are unaware that they are following the dictates of the "voice" because it is largely unconscious. Therefore, they follow the prescriptions of this internal parent to their own detriment, with important negative consequences in their everyday interactions with their offspring.

As described throughout this work, parents possess diametrically opposed views of themselves. All people suffer to some extent from a sense of alienation from self—a conflict that goes beyond such a descriptive word as ambivalence. They have an alien point of view, imposed originally from without, that reflects their tendencies for self-limitation and self-destruction. This alien view is not only antithetical and hostile toward the individual, but is also cynical and suspicious about other people. The "voice" represents a systematized pattern of negative thoughts that is the basis of a person's maladaptive behavior.

The voice exists primarily on an unconscious level. However, many people are aware of negative thoughts in the form of a running commentary or internal dialogue that criticizes them in times of stress, increasing their nervousness and undermining their self-confidence.

A woman preparing to attend a formal social function feels especially self-critical: "Look at you, you're so nervous! You're such a shy, awkward person." A father worries silently: "You're not going to get that promotion. You're not a good provider for your family!" A young mother with a new baby anxiously questions herself: "Why is he always crying?" and then answers with a self-accusation: "Because *you* don't know how to take care of a baby."

Many people berate themselves for making mistakes or for failing to live up to their own expectations. A student depreciates himself: "You really must be stupid to fail such a simple exam. What makes you think you can make it in college?" The athlete in the midst of a temporary slump castigates himself: "You've really lost it. You should have quit while you were still ahead. It's too late to make a comeback now." These thoughts are but the tip of an iceberg. They are isolated fragments of a profoundly destructive way of thinking that is operating on a subliminal level in every person. Acting on these thoughts leads to self-fulfilling prophesies and negative consequences. The voice is made up of a series of thought patterns and attitudes that do *not* reflect a person's self-interest. These hostile thoughts represent an overlay on the personality that is *not* natural or harmonious, but learned or imposed from the outside world during one's formative years.

The Voice as Distinguished from a Conscience

The voice is *not* a conscience or a positive guide, even at those times when it holds up morals and ideals to an individual as "shoulds" or rules to follow.[1] To the contrary, it is a discordant force within the personality. The self becomes its *object* of attack and punishment. One important distinction between the voice and a value system lies in the fact that it often punishes the person with self-recrimination and remorse for the very actions it has influenced or promoted. The alcoholic who succumbs to a voice urging him to have a drink to relax after a hard day at work, later, in the throes of a hangover, will viciously attack himself for having no will power. Although the voice may at times relate to moral considerations, its internal statements against the self often occur *after* the fact and are typically harsh and judgmental, rather than helpful or supportive of constructive behavioral change.

The voice cannot be conceptualized as a constructive guide because in its extreme forms it may actually command the psychotic person to commit suicide or homicide. Occasionally, this injunction is carried out. In other instances, the voice tells the depressed person to commit suicide in order to escape the psychological pain that, ironically, originated in the destructive thought process of the voice. It is clear in these extreme cases that the individual's rational thought processes were completely subsumed by the voice, leading to irrational and destructive actions. Furthermore, in our investigations into this hostile thought process, we have determined that there is a persecutory element to the voice, present even in "normal" people, that does not resemble the qualities ascribed to a conscience.

The voice process supports self-denying attitudes and persuades the individual to give up his natural wants and drives by rigidly adhering to conventional, or distorting, values and mores. The author sees society and social mores as a pooling of the combined defenses of all its members. Therefore, many societal values support and validate the restrictions of each individual's voice. Because so many of us have been taught as children to conform to unnecessary rules and prohibitions at our own expense, these particular voices are very common in our culture. We have learned to be selfless. We feel guilty for having wants and needs. We carry an internal parent within, telling us to ration pleasurable experiences, to be self-sacrificing, and to put off until some future date the gratification of our desires.

Evolution of the Voice Concept

Clinicians (Beck, 1976; Butler, 1981; Ellis & Harper, 1975; G. Kaufman, 1980) have long been aware that there are self-destructive thought processes involved in emotional disturbances and that these thoughts profoundly influence maladaptive behavior. However, clinicians have not taken fully into account the fact that a good deal of negative thought processes are the result of parental abuses. They fail to recognize the intensity and pervasiveness of the feelings, especially the anger or rage associated with illogical or negative thinking. In the following pages, we will describe a valuable and unusual procedure, termed *voice therapy*, that we have used to elicit and bring to the foreground the contents of this subliminal thought process.

The techniques of voice therapy bring out the full extent of the feelings associated with the negative thought process, provide insight into its sources, and are therefore different in many respects from other cognitive approaches to psychotherapy. A number of clinicians, among them R. D. Laing, Joseph Richman, Pamela Butler, Nolan Saltzman, Giovanni Liotti, and Richard Seiden, have acknowledged the procedures as being valuable both in the practice of psychotherapy and as a research tool for studying self-destructive behavior in a wide range of patients.

Early Studies of the Voice

In my early work with schizophrenia, I observed that the patients' hallucinated "voices" had a harsh, parental, prohibitive tone. These voices represented exaggerated manifestations of the negative thought process found in neurotic patients. Psychotic patients often imagine that other people hate them and accuse them. Similarly, they hear voices degrading them and commanding them to commit self-destructive acts. M. A. Sechehaye (1951), in her brilliant and moving account of a young schizophrenic patient, Renee, points out how voices instructed the girl over and over again to hurt herself. When Renee gave in to these voices and acted out physical abuse on herself, they became even more intense and derisive in their attacks.

Schizophrenic patients do not *think* voices, they actually hear them. The patient no longer recognizes the thoughts as his own. He has projected them onto other people, experiencing them as originating in the external world. Many patients we worked with reported that these auditory hallucinations or voices reminded them of parental reprimands or orders. The split personality commonly conceptualized as characterizing this illness can be understood in terms of a split or division between the harsh parental figure assimilated into the patient's personality, and the "weak, bad child" part that is attacked by the internal parent. This split also exists in the "normal" or neurotic patient, although to a far lesser degree.[2]

Voice Therapy

In voice therapy sessions, we encourage patients to verbalize negative thoughts toward themselves and express the feelings connected to these self-attacks. First, we generally ask them to recall what they were *telling themselves* in situations that typically made them anxious or depressed. Most patients can learn to verbalize their self-critical thoughts in the second person, for example, saying, *"You're* so stupid," rather than saying about themselves, "I'm so stupid."

Patients report that putting their hostile thoughts in this form feels more authentic. These negative thought patterns appear to occur more in the form of statements directed *toward* or against oneself rather than about oneself. Therefore, they lend themselves to expression in the second person. Verbalizing the attacks in the second person helps patients to separate these thoughts from other, more rational thoughts and positive attitudes. They are then better able to clarify their own point of view about situations and about themselves.

An example of a patient verbalizing her self-attacks will clarify the concepts as applied in a voice therapy session. A depressed young mother who was very constricted and inhibited was encouraged to express her self-critical thoughts. As she verbalized these self-accusations, her anger came more to the surface.

PATIENT (verbalizing her voice): Here you go again. Here you go again, stirring up trouble. Here you go again, bothering people.

As she spoke, her voice became loud and angry. Tears came to her eyes; her voice began to tremble, and she appeared on the verge of tears:

Just keep your mouth shut! Quit bothering people! Shut up! Can't you see that you make people feel bad? Can't you see what a bad effect you have on your family? Don't you see how bad you make them feel, all under the guise of caring!

At this point, the young woman was in effect yelling loudly at herself. A new tone crept into her voice; a snide, degrading, sarcastic outburst of fury was followed by deep sobbing:

All under the guise of caring! Caring! You don't care for anybody! You never cared for anybody in your whole life! (*cries*)

This woman had come alarmingly close to acting on the content of this thought process by almost leaving her husband and children, rationalizing that they would be better off without her. It was evident that her plans for carrying out this self-destructive action followed along the lines of the thoughts she verbalized in the session.

COMMONALITY OF VOICES

The voice represents an alien view of life, a bias that is common in every person. There are a number of common threads underlying a "normal" person's self-criticisms, as well as the more seriously disturbed patient's self-destructive urges. In our clinical work, we observed a significant overlap in the content of the negative thoughts or voices expressed by subjects. Because most of our subjects had been raised in the same culture, their voice attacks reflected common restrictions, prohibitions, and warnings. Therefore, virtually every individual in our experimental group was able to identify and empathize with the person who was verbalizing his self-attacks in the session.

Origins of the Voice

In the process of verbalizing their self-attacks, many of our subjects identified these thoughts as statements they remembered their parents actually saying to them as criticisms and warnings. Others recalled parental attitudes they had picked up in their parents' tone of voice, body language, or other cues. Even more remarkable were the changes in appearance, speech, and mannerisms that our subjects displayed as they expressed these angry verbal attacks against themselves. We were able to examine the speech patterns of parents and their teenage or adult children, and we noted that the self-attacks expressed by our subjects were similar in style to their parents' mannerisms, phrasing, accents, and colloquial expressions.

We began to understand the connection between the participants' verbalizations of their self-attacks and the kinds of negative parental statements and attitudes they had assimilated as children. The role of the voice in the transmission of parental defenses was clearly demonstrated time and again in group and in individual voice therapy sessions. We conjectured that what we were observing in these sessions were the remnants of parental warnings, directions, commands, labels, and negative feelings that had been a part of the socialization process for these people. The profoundly abusive attitudes and the disrespect expressed by our subjects against themselves seemed to have been incorporated into their thinking processes early in their lives.

The intensity of anger and sadness that accompanied verbalizations of the voice was also an unexpected phenomenon. A wealth of unconscious material and feelings was unearthed by the participants, followed by powerful insights. Individuals were able to identify and understand the origins of self-limiting behavior and the source of their lack of self-esteem.

Patients and subjects became aware of how they maintained certain undesirable behaviors in order to validate the bad child image they had assimilated in their families. It became increasingly clear to us that this thought process originated during stressful periods in each person's early life.

A teenage girl came to therapy complaining about being in a constant state of confusion. She had gained an unusual amount of weight, was extremely self-depreciating, and was engaged in self-destructive behaviors (compulsive eating and purging) that were causing her parents and friends considerable concern. She had recently become involved in a life-style that her parents feared was potentially disastrous for her.

This adolescent revealed that she thought of herself as uncoordinated and incompetent and felt as though she could do nothing right. She felt that she had no control over her actions whenever she was under pressure. Indeed, she often acted confused, overwhelmed, and helpless. In a group session, she recalled an incident from early childhood that she believed must have contributed to her sense of worthlessness.

PATIENT: When I was three or four, I remember my mom getting really furious at me for dropping a thermometer. I didn't do it on purpose—I was just carrying it to her, and I tripped and broke it. She jerked me up and threw me almost across the room—she was really angry. I remember being really shaken up.

Later, my mom explained that she was worried that I might get some of the broken glass on my hands—that there was poisonous stuff inside—that she was just trying to protect me. But she was *so* angry; that incident really stands out in my mind. I remember it so clearly.

Later in the session, she verbalized a vicious, derisive voice that degraded her each time she made a mistake. She became aware of the extent to which she still blamed herself for being rejected by her family:

PATIENT: Any time I make even a tiny mistake these days, I tell myself:
   "People are going to be angry at you. How can you be trusted? You're such a little klutz! You can't do anything right. You're always forgetting things. You're so unreliable, no wonder no one trusts you!"
   I still can't get it straight. I still think there was something about me that made them not like me. I'm always confused about it. I just can't get it clear in my mind. (cries)

THERAPIST: Even today you can't get free of that way of seeing yourself. It just seems to go on and on, that feeling that you're to blame. Maybe with this insight, you'll be able to get some clarity and see where this view of yourself came from.

In the example of this adolescent, her mother's explosive anger and destructive outbursts fostered a deep-seated sense of inadequacy and a feeling that she was bad. Following this session and others, the patient began to show improvement and was better able to control her impulsive acts.

As was the case with this young woman, the majority of our subjects and patients became acutely aware of the extent to which they had accepted critical views of themselves at face value. They became very knowledgeable about how they acted out undesirable behaviors and preserved personality traits that confirmed feelings of being unacceptable and unlovable. Uncovering the sources of this hostile point of view and expressing the emotions associated with specific self-punishing thoughts shattered deeply held misconceptions, relieved feelings of guilt and remorse, and, in most cases, aroused feelings of compassion in each person for himself.

THE ROLE OF THE VOICE IN THE CYCLE OF CHILD ABUSE

The role of the voice in the cycle of physical and emotional child abuse is a three-step process: (1) To varying degrees, all children suffer trauma and rejection in their formative years. Particularly during times of stress, they incorporate an *internal parent*, represented by a destructive self-critical thought process or negative voice. (2) Children retain this hostile voice within them throughout their lives, restricting, limiting, and punishing themselves. (3) When they become parents, they are compelled to act out similar abuses on their children, who, in turn, incorporate the punishing attitudes as a self-depreciating thought process, thereby completing the cycle. The voice is an attack on one's self. It is an attack on one's interests, on one's wants, on one's priorities, on one's mate, and especially on one's offspring. In the following pages, we will demonstrate how typical self-critical thoughts and attitudes reported by volunteer associates and subjects in our voice therapy groups affected their children.

In one case, Wally, a participant in the group, verbalized voice statements that chastised him for the way he was talking in the group meeting:

WALLY: I was trying to figure out why it's hard to talk in this group and usually it's my voice attacks that keep me quiet. Like right now I have a voice that people aren't interested in this. It tells me: "People really don't want you here in this talk—you look bad."

I have to give a lot of presentations at work. I know some of the attacks there: "You're boring people. What you have to say is worthless, it doesn't mean anything. You really haven't researched this sufficiently to come up with anything new or creative."

I also have attacks about my physical appearance: "You look tired, you look old, you're not dressed right, you're slouching, you're not speaking clearly."

As Wally spoke, his voice became louder until he was angrily berating himself with words such as:

WALLY: "You'd better say this goddamn voice right, buddy. You say it right! If you don't say it right, just shut up!"

This is something I'm always telling myself. I've got this voice all the time: "Just say it right. You'd better be right, or don't say anything!"

I start putting this pressure on myself where I say to myself, "You'd better be better next time. Just say it better next time!" (*angry tone*)

In observing Wally's son, Danny, it was clear that he had assimilated the same overly critical, nagging voice that Wally verbalized in the group. The impatience and perfectionistic attitudes that were characteristic of Wally were apparent in Danny when he talked recently in an adolescent discussion group:

DANNY: I know I must hate myself unconsciously, because I react to criticism so badly. Like when someone says something to me that rings a bell in my head, it's like I'll go to the extreme—I'm terrible—I feel like I'm a terrible person.

The other day Ron said something to me about being a little slow at a baseball game, and I just fell apart. I felt like I was terrible. I told myself, "You're nothing—you're a terrible person!"

In another case, the parents of a 6-year-old girl held strong negative views of themselves as being strange and different from other people. Both parents expressed their self-attacks and critical voices in the group sessions:

FATHER: The attack I made on myself after a friend criticized me went something like this: "You're such a quiet creep. You're second class. You should just stay in the background, because when people get to know you, they'll find out that you're not fit to be with, that you're a shit person, and everything about you is shit."

So if someone says anything about my little girl, I put it into that same attack. It's like she's shit, too. (*sobs*)

It's interesting that I really felt a lot when I said that attack, that my daughter was shit because I was shit. I didn't know how much I wove her into the way I feel about myself. I realize how much I want to change that image, for myself, but also for her, because I felt so bad when I gave words to that feeling.

MOTHER: I was with my daughter the other day, and I wasn't feeling very good about myself at the time. I noticed she looked really happy. She had been swimming with her friends and she was really lively and excited. But right away I started picking her apart in my mind like: "Look how awkwardly she moves. She's not *really* happy; she's phony and silly." I suddenly realized that I was tearing her apart in the same way I had been running myself down all day.

Both parents had experienced chaotic childhoods. The father remembered little of his upbringing other than the endless arguments and physical abuse he and his siblings witnessed between their parents. The child's mother had been raised to fill the role of the "sick one" in her family, and she was now passing on this role assignment to her own daughter by searching for minor flaws or weaknesses in the child, both real and imagined.

Because they were distressed by signs and symptoms of disturbance in their daughter, these parents asked another couple, close friends, to help them by becoming involved in caring for her. There was gradual improvement in the little girl subsequent to her being cared for by these substitute parents. Therapeutic interventions were also undertaken with the natural parents, and they have shown considerable progress as a result of identifying the destructive ways they had been viewing themselves *and* their daughter.

In another example, a young mother manifested extreme fears about her infant son's health and his developmental progress. Her obsessive worries that he was not developing properly caused her considerable distress. She revealed that she constantly compared her son's physical abilities with those of other babies his age, telling herself: "He's slow for his age; he's not getting enough to eat; something is wrong with his formula"; and so forth. Her fears about leaving the child with a sitter or relatives took the form of such thoughts as *"They won't know when to feed him; they won't feed him enough, or know when he's cold or hungry."*

Later, the woman recalled her mother's exaggerated focus on proper diet and physical fitness and realized that her own nervous attention on her young son's food intake and physical development was no different from her mother's compulsive focus on *her* health as a child. In recognizing the origins of her obsessive ruminations in relation to her baby, she was able to relax her vigilance and began to take pleasure in her interactions with him.

INTERGENERATIONAL TRANSMISSION OF SELF-DESTRUCTIVE TENDENCIES

In our 12 years of interest and investigation of the manifestations of the voice process, we found that virtually every individual we interviewed could identify with the concept of the voice. In addition, they were familiar with the negative influence these thoughts had on certain areas of endeavor. Seriously depressed individuals and suicidal patients in particular were unusually aware of the voice process. They encountered voices of self-recrimination and self-attack very directly in their daily lives.

In a number of cases in which the voice reached proportions threatening to the physical integrity and lives of the patients, we found that these individuals had incorporated especially vicious, hateful feelings and malicious attitudes from their parents during traumatic incidents of physical and emotional abuse during childhood. For example, Mrs. S., a young woman who survived a serious suicide attempt, recalled an incident from her childhood when her mother hit her repeatedly until she began to bleed. In an interview several years later, she described the events that led up to her trying to kill herself. Here she speaks of the viciousness and malevolence of her voice:

MRS. S.: The voice about killing myself was vicious. It took the form of "You'd better do it. It's the only thing you can do. You'd better do it! I hate you! I hate you!"

I just had a thought in relation to my mother, remembering feelings directed toward me when she would get angry with me. [Relates the incident mentioned above, when her mother punished her.]

I remember the hatred. Her hatred was being directed toward me. "I hate you. I hate you!"

And that was like that voice—my own voice. It turned into my own voice, hating myself. That's when it was vicious.

In another patient who had made several suicide attempts, it appeared that parental death wishes had been incorporated as an internal voice in somewhat disguised form. The patient's father had physically abused her on several occasions and had once actually tried to strangle her. This very disturbed woman held a bizarre belief that she was filled with poison. After one suicide attempt, she said that she had obeyed a voice that ordered her to "slash your wrists, get rid of the poison." In this extreme case of pathological acting out, the father's death wishes toward his daughter had been translated into action by her. Other researchers and clinicians (Rosenbaum & Richman, 1970) have reported unconscious death wishes as being prominent in the parents of individuals who were recovering from suicide attempts.

Rheingold (1964) has described a number of mothers who reported being disturbed by death wishes and destructive impulses they felt toward their children. In one case, the mother of a 4-year-old girl "suddenly had the idea, 'What if I would harm my daughter?'" Following this disconcerting thought, she sought professional help because of extreme nervousness and recurring thoughts of suicide. She was too unnerved by these impulses to move into a two-story house for fear she might jump out of a window. Rheingold goes on to describe the thoughts of his patient:

[PATIENT:] "I get shaky, I feel feverish, I bite my nails all day long. *Someone keeps talking to me in my own mind telling me to grab her (daughter) and knock her down or choke her* [italics added]. I argue with myself but I'm afraid I'll do it. Am I going crazy? Should I send her away?"

[RHEINGOLD:] All I had to do was to ask who that "someone" in her mind was to evoke a flood of recrimination against her mother. She revealed the usual story of a vindictive, sex-repressive mother. In her second visit, 13 days later, she reported that she had felt better after the first one and now was cheerful and "tickled" to have her daughter. (p. 65)

Rheingold emphasizes that the major factor contributing to the patient's improvement was her realization that these "bad thoughts" originated in the attitudes and actions of her own mother. By identifying and separating the voice and uncovering its source in the painful events of her own childhood, this mother was able to achieve a normal adjustment as a parent and no longer was troubled by persistent thoughts of getting rid of her daughter, nor did she have further impulses to kill herself.

Defensive Functions and Objectives of the Voice

The voice statements verbalized by our patients indicated a basic division or split in the person between feelings of positive self-regard and strong negative attitudes toward self. We were able to observe the overall effect of the self-limiting prescriptions of the voice on the child's, and later the adult's, behavior. In the following sections, we will examine the general predilections or biases of the voice process in adult individuals. The reader will note that the parental defense patterns listed in the previous chapter are strongly influenced by this negative thought process.

The Voice Promotes:

1. *Hostile attitudes toward self and others.* We noted that the voice not only serves the function of attacking the self, but it is also directed against others. Depressed, self-critical patients also tended to feel cynical toward friends, family, and associates. In therapy sessions, patients frequently alternated between expressing *self*-attacks and verbalizing harsh or suspicious attitudes about other people. They anticipated rejection based on these two aspects of the voice.

In the first case, patients and subjects reported self-depreciating statements, such as "Why should he want to be *your* friend? *You're* not very attractive or intelligent"; or "Why should she like you? You're not in her league; there are other men she'd much rather go out with."

In the second instance, people were cynical toward *others* based on certain negative beliefs and biases. They tended to have such thoughts as "*He's* so critical and judgmental! Why would he want your friendship? It's impossible for *any* woman to live up to his expectations"; or "She's just leading you on; she doesn't really care about you"; and, more generally, "People don't really care. *They* don't understand."

In our clinical experience, we found that both kinds of negative views (toward self and toward others) contribute to a posture of alienation by influencing a person to avoid relationships that might challenge his defense system. Both attacks lead to a decline in personal relating and a tendency to withhold positive responses from others.

2. *Isolation and solitary activity.* The voice encourages time alone and then uses the time to undermine or attack the self. This is very different from time used for creative work, artistic achievement, or relaxation from the stress of everyday living. Instead, isolation of this type is used to act out self-nourishing habit patterns for which people later punish themselves. It is surprising how many individuals "listen" to voices telling them to be alone so they can "relax" and to seek privacy and self-comfort.

Thoughts influencing isolation can be difficult to counter because they appear to be reasonable. Yet extended periods of isolation from social contact can be detrimental to mental health, as noted by many researchers (Gove & Hughes, 1980; Seiden, 1984). A number of patients who were in suicidal crises revealed voices that urged them to seek solitude, then bombarded them with extremely degrading attacks and urged them to kill themselves with such injunctions as "You don't really matter to anyone. Who would care if you weren't around? This is something you really should do. It's the only way out." On the other hand, patients reported that suicidal thoughts were diminished or largely absent when they found themselves in social situations where it was necessary for them to interact with other people. Time spent in isolation and a lack of shared activity in both children and adults often permit the voice to gain ascendancy.

3. *Self-nourishing habit patterns.* The voice process influences a person to satisfy and soothe himself with food, drugs, and deadening habit patterns and routines. Alcoholics, drug abusers, and people with eating disorders have all reported voices that seductively influence them to indulge their addiction or self-destructive habits. Later, they are tortured by vicious self-critical attacks for indulging their habit and by increased feelings of depression. This painful cycle of events predisposes the individual to more drug or substance use, thereby strengthening the addiction. The voice operates in both phases of the cycle, encouraging the indulgence and then chastising the person for the regression.

4. *Self-denial and self-limitation.* By encouraging people to defer their wants, the voice fosters asceticism and self-denial, limiting their pleasure and enjoyment. It warns of negative outcomes for people who are pursuing personal and avocational goals, which increases their tension in performance situations, and often leads to a self-fulfilling prophecy of failure or limitation. This *seemingly* self-protective voice interferes with basic expressions of the self and diminishes rather than enhances a sense of personal identity. For example, several subjects reported voices that told them that they were too old for sex or that lively activities were too strenuous for them. Self-attacks related to seeking pleasure and happiness were quite common. These voices led to a self-denying approach to life, labeling desires and wants as selfish or hedonistic.

Many people turn their backs on strong wants and motives that have personal significance in their lives. They fail to realize that their decisions are based on an unconscious negative thought process that makes use of practical issues as rationalizations to support a basic theme of self-denial.

5. *An inward, withholding life-style.* The voice calls an individual a "sucker" for extending himself or herself in personal relationships or vocational pursuits. This overprotective voice is similar in many respects to the voice that fosters the self-denying attitudes described above. Most of our subjects have verbalized voices that warned them not to be open and vulnerable in their dealings with other people. Voice statements such as "Don't be a fool! Don't be so naive, so trusting, so gullible! People will take advantage of you whenever they can. Why should *you* be the one who's always giving?" were common in the majority of our subjects.

6. *Regression and childish manipulations.* The voice fosters an image of the "noble" child within each person, wherein one perceives oneself as an innocent victim of other people. It encourages childlike behavior, dependency, and ploys that pull others into a parental, caretaking role. Many people have exposed voices telling them that they were misunderstood and exploited. For example, "He (the employer) doesn't know how conscientious you are or how hard you work." This voice also tells an individual that he has "certain rights in life" or that he "deserves love," and so forth, in a manner that leads to a self-righteous, victimized, or paranoid orientation.

7. *An antifeeling orientation.* The voice accuses people of being overemotional, overly sensitive, or thin-skinned, when they feel hurt

or disappointed. One father often wondered why he felt cut off from his feelings in situations that aroused strong emotional responses in other people. He uncovered a voice that told him "Don't you cry— boy, don't you cry. You'd better not cry. If you don't stop, I'll give you something to cry about." He realized that his own father had taught him, both by example and through direct instruction, that men were not supposed to cry or show emotional responses that could be considered signs of weakness.

8. *A fantasy process of internal gratification.* The voice militates against close personal relationships, honesty, openness, sexuality, and the fulfillment of one's potential through goal-directed behavior. Indeed, it tends to support a fantasy process of self-sufficiency over real relating and actual gratification in the external environment. As such, it furthers maladaptive responses and has a decidedly self-destructive dimension.

9. *Relationships that are characterized by dependency bonds.* The voice functions to promote the fantasy bond over a real relationship. In this type of destructive dependency relationship, there is very little genuine affection between partners, but there is a good deal of manipulation, obligation, and control.

10. *Guilt in relation to moving away from destructive ties.* The voice also fosters guilt in individuals who are moving away from restrictive coupling or enmeshed family relationships. For example, participants in voice therapy groups invariably report self-attacks such as "Why do *you* think you're different from us?" (meaning the family) or "Who do you think *you* are?" whenever they find themselves different or better off than their parents or spouse in any area of endeavor. Many have voices deriding their happiness and their excitement about achievements, particularly in areas where they surpass the parent of the same sex.

11. *Vanity—an idealized image of self.* The voice builds up an individual's self-importance and supports an inflated self-image. It "tells" him that he is exceptional and special and able to perform at unrealistically high levels. Later, the voice severely castigates him for falling short of these standards of perfection. Some of our subjects initially found it difficult to recognize the profound and insidious destructiveness of this seemingly positive voice. Later, they realized how this thought process set them up for subsequent feelings of failure and self-recrimination.

Vanity generates both gratification in fantasy and intense self-attacks when failure occurs. To illustrate, Larry, a 45-year-old long-distance runner who previously had been able to run 12 miles, set a goal for himself of completing a 26-mile marathon. He trained for months, telling himself, "You're really good. You can do *anything* if you really want to." When he was forced to stop at the 20-mile marker because of exhaustion, he sank into a deep depression that lasted several weeks. Later, in exploring the sources of his "bad mood," he reported thinking extremely self-depreciating thoughts:

LARRY (verbalizing his voice): "You quitter! You can't finish anything. You didn't have to quit. You could have seen it through to the end. You didn't have to stop, but you quit, just like you do in everything else you try!"

Although he was 45 years old, he compared himself unfavorably with teammates half his age and thought:

"*They* finished the race, but not you. You trained longer and harder than they did, but you quit. You just don't have the guts, the motivation, the right stuff. You *could* have done it, you quitter!"

Still later, in analysis, he realized how ridiculous this comparison was. In a session, he recalled how his mother had built him up to compensate for her lack of real interest in him. He became painfully aware that much of his effort in relation to running and, indeed, to other areas of endeavor had been for his mother's benefit, as well as an attempt to earn her approval, rather than for his own satisfaction. His real achievements brought him no pleasure, because in a sense they had become a way of feeding his mother's desperate need for recognition and glory.

12. *Self-destructive voices and suicidal ideation.* We have found that the voice operates along a continuum, ranging from mild self-criticism and cynicism about other people to thoughts that promote self-denying and self-limiting behavior—to vicious self-recriminations that are accompanied by intense rage and sometimes even by commands to injure oneself. As an individual follows each prescription of the voice, as he allows the voice to assume more and more control over his actions and the way he perceives himself, he becomes more and more self-destructive.

A number of patients revealed extremely savage voices commanding them to mutilate themselves or perform careless acts that would lead to accidents. One man, a carpenter, who had become very nervous while working alone late at night, heard a voice that urged: "Go on, see how close you can get your fingers to that saw! Go ahead! Just run your hand right under the blade!" When the man recounted this self-attack in a session, his tone of voice assumed a loud, angry quality, totally devoid of feelings of concern or self-interest. After expressing this powerfully spoken attack, the patient broke into deep sobs. Malicious commands, such as the thoughts that tortured this man during his isolated work, undoubtedly contribute to accident-proneness in many people.

We also noted that each individual has a potential for suicide within himself, as well as a desire to live a constructive life. The degree to which a person actually acts out self-destructive urges depends on a number of variables, but it is strongly influenced by the depth of the voice process. When people allow the voice to acquire ascendancy over their actions, they are increasingly debilitated and become involved in a negative cycle of self-hatred, self-recriminations, and depressive states.

The Concept of the Voice as a Diagnostic Indicator of Suicide Potential

By understanding the thought process that regulates the myriad forms of self-destructive behavior, clinicians can assess with a higher probability the risk of suicide in disturbed adolescent and adult patients. A number of assessment tools exist for this purpose, among them Beck's Suicide Intention Scale (Beck, Rush, Shaw, & Emery, 1979) and Pfeffer's (1986) Child Suicide Potential Scale. The explanatory power of the concept of the voice adds still another increment to our ability to determine the suicidal potential in high-risk patients. (The chart, *The Continuum of Negative Thought Patterns*, in Appendix B lists voice attacks underlying various forms of self-limiting and self-destructive behaviors in terms of the degree of suicidal intention they appear to reflect.)

An individual can remain stabilized at a certain level on the continuum for years. People can lead ascetic lives of selflessness and self-sacrifice and never move toward suicide. However, one would be alarmed if a self-denying person had thoughts urging him to hurt himself or influencing him to stay away from friends or family. Giving up an activity that has always been especially meaningful to the individual is another danger sign. Thoughts and rationalizations that morally justify self-destructive behaviors, such as running away and substance abuse, are signs that the patient has submitted to the voice and adopted this alien view as his own. As the self-destructive thoughts gain ascendancy over his rational thoughts of self-interest, he wholeheartedly *believes* the negative, self-depreciating statements about himself and other people.

The depressed and/or suicidal person gradually loses contact with his real self and feels hopelessly estranged from others. Despair and helplessness are expressed by thoughts verbalized by many suicidal patients, "What's the use? Nothing matters any more." As he increasingly submits to the alien voice or personality of the introjected parental image, he now reacts to the self as if *he* were the incorporated other. If that person (parent) wished him dead, he may well oblige by killing himself.

CONCLUSION

In understanding the implications of the voice process and its prescriptions for behavior, one can begin to counteract its destructive practices. The voice process favors a negative self-image, isolation, self-denial, self-nourishing habits, and a sense of alienation. Child-rearing practices which support the formation of this type of thinking process foster behaviors that are detrimental to the child's development.

Ideally, parents strive to avoid actions that give children the feeling that they are bad. They would not support destructive tendencies toward isolated solitary activities, nor label children's wants as greedy or selfish. On the other hand, parents would support their children's direct pursuit of goals in a social context and would teach them to control and eliminate acting out, regressive, and manipulative behaviors. When children do act up and misbehave, parents can teach them to change their behavior rather than label themselves as bad or hate and punish themselves. We particularly discourage all parental behaviors or child-rearing philosophies that support the formation of hostile voices or negative internal dialogue.

NOTES

1. *The concept of the voice as distinguished from a conscience*: Freud tended to use the terms *superego* and *conscience* interchangeably in many of his writings (see "The Ego and the Id" [1923/1961]). Another example can be found in Freud's last work, "An Outline of Psycho-Analysis" (1940/1964), in which he states:

The torments caused by the reproaches of conscience correspond precisely to a child's fear of loss of love, a fear the place of which has been taken by the moral agency.... The super-ego continues to play the part of an external world for the ego, although it has become a portion of the internal world. (p. 206)

In "The Concept of Superego," Joseph Sandler (1960/1987) traces the progression of Freud's thinking related to the superego and the ego ideal. According to Sandler, the functions of a "conscience" were ascribed to the superego by Freud, and the superego "exercises the 'censorship of morals'" (p. 20).

Loewenstein (1966) clarifies the distinction between superego and conscience in his essay "On the Theory of the Superego: A Discussion":

One characteristic of the superego is today often neglected: namely, the fact that...its contents and functioning often differ widely from the consciously adopted moral code of the individual. (p. 300)

2. *The controversy over formulations about superego and split-ego functions*: In his essay "On Narcissism," Freud (1914/1957) wrote about his early formulations concerning functions of the superego, ego-ideal, and conscience:

A power of this kind, watching, discovering and criticizing all our intentions, does really exist [italics added]. Indeed, it exists in every one of us in normal life. (p. 95)

However, in a subsequent paper, "Mourning and Melancholia," Freud (1917/1957) located this critical agency in the ego. He postulated that in melancholic (depressed) patients "the critical agency...is here split off from the ego," causing great suffering. "We see how in him *one part of the ego sets itself over against the other* [italics added], judges it critically, and, as it were, takes it as its object" (p. 247).

Psychoanalysts since Freud's time have continued to postulate a dynamic conflict between the self and a tyrannical thought process consisting of an internalized representation of parental attitudes and wishes (Beres, 1966; Rapaport, 1951; Westen, 1986). A number of these theorists have emphasized the concept of the superego (Novey, 1955), whereas others have based their views on the *split-ego concept* postulated by Freud in "Mourning and Melancholia":

A newly developing persecuting ego-function [the *antilibidinal* ego] develops in which the psyche directs its energies to hating its infantile weakness and striving to subdue it rather than protect it. (Guntrip, 1969, p. 188)

Our concept of the voice is more closely aligned with the orientations of Fairbairn and of Guntrip than with the formulations of classical psychoanalytic thinkers. It is more important, however, to recognize the extensive effects of the process of introjection and the associated hostility toward the self than to hypothesize about or categorize the structures involved.

CHAPTER 6

Typical Abuses in Childhood and Their Effects on the Adult Personality

> I consider many adults (including myself) are or have been, more or less, in a hypnotic trance, induced in early infancy: we remain in this state until—when we dead awaken, as Ibsen makes one of his characters say— we shall find that we have never lived.
>
> R. D. Laing (1969/1972), *The Politics of the Family* (p. 82)

There are many forms of child abuse, other than physical or sexual abuse, that are more damaging to the child and more devastating to family life than most people realize.[1] Although physical incidents are reprehensible and tragic, not enough attention has been paid to other forms of mistreatment that have adverse effects on the child's personality, spontaneity, and sense of self (Ney, Moore, McPhee, & Trought, 1986). Indeed, no child enters adulthood without suffering a certain amount of damage in basic areas of personality development that disturbs psychological functioning and yet leaves no visible scars.

Children are often the victims of parental hostility, neglect, cruelty, or outright sadistic treatment. Their emotional suffering can exceed distress caused by physical beatings (Garbarino *et al.*, 1986; Rohner, 1986). In thinking about psychological abuse, as well as sexual and physical abuse, it is important for parents to remember that *they* were once children themselves who were vulnerable to trauma and mistreatment. However, most parents avoid looking into their childhood for the roots of the problems they later experience with their own offspring. Admittedly, it causes pain to examine one's past and uncover memories one wishes to forget, but the results of such a retrospective exploration can be valuable and even curative when these recollections are expressed and understood.

TRADITIONAL VIEW OF CHILDREN

Although psychologists are aware of the harmful effects of parental mistreatment, very often their own defenses cause them to minimize the role that traumatic experiences play in shaping people's lives. Furthermore, many people assume that certain forms of physical punishment and emotional abuse are an inherent part of disciplining and socializing children and are therefore a basic part of child-rearing (J. Kaufman & Zigler, 1987). Bruno Bettelheim (1985) called attention to this incorrect view of discipline in his essay, "Punishment versus Discipline":

> The majority of those [parents] who have asked my opinions on discipline
> have spoken of it as something that parents impose on children, rather
> than something that parents instill in them. What they really seem to have
> in mind is punishment—in particular, physical punishment. (p. 51)

Alice Miller (1980/1984, 1981/1984) has dramatically illustrated in her writing that many socially accepted and culturally determined methods of rearing, educating, and disciplining children have provided parents with the rationale for committing cruel acts of physical and psychological abuse on their offspring. The results of such forceful measures of discipline and subtle forms of social control have been described by Miller in her book, *For Your Own Good*. In this work, she examines several case histories of disturbed individuals. Notable among them was an examination of Adolph Hitler's childhood, as well as an analysis of the typical upbringing of youth in pre-World War II Germany. The following childhood recollection was found in the diary of another famous Nazi, Rudolf Hoss, the Commandant at Auschwitz.

> It was constantly impressed upon me in forceful terms that I must obey
> promptly the wishes and commands of my parents, teachers, and priests,

and indeed of all adults, including servants, and that nothing must distract me from this duty. Whatever they said was always right. These basic principles by which I was brought up became second nature to me. (Miller, 1980/1984, p. 68)

In my work with parents and with adult patients who had been abused as children, I have been impressed by the pervasive misconceptions of discipline noted by Bettelheim and Miller. In addition, many parents have been so hurt in their own development that they are unable to lead lives of integrity and self-discipline and are therefore incapable of serving as *models of mature behavior* for their children. Consequently, their "discipline" reflects the well-known policy, "Do as I say, not as I do," an extremely ineffective method of socialization.

Many forms of incidental damage to children occur on the periphery of parents' consciousness. There are several reasons for parents' lack of sensitivity to the kinds of incidents that might be hurtful to children. Two principal reasons are particularly relevant to this discussion. First, as we noted earlier, many parents were treated harshly as children and have rationalized their own parents' mistreatment of them. Second, there is a belief prevalent in our society that children belong to their parents in the sense of being their property. This notion negates to a considerable extent children's inalienable rights as human beings.

Painful Experiences in Growing Up

For several years, participants in our parenting groups have been examining the particular forms of maltreatment *they* encountered in their upbringing and the ongoing influences these experiences still exert on their present-day behavior. In a sense, these individuals have partially "awakened from the trance" of which Laing wrote and, as a result, have been able to recall incidents of humiliation, exploitation, and harsh discipline that contributed to the tense atmosphere that prevailed in their homes.

As I have listened to these people describing specific occurrences of abuse or the long-term, unrelenting anguish of their early years, I have been surprised and disconcerted by the amount of pain they had experienced as children. In addition, I have been able to clearly observe manifestations of suppressed childhood pain expressed in their present-day relations to self and others. I have observed the extent to which early events were still affecting the lives of these people, despite the fact that they represented a "normal" population in terms of achievement, overall personal development, and absence of serious pathology.

In our clinical experience, my colleagues and I discovered that people generally deny or underplay their hurt feelings in relation to childhood trauma. People mold their present-day environments in order to avoid reexperiencing painful memories. Gradually, however, the individuals in our parents' discussion group developed a depth of feeling and a compassionate understanding of the events and interactions that hurt them in their formative years.

Case Studies: Analysis and Discussion

My associates and I found that many of the group participants had been sexually molested by adults in their families and that many were also beaten, often routinely, by their parents. A number of women revealed sexual abuses by their fathers, stepfathers, or other relatives—incidents that ranged from seductive tickling, sexual play, and stimulation to incidents of intercourse. In one case, sexual activity, including mutual masturbation, was part of an ongoing sexual relationship between a father and daughter, which started before the young woman, Cynthia, reached adolescence and continued into her adult life.

One morning, when Cynthia was about 10 years old, she was lying in bed between her parents. After a while, she became aware of her father's hand under the covers touching her genitals. Cynthia remained quiet, pretending that nothing was happening; her mother was still in bed. Later, her father told her to come out to the workshop with him, where he caressed her until she had an orgasm.

Cynthia continued to go to the workshop with her father at frequent intervals, on the pretext of helping him. One day, several months later, Cynthia told her mother everything. That night, the little girl could hear angry conversation between her parents. She heard them talking about divorce and felt very guilty as if she had caused her family a tremendous problem.

Cynthia's mother began to keep close watch over her, and she was not allowed to go to the workshop. For several weeks, this routine continued, and her parents' relationship seemed more harmonious to Cynthia. She started to feel that her mother cared about her and that she would protect her. Then, one evening while she was helping her mother in the kitchen, she was shocked to hear her mother say, "Cynthia, go to the workshop and help your father." Stunned, she obeyed and walked silently to the workshop to resume the sexual relationship with her father, which continued until she was married.

The effects of this incestuous relationship were long-term. The secrecy and complicity that pervaded Cynthia's family life had taken their toll and seriously interfered with her adjustment as a wife and later as a mother.

A number of men in the parenting talks also reported being fondled seductively by their mothers during bathing. Others revealed incidents of seduction by maids or sitters. Sexual play and intercourse instigated by these older women frequently led to feelings of guilt and inadequacy. It is important to emphasize and understand that the secrecy and shame surrounding incidents of sexual abuse often had a more damaging effect than the actual sexual acts, which were problematic in themselves.

Cases of regular beatings were common among individuals who spoke of their childhoods in the group; several individuals reported anticipating daily physical punishment. In many instances, these beatings appeared to have very little relationship to actual discipline.

For example, one man, Mr. A., related incidents of daily physical and verbal abuse that could be traced to his mother's bad moods and temper tantrums, rather than to realistic disciplinary action. Mr. A. could not recall what he had done to deserve the severe beatings and repeated tongue lashings. Here he talks about these incidents in a parents' group:

MR. A.: My father used to beat us pretty often for almost anything that we did that he considered wrong. I didn't feel as bad from his physical beatings, because that was pretty common where I grew up—you know, if kids did something wrong, they got beatings—but I felt *more* hurt from the way my mother talked to me.

I would always be trying to figure out what I did wrong—"what did I do?" It's like she would yell at me at the top of her voice. And it was always something real crazy. It was like a tantrum that she was throwing, like "I'm going to *kill* you if you do so and so again."

TYPICAL ABUSES

A disease that is kept hidden behind closed doors and shuttered windows, whose existence is ignored or denied, can never be cured....

I was told again and again that I was exaggerating the problem. I was even told that maltreatment of children was a figment of my imagination, that its incidence was very low....

At that time, we had no statistics; we only had our gut reactions to personal experiences. It was difficult for those of us who believed child maltreatment to be a major disease to convince those who did not.

But I think, in the course of the past ten years, we have had a measure of success. (Fontana, 1983, pp. 30-31)

In the sections that follow, we will describe several individuals' recollections of the hurtful treatment they received as children. We cannot stress too strongly that, without exception, *every* participant in our parenting groups revealed stories of emotional abuse, neglect, and maltreatment similar to those recounted here. Many of these incidents had been buried in the person's unconscious or had been pushed into the background and given little importance. Some individuals spoke of brutal, sadistic acts on the part of parents, whereas others related stories of living for years in a torturous home atmosphere, constantly anticipating parents' explosive anger.

As more participants uncovered deeply repressed memories of the past, they spoke less matter-of-factly and began to experience the outrage, humiliation, and grief of being treated harshly and cruelly as children. With the full realization of what had happened to *them*, these parents were able to allow a process of healing to occur that has freed them, to a considerable extent, from the compulsion to repeat similar abuses on their own children.

Parental Indifference or Coldness

Two cases strikingly illustrate parents' indifference resulting in gross neglect. In one case, a 6-year-old girl was sexually molested by a neighbor. Confused and scared, she haltingly tried to tell her mother about the incident. The mother, completely oblivious to obvious clues that something frightening had just happened to her little girl, ignored her attempts to communicate and sent her back outside to play. Her lack of understanding and indifference had a nearly tragic ending. Later that same day, the distraught youngster became overtly self-destructive, running carelessly into the street, almost as though she wished to get hit by a car. Finally, a motorist who narrowly missed the child stopped his car and took the little girl to her mother. Still insensitive to the fact that earlier her daughter had been very upset and had tried desperately to tell her something, the mother punished her severely for running into the street. The girl recalled that she had been seriously depressed for years afterward, and often thought about suicide.

In another incident, a man recalled that when he was a boy his mother had allowed him to ride his bicycle down a dangerously steep hill. Speeding out of control down the hill, he rode through an intersection and sideswiped a truck. In describing what happened next, he said:

I was very scared, but I picked up my bike and started walking home. The man driving the truck called an ambulance because I was scraped and bleeding. The ambulance came, but I just kept walking and finally got home. I banged on the back screen door, but my mother wouldn't respond to me because I was crying. She said, "Stop crying, then I'll let you in."

I kept crying and crying until finally the ambulance driver broke the door down. Both the truck driver and the ambulance driver were furious at my mother for letting me drive my bike in that neighborhood, because I was only 6 years old and there was no way to control a bike on that hill.

I recently went back to my old neighborhood and looked at the street. I can remember more about the incident now. It took place on a very steep hill, right near an elementary school, and the intersection was always congested with traffic. I would never—(crying)—I would never think of letting a child ride a bike unattended in that area.

As was true in the case of the sexually abused girl described above, the neglect evidenced in this case might also have ended tragically. Until this man talked about the details of the accident, however, he had been unaware of his mother's indifference to his whereabouts and his safety. In fact, only in the course of talking about this event did he remember that the two drivers who had tried to help him had been outraged at his mother for allowing him to ride his bicycle unsupervised in his neighborhood. Recalling the men's emotional reaction to the incident brought about a painful recognition of his mother's indifference, rejection, and covert hostility. Furthermore, this man gradually gained insight into some of the initial sources of his careless and unfeeling attitudes toward himself and his apparent lack of regard for his own personal safety.

Sadistic Mistreatment during Socialization of the Child

The participants in the parents' group reported many incidents of unnecessarily cruel and sadistic treatment while their parents tried to socialize them. Many men and women remembered that they were often treated harshly for minor infractions of rules or for being messy or dirty. In each case, there appeared to be no justification for the severe measures employed to "teach the child a lesson." The examples cited below were excerpted from a parenting group session in which the participants were exploring events they recalled from their childhoods:

LARRY: I remember a lot of times my dad saying things to me like "You won't be that way," or "You won't act that way," or "I won't hear this about you," you know, "*My* son won't act that way." And I would just be terrified, because he'd be yelling and hitting me about something that I had done that had embarrassed him.

ROBYN: In my family, the kids were singled out in different ways for the abuse, like my brother and I were treated very differently. He got beatings, and I remember being really little and watching him being beaten. I remember both of my parents beating him at the same time, really heavy beatings, and it was agony for me to watch it. He'd be playing with other kids and a fight would be going on, and my mother would automatically assume that it was him, and she would go into a rage and beat him.

LOU: My mother would get hysterical if we spilled something at the dinner table. She would say: "Don't upset your father." But it was *her* hysteria that upset him. My whole family was controlled by this kind of interplay between my mother and my father. I don't think my father could have cared less if a kid spilled his milk, but once my mother got furious about it, then we kids got caught in it and were the innocent scapegoats in those situations.

MARY: One day when my sister and I were very small, we took a putty stick and wrote our address on some old furniture stored in our garage. It was very innocent; we had just seen the Wizard of Oz and were pretending that if everything had blown away in a tornado, we would still have our address written down on things, so that people could return everything to us. We went in the house and told our mother about what we were doing, thinking that we had done something really responsible. And she went insane. She started hitting us with a fly swatter, and she beat us and beat us. I remember we were bleeding, and I just couldn't understand it. And I know that even now, I try to figure out ahead of time if what I'm going to do is the right thing, if it's going to be acceptable. I'm afraid I'm going to make the wrong move.

The people in our groups became increasingly sensitive and aware of prevailing patterns of emotional and physical child abuse. They reported harsh, punitive behavior that they casually observed in everyday interactions involving strangers, incidents that occurred in public in which parents humiliated and degraded their children.

ALMA: I was in the shoe store the other day, and a lady picked up this awful-looking pair of shoes and asked her little girl if she liked them. The little girl said, "No, I don't," and the lady said sarcastically, "Well, I'm going to get them for you anyway."

Then they went to another part of the store, and the little girl accidentally bumped against someone—she wasn't looking—and her mother grabbed her really roughly, and the hatred just poured out of her. And then she turned to her friend and commented, "I *hate* her—she's disgusting. She does this all the time!"

FRED: I heard loud voices. It appeared to be a man yelling at a young boy. Looking in the apartment window, I saw him hurl his child across the room.

SANDY: I remember an incident where a woman was screaming every kind of verbal abuse, foul language, and name-calling at a youngster at the top of her lungs. The little girl, about 7 years old, withered before her as her mother held her and shook her violently.

SUE: I was walking behind an older woman with two little girls, and she was almost yelling at them saying, "The reason I'm taking you is because you're driving your mother crazy." And they both said, "No, we're not." And she said, "Yes, you are, you're driving her crazy." Then I think she realized what she was saying and tried to throw in something totally the opposite and she said, "But you're both wonderful children." It's like she switched back and forth—it was really painful to see and hear.

Threats of Punishment

Threats of abandonment or of being sent away are more common than one would assume. John Bowlby (1973) reports that threats of this sort are widely used by parents and frequently lead to serious school phobias.

A man in one of our groups reported that when he was 10 years old, he was blamed for an injury to his sister, which was, in reality, the result of his father's angry outburst.

CHARLES: One night at dinner we were all sitting around the table. My father was lecturing me about how I was lazy and no good. As he got more and more into it, he became more and more enraged at me. Finally, he pounded on the table with his fist, and a fork flew up from the table and hit my sister near her eye, cutting her face and drawing blood. At this point, he lost control, grabbed me and shook me and threatened to throw me in the street and never let me come back home. He screamed, "Look what you've done to your sister." I was totally confused and terrified.

In the aftermath of the accident, rather than attending to his daughter, the father ordered the son to pack his bags and leave the house. Terror-stricken, the boy pleaded with his father to allow him to stay, but to no avail. Only when the father was actually driving the boy to a bus stop did he finally relent and grudgingly agree to the boy's return.

Bowlby (1973) has pointed out that stories such as this appear only rarely in case reports or in the literature, because "parents are loath to talk about them." He goes on to describe various threats, including threats that the child will be sent away to a reformatory for misbehavior, threats that the mother and the father will go away, threats that the mother or the father will become ill or die, as well as impulsive angry threats to desert the family, "made usually by a parent in a state of despair and coupled often with a threat to commit suicide." These threats and others like them are not accidental or innocent. Many times they are conscious manipulations used by parents as strategies of discipline and control.

Verbal Abuse, Ridicule, Name-Calling, Labeling, and Condescending Ways of Talking to Children

Many times children are ridiculed at vulnerable stages in their development. Just as often they are criticized, attacked, or put off when they express spontaneous affection toward their parents. We have interviewed many women who recalled rushing up to their fathers only to be ridiculed and reminded by their mothers that "nice girls don't act like that." Several men remembered that they were brushed aside as children by an embarrassed adult when they were expressing affection and told that they were "too old for such things."

Many people remembered being defined and labeled in pejorative terms by their parents and relatives. Here a young man talks about certain labels that were applied to him in his upbringing:

YOUNG MAN: I was thinking about the words that I was called in my family. I know that these terminologies are deep in me. They are a basic, integral part of my image of myself that I still carry around to this day, like the word "bum" really gets to me. "Bum—you're a bum."

When I think about it in light terms, I laugh, but I mean I *really* feel like a bum. If I'm driving along and I see somebody on the street, a bum, I think to myself, "That's you. There you go, five years from now when you finally lose it."

Another term is "simple shit." "You simple shit." It's a feeling of being so dirty, dirty beyond belief. I can't tell you how many times these words were said to me, but they're deep inside and really express my image of myself.

Other subjects recalled that their parents made condescending remarks about their activities. For example, the parents described romantic relationships as "cute" or as a "childish infatuation." Several people were made fun of for being shy, quiet, or reserved. One woman, Lisa, recalled that her sister was adored, indeed almost revered, by her parents and relatives, while she was humiliated and insulted. She was made to feel "second-class" and unacceptable in her own family, and this feeling has persisted into her adult life.

LISA: I was made fun of for practically everything I did. If I cried, I was called names of being a child that always cries, "red eyes." If I had to go to the bathroom a lot because I had trouble—this is very hard to say—I was called names and told that the toilet was my room. If I asked for more food, I was called "big eyes." I was referred to as the "yeller," and a "nervous child."

My mother took delight in telling me that "from the time you were born, you were so terrible that you cannot be my child—they switched you in the hospital." I was watched in an unfriendly way. Whatever I did was commented on. I was called a lot of terrible names since very early in my childhood.

Later, when I was about 13 or 14, my mother had a big family dinner. Afterwards everyone was going to visit my mother's cousin, who was in a higher social class—he was an architect and had a beautiful home. When everyone was ready to go, my mother told me I wasn't allowed to go, that I had to stay home and do the dishes. I begged her to go, but she was determined that I should stay home.

Then everyone left to take the bus to my cousin's house. I ran behind the bus for about two miles and got there not long after they arrived. I pleaded to stay and promised to do the dishes later. My mother chased me down the street, yelling at me to get home to the dishes. I ran all the way home crying. I was so depressed because not one person among all my relatives offered to let me stay.

Misleading and Lying to Children

Many of the individuals we talked with revealed stories of being misled about important issues, such as death, birth, sex, illness, and separations. They were lied to or told fantastic stories about people who had died. When their pets were "put to sleep," their parents reacted dishonestly, causing distrust and suspicion. One woman was told that her dog had been sent away to a ranch, where it had "fallen in love with another dog and now had puppies." Years later, she found out the truth, that her pet had been hit and killed by a car. This woman was deceived by her parents about many other important issues. She developed a strategy of lying and deceitfulness herself and has found it difficult to break this pattern as an adult.

Other participants in the discussion group disclosed that they were confused by parents who attempted to cover over mistakes by blaming their children. In one case, a young girl spent the better part of a family vacation searching for car keys her father accused her of losing.

YOUNG GIRL: All I remember is how horrible the next three days were while my father screamed at me and my dumbness, and I frantically tried to find the keys. He constantly reminded me of how this was ruining our vacation, of how much it was going to cost him to get a locksmith to leave town and come to this remote camp and break the lock and make new keys. I can remember how I hated myself as I ran through the camp asking everybody if they had seen the keys.

Suddenly the keys were "found." My father told me that some furry animal or a bird must have found the keys and picked them up and put them in a nest and they just now dropped out and were found. I never thought to question him, because I was so relieved that things were calm again. I was very gullible and believed his facetious story at the time.

Just recently I mentioned the incident to my sister. She told me that my father had found the keys under his bunk, where they had fallen out of his pocket, but he had never told *me* the true facts. He just couldn't admit to me that he was at fault.

Overbearing, Proprietary Interest in the Child

As we have seen in previous chapters, a build-up of the child's vanity is more often than not a compensation for the parents' lack of genuine regard for the child. Because most parents implicitly believe that their offspring belong to them, many brag excessively to their friends about their children's accomplishments and live vicariously through their achievements. These parents also falsely praise their children, offering them flattery and special treatment as a substitute for the real love they do not give. Vanity and an exaggerated sense of self-importance connect such individuals to their parents. Children, and later adults, come to need the false praise or build-up. Their vanity belittles their *real* achievements and real appreciation of these achievements by others, and often leads to a sense of failure. Here, Barry describes how his mother exploited him and built him up for her own self-enhancement:

BARRY: I was never hit or beaten, ever, but I do know that my mother took over my entire life from a very early age and that I just became a performing object. I was 2 or 3 years old and she was teaching me how to read and giving me dancing lessons. My entire life was out of my hands. I was always performing. If there was a party, I'd be waked up and called into the living room and I'd have to read something or do a dance.

It was an endless succession of performances, and I know that now I can't go into a room with people in it without thinking about what I'm going to do. What am I going to do to please these people? What am I going to do to make people like me?

Parental Inconsistency

Parental inconsistency is sometimes more damaging than consistent ill treatment. Parents tend to respond to the child more in terms of their own moods (which vary considerably) than what the child's behavior calls for. Children react more strongly to negative experiences than positive ones. When treated inconsistently, they develop a deep distrust of positive responses. Some parents invariably punish their children or become particularly withholding from them following close personal interactions with them.

One woman related a story in which her father appeared to have a negative reaction after his initial generosity toward her.

WOMAN: Once, my father, who rarely did things with me, drove all the way back from the market to get me, because he saw that they were having a special event. Howdy Doody, from the TV program, was there, and my father knew that I loved him. I was very impressed that he drove all the way back home to pick me up. I remember feeling really happy.

   But when we started to get out of the car, I had one of those army belts on over my clothes, and he wanted me to take it off before we went into the market. It got caught on something and I couldn't get it off. He started yanking at it and yelling at me to get it off quick. It was a horrendous experience, and yet it had started off with such a nice feeling from him toward me.

Other individuals remembered being told "No!" automatically when they asked their parents for anything. Some mothers and fathers take a sadistic delight in refusing to let their children do anything they want, on principle. They set up unnecessary rules and regulations without apparent rhyme or reason.

SITUATIONS THAT AROUSE ABUSIVE RESPONSES

In a parents' group, we discussed specific incidents with children that aroused aggression in parents. The majority admitted that they experienced irrational or uncontrollable feelings of rage under certain conditions; for example, when their child was whining or constantly crying, when children were chronically ill, or when children appeared helpless, vulnerable, or incompetent.

Parents felt the wants and needs of their infants as demands, as unwanted intrusions. The cries of babies and parents' inability to comfort them led to anger and physically insensitive or abusive treatment. One patient was so distressed by his baby's cries that he put a pillow over its face. The baby suffered severe brain damage from this suffocation. This terrible example is a dark manifestation of a common response to the parental discomfort aroused by incessant crying.

We have found that abuses before the child develops language are particularly shattering to the child's psyche and very guilt-provoking for parents. Parents sense they are taking advantage of the child's helplessness and vulnerability. Abusive incidents suffered by preverbal youngsters are especially difficult to work through, because there were no words at the time, only primal feelings with no acceptable outlet. Other studies (Wilkie & Ames, 1986) support our observations.

Messiness, incompetence, and errors of judgment arouse rage in parents raised in a regime of cleanliness, who hate their own ineptness, and who have perfectionistic standards of behavior for themselves. The perception of a child's vulnerability and helplessness triggers feelings of tension and hostility. A helpless, dependent child brings out abuse in people who have underlying sadistic impulses that they otherwise manage to keep under control.

For example, one mother who severely punished her 3-year-old son for getting his clothes dirty, when asked what about that situation had aroused such intense anger, answered:

MOTHER: His vulnerability, mostly. I remember that he looked so small. He looked like he couldn't defend himself. He looked like he was feeling bad, but mostly he looked small, dependent on me, and I felt that I had nothing to offer him. So I was very angry.

Noise levels, excited exclamations, and laughter of children often arouse discomfort, even hatred, in reserved and controlled parents who were forced to stifle *their* laughter when they were children. One man, whose spontaneity was squelched by overly critical parents, now finds himself, without thinking, sarcastically asking his 4-year-old son, "What are *you* smiling about? What's so funny anyway? Why are *you* so happy?"

Children who are handicapped or chronically ill often arouse feelings of anger and rejection in parents; yet these feelings are conventionally unacceptable. Insecure, self-critical parents both attack and blame themselves for the child's disability, and take it out on the child.

To illustrate, an associate told me that when he was very young, he had been seriously ill for several months. His father, a physician, was humiliated that his son was sick for so long. Later, his mother told the youngster that his father somehow blamed her for the illness and had said he would kill himself if the boy died. As an adult, this man felt humiliated and self-hating whenever he became ill and dreaded going to the doctor even for routine physical examinations.

In the following segment from a parenting group discussion, participants talk about the particular behaviors and characteristics in children that typically arouse anger in them (see also Silver *et al.*, 1969):

TOM (father of a 3-year-old boy): When I see children fidgeting or playing with their hands, it makes me angry. Also silliness that leads to things like spontaneous clapping and liveliness, I always interpret as silliness.

ELIZABETH (18-year-old girl): I get the most irritable with D. (the youngster she baby-sits) when he's eating—when he won't eat his dinner. I remember that it was a torture for me when *I* was little—being at the dinner table. Because if I didn't finish something, if I didn't eat it right, I got into trouble.

If we are at a restaurant, I say kind of under my breath but angrily, "Better eat your dinner, better eat all of it. You ordered it! Don't just sit there! Eat it all now or you're going to get it!" Where he could hear it, but nobody else could.

DR. F.: I think that there's an echo of that in every parent. But also shame about letting it show. It's like an externalization of what you felt or feel even now toward yourself. And in situations where it's clearly obvious that the child is inept or slow, then there'd be a really abusive feeling stirred up.

MARTHA (mother of a 25 year-old man): When I brought up my son, as long as I could be by myself, so to speak, isolated, I wouldn't mind. If I was in the kitchen and he was watching TV, it was all right. But if he wanted to communicate, if he wanted to ask me something, I got irritable without even knowing why. If he would look up at me, I could see in his eyes that he wanted something from me, simple, like being with him or helping him with something, I would get furious and I never would know why.

As noted, parents react in anger to positive expressions of affection from their children. These responses arouse painful, repressed feelings of sadness.

A mother of two boys talks about angry reactions she had to her older son's enthusiasm and affection when he was an infant:

MOTHER: Lots of times Malcom would wake up from a nap, and he would have a bright look on his face toward me. But I would choose something to get really angry at him for, in the crib, even at that age.

When I would walk into the room to pick him up, like if he was crying, and he would see me and he would have that bright look, I would say, "Stop crying!" That would be my response. But he had already stopped crying because he was happy to see me. And I know that he's grown up with a deep sense of being bad. That's a painful thought.

When parents react to provoking circumstances with their children by becoming angry and abusive, these frightening outbursts are often followed by feelings of contrition and apologetic behavior. This vacillating pattern is very confusing and upsetting to the child.

Many mothers are overprotective and overly permissive to cover up their anger or rage (Epstein, 1987). They retreat from disciplining the child and threaten the child with comments like "Wait till your father gets home. He's really going to give it to you." These mothers act out suppressed anger by utilizing and involving fathers as the punishing agent, reinforcing the concept that "men are mean." Many men who feel protective toward their wives are drawn into the punitive role and act out this function to their own detriment and thus experience considerable guilt. They come to believe that they *are* mean, harsh, and unfeeling by nature.

This situation is exemplified in the following case history. One mother in a family that I have known for several years had suffered physical and mental abuse in her childhood and, as a consequence, was overly indulgent with her three children. She confided that she had vowed she would never physically punish her children or raise her voice to them in anger. Therefore, she refused to discipline them, yet warned them repeatedly that their father would punish them when he returned home from work each evening. Her husband filled the role of harsh disciplinarian, while she was perceived as an easygoing, "good" mother by friends and neighbors.

The fact that this woman had disowned her own aggression and was using her husband to carry out her hostile urges toward her children became apparent to her only after her children were adults. Here she relates a painful incident that had occurred when one of her daughters was 1 year old:

MOTHER: Linda learned to walk very early, at 10 months, and started exploring things, some of them dangerous. She would go into the street, put objects into her mouth, and play with the knobs on the stove. I thought of her lack of response when I would tell her "No" as rebelliousness or defiance, a quality I envied and hated at the same time, since I had become so compliant and obedient myself as a child.

One incident, which I vividly remember, occurred one night just as my husband was coming in from work. Linda had been deliberately disobedient for the third time that day. I complained bitterly to my husband that Linda was uncontrollable and that I didn't know *what* to do with her!

He grabbed her and holding her arms tightly, shook her hard. He yelled right into her face that she was going to mind "or else!" Linda was terror stricken; her eyes widened and she cried and screamed. He held a hand over her mouth and ordered her to stop crying. Of course, she couldn't and he became even more angry. Finally, I timidly asked him to stop because I felt too guilty about what was happening. But, at the very beginning of the scene, when he began shaking her, I remember feeling glad and excited that *he* was angry, that he was punishing her.

THE EFFECTS OF PARENTAL MISTREATMENT ON ADULT CHARACTER STRUCTURE

The two case histories that follow illustrate the ongoing effects of early emotional trauma.

Case Report

Mrs. C., an attractive 39-year-old woman with a lively sense of humor, is seemingly outgoing and friendly. Nonetheless, despite her facade, many aspects of her physical appearance, posture, and mannerisms reveal the indelible mark left by the abuse and mistreatment she suffered during her childhood. Uncomfortable in social situations, her painful feelings of awkwardness are evident in her posture and in her hesitant manner of talking that detract from her overall appearance. The results of a chaotic childhood marked by physical abuse, indifference, disrespect, and repeated separation experiences led to problems in her personal life and a limited ability to function in her career. Until recently, she experienced overwhelming feelings of claustrophobia in the office setting and often felt compelled to leave work in order to relieve her anxiety. She was unable to understand these symptoms until she developed insight into the traumatic events of her childhood.

Mrs. C.'s close relationships were unstable, and she found it difficult to commit herself to family life. Recently, problems in the relationship with her 6-year-old daughter catalyzed Mrs. C.'s desire to uncover the history of what had happened to *her* as a child. Gradually, the details of her early years became more distinct in her mind as she examined her past and present relationships.

Background. Mrs. C.'s mother had attempted to smother her when she was about 2 years old. Following the little girl's recovery from the incident, her mother abandoned the family. However, she returned when Mrs. C. was 9 and continued to physically abuse her daughter, verbally degrade her, and depreciate her worth. In a group discussion, Mrs. C. recalled her angry reactions to the verbal abuse. (She recalled these incidents of verbal abuse *before* she was able to remember the attempted suffocation by her mother.)

MRS. C.: The most disrespectful thing my mother did was that she would refer to me as "it" instead of referring to me as "her." When I was around her, I would stammer when I talked and she would say—I remember clearly her saying this phrase—"Well, don't worry, 'it' can't talk plain," to her friends. I would get so furious because I think that that's the way she thought of me. She thought of me as some weird "thing." She didn't think of me as a person.

At times, Mrs. C. still tends to think of herself as an object of derision. Although she has strong opinions, she is fearful of expressing her views or displaying independence in her work. She often becomes the "comedienne," relying on jokes rather than running the risk of being taken seriously. Easily embarrassed, she suffers deeply from feelings of humiliation in situations that remind her of earlier interactions with her mother.

The most significant factor here in relation to child-rearing is the repetition of Mrs. C.'s mother's desertion. When Mrs. C.'s son, Mark, was 2 years old, she ran away and left him in the care of her husband. Like her own mother, she became frightened of the hostile impulses she felt toward her child. In the following sequence, excerpted from a parents' discussion group, she relates the story about abandoning her son. Incidentally, a few weeks following this particular group meeting, Mrs. C. recovered the memory of being smothered by her mother.

MRS. C.: Before Mark was born, I had made all sorts of vows that I was going to give my child the things I felt like I was lacking in my childhood. I was going to be a "nice" mother. But then, when he was born, very quickly I felt the same rage towards him that I felt towards myself. It wasn't like when he was 3 years old, it was when he was about a week old. I was so terrified by that feeling that I didn't know what to do. I was totally confused.

DR. F.: How did it feel? What did you feel?

MRS. C.: In the afternoon he started having colic, and about 5 o'clock he would just start crying and crying, and I would just feel like I would want to drown him, or I would want to just choke him, or I'd want to put a pillow over his head, or just something to stop him from crying. Luckily I had a next-door neighbor who came over and helped me.

I knew that there was something really wrong, and so I started planning to leave as soon as I had that feeling. When he was about 2 weeks old, I started planning in my mind to leave and to leave him with my husband, because I was terrified of what would happen. I had the feeling that I wasn't any good for him and that I needed to get out of there in order for him to live.

It wasn't until years later that it dawned on me that I had the same pattern as my mother and that I had hurt him by leaving in much the same way that I had been hurt by my mother's leaving *me*. But also it wasn't until years later that I really admitted that *I was hurt* by her leaving. I felt like it was my fault, and I felt rejected. I know that's the way my son feels, too, because no matter what I say, I can't convince him that it wasn't his fault that I left.

Later, Mrs. C. spoke of her change in attitude toward children since she had revealed the details surrounding her desertion of Mark.

MRS. C.: Since I've been talking about these abusive feelings in the parents' talks, I've felt different. I don't feel so afraid. Before we talked about these feelings, I felt almost terrified all the time to be around children, and particularly my own children. Now that I've told the "truth" about how I really feel, it's not like I'm a bad person, so

I think that I relate better to children in general, but especially to my daughter, Jane. I relate to her more as a person.

Uncovering the full story of the traumatic events that occurred in her own childhood has led to improvement in many aspects of Mrs. C.'s relationship with her husband and children. Her claustrophobic feelings and other symptoms of anxiety, which were probably connected to the original trauma of near suffocation, have lessened to a considerable extent. In addition, Mrs. C.'s fear in social settings has significantly diminished, and she now finds it far easier to express her opinions and ideas.

Case Report

The case of Cynthia, whose ongoing incestuous relationship with her father was described earlier, clearly demonstrates the effects of this sexual abuse on her adult behavior, as well as the secrecy and duplicity that characterized her family constellation. Cynthia entered therapy at 25, suffering from feelings of emptiness, frigidity, and compartmentalized feelings about her sexuality and her body. Originally, she sought professional help out of a concern for her two daughters, who were exhibiting symptoms of profound psychological disturbance.

In her first sessions, Cynthia had trouble talking about herself, so her therapist suggested that she write a brief biography of her life. The following week she worked conscientiously on this autobiography. She tried to recall every important detail about her childhood, as well as the things she was experiencing in her current life. Significantly, she neglected to write anything about the sexual relationship with her father.

Much later, recalling her years in therapy, Cynthia further explores the shame and guilt that had led to her secrecy:

CYNTHIA: I had been in therapy several months when I brought up the subject of my sexual relationship with my father. My therapist was the first person I had ever told. Somehow, in telling him the story, the reality of it began to dawn on me. It's like I was telling *myself* for the first time what I had been doing. In the years of silence, I had been keeping my sexual life almost a secret from myself. Secrecy, lies, and covering up had become a part of my life.

Secrecy was also evident in our family's conversations. We always talked about the workshop on a superficial, false level. My father and I pretended to everyone and even to ourselves, I think, that we were talking about practical work that had to be done. We deluded ourselves about being sexual and acted as if it were *not* planned, but "just happened" or maybe didn't even happen at all—that's the way I would think about it afterwards.

I rationalized away my guilt by insisting that my father never had actual intercourse with me, and so I was able to preserve my "virgin" status. But I worried endlessly that the relationship had damaged me sexually and that I would never be sexually "all right."

My mother, who seemed to condone my trips to the workshop, warned us constantly about other "family secrets." She always reminded me and my sisters to never talk to my father about the war, which she felt had been traumatic for him. We were also not supposed to mention our grandfather to my father, because my grandfather had committed suicide.

Cynthia's continued pattern of lying and other impulsive behaviors indicated a character disorder that was not only connected to the sustained pattern of sexual abuse, but was also related to the secrecy and collusion in her family. Her pattern of lying and secrecy continued after she revealed the secret of the incestuous relationship with her father to her therapist. During therapy, she began to act out sexually and dishonestly withheld information about her extramarital affairs. Many years of therapy were required before Cynthia felt that she could live openly and could safely abandon her pattern of lying and deceitfulness.

Note that the patient, like many women, unconsciously chose for a husband a man very similar to her father, despite the trauma in the family. The interplay between the powerful, unconscious needs existing in each partner and the interlocking defense patterns of this patient with those of her husband were indeed remarkable, yet each had selected the other based partly on these unconscious elements. Cynthia was unaware that her husband felt sexually insecure with her and with women in general and that he was fascinated by, and attracted to, preadolescent girls.

In the cases of both Mrs. C. and Cynthia, the mother, who is generally thought of as being naturally protective and nurturing, failed to provide the necessary protection and understanding. Both mothers failed to provide the support and care necessary for the security of their child. The significance of this failure in terms of the child's later development is stressed by Brandt F. Steele (1986) in his chapter dealing with child abuse. He noted that the ability of some children to recover spontaneously from severe childhood trauma and to later develop a resiliency and ability to cope adequately as adults appeared to be related to the presence of a person in the child's environment who would protect the child from further trauma or who would assist in the healing process. Other clinicians who have addressed this question of resiliency include Garmezy (1971), Rutter (1981), Farber and Egeland (1987), and Anthony (1987). However, Anthony concluded that these resilient or invulnerable adults still "seem to pay a psychological price for their apparent immunity from psychiatric illness" (p. 180).

CONCLUSION

Physical, sexual, and emotional abuses suffered by children in the course of a so-called *normal* upbringing are more prevalent and the effects are far more destructive and long-lasting than previously recognized (Emerson & McBride, 1986; Finkel, 1987; Jones, 1982; Shearer & Herbert, 1987; Zigler, 1980). We have traced the roots of adult character defects and neurotic symptomatology to these early experiences. It is painful to imagine what the people whose stories were recounted throughout this chapter could have become in the absence of the traumatic events that damaged them. It is appalling to consider the loss of vital aspects of a person's personality and the tragic waste of unlived lives and destinies not lived out, because of unnecessary, routine trauma in early life. People desperately need to protect an image of their parents as adequate, loving, reasonable, and "good," in spite of the evidence documented here and the accumulating data on the mistreatment of children (Garbarino & Gilliam, 1980). Consequently, they repress and block out the harmful events of their formative years.

NOTES

1. Statistics on child abuse show 1,928,000 incidents of physical child abuse and neglect in the United States during 1985 and as many as 225,000 victims of sexual abuse each year (California School of Professional Psychology, 1987).

CHAPTER 7

Idealization of Parents at the Child's Expense

The main task to be accomplished, if we are to liberate ourselves from the family in both the external sense (the family "out there") and the internal sense (the family in our heads), is to *see through* it.
David Cooper (1970/1971), *The Death of the Family* (p. 16)

SOCIETY'S GLORIFICATION OF PARENTS

The nuclear family is regarded as the bulwark of society by most people. Its image must be protected at all costs. Except in cases of blatant child abuse, parents' rights over their children's lives are held sacred and inviolable in most courts of law.[1] Our failure to recognize the child's inherent rights goes hand in hand with the conventional wisdom that parents have unconditional love for their children and know best how to raise them. In supporting the sanctity of the family and in protecting parents' rights over their children, we often unwittingly condone the harm done to children "for their own good."

A father of three grown children became painfully aware that he had acted on the premise that any disciplinary measure he had used in raising his children was justified by societal conventions.

FATHER: I know that with my children, I was sure that "right" was on my side. And with a vengeance, you can really bore in, and it's approved, and this is the way it's done.

But sometimes that veneer would crack, and an explosive rage would come out at the kids, and that would be the shocking part—"what am I, a monster?" And you can't take that rage back when it happens.

But most of the time, right is on your side, I'd say, in most households. You say, "You've played enough for one day." "It's time for your nap now." "Don't disturb other people." Just stamp them out. This is the stamp that this child, this person has to be put into. But a lot of society is on the side of wiping these people out.

This man had been raised in a family dominated by a tyrannical father. He had accepted the imposed role of scapegoat by other family members and still blamed himself for his father's explosive temper.

To some extent, almost all of us have grown up idealizing our parents to our own detriment. This pseudopositive view is difficult to alter or refute because it fits so closely the bias of our culture. Indeed, merely to expose the truth about the destructive effects of family life, even without blaming parents, is a violation of our societal code.

There is a taboo in our society against tampering with our traditional, overidealized view of family life. The rationale behind this taboo appears to be based on the following logic: The family's primary function as an institution is to teach children the values, mores, and standards of society. Therefore, it is in our best interests, as members of that society, to protect the family's image as "good," stable, and enduring—often at the cost of reality.

On a deeper emotional level, the need to maintain an exaggerated pseudopositive image of parents and family is based primarily on guilt and fear. Family members conspire to protect the picture of the "happy family." Their collusion stems more from a deep *fear* of the consequences of revealing the truth than from a conscious, rational motive of preserving the traditional values and mores of our culture. R. D. Laing (1969/1972), writing in *The Politics of the Family*, exposed the confused, entangled "rationales" behind this protection of family goodness and love:

> One requires collusion to play "Happy Families." Individually, I am unhappy. I deny I am to *myself*; I deny I am denying anything to *myself* and to the others. They must do the same. I must collude with their denial and collusion, and they must collude with mine.
>
> So we are a happy family and we have no secrets from one another. *If* we are unhappy/we have to keep it a secret/and we are unhappy that we have to keep it a secret. (pp. 99-100)

Laing (1967) emphasized the mystification inherent in this form of collusion and described the implicit oath of loyalty that prevents family members from exposing the myth of family unity and love. In another work, *The Politics of Experience*, he stated:

> In this group of reciprocal loyalty...each freedom is reciprocally pledged, one to the other....
>
> A united "family" exists only as long as each person acts in terms of its existence. Each person may then act on the other person to coerce him (by sympathy, blackmail, indebtedness, guilt, gratitude or naked violence) into maintaining his interiorization of the group unchanged....
>
> Any defection...is deservedly...punishable; and the worst punishment devisable by the "group men" is exile or excommunication. (p. 87)

Collective forms of collusion that protect the family's "good name" are evident in many segments of our society. In the field of psychology over the past several years, we have witnessed an unfortunate movement toward rationalizing away potentially damaging parental behaviors by debunking the idea that the attitudes and behaviors of parents constitute important factors in the child's later emotional development. In our opinion, this movement is clearly an effort to protect parents and declare the family off limits to objective scrutiny and realistic appraisal. This development may well be an overreaction to the practice of "blaming parents" prevalent in the 1950s—an unprofessional attitude unnecessarily hurtful to parents. However, the change in position toward the other extreme of denying children's vulnerability and protecting parents has had a negative impact on the field of mental health.

Albert Rosenfeld (1978), in his article "The 'Elastic Mind' Movement: Rationalizing Child Neglect?" strongly disagrees with proponents of this new movement and quotes prominent psychoanalyst Gilbert Kliman's opposition to this trend:

> We in our culture...are finding it increasingly difficult to bear the pain of our children.... So we must *rationalize our collective neglect of children by denying that the neglect does them any harm* [italics added]. (p. 28)

Another unfortunate trend in the psychological community is reflected in the view that some children are innately "difficult" or "bad." In their book, *Crime and Human Nature*, Wilson and Herrnstein (1985) state that "criminal behavior, like all human behavior, results from a complex interaction of genetic and environmental factors." However, they stress that "individuals *differ at birth* [italics added] to the degree to which they are at risk for criminality." They believe that "there is *some* psychological trait, having a biological origin, that predisposes an individual to criminality" (p. 70).

THE CONCEPT OF THE GOOD MOTHER/BAD CHILD

> Intellectually and—more to the point, in fact—emotionally, people continue to think of mother love as an absolute.... Deep down we are repulsed to think that mother love is not immune to all defects or variations of character...perhaps because we refuse to question what we prefer to believe is the absolute and unconditional love for us of our own mothers. (Badinter, 1980/1981, pp. xxii-xxiii)

Most individuals develop an idealized view of their parents because, as children, they were dependent on their parents for a long time for satisfaction of basic needs and, indeed, for their very survival. Consequently, they needed to see their parents as good and powerful, or their situation would have seemed truly and completely hopeless.

Schizophrenics tend to protect an exaggerated image of their parents' goodness and strength. In answer to the question, why must the child preserve an image of the parent as good, when it seems to be to his own detriment? Arieti (1974) replies:

> In early childhood the parent, generally the mother, is the person who connects the child with the environment; she is the Thou, the representative of the interpersonal world. The child must accept her in order to fulfill his inborn potentialities for full maturation and socialization.

> If she is not good, his need and desire to accept the world will be thwarted, and certain tendencies toward autism and arrested socialization will manifest themselves. (p. 95)

The child who is *not* accepted by the mother (or the most significant person in early life) tends to feel unworthy and unlovable. To avoid the desolation and hopelessness of feeling totally rejected and unlovable, the child constructs and preserves an ideal image of the mother, in the hope that she will fit it some day and approve, accept, and love him or her. The alternative, to accept the truth of her rejection and her inadequacy, is to give up the possibility of ever getting the gratification denied.[2]

Idealization also helps the child suppress and deny anger at his withholding or rejecting parents. Rage toward parents threatens to overwhelm the undeveloped ego and leads to terror of disintegration and annihilation. To avoid this debilitating rage and potential fragmentation, the child exaggerates the positive traits of his parents and blocks out awareness of their weaknesses or inadequacies.

It is important to stress that these dynamics operate not only in cases of severe pathology, as in schizophrenia, but that they are also a vital part of *each person's* defense system to varying degrees. The idealization process is a prominent feature in schizophrenic reactions. However, it is also a key factor in the strong resistance of neurotic and normal individuals to making constructive changes in their lives (Bloch, 1985).

Many children suffer deeply from subtle parental rejections and try desperately to maintain an image of their parents as loving and good. The more rejecting the parents, the more the child needs to perceive his parents in a favorable light. If parents are punitive and frightening, the child feels that it is not that the parents are bad, but him. The unfortunate child learns to evaluate him- or herself as in the rejecting parents' view, and develops strong feelings of self-hatred and a negative self-image.

In her work with children, Violet Oaklander (1978), author of *Windows to Our Children*, observed that:

> Almost every child I see in therapy does not think too well of herself, though she may do everything she can to keep this fact hidden. Young children do not place blame for their problems upon their parents or the world outside. They imagine that they themselves are bad, that they have done something wrong. (p. 57)

The case of Sharon C. exemplifies the important link between the idealization of parents and the corresponding lack of self-esteem characteristic of so many children.

> Sharon recalled that when she was about 13 years old and was starting to develop physically as a woman, her father began abusing her. Almost every night, he would wake her up, call her names, and hit her on her arms and face.
>
> She remembered that at the time, she believed he must be right in punishing her, and she would try to think of something she had done during the day that had made him angry. In general, she would be unable to think of anything; however, the next morning she would apologize to her father for upsetting him and for being a "troublemaker."

If Sharon had *not* taken the blame for the abusive treatment she received, if she had perceived her father realistically as abusive and unreasonable, she would have had to experience the profound fear of knowing that she was at the mercy of a seriously disturbed, even potentially dangerous, person controlled by impulses out of his control. It was less threatening for her to be the scapegoat, thereby making his insane actions appear to be rational.

IDEALIZATION OF PARENTS AND THE FANTASY BOND

Adults still tend to preserve an idealized view of their parents because this positive image is a vital part of the fantasy bond—the process of parenting oneself in imagination. To develop a more realistic view of one's parents and family interferes with the self-nourishing process, creating anxiety. As patients progress in therapy and begin to perceive the weaknesses, inadequacies, and rejections of their parents, their internal system of self-parenting often breaks down. They recognize that they are no longer able to lean on the now diminished parental image for support. Most people mistakenly feel that maintaining a positive image of parents and the family *is essential* to their security. Yet, paradoxically, this preservation ensures the perpetuation of the "bad child" image and feelings of being unlovable.

IDEALIZATION OF PARENTS IN DISTURBED AND IN NORMAL INDIVIDUALS

In our work with schizophrenic patients, as well as with less disturbed individuals, we have found that there is a tendency to protect a positive image of one's parents by maintaining negative thoughts, feelings, and attitudes toward self. We have recognized that even people who openly criticize and blame their parents for their misery and symptoms still cover up aspects of an unconscious, underlying process of idealization.

A prominent businessman and politically influential figure was completely ineffectual in his attempts to prevent his mother's continual intrusions into his life, although he acknowledged his negative feelings toward her. She repeatedly humiliated him in public despite his requests and pleas that she was not to attend functions where he was a speaker. Although he constantly complained about his mother's intrusiveness, he was powerless to break away. It was ironic that this man, who made major decisions that affected the lives of many people, had so little influence on his mother. His fear of her calls and his childish or indirect ploy of instructing his secretary to lie about his whereabouts to his mother stood in sharp contrast to his directness in dealing with associates, friends, and employees.

On one level, this man continued to have a distorted view of his mother, perceiving her as powerful and strong. He maintained his guilt and self-hatred in relation to her and refused to face the truth that his mother was a confused, incompetent person who had been unable to provide him with the care he had needed as a child.

Many therapeutic interventions are directed toward disrupting idealizations of parents. Techniques such as "direct analysis" of psychotics, primal therapy, feeling release therapies, and voice therapy, all expose the truth of painful childhood experiences at the hands of insensitive, rejecting, or inadequate parents.

CASE ANALYSES RELATED TO THEORETICAL VIEWS

Psychotic Patients

In schizophrenics, the idealized image of the mother or parent has been internalized as part of the good parent/bad child split. This division severely impairs their intellectual and emotional organization, leading to extreme maladjustment. These psychotic people see themselves as possessing godlike superiority and as being the lowest, most unworthy creatures at one and the same time. The exaggerated ambivalence of these patients reflects grandiosity and feelings of omnipotence, as well as wretched feelings of inferiority and inadequacy.

A paranoid schizophrenic man was under the delusion that he was "god," and, at the same time felt he was completely worthless and despicable. A major symptom was his hallucinated pyramids. This had troubled him for some time. In one session, the patient was instructed to tell the therapist everything he knew about pyramids. The therapist interpreted the pyramids as representing the patient's mother's breasts that had been hard and cold like stone, because there was no love. The patient was asked to repeat the interpretations. He did. He left the session very impressed and excited by the interview, expressing the idea that maybe he could get better by talking to the therapist—an attitude sharply in contrast to his usual resentment of therapist and therapy. The patient's hallucinations began to disappear. By breaking into the patient's idealized image of his mother, the therapist could relieve the patient's more serious symptoms. Later, this man came to understand that his mother was incapable of loving him and caring for him, and that this was a token of her inadequacy as a mother, rather than an indication that he was worthless and unlovable (Firestone, 1957).

Psychosomatic Illness

In my clinical experience, I have had occasion to treat several patients with severe asthma. Their symptoms were relieved when I exposed undesirable qualities in the patients' parents. In one case, I had to affirm and speak out the patient's anger toward her mother on behalf of that patient, while she was having a severe asthma attack. Facing her hatred toward her mother, that is, hearing her anger externalized, was enough to break into the image of the "good mother" and cause a temporary remission of life-threatening symptoms. My records from the early phase of this patient's therapy illuminate her compelling need to perceive her parents as competent, loving, and "good."

Leora was 11 years old and had intractable asthma when I began to treat her. She had been sent home from the Jewish National Home for Asthmatic Children in Denver because, after a year and a half of treatment, they had been unable to control her symptoms. In effect, they had sent her home to die, because there was nothing more they could do to help her.

I was chilled by the depths of Leora's despair during the initial weeks of our sessions. She really wanted to die and wished to be released from her psychological as well as physical symptoms.

In one early session, Leora reluctantly showed me one of her poems: "A room ready to listen to my stifled sobs, to share the joys and sorrows of my heart."

She hesitantly told me: "I sometimes see things like I can't tell you. Right now I keep everything in a secret world."

DR. F.: If you could only let it out.

LEORA: A world—like my parents really adopted me—not like the other kids. I have another poem: "I sit in bed, chained as a dog to a leash."

I can't really talk about my parents. They are good people who really love me. (*Leora begins wheezing heavily.*)

DR. F.: Then why do you feel that you are adopted? Something sounds mighty fishy to me. You know what I feel—that you are the biggest sucker.

LEORA: What do you mean?

DR. F.: You're covering up for them, your parents, somehow. You don't want to tell the real story. You want to believe that they are good and of course feel that you are bad and evil. And yet you pay them back.

LEORA: How?

DR. F.: By being sick and making them climb the walls. Then they feel rotten, but what's the good of it? You are the sucker.

LEORA: You're crazy, Doc. You really don't know what you are talking about. I sometimes don't like to talk to you.

In the months that followed, the anger came and the wheezing stopped, mostly. Leora was angry at everything—her parents, me, her little sister—and so the internalized anger and self-hate began to flow in another direction—outward. And it splattered all over the place. She became a real bitch, and her mother got very angry at her and insisted that she answer her as "Yes, mother dear," or choke. Very often, Leora obliged....

In looking back over my notes at the time treatment began, I described Leora as having a strong negative image of herself. She was clinging desperately to this negative self-picture and could not accept her hostile feelings toward her parents; she was very defensive about these feelings, often developing symptoms at the times when her anger was aroused. She was especially reluctant to accept any inadequacies in her mother because her illness made her extremely dependent upon her on a reality level for shots, medications, etc.; thus, if mother is "bad," she would surely die.

Leora was very depressed and had learned to internalize her anger and to develop physical symptoms instead. That's why I called her a sucker. I knew that if she could begin to accept her anger, she would ease up on her physical symptoms, as many of the children at the hospital had done. This is what happened with Leora. As the anger came out she began to feel better. However, this was not a smooth or continuous process. There were periods of regression and anxiety followed by remorse and depression and sometimes serious attacks requiring hospitalization and emergency treatment.

In the incident mentioned previously, I had been summoned to her side because she was failing rapidly. Her mother called me on the phone and begged me to hurry over. When I arrived, Leora was very weak and frightened. I tried to get her to reaffirm her anger toward her mother, related to an incident of the previous week. I was frightened of this approach at this time but it just came out of me. I voiced the anger that Leora was feeling toward her mother. I held her hand and tried to give her my strength. Finally, I had to go, and I was not too encouraged by her reactions. There was only minor improvement.

I went back to my practice and got involved in my regular duties. The phone rang and it was Leora's mother. I was scared and anticipated bad news. I thought this was the end. She asked me; "What did you do with her?" I got more frightened, feeling that she was angry and critical of me, meaning that things must be pretty bad with Leora. But it was just the opposite. The news was good. She was feeling fine and the mother was thankful. The paradox was amazing. What had I done with her daughter? I had helped her face her hatred toward her mother so that she might live.

In another case, a similar remission of symptoms was accomplished when an associate urged a 14-year-old girl, who was in the throes of a severe asthma attack, to call her mother names in anger. It had been necessary for the mother to carry her frail, underdeveloped daughter to the session because the girl lacked the strength to walk from the car to the waiting room. Unable to speak because of her continuous wheezing, the young patient listened as her therapist verbalized the anger she felt at her mother's hypercritical attitude toward the girl and the way she had restricted her activities the previous week. Less than half an hour later, the girl was breathing easily and was able to walk on her own to the waiting room. Her mother expressed amazement and prevailed upon the therapist to describe what she had done to accomplish this "miracle cure."

PROTECTION OF THE PARENT BY IMITATION

The preservation of an idealized image of one's parents is made possible because the most undesirable and rejecting traits of the parent are repressed and blocked out of the child's awareness. Often these traits are projected onto others, fostering disturbed relationships. Many children avoid seeing negative characteristics in their parents by taking on these same qualities themselves and acting out their parents' destructive habit patterns. As adults, they continue to deny these qualities in their parents by imitating their parents' behavior.

This type of identification and imitation is demonstrated most often in people's actions and attitudes toward their *own* children. Occasionally, other family members are affected by this defensive form of imitation.

A teenage boy exposed the details of his father's neglectful behavior. He later manifested the same neglect in relation to a younger sibling.

In a discussion group, 16-year-old John revealed that when he was 5 or 6 years old, he had been left at school for hours because of his father's forgetfulness. He recalled feeling terrified at those times. The boy felt relieved to have finally told the story, although he realized it was painful for his father to hear.

Coincidentally, two days later, John himself forgot to pick up his 4-year-old brother at nursery school. Prior to this incident, the teenager had been completely reliable in performing this task. This event, following so closely upon John's exposure of his father's neglect, was clearly an unconscious imitation of his father's behavior. Several days later, the youngster could barely recall the story he had recounted in the group meeting; instead he was preoccupied with self-punishing thoughts and recriminations in relation to his own behavior.

Long-term effects of this particular form of protection are evident in the case of Karen, a woman who believed, on a deep level, that she was incapable of being a "good mother." Her hostility toward her son, which she attempted to hide by overprotecting him, was perceived by Karen as reflecting her basic attitude toward all children. In a parents' group, Karen began to remember incidents from her childhood that clearly revealed her mother's hatefulness and coldness toward her.

KAREN: I realized when we were talking last week that a very common thing my mother said to me was—she must have said it ten times a day—she'd say, "I'd like to break your neck."

I got so used to her saying it that I didn't even think it was anything unusual. She'd say, "I'd like to break your neck, you little brat!" That's how she would talk to me a lot of the time. Saying it right now, it would seem like an exaggeration, but actually it's not. I clearly remember the feeling of it. And it wasn't how I said it just now. It was *angry*—like she wished that she really could do it.

A number of important insights followed this session as Karen uncovered more painful memories which she had repressed since childhood. Subsequently, she noticed a change in her attitudes and feelings toward her son. The recognition that her behavior and attitudes had been a compulsive, unconscious imitation of her own mother's treatment of her as a child was an important step in Karen's developing a better relationship with her child.

Some clinicians consider it questionable to disrupt a *false* positive idealized view of parents (Lidz, 1983). Many professionals avoid tampering with well-entrenched forms of self-deception (especially when the issues involve perceptions of the patients' families), rather than use sensitive timing to help adolescents work through disillusionment with their parents. They believe that illusions fulfill vital psychological functions. These psychotherapists directly and indirectly support idealization, to the detriment of their patients over the long term.

This is not our position. The anxiety, anger, and guilt aroused after exposing the truth about parents is an essential part of therapy. We feel that these reactions must be worked through in successful therapy. In general, we are opposed to the reinforcement of any process of self-deception. Defenses and illusions distort life experiences and cause many unnecessary problems and pain in relationships (Goldberg, 1972).

RESISTANCE TO SEEING PARENTS OBJECTIVELY

Fear and Guilt about Hurting Parents

Most patients tend to progress in therapy until they reach a point where they begin to seriously resent the damage they sustained as children. They become fearful and guilty when they experience intense anger, grief, and outrage. These strong responses have long been suppressed through idealization. When this basic defense is disrupted, feelings of rage emerge and threaten again to overwhelm the patient. When these people feel and begin to express their rage at their abuse, they tend to turn away from their memories and insights. They turn their backs on themselves, internalize their anger, and direct it against themselves. They go back. They regress.

Most patients do not confront their parents directly. They experience deep feelings of guilt and become fearful of causing their parents pain, even in the absence of confrontation. Insights that seemed so powerful and dramatic at the moment of discovery frequently fade from the patient's consciousness after a few days or weeks. Other patients deny the pain they suffered in their families by attacking themselves with such voice-thoughts as "Why are you blaming all your unhappiness on your parents?" or, "You're only trying to make excuses for your own behavior."

One man revealed specific childhood abuses and humiliations. He still imposed limitations on himself as an adult and invariably berated himself after each disclosure:

PATIENT: "Why don't you grow up? Here you are, 45 years old, and still trying to work out your problems. Still shy and strange and neurotic! What are you trying to do, blame your father? Make your father look bad?"

He felt confused and hated himself until he identified these self-accusatory thoughts. He had to identify this insidious "voice" before he could get to good feeling about himself and gain his clarity.

It is necessary to account for one's unnecessary suffering in childhood. However, one need not maintain an attitude of "blame" toward one's parents or act out destructive, hostile behavior. Yet, patients still feel guilt about reaching a realistic, albeit critical, picture of their parents and developing a compassionate view both of them and themselves.

A young woman wrote a powerful, expressive letter to her parents describing her view of her childhood and her perceptions of family members. The guilt she experienced about sharing this realistic perception with her parents eventually led to a serious regression. The letter was very direct and honest, and compassionate and understanding in tone. She empathized with her mother in her tendency to overprotect members of the family:

> I just remembered that *your* mother treated you the same exact way [overprotectively]. She pre-wrote you weekly postcards when she went into the hospital, not letting you know what was going on, and then telling you a month later (when she was okay) that she had been operated on. So you grew up feeling that you needed that protection and later believing that my sister and I and even my father needed it, too.

In the closing lines of her letter, she wrote of her desire to develop further as an independent person with her own identity. The following excerpt demonstrates that she had begun to perceive her parents realistically as people with problems like her own.

> Telling you the truth about myself also destroys the old image that I have of myself—the one that you still cling to. And I am also more able to see you as two people whom I spent many years of my life with...but also as *people with your own thoughts and feelings and struggles*, separate from me.

For months, this young woman waited for a reply. None came. As the months passed, she developed serious self-destructive behavior patterns, isolated herself from her close friends, and some time later made an almost fatal suicide attempt. Her guilt about the pain she imagined she had caused her parents by writing the truthful and compassionate letter turned her against herself, and her subsequent regression nearly ended in tragedy.

Fear of Retaliation

Children and adolescents are afraid to be punished by parents and other family members for revealing the truth about the family. Because of the dishonesty and pretense involved in preserving the fantasy bond, personal communications within most families are typically indirect and manipulative. This is especially true of candid statements that might diminish images of parental wisdom and strength. Any suggestion that a parent might be inadequate or weak, any hint that maternal love is not an inherent, feminine quality, any indication that the husband is not preferred at all times to all other men by his wife threatens the parents' imagined connection with each other and with their children. For these reasons, many children are afraid to speak their minds on these subjects.

Clinicians have noted that patients and their families typically agree to keep silent on certain issues in order to protect the family image. Lidz, Cornelison, Carlson, and Fleck (1958/1972) described the process of "masking" within the families of seriously disturbed patients. According to them, "masking" confuses communication and involves the "ability of one or both parents to conceal some very disturbing situation within the family and to act as if it did not exist" (p. 285). They contend that "some degree of masking may exist in all families." Such defensive masking stems from dread of retaliation from the members of the family for coming out with the truth.

Artist Mary Barnes (Barnes & Berke, 1971), in an autobiography about her psychotic condition, revealed the discrepancy between the outward impression given by her parents to the world and their underlying hostility, which they kept confined to the privacy of the family home:

> My family was abnormally nice. Friends, relations and neighbours thought that we all lived happily together. Mother and Father were devoted parents.... Mum and Dad were always considerate and polite to each other.... They never shouted. The air was cold yet a storm was always brewing. (p. 5)

Mary goes on to explain the origins of her brother's emotional breakdown:

> He was caught, stuck in his anger. No one knew he was angry.... The tangle of the emotions of my family was so intense that automatically one member struggling free must be killed, annihilated, rather than the grip be loosened. *Such was the fear of truth* [italics added]. Madness was a step on the way to truth. It was the only way. (p. 8)

In a similar vein, a father in one of the parents' groups recently expressed sentiments of regret and anger about the restrictive regime under which he lived as a child. No disagreement had been allowed, especially if it threatened his family's myth of superiority and status.

FATHER: When I was growing up, it seemed like we were an ideal family, a happy family with the two parents and a girl and a boy, but there was a strong need to preserve that image, and if I did anything, especially in public, to make it seem as though it wasn't that way, I felt almost like I would be killed or kicked under the table or something like that. I would have to suffer for it in some way. It was really important that we maintain the image that we were a perfect family, especially that we were a really happy family—and it wasn't always true.

Somehow that whole attitude spilled over when I had my children. It was important that we project the image of being a happy family, and it would make me really angry if anything happened to detract from that in any way. If the kids would act up or be bad in school, or anything that would reflect the idea that we weren't a perfect family would infuriate me.

Adults who have discussed their problems and personal feelings with their parents have often been met with strong resistance. This resistance can take various forms: vindictiveness, denial, anger, indifference, tears, and, in many instances, the threat of an emotional breakdown.

A colleague was asked by family friends if their 19-year-old son could visit him for the summer. The teenager was having problems at school, and his parents were concerned about his rebelliousness and generally defiant attitude. They were hopeful that my associate would have a constructive influence on the boy. The summer passed pleasantly, and the young man became involved in the family activities of his host. Gradually, he relaxed and began to drop his angry stance. According to my associate, the boy also talked openly about the disharmony in his family.

When he returned home in September, the young man decided to tell his parents some of the discoveries he had made about himself over the summer months. Evidently, he had little opportunity to say much, because his mother burst into tears immediately, acting as though she had been accused of being a terrible mother. She was inconsolable for the next several days. The boy was compelled to reassure her over and over that she was a "good" mother.

It appeared that by selling out on his perception of his family and especially his mother, this adolescent damaged himself psychologically. The following week, he left for college in a depressed state. The next semester he changed his major to that of law, the profession his parents had urged him to pursue, and turned his back on his own career choice. Another painful consequence of this family scene gradually became evident when my associate realized some time later that he had been rejected by his old friends. He was forced to conclude

that they blamed him somehow for "influencing" the boy and sup-
posedly turning him against his family.

Fear of Being Ostracized by Society—Being Labeled "Crazy"

If anyone in a family begins to realize he is a shadow of a puppet, he
will be wise to exercise the greatest precautions as to whom he imparts
this information to. It is not 'normal' to realize such things. There are a
number of psychiatric names, and a variety of treatments, for such realizations. (Laing, 1969/1972, p. 82)

As discussed earlier, there is a strong taboo in our society against
perceiving one's parents realistically, even in the absence of blame.
There is strong social pressure *not* to tell the truth of what happened
in one's family, *not* to attempt to account for the long-term effect of
growing up in a destructive parental atmosphere, and *not* to fathom
the underlying pain that shows up in neurotic symptoms. Patients
attack themselves by believing that they are distorting their personal
experiences and accuse themselves of oversensitivity. They feel that
they are immature or childish for feeling hurt. However, in spite of
strong resistance, patients in therapy often reveal the family secrets;
that is, they expose the truth about parental cruelty and inadequacy,
only they do it behind closed doors. The ethic of confidentiality is not
only the basis of trust, but it protects the individual against expected
retaliation by parents and from society. One must question *why* patients'
revelations need to have taken on such a secret connotation.

Many parents react fearfully or defensively when their adult children enter therapy. Sometimes very angry scenes are generated as a
result. In other instances, parents attempt to rationalize their behavior,
such as in the following sequence:

Robert, a quiet, unassuming man of 25, entered therapy with the presenting symptoms of obsessive paranoid thoughts in relation to his employer. He was unable to
concentrate on the task at hand but was constantly worried that his boss would spot
a flaw in his work.

It happened that the patient's father visited him during the early months of therapy.
When he discovered that his son had recently started seeing a therapist, the father
revealed certain incidents where he had reacted irrationally and punitively toward his
son when he was a very small child. He was terrified that Robert might have remembered the events. He attempted to reassure his son that there had been extenuating
circumstances contributing to his cruelty; that is, he still tried to protect his own image
of being a "good" father by rationalizing his behavior.

The patient had *not* remembered the events described by his father, but was gratified to have the information. His father's "confession" about his cruel treatment of his son in relation to strict, unreasonable standards for cleanliness and orderliness gave Robert a clue about the origins of his deep-seated suspicion and fear of disapproval.

In another case, a mother refused to pay for her 17-year-old daughter's sessions when the therapist would not discuss the personal details of the daughter's case with her during a consultation that the mother had requested. When the mother discovered that the therapist implicitly stood behind individual rights rather than supporting the sanctity of the family, she retaliated by forcing her daughter to terminate therapy.

Separation Anxiety in Relation to the Family

Breaking the idealization of the family is not only threatening to the self-parenting process and to one's own self-esteem, but it arouses also intensely defensive reactions. People derive feelings of security from identifying with the "good" parent and find gratification for their vanity in "belonging" to a "special" family. The embarrassment and humiliation suffered by many young people when their families are seen as odd and different is a sign of their strong resistance to having the idealized image tampered with (Goleman, 1985; Lidz, 1983).

People who are moving toward independence often become threatened by the implied separation from parental figures. They experience a sense of loss of the persons or parent on whom they previously depended. Patients in psychotherapy who begin to develop a more positive view of themselves usually feel considerable anxiety because this change in identity disrupts the bond with their families. When they pierce the shell of their defensive protection of the family, the subsequent anger and symbolic "death wishes" toward their parents threaten their security and arouse guilt and fear. At this crucial point in therapy, patients tend to retreat, and serious regression can follow.

Guilt about Surpassing One's Parents and
Moving toward Independence

In cases in which patients surpass their parents, particularly the parent of the same sex, there is usually considerable guilt. I have treated several individuals who regressed and became self-destructive *after* achieving more in life than their parents. In many of these cases, patients expressed the feeling that they were "leaving their parents behind" or abandoning them. Many felt guilty as though they had broken an implicit pact or agreement.

Some parents interpret their offspring's moves toward independence as being critical or disapproving of the family. Indeed, clinicians are very familiar with the self-destructive or suicidal young person whose independent strivings cause his parents excessive pain and anxiety. In his book, *Family Therapy for Suicidal People*, Joseph Richman (1986) emphasized the negative impact that this parental distress can have on an adolescent's adjustment:

> The [adolescent's] formation of outside friendships and relationships is labeled [by the parents] as disloyalty. (p. 32)

> [The suicidal person] is alienated and isolated both outside the family and within it. It is that combination that often produces the particular pattern that is fundamental to a suicidal resolution. (p. 133)

The dynamics described by Richman are based on the family's fear of disrupting the illusion of connection or the fantasy bond, of which the idealization process is an integral part. Indeed, this imagined connection is felt to be a survival mechanism for family members (parents) who have suffered profound losses through death or divorce in *their* early experiences.

Individuals who are breaking away from a symbiotic family constellation, whether through forming "outside" friendships, going away to college, or surpassing a parent's accomplishments with their own achievements, can arouse intense feelings of separation anxiety in other family members. To most parents, a united family is the ideal, and "missing" members signify a flaw or weakness in the family structure. The coercion and manipulations, designed to pull the "deviant" or wayward individual into the family unit through playing on his guilt, can have devastating effects. One such effect, Murray Bowen (1978) contends, is that family members tend to withdraw from outside relationships as the level of tension and anxiety increases within the family's "emotional system."

Sabbath's (1969) description of "the expendable child" can be seen as part of this pattern of isolation within the family. A child pushed out of the family is also kept from outside relationships. The guilt and confusion inherent in trying to see through this double bind can lead to serious symptom formation.

The powerful defense of idealization prevents people from "seeing through" the manipulations and machinations of parents and families. It is a fog to cloud the reality of family life as many have experienced it. With seriously disturbed individuals, the cost of this blindness is tragically high.

CONCLUSION

Idealization of parents and family is a powerful defense formed in early childhood that people carry with them into their adult lives and extend to their mates. As long as an individual holds on to an exalted, overly idealized picture of his parents, he is unable to develop positive feelings of self-esteem. The two defenses are closely linked, and both are very resistant to change. Maintaining a negative view of ourselves and an exaggerated positive view of our parents insulates us against intrusions into the fantasy of self-sufficiency and pseudo-independence. Breaking into this primary defense brings people face to face with feelings of separateness and aloneness. Although one can hardly help but experience considerable initial anxiety in adapting to a more realistic view, such anxiety is positive and well worthwhile. If we can face the truth and give up our illusions, we feel more ourselves, more vital, more excited about life, and have a stronger sense of identity.

NOTES

1. Other cultures and societies do not necessarily conform to Western conventions regarding the sanctity of the family versus protecting the rights of children. For documentation of legal and ethical standards in two countries, Sweden and Communist China, that support children's rights, see Norma Feshbach's (1980) chapter, "Corporal Punishment in the Schools: Some Paradoxes, Some Facts, Some Possible Directions," and Jill Korbin's (1981) "'Very Few Cases': Child Abuse and Neglect in the People's Republic of China."

2. In *A Concept of the Schizophrenic Process* (Firestone, 1957), I expanded the "good mother/bad child" and the "bad-me" concepts delineated by Arieti and Sullivan in developing a theory of schizophrenia and extending the application of the concept to its central role in the defensive process for *all* individuals. Other theorists (Fairbairn, 1952; Kernberg, 1975) have noted the importance of the defensive idealization of parents and family in the etiology of neurosis.

CHAPTER 8

The Mother-Daughter Bond

A woman may bring any number of assets to marriage—compassion, wisdom, intelligence, skills, an imaginative spirit, delight-giving femininity, good humor, friendliness, pride in a job well done—but if she does not bring emancipation from her mother, the assets may wither or may be overbalanced by the liability of the fear of being a woman.

Joseph C. Rheingold (1964), *The Fear of Being a Woman* (p. 451)

THE CENTRAL ROLE OF THE MOTHER

In our culture, the role of the mother as the primary caretaker of children has important implications because she exerts a profound influence on the family. Some degree of frustration is inevitable in a child's early interactions, because no person can successfully anticipate the needs of another at all times. However, when this frustration is compounded by immature or rejecting mothering, it leads to a combination of intense rage and emotional hunger in the child. These negative feelings have no acceptable outlet in most cases and therefore manifest themselves in the building of defenses, passive aggression, and the withholding or holding back of positive responses.

In the case of female offspring, where the identification is strongest (Deutsch, 1944), the daughter's hurt or angry response is transformed into a form of withholding that resembles the mother's personality traits and defense patterns. Paradoxically, the more the daughter resents the mother and suffers at her hand, the more she tends to imitate her behavior and attempts to form an imaginary connection or bond with her.

It is important to note that women who have been deeply hurt in their relationships with rejecting mothers do not *consciously* want to imitate them. In fact, they are often very critical of their mothers' inadequacies, negative characteristics, and general style of relating. Indeed, the process of identifying with and of introjecting withholding patterns is largely an unconscious phenomenon. Over a long period of time, the daughter's holding back of positive responses and pursuits becomes automatic and involuntary, and the pattern is repeated with *her* children.

Repercussions of the mother-daughter bond have a destructive effect on women's relationships with the men in their lives and later on the children in the new family. However, it is most important to emphasize the powerful limitation this bond imposes on each woman's sense of self. Its stultifying impact on their feelings of self-worth, achievement, and personal power is far greater than most clinicians realize. In addition, this problem is compounded because women tend to feel guilty, depressed, and demoralized to the extent that the symbiotic tie with their mothers interferes with their most intimate relationships.

In exploring this controversial, emotion-laden topic, I hope that the reader will look at the subject objectively, with feelings of empathy for both men and women. Clinical analysis of data, combined with compassion, will help to prevent the misuse or misunderstanding of our data in the direction of anti-female, anti-mother bias, or defensive sexist attitudes on the part of men or of women. I feel strongly that sexist attitudes and stereotypes applied to either sex are psychologically damaging and are responsible for a great deal of human misery.

ANXIETY AROUSED BY SEPARATING FROM THE MATERNAL BOND

We offer men our bodies if they will marry us; afterward, we are mystified because we are less interested in sex now that he is "ours." What we wanted all along wasn't sex, but closeness. *Mother most rewarded us with symbiotic love when we denied our sexuality.* Sex, even with its infinite pleasures, becomes merely a means to an end; nothing is sweeter than symbiosis. Grown women, we find we have manipulated ourselves out of our own sexuality. (Friday, 1977, p. 83)

The process of individuation, whereby children increasingly differentiate themselves from their mothers, occurs naturally throughout children's lifetime. Each step is generally accompanied by reminders of existential aloneness and separateness. The developmental task is characterized by feelings of anxiety in children of both sexes. The son, in differentiating himself from the mother, gradually shifts his identification to the father. The daughter remains finely tuned to the mother. For their part, mothers generally find it easier to identify with their daughters than with their sons. Genevie and Margolies (1987) reported, for example:

> Our findings show that mothers form this primary relationship more readily with their daughters whom they view as extensions of themselves: more dependent, more emotional, more bonded by the primary mother-child tie. (p. 291)

Thus, each step in a woman's development toward sexual maturity is filled with conflict. She is torn between expressing her love and sexual desire in relation to a man, which separates her from her mother, and holding back these responses, which affirms the maternal connection. Furthermore, as she matures, the daughter may actually fear retaliation from the mother for seeking adult sexual fulfillment.

In my own clinical work, I have found that both separation anxiety and fear of the mother's envy or vindictiveness are experienced by women at crucial points in their sexual development. In his book, *The Mother, Anxiety, and Death*, Joseph C. Rheingold (1967) has drawn attention to this aspect of the separation-individuation process:

> In the psychotherapy of women one regularly discovers an association of the masochistic or hostile dependent kind of relationship with the mother and the fear of mutilation and annihilation as punishment for feminine self-fulfillment—indeed, for just being a female. (p. 96)

In an earlier work, Rheingold (1964) contended that most young girls are terrified of the mother's feelings of hostility and jealousy, and, as a result, they attempt to turn to the father for protection. However, this move toward the father is similarly fraught with danger because of the mother's envy, and the girl retreats once again. In her book, *Between Women: Lowering the Barriers*, Paula Caplan (1981) describes how daughters often adjust to their mothers' envy:

It is a heavy burden to feel envied by one's mother. This is especially true because anger so often accompanies envy.... How does a daughter deal with her mother's competitiveness with her or jealousy of her accomplishments? Often, she does one of two things (or tries both at different times): she reduces her efforts to achieve (or at least begins to conceal them from her mother), and she puts emotional or physical distance between herself and her mother. (p. 120)

In describing adolescent girls who have already begun to renounce their sexual identity in order to appease their mother's anger, Rheingold wrote:

We observe many more girls who exhibit the "mutilated" state that becomes so distinctive in adolescence and adult life. They wear a hurt, intimidated look, seem burdened with distrust and guilt, and show not a trace of femininity or any other kind of self-affirmation. (p. 266)

As a clinician, Rheingold demonstrated an unusual understanding of the conflict that prevails in women throughout their lives: on the one hand, women desire sexual fulfillment and independence; yet, at the same time, they are drawn back to the mother through fear of her retaliatory powers:

The girl has no choice but to enter into the rivalry.... The threat of retaliation, however, forces her to abandon her aspirations and surrounds all woman-roles with danger. (p. 267)

A woman begins fleeing her mother in early childhood and never ceases trying to deliver herself from the psychic bond to her.... The drives to attain freedom never succeed.... She is always her mother's daughter. (p. 272)

Rheingold's interpretations of his findings are consistent with the hypotheses my associates and I have derived from our clinical material: most women do indeed remain their "mother's daughter," bound to the mother *not* by natural affection, but by fears of aloneness or vindictive retaliation.

GUILT ABOUT SEPARATING FROM THE MATERNAL BOND

A self-denying mother arouses powerful feelings of guilt in her children. By denying herself gratification, fulfillment, or sexual pleasure, a woman not only hurts herself, she also imposes subtle restrictions on her daughter's life. Her daughter, out of a sense of guilt, turns her back on her own development and retreats from an adult, womanly posture.

This guilt becomes more evident as young women take tentative steps toward independence or move away from emotional ties with the family. As noted earlier, bonds or fantasies of connection between parents and children function as powerful agents of security; indeed, the fantasy bond (the imagined merger with the mother) is often more important or preferential to family members than any real security that could be found in genuine, loving relationships. Breaking a bond is symbolic of a break in a lifeline (letting the other person die), because one has difficulty maintaining a bond or illusion of connection without collusion or cooperation from one's partner in the bond. In the case of the adolescent girl, the guilt involved in breaking away or "leaving her mother behind" is often intense and debilitating, especially when her mother is depressed, self-hating, self-destructive, or childlike in her orientation.

Guilt Reactions in Adolescent Suicidal Behavior

Joseph Richman (1986), in his book, *Family Therapy for Suicidal People*, explained that many mothers exert a strong pull on their adolescent daughters. In treating adolescents in suicidal crises, Richman noted that one symptom of a disturbed symbiotic relationship (which I have defined as a fantasy bond) between mothers and daughters was a breakdown in the mother's capacity for empathy:

> Empathy is a recognition of separateness, and, therefore, of the unbearable loss of a symbiotic relationship. Such symbiosis can only be maintained through a denial of difference. (p.19)

Richman pointed out that an important source of guilt manifested by suicidal adolescent girls lies in the mother's inability to tolerate separation experiences. As a result, these mothers tend to interfere with their daughters' strivings. Richman found that some mothers strictly control their daughters' activities; at the same time, they deny the fact that they are attempting to limit their freedom. Indeed, many mothers act as though they and their daughters are one, that they are uniquely attached or mystically united. Agreement on all issues is mandatory in order to maintain the unrealistic tie.

In his analysis of several "symbiotic" families in which one of the offspring had become suicidal, Richman wrote:

In a disturbed symbiotic relationship the development of uniqueness or individuality in a key member opens up the threat of separation and must therefore be opposed or "corrected." The intensity of the sense of threat is one of the major ingredients of symbiotic anxiety. The presence of a symbiotic relationship under threat can also be recognized *when difference is denied* [italics added].

The mother of Joan, a 25-year-old suicidal girl, said during a family interview, "Joan confides completely in me." "No, I don't," Joan replied. "Yes, you do," her mother responded. (p. 19)

As is demonstrated in Richman's work, intense feelings of guilt, anger, and confusion accompany a young woman's attempt to separate herself emotionally from a mother who is desperate to maintain this illusion of oneness and fusion. These reactions often play a significant part in precipitating a suicidal crisis in adolescent girls who are breaking away from "symbiotic" family constellations.

Manifestations of the Daughter's Guilt in Her Adult Life

As noted earlier, the children of mothers who withhold feelings of love suffer from unsatisfied longings, emotional hunger, and rage at being rejected. Children, and later adults (of both sexes), generally feel guilty about feelings of hostility toward their parents and subsequently turn their rage against themselves.

The daughter's guilt about the anger she feels toward her mother causes her to hate herself. When, because of hurt and rejection, she is forced to renounce the loving feelings she originally felt toward her mother (the most important person in her life), she becomes disoriented and resentful. As a young girl, she learned by observation and imitation to be like her mother and feels strange or uncomfortable when she is different from her role model. Guilt reactions cause women to turn their backs on important personal and vocational goals if these pursuits differ from or threaten to surpass their mothers' achievements. Kim Chernin (1985) commented on her observations of guilty women in her book, *The Hungry Self* (a study of eating disorders):

The contrast for most women between their life of possibility and their mother's life of limitations continues to haunt them through every stage of growth and development, making separation a perilous matter, for it involves inevitably this problem of surpassing a woman who must, in her lonely sense of failure at life, perceive the daughter's movement into the world as a betrayal and abandonment of the identity they share. (pp. 57-58)

A number of recent studies tend to confirm my hypotheses about women's guilt reactions. Empirical data have shown that a mother's negative, discouraging responses to her daughter's aspirations often contribute to these guilt feelings. One study (Suitor, 1987) suggests that mothers who exhibit a lack of support or negative reactions may well foster serious self-recriminations and regression in upwardly mobile or successful women, particularly when they surpass their mothers' level of education and achievement. In our experience, we have found that women manifest intense guilt reactions when they achieve success in areas where their mothers failed, and that they often compensate by regressing in other areas. This is a primary factor contributing to women sabotaging their successes and achievements.

The following case history illustrates long-term regressions that can occur when women develop personally and vocationally and symbolically leave the mother by leading different or "better" lives.

After a year of individual therapy, Carol B., a dark-haired, serious, reserved young woman of 24, began to question her mother's authority and challenge her image as the "perfect" mother. Carol's mother was a highly respected chairperson of the history department at a nearby college. She had divorced the patient's father when Carol was 3 years old. The mother moved in a large social circle of women associates and friends. Her current life was completely devoid of male companionship and, according to the patient, her mother spoke of men with derision and bitterness.

In early sessions, Carol, an unusually perceptive and intelligent person, rapidly gained emotional and intellectual insight into the dynamics of the relationship with her mother. Carol spoke in her therapy group about her mother's rejection of her father and her need to control family members. In addition, she noted her mother's sexualized involvement with dependent and ingratiating women. Altogether, her insight was clear, compassionate, and powerful.

During this period, Carol gradually unfolded as a woman. Her previously drab, unfeminine appearance and quiet reserve were replaced by a brightness, vitality, and lively sense of humor. Gradually she developed a stronger sense of identity as a sexual woman, in stark contrast to her mother's asexual orientation. Carol moved out of the family home into her own apartment, and decided to pursue an advanced degree in psychology. She lost weight, began to dress stylishly, and for the first time became involved in a sexual relationship with a man for whom she cared a great deal.

At this point in her therapy, Carol appeared on the threshold of changing deep character defenses of submission and catering to her mother, attitudes she had extended to other women who served as symbolic substitutes for her mother.

One day, Carol's mother visited her at her apartment, and the patient found herself excited by discussing her career plans and some of the insights she had gained in the course of her therapy. She was totally unprepared for her mother's angry reaction. Stunned, Carol listened as her mother unleashed an irrational diatribe against her and her therapist for his "bad" influence on her. At first Carol attempted to defend her point of view; however, the combination of her mother's hysterical anger and tears effectively brought Carol "back into line." The next day Carol spent hours on the phone reassuring her mother and reestablishing the bond with her.

Already torn by guilt about achieving more satisfaction in her personal life than her mother, the patient was unable to recover her good feeling after the incident. She began to deny or repress the insights she had gained in therapy. She "forgot" important perceptions she had about her mother's controlling posture and destructive role in the family. She lost sight of her mother's manipulation through weakness and negative power.

It was disheartening for those who knew Carol to see the rapid deterioration in her self-confidence following the meeting with her mother. Several weeks later, Carol dropped out of her therapy group. Some time later, she terminated individual therapy and gradually withdrew from the relationship with the man whom she had planned to marry.

In turning against her realistic perception of her mother's hostility and inadequacy, the patient suffered a serious regression. Eight years later, a follow-up showed that Carol still lived alone, physically separate from her mother, yet emotionally tied to her.

This case is not unusual. Guilt reactions precipitated by breaking bonds often predispose serious regressions. In another example, a patient who was progressing well in therapy and changing her hostile, suspicious views of men received a phone call from her sister. The sister, who was seriously disturbed psychologically and cynical toward men, had played a significant role in raising our patient and meant a great deal to her. After the patient told her sister about her progress and her optimistic outlook, she asked her sister how *she* was feeling. The sister's bitter reply was, "You really want to know? I'll tell you how I feel—I'm so depressed I feel like killing myself." Her sister's response acted to turn this patient against herself.

Within a week of this unpleasant call, this patient, torn by unbearable guilt feelings about her sister's misery, suddenly left her boyfriend and resumed an isolated life-style. It was literally impossible for her to tolerate her guilt about the contrast between her own happiness and her sister's depression and hatred of men. She refused to break the bond with her sister and instead sacrificed her own pursuits.

Women's Guilt in Relation to Symbolic Substitutes

Female anxiety and guilt about ambitious strivings and the exercise of competence are so ubiquitous that the "fear of success" syndrome has become a household word. (Lerner, 1988, p. 195)

Many women fear the loss of the mother as represented by symbolic substitutes in their present-day lives. We found that women take their cues from other women in their surroundings in terms of their emotional state or their tendencies to be self-denying. Rather than compete with another woman who is depressed or distant from the man in her life, a woman is more likely to withdraw and become self-denying herself. She is often too guilty to separate herself from less fortunate women and maintain her own pursuit of sexual fulfillment or other personal goals. She tends to respond adversely to unconscious social pressure exerted by other women who have given up their independence. When the women in her interpersonal environment act weak and defensive, it has a detrimental effect on her personal life and goal-directed activities.

Most women are afraid to be nonconformists, that is, to stand out from the "sisterhood." For example, the stereotyped attitudes toward men expressed by women in neighborhood conversations over coffee, in club meetings, and in office settings are rarely, if ever, challenged by women who disagree. Cynical and/or condescending views about men are accepted as foregone conclusions by many women who use these conversations as a forum to verbalize attitudes that justify their withdrawal and withholding. Moreover, there is increasing social pressure from the media and literature supporting a sexist, prejudicial view of men that holds them accountable for women's dissatisfaction in marriage.[1] This distorted societal view, in turn, exerts a strong pull on each woman to feel victimized or exploited by men.

SIGNIFICANT EVENTS THAT AROUSE ANXIETY AND GUILT IN WOMEN

Marriage

Just as the fate of personality development hangs largely on the effect of mother on child, so, I believe, the fate of a marriage hangs largely on the effect of wife on husband.... Overwhelmingly the flow of crucial influence is from the woman to the man, requiring adaptation or defense on his part. (Rheingold, 1964, pp. 421-422)

The concept of marriage has very different unconscious significance for men and women. For men, marriage symbolizes the fulfillment of their desire for close, affectionate contact with the mother that they have longed for since early childhood. For women, marriage symbolizes a step *away* from the mother and a loss of the hope of ever satisfying their longing for maternal love. In this sense, men and women have a conflict of interest and are unconsciously at odds with each other after the early stages of their relationship.

Both extensions of the bond are unhealthy. It is ironic that women are drawn to marriage as an imitation of their mother, yet, at the same time, they fear this move toward further individuation and see their independent actions and mature expressions of sexuality as replacing the mother. Their attitudes toward marriage are necessarily ambivalent. Their defenses alienate them from men and predispose a destructive bond in place of genuine intimacy.

Men also tend to act out aspects of the bond with their mother in their relationships with their mates, which exerts a negative impact on the marriage. They interpret their partner's positive or negative sexual responses as symbolic of the mothering they are unconsciously seeking. Many men behave in a childlike manner in relation to their mates, seeking definition, and are either submissive or domineering. Often they are emotionally hungry and willing to sell out on their own point of view when the women in their lives are unresponsive, depressed, or self-hating, in order to maintain the bond.

Rheingold's (1964) thesis supports my own view of this basic difference and its impact on the couple's relationship:

> This [initial] level of compatibility is not attained or long maintained because marriage attempts to integrate mutually alien worlds of being, that of the man and that of the woman. (p. 423)

Rheingold then stressed the fact that marriage once again arouses a woman's fear of her mother, a familiar sense of dread that she has lived with since infancy.

> Marriage is a crisis for the woman.... Next to pregnancy and becoming a mother, marriage poses the greatest threat because it represents two bold acts of self-assertion: assuming the status of the married woman and entering into a publicly announced heterosexual relationship. (p. 437)

Rather than cope with the separation anxiety and guilt inherent in moving away from the mother, many women find themselves experiencing a renewed closeness with their mothers following the wedding ceremony. Nancy Friday (1977) commented on this "reunion" in her book, *My Mother/My Self*:

> The truth is that in marriage we become the little girl who once took down the cookie sheet and imitated mommy. We also become mommy....

> We do not mean to ally with her, but whose standards are we living up
> to when we give up our identity? Did he ask it of us? (p. 345)

In her interviews with over 200 men and women, Friday reported that the majority of the wives imitated their mothers' style of relating. Most husbands validate this finding. For example, one man who was interviewed recently stated the principle succinctly: "The longer we're married, the more like her mother she becomes."

Most women sacrifice their sexuality in order to hold on to the mother and relieve their unconscious fears of punishment. In this sense, they are fearful of becoming mature women. When this happens, women take on a sameness with the mother that makes them hate themselves. Their goals and personal relationships are contaminated by feelings of unsatisfied emotional hunger, and their feeling for the men in their lives is distorted.

Many women who profess goals of future marriage and family tend to be disturbed at the actual prospect of becoming involved in a long-term relationship with a man or the thought of having a child. In our clinical experience, we are familiar with countless cases where women reported having perverse or angry responses to acknowledgments of love from the men in their lives. In one instance, a woman was shocked at the sarcasm she expressed in reaction to her lover's talking about his wish to make a serious commitment to the relationship. The couple had just spent a romantic evening together when the young man spoke sincerely of his growing desire to marry and start a family. As the couple talked about the possibility of having children, the woman suddenly burst out angrily: "Well, you know, *you'll* have to take care of the kids, *too*; I'm not going to do it alone!"

Both people were startled by this uncharacteristic response. In retrospect, they were painfully aware that this "slip of the tongue" had been a portent of things to come. After the couple married and had a family, this woman became increasingly hostile toward her husband and progressively withheld feelings of affection.

In another example, a woman responded coolly to a marriage proposal. She condescendingly replied, "Oh, really!" in relation to her boyfriend's declaration of love and commitment to the relationship. The man immediately felt humiliated and tried to cover his embarrassment and hurt. Later, after the couple chose an engagement ring, the woman showed the ring to her mother. The mother's comment, "Where did he buy that ring, at a discount department store?" was spoken in a derisive tone that was very similar to her daughter's cool response to the marriage proposal. In this manner, cynical and distrustful attitudes toward men pass between mother and daughter.

Becoming a Mother

Having a child of one's own is in itself the ultimate fulfillment of womanhood. Nonetheless, it symbolizes a separation from or a release of one's own mother, which can arouse considerable anxiety. Becoming a mother implies a permanent loss of one's mother. Starting a new family effectively signals the end of childhood, causing many women to cling to dependent, childlike patterns of behavior during the pregnancy and following the birth of the baby. Conventional views of women's helplessness and need for protection generally support a woman's return to dependency and self-indulgence during this critical period. Yet, soon after the baby is born, there is a complete change in the emotional climate. Now the woman is expected to take care of and nurture the baby. The abrupt change from being taken care of to being a caretaker may foster a wide range of regressive behaviors and is a significant factor in postpartum depression.

Fear and Unconscious Hostility in the Pregnant Woman

Developmental psychologists Klaus and Kennell (1976) have suggested that pregnant women have many fears that form the basis for the wide variation in quality of mother-infant relation.

> The production of a normal child is a major goal of most women. Yet most pregnant women have hidden fears that the infant may be abnormal *or reveal some of their own secret inner weaknesses* [italics added]. (p. 42)

Berry Brazelton (1973), a well-known pediatrician and child developmentalist, observed that

> prenatal interviews with normal primiparas [first-time mothers] in a psychoanalytic interview setting, uncovered anxiety which often seemed to be of...pathological proportions.... The unconscious material was so loaded and so distorted, so near the surface, that before delivery one felt an ominous direction for making a prediction about the woman's capacity to adjust to the role of mothering. (p. 260)

In her book, *Children in Jeopardy*, Elizabeth Elmer (1967) documented the high incidence of child abuse occurring in the *first months* of the children's lives by mothers who were operating under the stress of having many young children to care for or who were pregnant with another child at the time. She suggested that pregnancy is a "biologically determined maturational crisis that is not always resolved with the birth of the baby" (p. 78).

Rheingold (1967) observed similar phenomena in well over 2,500 cases of pregnant women he treated during a 10-year experimental study. He found that the mother's ambivalence usually continued unabated long *after* the child was born, although the more negative aspects were either completely forgotten or partially repressed. He suggested that even "normal" mothers transmit their basic conflict about being a mother as well as their repressed hostility to their infant, instilling in the child a deep sense of anxiety and insecurity.

Postpartum Disturbances

Regression during pregnancy generally continues until delivery, when there is either movement toward recovery or a more pronounced regression. The dynamics of postpartum depression indicate intense emotional reactions to the sudden shift from a childlike mode to the reality and responsibilities of being a parent. These depressive reactions sometimes reach psychotic proportions.

In a case report, Rosberg and Karon (1959) described in depth a classic example of postpartum psychosis. A number of important factors in this case relate to our own findings: (1) It became clear through analysis that the woman's husband had, in many ways, replaced her mother as the center of her emotional life (the primary feeder). (2) Sexuality was symbolic of oral gratification (vagina/mouth; penis/breast; semen/milk).[2] (3) Pregnancy represented a symbolic solution to frustration on an oral level. The physical changes that were manifested signified oral gratification (stomach filled with milk). (4) The actual childbirth represented a catastrophic loss of gratification and a premature demand to feed another. This series of hypotheses casts light on some of the unexplained characteristics of postpartum disorders.

One further complication that often occurs at the time immediately after the delivery, when mother and child return home, is the appearance of the maternal grandmother on the scene. This occurrence generally tends to precipitate regressive trends in the new mother. Instead of relieving anxiety, it often causes additional tension. Rheingold (1964) reported similar findings:

> I cited the case of the woman who irrevocably renounced her child (and her marriage) after a visit from her mother. (pp. 564-565)

> According to her husband, all went well until the patient returned home after confinement and her mother came for a week's visit.... [The patient] grew nervous and paced the floor at night. [The woman later divorced her husband.] (p. 69)

Early Feeding Experiences

Helene Deutsch (1945), in her classic work, *The Psychology of Women, Vol. 2*, has suggested that the nursing mother may regard her child as an enemy and his oral needs as aggressions. More importantly, she may also fear her own aggressive reactions to her infant and may therefore fail in her attempt to breast-feed him in order to escape the situation and protect the child against her aggression. We have interviewed a number of mothers who reported that they resented feeding their infants. Several mothers revealed that they had initially enjoyed breast-feeding, but soon found themselves giving up what had been a pleasurable experience for them, often for no apparent reason.

For example, Janice stopped breast-feeding her 3-month-old infant daughter following her mother's visit. Later, in a parenting group, she recalled that her mother was unable to breast-feed her or her younger brothers:

JANICE: When my daughter was 3 months old and my parents came to visit, I was too embarrassed to breast-feed in front of my mother. And then, right after that, I thought of a bizarre reason to stop breast-feeding, you know, that it would be better for her to be on a bottle. So I stopped breast-feeding without ever making the connection that it followed that visit.

It's interesting, because my mother couldn't breast-feed me. And I have brothers who are much younger than I am, and so I remember watching her trying to breast-feed them.

One scene I remember clearly was when I was 7 years old, standing in the doorway, and my mother holding my brother when he was a baby and trying to feed him. Her milk would flow until the baby would start to suck, and then it would stop—that's how withholding she was.

And I remember my father being angry at her for what she was doing. I mean, he just couldn't help being angry. He saw it happening right in front of him, you know, that she wouldn't feed the baby. And I remember standing there. I didn't want to see it; I wanted to turn around and walk out of the room, but my feet were frozen. I couldn't move; I was just frozen standing there staring at that scene.

OTHER ISSUES IN THE PSYCHOLOGY OF WOMEN

Sexual Components in the Early Maternal-Child Attachment

We have observed that the majority of women, like men, reported that they were physically and even sexually attracted to women and that this basic attraction did not appear to be a signal or sign of abnormality.[3] This attraction is based on the early physical attraction to the mother and is part of the child's earliest feelings. Although men, too, are physically attracted to other men, their attraction does not appear to be as powerful or compelling. This difference is due only partly to the cultural taboo regarding physical or affectionate contact between men.

The daughter's initial attraction to the mother can be frustrated early in the relationship. Some clinicians believe that social taboos against a baby daughter's expressions of affection toward the mother are stronger than against the son's.

> [Women's] feelings for their baby daughters may frighten them if they label them sexual. This can lead mothers to limit their physical contacts with their young daughters severely. (Caplan, 1981, p. 59)

Other researchers have observed that many mothers are more hesitant about expressing affection to their daughters than toward their sons and that this reluctance has a damaging effect on the girl's later sexual development. Sirgay Sanger, in a personal communication to Nancy Friday (1977), stated:

> The subtle deprivation of physical demonstrations of affection that little girls often suffer from their mothers makes women more vulnerable to fear and the loss of attachment.... It makes women greedy to hold on even to men who treat them badly, more possessive and competitive for whatever crumbs of love may be available to them. (p. 58)

Sanger's interpretation corresponds to our findings regarding the damaging effects of maternal withholding on children, especially on female offspring. When we use the term *withholding*, we imply that mothers actually hold back positive responses from their daughters. The implication is that these feelings really do exist, but are, for one reason or another, not manifested or expressed. The daughter's peripheral awareness that affection is potentially available causes her to develop powerful longings and emotional hunger for physical contact.

In cases in which the woman was loved and cared for initially and later was not responded to or inconsistently responded to, a pull is exerted on the young girl that has an addictive quality. She feels compelled to try to recapture the love she once experienced, and this desperate search persists into her adult life, distorting her relationship with her husband and children.

Effects of Repressing the Original Physical Attraction to the Mother

A mother who is intolerant of accepting love *from* her daughter creates a feeling in her that her physical touch is unacceptable or even repulsive. This deep-seated belief is one reason why a woman develops a strong feeling of being unlovable and sees herself as different from other women, undesirable, or unattractive to men. In addition, reactions of rage because of the early frustration of her desire for physical contact can lead to an immature fixation on the mother or substitute objects and a variety of sexual disturbances. Perversely, the anger generated causes the young woman to rely heavily on repression and to move closer to her mother. This alliance plays a significant role in her sexual withholding as an adult.

Sexual withholding refers to the holding back or blocking of one's natural sexual desire and its expressions: physical affection, touching, qualities and physical characteristics that are attractive and appealing, and all other aspects of one's natural, healthy sexuality. Most women are very ashamed of holding back sex and physical affection from the men they profess to love. Other women refuse sex outright or offer a variety of excuses. When women "hold back their natural responsiveness or enthusiasm for sex, a shadow is cast on the relationship, and the effects are profoundly detrimental to *both* partners" (Firestone, 1985, p. 373). A sexually withholding woman tends to hold back affectionate responses from her children as well or may feel very awkward expressing physical affection. Her inhibited response to her children is very similar in style to the manner of withholding she manifests toward her husband.

Women's sexual withholding has a powerful manipulative effect on the men in their lives. In general, the extent to which a man is sexually attracted to the woman in his life is very dependent on her honest, sexual wanting. Men tend to blame themselves for any lack of sexual attraction to their partners regardless of circumstances. Even when they are outwardly critical and fault-finding with the women in their lives, men are intensely self-critical and self-destructive on this issue.

Although many women eventually become withholding in long-term sexual relationships, nevertheless, there are numerous disguised manifestations of this pattern such that even a woman who is overtly sexually aggressive may be acting in a way to provoke rejection without being aware of her actions. These women tend to blame men for not making love to them and have evidence to back up their complaints. However, most men find it difficult to respond when the woman's seductive behavior does *not* reflect an honest desire for sexual intimacy. At this point, most men resort to sexual fantasy or increased physical movement in order to attempt to complete the sex act.

In many cases, insecure women have a strong need to control every aspect of the sex act, that is, the time, the place, the position, and the movements and frequency of the couple's sexual relations. My clinical experience has shown that many women attempt to control the amount of sexual gratification they receive from their partners, even when they find sexual experiences fulfilling.

The psychodynamics involved in sexual withholding are similar in some respects to those manifested in postpartum disturbances, although the symptoms may be less dramatic. The withholding woman has reverted to a regressed state, in which she desires to be fed, symbolically. In effect, she is striving for an unfeeling, automatic connection similar to what her original bond with her mother turned out to be, and tends to lose empathy and genuine feeling for her husband. Although she may remain adult or mature in her work or career (behaving logically and rationally), on a deeper emotional level she has reverted to an immature state of being. She is once again her mother's daughter, guilty about sex, distrustful of men, and self-hating. Renouncing her independent strivings leads to increased dependence on maternal substitutes and symbolic reinstatement of the bond with her mother.

THE EFFECT OF MATERNAL DEPRIVATION ON
THE MALE CHILD

Maternal withholding also has important consequences for men, although the effects may manifest themselves in a form different from that in women. The resulting damage to men leads to a variety of personality disorders. Many men become desperate, dependent, and clinging to the rejecting mother. Later, they tend to become very possessive or jealous. Still others cut off their feelings, wall themselves off, and act critical and superior to women. Since they are uncomfortable with hungry, childlike feelings, they attempt to cover them up by acting tough and macho.

The young boy who is hurt and angry learns to hold back or suppress his affectionate feelings for his mother. He internalizes his anger and becomes self-hating. Later, there is considerable guilt if this anger and distrust lead to dominating or controlling responses toward women.

If his mother manipulated and controlled the family through weakness, the son tends to take her side and develops angry feelings toward his father and against men in general. In a sense, he turns on himself as a man. He develops an acute sensitivity to his mother's moods and expressive movements. Later, in his adult relationships, he is tuned in to his mate's variations in mood, and any restraint on her part arouses primal feelings of rage and guilt that lead to serious tension in the couple.

The case of Dr. N., a 38-year-old dentist with a large successful practice, illustrates these dynamics. In a couples' group, Dr. N. spoke about the insights he had gained into the probable origins of his deep rage toward women and the feelings of self-hatred and disgust he had about himself as a man:

DR. N.: I'm just beginning to get a sense of where my feelings of being unattractive to women come from. I hate to admit this, but the feeling is that sometimes my wife can't stand for me to touch her, that I'm repulsive to her somehow. I know that these feelings have a lot to do with the way my mother felt toward me.

I have a distinct feeling that she tried to raise me to be a girl, because I know she had no use for me as a boy. I know she really hated my masculinity—my body. Once, when I was about 10, I was going down the hall toward my bedroom, and my bathrobe was half open. She had to pass me in the hallway, and she glanced at me and made a sound like she was disgusted. She quickly looked the other way and almost ran past me, yelling at me to keep my bathrobe tied.

I also remember that she was condescending to my father, belittling, cold, indifferent. Nothing *he* said mattered at all to her; she just sort of ignored him.

Sometimes when my mother was confiding to me about her dissatisfactions with my father, I so much wanted to yell at her, "Stop talking about Dad like that to me!" But I never had the guts to do that. Mostly I just listened, agreed with her, and felt sorry for her.

Later, in the same couples' group, Dr. N. connected these painful memories of his childhood to the current difficulties in his marriage. He frequently took on his wife's point of view *against himself* in a way reminiscent of his childhood commiserations with his mother against his father.

DR. N.: I'm so confused by my wife's erratic behavior sexually that I can't concentrate during the day on my practice. Each morning I feel drained and exhausted. Sometimes when we make love, which isn't too often, I find myself identifying with her, imagining how *she* must feel making love with me. I start thinking that I'm not touching her sensitively or in a way that would make her feel good. That's when I start feeling that she's repulsed by my touch. It's a terrible feeling.

Sometimes I feel such a rage toward my wife that I'm afraid to even touch her. Last week, I became so angry at her refusal to make love that I actually hit her. I've felt terrible since then—completely despicable.

By unconsciously selecting a woman very similar to his mother, Dr. N. maintained his mother's view of men (and of himself). When making love to his wife, he often picked up her unspoken critical thoughts about him and, at those times, experienced difficulty in completing the sex act. He completely blamed himself for the failures, accusing himself of being inadequate, weak, and physically unappealing.

Men who become sexually withholding tend to feel hesitant in their approach to women, as did the patient described above. Their hesitancy covers intense feelings of repressed anger. Sometimes the man is sufficiently provoked and this rage surfaces, leading to explosive outbursts. When this occurs, the man experiences deep feelings of remorse, guilt, and self-hatred for extended periods of time.

Withholding men often manifest personality traits of passivity and meekness, acting humble with false humility and deferring to their partner's wishes. Symbolically, they are still trying to placate their mothers by their submissive behavior.

Women who mistakenly choose this type of man over men who are genuinely strong often falsely equate real strength with meanness and confuse or misinterpret passivity with sensitivity or kindness. Unfortunately, these passive, submissive men are often cynical, superior, and hyper-critical toward women, exhibiting deep-seated hatred and resentment.

Some men develop such strong patterns of withholding through their contact with a controlling, self-denying, or self-sacrificing mother that they learn to manipulate others through weakness. They maintain a woman's point of view that men are hard and mean and attempt to control others by falling apart emotionally, sulking, or becoming moody and jealous as a form of retaliation. These men play the victim in their relationships with both men and women. This defensive posture leads them to compete with their partners as to who can be the more unhappy, self-destructive, or confused. Initially, they were the objects of this type of manipulation, but now they have learned to play a similar game. They utilize their unhappiness, personal suffering, and self-hatred to inspire guilt reactions and fear in their mates and associates.

RHEINGOLD'S THESIS REGARDING MATERNAL DESTRUCTIVENESS

> I can only declare, with Spinoza, that "I have made a ceaseless effort not to ridicule, not to bewail, nor to scorn human actions, but to understand them."... I enter the plea...that no one is to blame. The hurtful adult was once a hurt child, and the transmission of destructiveness is not willed. To traduce mothers is to add injury to injury. (Rheingold, 1964, p. viii)

Rheingold (1964) emphasized that the influence of the mother becomes evident quite early in a child's life. Whatever nurturant tendencies a mother may have, she still has a certain hostile or aggressive component to her personality that exerts a harmful influence on her infant. In his commentary on the infant's vulnerability to the mother's hostility and the life-long effects of the anxiety-provoking, toxic interactions with her, Rheingold stated:

> The infant is maximally vulnerable to the noxious influence because of its preternatural perception of the mother's mood and wishes and its almost total lack of defensive devices. It experiences basic anxiety and acquires a basic ambivalence toward life, which together with the innate dispositions and the vicissitudes of being, determine its character organization, modes of adaptation, patterns of behavior, and liability to disorder. (p. 132)

Rheingold's major thesis (1967) is as follows (pp. 105-106):

1. Maternal destructiveness is universal. Every mother exerts both salutary and harmful influences. This fact is objective and not a moral judgment.
2. The range of pathogenic influence has been underestimated.

> What is not fully envisaged...is that the more overt manifestations spring from certain impulses, usually repressed, and that these impulses have deleterious effects even in the presence of a conscious benign disposition toward the child. (p. 105)

3. There may also be an underappraisal of pathogenic consequences of maternal destructiveness. "The total evidence at hand seems to permit one to say that it enters causatively into a greater range of disorders than any other factor" (p. 106).

Rheingold's keen insight into the psychology of women and their extensive influence on their offspring may be found in his two well-documented volumes, *The Fear of Being a Woman* (1964) and *The Mother, Anxiety, and Death* (1967). It is remarkable that these two books generally failed to have an impact on the field of clinical and developmental psychology, psychiatry, and pediatrics. The reasons are obvious: Rheingold's thesis is painful to contemplate and conflicts with the idealized image of motherhood in our culture. Therefore, most clinicians have been resistant to integrating these ideas into their thinking.

Rheingold (1967) also described two methods whereby clinicians circumvent the truth of childhood trauma attributed to maternal influences: (1) the use of the terms *constitutional* and *temperamental* to direct attention away from the possibility that mothers are responsible for their child's neuroses,[4] and (2) Freud's instinct theory that there is an inherent tendency toward self-destruction (termed "death instinct") in the infant that is responsible for his later neurosis. Other theorists, among them Sandor Ferenczi (1929), Adelaide Johnson (1951), and Norbert Bromberg (1955), reported findings that tend to support Rheingold's thesis.

John N. Rosen (1953) developed the concept of the "perverse" mother in describing pathogenic influences on schizophrenic patients. He observed that these mothers appeared to manifest "a perversion of the normal mothering instinct." Rosen compared them with examples of "perverse mothering" in the animal kingdom. According to Rosen, because of her own neurosis, problems, and failures, the "schizophrenogenic" mother is similarly unable to assume the role of mother, and thus seriously jeopardizes the psychological adjustment of her child.

My associates and I concur with Rheingold (1967), Rosen (1953), Rich (1976), Badinter (1980/1981), and others in their theoretical awareness of maternal destructiveness. We have found that when we developed an accepting and compassionate atmosphere, women have had the courage to reveal their destructive thoughts and feelings toward their offspring. In their openness and candor, they supported Rheingold's conclusions based on his clinical data. They confirmed the fundamental ambivalence of mothers' feelings, both nurturing and hostile, that had a profound effect on their children's mental health.

CONCLUSION

Because the mother is generally the key figure in the family, she plays a central role in its psychological well-being. The withholding tendencies in the mother have an enormous impact on her sons and on her daughters and are perpetuated within the context of the new family, when the daughter emerges as the most significant figure.

We have found that self-awareness of hostile as well as nurturing feelings can have a constructive effect on a mother's efforts to minimize damage to her offspring. We have observed progress in women as they have come to understand the division in themselves between their strivings toward independence and sexual fulfillment and the debilitating tie to their mothers. As they break down this bond, they allow themselves more fulfillment and manifest a strong identity. Learning to deal with this side of her personality and understanding the sources of this aggression *relieves* a woman's guilt feelings rather than creates further guilt reactions and self-hatred. Recognizing the subtle manifestations and effects of maternal hostility has value as an explanatory principle and as a method for minimizing the detrimental effects.

When women are alienated from men and have strong sexist views, these attitudes have an even greater detrimental effect on them than cultural processes that deprive them of their full rights and potentiality. Indeed, guilt and anxious attachment to the mother that perseverate into adult life seriously impede women in their search for equality, maturity, and independence. Furthermore, we suggest that feminist literature and approaches based on malice and animosity toward men are extremely damaging to women, despite the fact that they represent a movement in the right direction, politically and economically. Thus, women walk a fine line in fighting for their rights as equals and, at the same time, not turning against a part of themselves that is basically loving and naturally drawn to men.

NOTES

1. *Time* magazine, in a cover story article, documented the various self-help books, published over the past decade, that focus on male "shortcomings" as the core problem for women in their relationships (Wallis, 1987).
2. Symbolic fantasies such as those described in the Rosberg and Karon case report have been uncovered in the analysis of less disturbed individuals. Silverberg (1952) and Klein (1948/1964) reported dreams and fantasies of neurotic patients, indicating that many people represent sexual intercourse in terms of oral symbolism.
3. Women's sexual attraction to other women, as described, appears to be a natural manifestation and is not necessarily connected to lesbian involvement or homosexual activity. Indeed, the latter relationships are typically characterized by strong love-hate tendencies and generally exaggerated dependency bonds.
4. Rheingold does not imply that biological tendencies or hereditary influences are inconsequential. He suggests that these factors can be overemphasized to lean on and to explain away the importance of maternal rejection or malevolence as a causative factor in neurosis.

PART II

CHILD-REARING TECHNIQUES

CHAPTER 9

GENERAL PHILOSOPHY OF CHILD-REARING

I came to realize that no teaching of theories will do; nor will any instructions on what exactly to do in a specific situation. (p. 15)

After all, behind all our actions in a given situation is the whole of our past life experience, which soon begins to influence our view of what we are doing to our child and of what he is doing to us. The same is true for our child; he, too, reacts to our intervention in terms of his past experiences, many of which we ourselves have provided or shaped. (p. 14)

Bruno Bettelheim (1962/1971), *Dialogues with Mothers*

In our work with patients and parenting groups, my associates and I have been continually concerned with the toxic aspect of interpersonal relationships that contributes to the defensive process in the child and the subsequent development of character neurosis in the adult. Recognizing how our patients were hurt in their upbringing and how they, in turn, damage their children has important implications for child-rearing. In identifying the trauma that children suffer, we have formulated positive attitudes and philosophical guidelines to child-rearing practices that we feel could minimize the damage. These basic principles are directly analogous to the feeling and tone that we consider essential elements of effective psychotherapy.

DIMENSIONS OF EFFECTIVE PSYCHOTHERAPY
AND THEIR RELATIONSHIP TO CHILD-REARING

The therapist's *honesty, integrity, and trustworthiness* [italics added] will be a constant issue... The therapist must offer a holding environment to the patient, a basic relationship that provides the latter with a sense of security, respect, and trust...and safety. (Langs, 1982, p. 28)

First, a basic principle of psychotherapeutic practice is that the patient is being offered a "sound listening-formulating process"—with subsequent "working through of the unique insights,...improved adaptation, symptom resolution, and growth" (Langs, 1982, p. 26). In the process, the therapist listens with empathy and compassion, attempting to understand both the "manifest and latent" content of his patient's communications. Therefore, the therapeutic process is essentially one of *inquiry*; the therapist suspends judgment while he intuitively searches, wonders, and questions himself concerning his patient and the genesis of his disturbance. "Why is he depressed?" "What events cause him to respond inappropriately?"

In the same sense, parents who develop a sense of inquiry in relation to their child are both fascinated by, and alive to, the emergence of a unique personality. When things appear to be going badly, they wonder what is troubling their child rather than automatically punishing inappropriate or "bad" behavior.

Second, in most effective therapies, there is a strong emphasis on freedom of speech and emotional expression. For example, the technique of free association utilized in psychoanalysis allows the patient to let his thoughts flow in a stream of consciousness unencumbered by the rules of logic. Within this framework, the patient not only learns to think creatively but also gradually comes to recognize that any thought or feeling is acceptable. Thus, in psychoanalysis and other psychodynamic therapies, the therapist directly and implicitly teaches his patient that feelings are *not* equivalent to actions; that is, that *any* feeling, thought, dream, or fantasy is morally acceptable and valid subject matter. At the same time, the experienced clinician sensitively teaches the patient to analyze the consequences of his behavior. Maladaptive responses and acting out behavior are exposed and evaluated in a nonjudgmental and nonpunitive atmosphere.

The analogy to child-rearing is clear; ideally, parents would permit and accept all of their child's feelings uncritically and, at the same time, teach him to control undesirable actions. They would learn to encourage *verbal* expression of hostile or destructive attitudes while rejecting nasty or abusive behavior. While helping the child to develop a system of values and behavioral standards, parents would emphasize the child's inherent right to his own freedom of thought and feeling.

Third, a good working relationship between the therapist and the patient is necessary for a successful outcome. Effective therapy takes place in the context of a respectful, equal therapeutic alliance between two individuals and not within a doctor-patient role-playing, unequal relationship. Ideally, the good therapist does not assume a posture of omnipotence and superiority; for example, he would not utilize his technical expertise to confound his patients with "all-knowing" interpretative statements. This tendency, which gratifies narcissistic needs in immature therapists, leads to feelings of inferiority in the patient and, concomitantly, to the patient's idealization of the therapist. Harry Guntrip's (1969) remarks concerning the curative factors in the healthy therapeutic relationship are particularly relevant here:

> The psychotherapist is not a *deus ex machina*, an authority diagnosing and prescribing from some position outside the patient's personal world. The psychotherapist must be primarily a human being who has faced and sufficiently understood himself to be worthy to be admitted into the patient's private pain and sorrow.... He knows, not just theoretically but in his own experience, what the patient is passing through. (p. 353)

The same conditions are applicable to parent-child relationships. Although the child is obviously not the equal of his mother or father in terms of physical size, power, knowledge, or competence, it is important that parents not utilize these differences to exploit, overpower, and intimidate their offspring. Parental omniscience tends to make the child feel unnecessarily small, weak, or inferior. In the same sense, children need a genuine support system, not the application of role-determined parental responses.

A fourth principle or characteristic of good psychotherapy is the therapist's consistency and stability; the therapist refuses to be alienated and maintains a relating posture. In addition, the rule of confidentiality encourages trust and a sense of safety in the patient. The therapist refrains from punishing or rejecting the patient for his communications, no matter how distorted or negative they are. This implies a maturity that allows the therapist to suspend his own needs and priorities during the session so that his responses to the patient's communications are consistently helpful.

In relation to child-rearing, we place considerable emphasis on parental maturity and consistency. Parents need to resist regressive trends in their own personalities in order to foster security in their offspring. Obviously, this task is even more formidable in the parenting situation, as compared with the therapy session.

Lastly, a very important dimension of psychotherapy lies in its nonintrusiveness; that is, the therapist acknowledges the basic worth of his patient and his right to an individual existence. Many patients enter therapy with the complaint that they feel unseen or "invisible" as a result of growing up with parents who failed to respond to them as persons in their own right. Others have pointed out how parents ignored and intruded on their boundaries and appeared to violate their rights as human beings.

The preservation of a sense of self is extremely important in psychotherapeutic interaction, as well as in parenting. Selective or conditional acceptance of the child is unacceptable. Part of this feeling of not being seen is often related to the lack of positive acknowledgment of one's bodily functions, sexuality, or gender identification. Therefore, the therapist's implicit validation of patients' sexual identity is important. In much the same manner, child-rearing practices that lead to the child's developing a healthy attitude toward his physical nature, as well as a strong sexual identity, are crucial to his overall development (Whitaker & Malone, 1953).

Characteristics of a Good Therapist

In addition to his or her specialized knowledge, the ideal therapist would be open and nondefensive, avoid a judgmental attitude, and be compassionate and forthright in communications. (Firestone, 1985, p. 385)

The personality of the therapist largely sets the tone and the emotional quality of the therapy process and therefore cannot be divorced from the dimensions of an effective therapy just described. Similarly, the personal characteristics of parents cannot be separated out from the emotional climate of the home. Several important personality traits of the effective therapist can be delineated. First, in order to offer his patients genuine help, the therapist would ideally be a person of integrity and personal honesty. The manner in which he conducts his personal life is very important, because if a therapist is defensive and lacks integrity in his personal life, he necessarily diminishes the amount of assistance he is able to offer his patients (Firestone & Catlett, 1989).

Effective clinicians serve as models for their patients, implicitly demonstrating by their own attitudes and behavior how to struggle against resistance and how to live less defensively with fewer self-imposed restrictions. Applying this principle to child-rearing, parents would then strive to act responsibly, with integrity, in *all* their associations and not allow hypocrisy and double standards to compromise their dignity and self-respect. Children are acutely sensitive to variations in parental behavior and, if forced to "swallow" parents' duplicity and lies, suffer severe blows to their own integrity.

Because he is cognizant of the inherent destructiveness of defensive life-styles and their projection or imprint on society, the therapist refrains from placing social conformity above the personal interests of his patient. Rather than attempting to remove or cover up emotional pain and fitting the patient into society, he helps patients learn to cope with the realities of life and maintain their individuality. Similarly, sensitive parents do not close off the means of expression that allow children to work through their problems, and they learn to deal with the inevitable frustrations of childhood. They are not overly concerned with appearances and conventional manifestations. Instead, they support the right of the child to maintain his feeling reactions and to cry and feel angry about unpleasant, stressful family interactions. Allowing the child the opportunity for self-expression offers a method or means of healing wounds to his psyche. This process is vital to the child's continuing psychological growth.

The ideal therapist does not fit the patient into a particular theoretical framework or model; instead, he is willing to experience the painful personal truths his patient reveals over the course of treatment. He is open to learning *from* his patient, to feeling with him, and tries to understand his fantasies, dreams, and unconscious processes. This open attitude and approach to the patient, together with the accessibility of his own unconscious material and inner life, permit the sensitive therapist to stay in contact with the deepest levels of the patient's verbal *and* nonverbal communication. The transpersonal interactions made possible by this deep level of understanding with a therapist, who is intuitively able to resonate with, or tune into, his patient, have been described by R. D. Laing as a moment of real meeting of two persons who are achieving a new transformation experience. By the same token, a person who is still in touch with the child in himself is capable of having a true empathic understanding of his child. This enables the parent to avoid harsh or judgmental categorization of the child's responses or traits. The accepted child will be spared painful primal feelings of being misunderstood or feelings that he is bad.

The well-trained therapist is knowledgeable about normal and pathological personality development and alert to symptoms of disturbance in the patient. Similarly, it is valuable for parents to be cognizant of the age-appropriate behaviors in their children for successive developmental stages. In doing so, they become aware of deviations or potential problems without reacting melodramatically or exhibiting hypochondriacal or overprotective reactions.

Finally, the experienced therapist anticipates the termination phase of therapy by continually encouraging the independent development of healthy ego-functioning in his patient. Excessive dependency on the therapist and patients' attempts to seek gratification or fusion with the therapist are discouraged. Instead, these inclinations or manifestations are interpreted with proper timing. In therapy, as in adolescence, the issues surrounding termination (leaving home) should be dealt with sensitively and compassionately.

The ultimate goal of therapy is to persuade the patient to challenge his inner world of fantasy and risk seeking satisfaction through goal-directed behavior (Firestone, 1985). Guntrip's (1969) views concerning the aims of psychotherapy are similar to my own; notably,

> to overcome our alienation from ourselves, from one another, and from our whole outer world, so that humans no longer hide away inside themselves, insecure and only half alive in an internal fantasy world that binds them to the past, but become able to emerge into real personal relationships and live a whole life. (p. 355)

In the same sense, the ultimate aim of child-rearing is to socialize the child in a way that allows him to move on to an independent life and separate from symbiotic ties with parents and other family members. Good parents, like good clinicians, take pleasure or pride in their child's movement away from dependency toward autonomy.

Differences between Psychotherapy and Child-Rearing

The proper functioning of a psychotherapist will be in important respects different from the proper functioning of a parental figure or friend. Thus, while the mode of relatedness should bear some resemblance to the sound

maternal role, it must also entail certain distinctions, since the therapist
is not entirely a parental figure. (Langs, 1982, p. 27)

There are obviously a number of significant differences between
the therapeutic venture and raising a child. First, the project of child-
rearing generally spans a much longer time period than does psychotherapy or psychoanalysis. Parents have more time to achieve their
goals, whereas therapists are limited by time considerations.

Second, parents have a potential advantage over therapists in that
they are in a better position to observe and to affect their child's life.
Living with the child gives parents far more exposure to the entire
range of the child's repertoire of behaviors than is possible for the
therapist to observe or even infer from limited contact with a patient.

Of course, parents tend to be more subjective and emotionally
involved with their children, whereas therapists can maintain more
objectivity with their patients. This distinction is potentially disad-
vantageous with respect to parent-child relations.

Parents, as contrasted with clinicians, are often plagued by guilt
feelings in relation to their offspring. In addition, negative attitudes
toward themselves and their productions often seriously interfere with
the appropriate perception of their youngsters. Parents also have the
expectation and the need to educate and socialize the child and influence his system of values. Ideally, in spite of these obstacles, the
good parent, like the good clinician, would learn to feel for his children and empathize with them, while at the same time preserving a
certain level of objectivity.

Third, parents, unlike therapists, have a total responsibility for
the overall well-being, both personal and financial, for their charge.
The full responsibility for a helpless and vulnerable human being
stresses an individual's capacity for maturity and understanding. In
that sense, problems of parenting are far more extensive and compelling. Indeed, parents' level of maturity and their capacity to feel
for themselves have the most profound effect on the personal development of their children and their future lives.

Lastly, parents have the opportunity of entering into a life-long
companionship with their child, a relationship based on the sharing
of a multitude of activities and experiences, in contrast to therapists,
who are restricted to a certain time frame, basic ground rules, and
boundaries that diminish the "real-life" quality of the relationship.
As such, therapists' personal needs, as contrasted with parents' per-

sonal needs, are less likely to enter into or interfere in their interaction with their patients. This arms-length relationship makes it easier for the clinician to grasp the overall picture and facilitates the therapeutic task. Nevertheless, in spite of their personal needs and essential subjectivity, enlightened parents would attempt to meet the challenges involved in positive child-rearing.

GENERAL PHILOSOPHY IN RELATION TO CHILDREN

In our observations and interactions with children over many years, we have been impressed with the early onset of strong defensive reactions. Once children have established these defenses, they have a significant investment in the self-protective process, choosing their inner fantasy world over real gratification and preferring activities that cut them off emotionally. Unless the need for these defensive patterns and self-destructive habits is consistently ameliorated, children will continue to act out progressively more sophisticated forms of this same behavior, and these traits will predominate in the adult. Therefore, it is essential that parents take steps to minimize the types of experiences that contribute to their children's confusion, pain, and suffering and to reduce the necessity for them to form powerful defenses.

These steps and the principles upon which they are based are similar in most respects to the dimensions of the positive therapeutic process described above. Our philosophical attitudes toward children and parenting practices are outlined in the sections that follow.

Parental Honesty

We are instructed to be honest. But instructed to operate on our experience in ways that can only be called dishonest. (Laing, 1969/1972, p. 107)

Just as it is necessary for therapists to maintain a high level of personal and professional integrity in relation to their patients, it is vital that parents *not* mislead their children. The process of misleading children or confusing their perception of reality can be more damaging than the negative experiences that are covered over. Distorting a child's perception leads to distrust and suspicion and is a key factor in mental illness. Furthermore, parental honesty, to some extent, prevents the child's idealization or build-up of his parents and family to his own detriment. It is of the utmost importance for a child to learn to trust his perceptions, and this can only be achieved in an honest atmosphere. In that sense, parents' integrity and truthfulness are necessary for survival in the emotional or psychological sense, just as food and drink are necessary for physical survival.

Respect for Separateness

And human minds reside quite separately from one another in single individuals. Minds can stimulate each other to produce a kind of joint creation, but each single mind must remain free to be stimulated and to develop its own ideas. Minds cannot be in slavery, however subtly or nobly defined, to the institutions other minds have created. (Harper, 1981, p. 6)

It is very important for children to be seen as human beings, with respect for their separate identities. As we have stressed throughout our work, children do *not* belong to the parents or their families, but to themselves; therefore, it is vital that, as professionals, we discourage parents from patronizing their children, categorizing them, or speaking for them.

Parents often talk *about* their children as if they were not there. How many times have you overheard a parent saying to a friend—in the child's presence—"He's always crying about something," or "She's such a shy child," or "I just don't know what I'm going to do about him!" How many times have you heard parents describing their child's "bad" behavior, while completely ignoring his presence in the room?

This type of treatment is especially dehumanizing and makes the child feel unseen, because he is not being acknowledged as a person with thoughts and feelings of his own. Ralph Ellison's (1947) description of a character in the *Invisible Man* is relevant: "Already he's learned to repress not only his emotions but his humanity. He's invisible, a walking personification of the Negative" (p. 72). Children who are "not seen" or responded to as separate individuals grow up to become caricatures of their parents and never discover who or what they might have become. Ellison's characterization of the conforming, compliant "invisible man" in our society accurately portrays the developing child who, in not being acknowledged for his uniqueness, often becomes a "personification of the negative" traits of his own parents.

Parents who respect the individuality of their children refrain from treating them as possessions or property. They do not attempt to live their lives through their children or feed off their achievements. When adults try to live vicariously through their offspring, the children grow up with tendencies to withhold their good qualities and special capabilities in a manner that seriously limits them in their adult lives.

It is important for parents to learn the meaning of "leaving the child alone" or "letting him be." Letting the child be is to allow him to feel that he is a person in his own right, distinct from other persons or family members. Parents who are respectful of personal boundaries avoid intruding into the life of their child by identifying too closely with his interests and aspirations or by making him feel that he must report his thoughts, feelings, and behaviors. They refrain from other intrusions, such as going through the child's belongings, reading his mail, fussing over his clothes, touching him excessively, and interfering with his personal relationships.

Parents' constant evaluations and commentaries, either positive or negative, on how their child stands, walks, sits, or speaks also overstep these boundaries. Furthermore, their evaluations *induce* the child to categorize himself as inherently "bad," "difficult," "special," "incompetent," "slow," "smart," "stupid," or a myriad of other labels they ascribe to him. A major danger in describing or categorizing youngsters is that they develop character defenses to fit their parents' descriptions.

R. D. Laing (1969/1972) has elaborated on the insidious power that the process of attribution has over children's lives:

> For example, a naughty child is a role in a particular family drama. Such a drama is a continuous production. His parents tell him he *is* naughty, because he does not do what they tell him. What they tell him he *is*, is *induction*, far more potent than what they tell him to do....
>
> "I keep telling him to be more careful, but he's so careless aren't you?"...
>
> If there is a smooth "normal" state of affairs, the structure is less evident, but not essentially different....
>
> "He knows right from wrong himself: I've never had to tell him not to do these things." (pp. 80-81)

Laing draws an analogy between these "induced attributions" and hypnosis in asking, "How much of who we are, is what we have been hypnotized to be?" (p. 79).

After recalling how she had been labeled and categorized when she was a child, one mother spoke out strongly against this common tendency in parents. She said:

You watch people all day long with their children and they're always defining them. "Oh well, he's a good boy, he's a smart boy, he's going to learn this, or he's so cute." Even if it's a "good" definition, I get furious.

It's the continual chipping away at the real person, the unique part of the child that's so infuriating. "Put your sweater on, take your sweater off, stand up straight, get in the car *quick*, hurry up."

Even if it's a constructive thing parents are trying to tell the child, I feel like saying to the parent, "So what? What right do you have to define it for him? Let him be his own person and give him whatever guidance you can, but you can't define his life for him."

Not "letting the child be" can cause extreme self-consciousness and social unease in adults. In effect, the adult who was intruded on as a child develops an exaggerated need for isolation and self-protection and is very often unable to enjoy companionship in close personal relationships.

David Cooper (1970/1971) ascribed importance to parental prohibitions and taboos against family members' experiencing their individuality and separateness:

There are numerous taboos in the family system that reach much further than the incest taboo and taboos against greed and messiness. One of these taboos is the implicit *prohibition against experiencing one's aloneness in the world* [italics added]. (p. 13)

A boy called Philip, at the age of six years, lived with his parents in a hotel owned by relatives. All his life he had been assiduously cared for. *He had never been left alone* [italics added] for a moment. But then one day, playing in the gardens, he rested his hands on a white-washed bird-bath and looked into the mossy water reflecting the sky. With a shock, he looked up at the sky, seeing it for the first time as if initiated into awareness of its reality by its reflection.

Then he realized in a moment of suffocation, which was also a moment of liberation, his total contingency and aloneness in the world. He knew that from that moment onward he could call to no-one, and that no-one could call to him in any way that would deflect the trajectory of his life project, which he now knew he had already chosen—although of course the details would have to be filled in.

His mother called out that supper was ready. He went in to eat, but for the first time he knew that he was no longer his mother's child but was, in fact, his own person. The point is that Philip could not say one word

> about his experience to anyone else in his family that would not be contorted into *their* terms or into some joke about *their* boy. (pp. 14-15)

Kahlil Gibran (1923) emphasized this theme in his philosophical treatise, *The Prophet*. His statements concur with our basic principle that children do *not* belong to their parents, only to themselves. Although these words have been much quoted, they make their point here:

> Your children are not your children.... They come through you but not from you.

> And though they are with you yet they belong not to you. You may strive to be like them, but seek not to make them like you. (p. 18)

Parents who demonstrate their respect for their offspring by following the spirit of these precepts have a positive effect on their child's development. Their children exhibit stronger characters, are centered in themselves, and are more likely to fulfill their unique human potential.

Constructive child-rearing includes encouraging children to be open and to take reasonable risks in expanding their world. Parents can offer their children creative, challenging experiences that enlarge the scope of their world rather than teach them a narrow, constricted range of interactions or self-protective habits. They can support the child in taking reasonable risks that lead to character development and would discourage him from developing a closed orientation toward life. Parental attitudes in this regard are paramount; if fathers and mothers are defensive and self-protective, they will encourage self-protective attitudes in their children.

When their own lives are characteristically dull and conforming, parents fail to provide vital or lively examples for their children to emulate. Men and women whose lives are shallow, insulated, desperate, or self-protective will not inspire their offspring to seek adventure or challenges. In order to teach a child to live "the good life," parents would have to genuinely value themselves, accept their feelings and priorities, and actively participate in their own lives.

Parents can compensate for their individual fears and weaknesses by encouraging other people—friends and relatives—to take an active interest in their children. By involving others, they can help avoid passing on their anxieties, fears, and other negative qualities to their offspring. Besides, being actively involved with other adults in addition to their own mothers and fathers helps children develop and expand their point of view and discourages a rigid, narrow approach to life. Indeed, movement toward an extended family, rather than strict reliance on the nuclear family unit, is an extremely important concept, because relating to significant other adults broadens the child's experience and acts to minimize and counterbalance specific negative effects of family interactions.

The Value of Being Personal

It is vital for parents to respond as real people to their children, rather than role-playing or acting patronizing, strategic, or phony in their interactions with them. It is impossible for parents to "learn how to talk to their children" in a manner that is contrary to their underlying attitudes or way of being. Indeed, any technique, attitude, or approach to child-rearing that treats children as objects to be manipulated by certain parental styles of communications is detrimental to their development. Many adult patients have complained bitterly about being treated as an object by their families.

Children need adults who relate to them directly; they need people who are open with them about their real thoughts and feelings. This type of interaction is not generally the case between parent and child. Instead, many parents question the child in an unfeeling manner, asking, "How was school today?" "Did you have fun?" or inquire about his activities in a rote or mechanical style that fails to lead to a real relationship. Very often fathers and mothers do not really listen to or respond sensitively to the answers to these questions, and children, in turn, learn to answer insincerely.

This type of parent-child relationship is best illustrated by a story a mother related about her interaction with her 8-year-old daughter. She began:

The other day JoAnn asked me if I would take her shopping with me—she really wanted to spend some time with me. So we got into the car, and by the time we had gone a few miles, I realized that I hadn't said anything to her. I thought: "This is really strange, because she really wanted to be with me, but I'm not being with her. I'm not saying anything."

As I thought more about this, I began to realize that there are two kinds of time for me. There is time with adults, where I'm aware that I'm with another person and I'm talking to that person. If an adult had been driving with me, I would have talked to them. Then I realized that the other kind of time is time alone or time with my children. But it's the same kind of time, time alone and time with my children. When I'm with them, it's exactly the same as when I'm alone. *I'm not being with a person.*

She went on to explain:

And then I thought that when I was planning to have children, if somebody had asked me two questions and said, "Which one of these alternatives describes what you felt when you thought about having children?: 'Do you want to have another person in your life who is close to you, that you can relate to, that you're involved with, that you care about, that is in your life every day? Do you want another person in your life like that?'"

The other question would be, "Would you like to have a new sofa? Would you like something new for your house, or something like that?" I'd have to admit that the way I thought about having children and the way I see most people thinking about having children is more like buying a sofa than having a new person in their lives.

I look at pictures in many family photo albums and see the parents standing there next to their children, but it's almost like they're standing next to an inanimate object. It's like the kids were props. That's the way it was in my family. I also hear people talking to children in ways that they would never talk to another adult.

It was interesting, because after I had that train of thought, the ride with JoAnn was one of the nicest times I've ever spent with her. I started talking to her, and it was more like a conversation that I have with one of my friends. We just talked about different things we had feelings about. It was much more like being with a person.

Children search the faces of their parents for genuine feeling contact. They have strong needs to feel the humanity of their parents, to see beyond the roles of "Father" and "Mother." Parents spend the majority of their time in a defended state and generally maintain a mask or facade. However, when they behave in a manner that is natural or personal and dispense with roles, they are experienced by their children as human and lovable. The child desperately needs to feel love *for* his parents, and if he is deprived of the opportunity, it causes him or her unbearable pain. The child who is kept at a distance or provoked into a negative or hostile posture toward his parents feels alienated and suffers intense guilt reactions. In a sense, he is bent out of shape psychologically and loses contact with himself. In addition, he is often punished and accused of, or defined as, not being a loving person. It is crucial that parents come to realize how important it is for their children to be allowed to love them. It is often difficult, however, for them to see the significance of this principle because most people place so little value on their real selves and natural attributes.

In general, we encourage parents to be personal in relating to children—to talk about their own feelings and life experiences, much as they would to a friend. This does *not* imply that they would "dump" their problems on their children or make immature demands on them for comfort or reassurance; rather, it implies parents' sharing their world with their children and allowing their children to share their world with them.

CONCLUSION

Individuals whose integrity has not been damaged in childhood, who were protected, respected, and treated with honesty by their parents, will be intelligent, responsive, empathic, and highly sensitive in both youth and adulthood. They will take pleasure in life and will feel no need to kill or even hurt others or themselves. (Miller, 1987, p. 25)

Throughout this chapter, we have pointed out a basic philosophy that can serve as a constructive guideline for child-rearing. These precepts are similar to those that underlie effective psychotherapy. In respecting their children as separate individuals, in supporting and encouraging their independence, and in relating to them directly with real feeling rather than hiding behind roles, parents can offer their children a firm foundation on which to build their lives, rather than forcing them into an inward, defensive posture. However, only to the extent that parents have developed integrity in the way they live their own lives will they be able to provide their offspring with the necessary model for mature, adult functioning. Parents' honesty and maturity are far more important in determining the healthy development of their children than any techniques prescribed by child-rearing experts.

Probably the most important principle discussed thus far involves the quality of the personal relationship between parent and child. In stressing the necessity of parents' building a *real* relationship with their children, British child psychologist Selma Fraiberg (1959/1968) wrote:

In the absence of strong human ties the child finds himself without positive motives for control of impulse.... The absence of positive human ties can brutalize a child as surely as repeated acts of sadism. (p. 296)

Rather than striving to preserve an image of being a "perfect" parent or even a "good" parent, mothers and fathers can offer their children much more by admitting their shortcomings and weaknesses, sharing with them the history of their own formative years, revealing their personal struggles as well as their successes, and in general relating to them as honestly as possible. Ultimately, parents' humanity and compassion for *themselves* are the most significant attributes for compassionate child-rearing.

CHAPTER 10

Discipline and Socialization

> In an environment that holds the baby well enough, the baby is able to make *personal development according to the inherited tendencies*. The result is a continuity of existence that becomes a sense of existing, a sense of self, and eventually results in autonomy.
>
> D. W. Winnicott (1986), "The Concept of a Healthy Individual" (p. 28)

The artist forms a general image in his mind and labors to implement his production. Similarly, child-rearing is a highly creative and imaginative task and, like other creative functions, requires considerable reflection and thought. We are not talking here about defining or shaping the child's personality in a specific mold that fits parents' expectations, as in choosing a career or modeling the child after a family member. These conventional images are usually based more on projections that reflect unconscious processes within parents, rather than on an objective view of the unfolding personality of the child.

Obviously, parents anticipate and visualize the kind of person they want their child to become. In a general sense, there are traits that they admire as well as a value system they wish to instill. However, rather than forming a set or a rigid image that is based on a restrictive view of the child, parents can learn ways of nurturing and guiding their children that facilitate the expression of their (the children's) natural qualities and personal style of being in the world. This goal implies parents' taking a sensitive, empathic interest in their child's development and perceiving him as a human being quite separate from themselves.

THE CONCEPT OF A MENTALLY HEALTHY INDIVIDUAL

> In terms of development it can be said that health means maturity according to the maturity that belongs to the age of the individual. (Winnicott, 1986, p. 22)

> Being and feeling real belong essentially to health, and it is only if we can take being for granted that we can get on to the more positive things. (Winnicott, 1986, p. 35)

> We perceive the healthy, adjusted individual as moving *away* from defenses, support systems, and painkillers toward openness, feeling, and emotional responsiveness, while changing from an inward, self-parenting posture to an active pursuit of gratification in the external world. (Firestone, 1988, p. 257)

According to Maslow's (1954) model, as healthy individuals satisfy their needs at one level, for example, the survival needs for food, sleep, and rest, they move to the next level of needs for social contact, productive work, and other self-actualizing activity. Other clinicians (Winnicott, 1986) have conceptualized the mentally healthy adult as one who has made an adjustment to society without "*too great a loss of individual or personal impulse*" (p. 27).

I conceive the mentally healthy individual as existing in a state of continual change, as moving in the direction of increased autonomy, self-fulfillment, and satisfying relationships, while necessarily experiencing more of both the joy and pain of living. The healthy adult pursues his priorities, that is, the activities and people that give his life its special meaning. At the same time, he is generous and giving of himself to others—not out of selfless, self-sacrificing motives, but because his generosity enhances his own good feeling about himself.

Parents who conceptualize positive qualities as goals for their children can learn to distinguish between experiences that encourage their development into effective, well-functioning, mature individuals, and socialization methods that tend to interfere with or disrupt movement toward these goals. No parent consciously wants his child to grow up to become a submissive person who is easily influenced, yet many people use scare tactics in training their children. What parent wants his child to become a cold or unfeeling person, yet countless parents inadvertently discourage emotional expression. Parents profess that they want their children to develop into strong, spontaneous, energetic individuals, rather than rigid, authoritarian persons taking orders from above and displaying senseless and unquestioning obedience. Yet so many parents unthinkingly support and live out inhibiting responses that shape their child's developing character in a negative direction. The goal of producing an active, healthy, independent adult can shape parents' attitudes, training procedures, and disciplinary measures.

OUR VIEW OF DISCIPLINE AND TRAINING

> The belief that there can be rules for dealing with one's child is inimical to an attitude of empathetic understanding, which can be derived only from our own experiences, which are as unique to us as are those of our child to him.... Since all rules are based on generalizations, they disregard what is individual, and hence make us overlook what is unique in our child and in our relation to him. (Bettelheim, 1987, p. 37)

Advice from child-rearing books related to discipline tends to interfere with a very personal learning process within the parent. The potential for this learning exists in the course of many parent-child interactions. This educational process begins when parents think through each problematic situation and attempt to discover for themselves the reasons their child is troubled or misbehaving, rather than automatically reacting with anger or restrictive prohibitions. Advising parents, even when the advice is sound, deprives them of this potential learning experience and detracts from the spontaneity of their personal reactions to their child. Telling a father or a mother what to do in a particular setting with an individual child is also reductionistic and reflects a view of both persons as objects to be manipulated or "fixed."

In addition, parents often find it difficult, if not impossible, to follow specific guidelines and suggestions for discipline that they read in child-rearing books or parenting manuals. For example, one mother, an experienced schoolteacher, upon learning that I was writing a book on child-rearing, expressed this difficulty, which is familiar to many parents. She said:

No matter how much I try to follow the advice I read in books, much of which is very good, when I'm in the actual situation with my children, I find I can't apply what I've read and I act in ways that I know are *not* "right" or helpful. Someone should write a book for parents explaining why it's so hard to apply this advice in *real* interactions with children.

The reader may well find that our philosophy proceeds along different lines from the usual child-rearing methods recommended by others in that they refer to *attitudes* that predispose action rather than specific how-to-do-it practical techniques. It is also important to emphasize that these recommendations and suggestions were derived from a series of parenting seminars, in which my associates and I and parents discussed pragmatic approaches to child-rearing based on sound mental health principles.

SOCIALIZATION

It is our view that the ultimate purpose of discipline is to help the child develop into a decent, likeable adult, capable of survival in a social milieu, rather than one who is submissive to the socialization process. With this goal in mind, we would recommend that parents with similar interest try to (1) avoid unnecessary restrictions, rules, and standards, (2) act as positive role models, (3) reward rather than punish, (4) avoid physical punishment, (5) avoid cynical, judgmental attitudes that reinforce a child's sense of badness, and (6) attempt to control their children's acting out of hostile, manipulative behavior.

Avoidance of Unnecessary Restrictions, Rules, and Standards

It is remarkable how few rules or restrictions are really necessary to accomplish parents' goal of effectively socializing their child; however, their goal can be better realized when those rules that *are* necessary and useful are consistently upheld. Rather than having a direct confrontation on petty or trivial issues, for example, "You have to eat your vegetables or you can't have dessert," parents can establish a limited number of rules that they would then firmly enforce.

Parents need to clearly state their standards and restrictions to the child. As the child matures, parents can explain the reasoning behind placing limits and emphasize the importance of leading a disciplined life. In situations where definite rules apply, parents would not act as though the child had a choice in the matter. For example, if they predetermined their child's bedtime, obviously they would not *ask* him each night if he wanted to go to bed, and then insist that he go anyway. Authority would be administered in a straightforward manner. Parents would state, "Now you are going to bed," if that was their intention; not, "Would you like to go to bed?"

Parents as Positive Role Models for Their Children

More important than specific training or disciplinary measures is the powerful modeling effect derived from the child's living day-in and day-out with parents who themselves consistently behave in a responsible manner. For example, there is no better method for teaching a child to be considerate of other people than for his parents to be considerate of him and of each other. The psychological processes of identification and imitation overshadow parents' verbalizations and prescriptions for good behavior. We agree in substance with Bettelheim's (1985) view:

> While most parents are ready to teach their children discipline and know that they are the ones to do so, they are less ready to accept the idea that they can teach only by example. (p. 57)

> We need not make any claim to be perfect. But if we strive as best we can to live good lives ourselves, our children, impressed by the merits of living good lives, will one day wish to do the same. (p. 59)

When parental "voices" are acted out toward others, they have a toxic effect on personal relations. Critical, judgmental, and abusive behavior damages both the parental person and the recipient.

> The...[toxic] person manifests an impressive variety of patterns with which he controls and manipulates others.... Toxic people oppress those around them.... Toxic people fail to see others as individuals or to respect the integrity of others. (Greenwald, 1973, pp. 35-36)

Certain personality characteristics are harmful while others are growth-enhancing in terms of their effect on people. Toxic personality traits in parents not only have a profoundly destructive effect on children directly, but these negative qualities are passed on to succeeding generations through the processes of identification and imitation. For example, a harsh, judgmental, or disrespectful father is likely to have a strong negative impact on his son, causing him to feel worthless and unlovable. In addition, these undesirable traits would tend to become a part of the boy's emerging personality *in the same general direction*, and he would tend to become authoritarian and parental with *his* child.

People who are paranoid, suspicious, and have a victimized orientation to life, who possess strong self-denying or self-sacrificing tendencies, or who are weak and passively conforming to authority, will have a destructive effect on others, especially their children. These people foster guilt reactions in their offspring when they fail to actively embrace life. Parents who themselves lead dishonest, empty lives will fail to provide their children with good role models. Phoniness, status-seeking, and class consciousness can foster vanity and feelings of superiority in children. Rigidity and a need to control would tend to produce a compulsive-obsessional personality structure in the child.

Tightness or lack of generosity, hostility and sarcasm, indifference, intrusiveness, irritability, and over-solicitousness are also toxic personality characteristics. Fathers and mothers who are domineering, overbearing, evaluative, or condescending behave in a manner that is against their child's psychological development. In contrast, the parent who is congenial, nondefensive, nonintrusive, consistent, and generous has a more positive impact on his child's personality.

Parents who reflect on these negative characteristics may become motivated to further develop themselves personally. As noted in the previous chapter, parents can best help their children not by sacrificing themselves for their children but by attempting to fulfill their own lives.

Rewards Rather Than Punishment in Facilitating Socialization

It is better for parents to reinforce their child's positive traits and desirable behaviors while keeping negative reinforcement (punishment) to a minimum. As noted in Chapter 4, learning theorists have studied the differential effects of reward and punishment on both human and nonhuman species and have arrived at a number of conclusions applicable to behavior modification techniques and, more generally, to child-rearing practices (Bandura, 1969; Skinner, 1953). The principles may be summarized as follows:

1. Positive reinforcement (rewards) tends to increase the frequency of the specific behaviors being reinforced.
2. Negative reinforcement (punishment) is not as effective as positive reinforcement in terms of its ability to extinguish the expression of undesirable behavior; at the same time, negative emotions (anger, fear, shame, guilt) are generally aroused, complicating the learning process.
3. Undesirable behavior may be extinguished after an extended period of time if the target behavior is neither rewarded nor punished, that is, if it is consistently ignored.
4. The withdrawal of positive reinforcers contingent on the child's acting out undesirable behavior tends to decrease that behavior.

Positive reinforcement responses, such as smiling, pleasure in the child's company, verbal praise, and physical affection, are significant for learning. Withdrawal of these responses and indications of displeasure can also mold the child's behavior. It is surprising how easily discipline is effected in a family milieu characterized by love and understanding. Indeed, the techniques described above are only truly efficacious when the child feels secure and loved. Children in that atmosphere are very anxious to please and do not generally present disciplinary problems.

Parents who are continually nagging, complaining, or lecturing are usually unsuccessful in socializing their child. These particular methods are extremely ineffective forms of punishment; they arouse the child's resentment and anger while failing to control his behavior. In general, a combination of verbal approval, tangible rewards, affection, *genuine* acknowledgment (not false praise), and some form of negative consequence for misbehavior is conducive to successfully disciplining children.

Parents who are responsive to the ways in which they were hurt as children are likely to avoid making evaluative, judgmental pronouncements about their children's behaviors. Labeling or categorizing children's behavior as "good," for example, such questions as "Were you a *good* boy today? Did you do your homework?" or as "bad," "You're *bad* if you don't do as I say" or "You're *bad* if you cry," are not recommended. Evaluative statements differentiating good and bad behaviors tend to support the formation of a narrow view of human nature and to discourage the child from developing his own standards. A good and bad dichotomy fosters conformity in the child and has an inhibiting effect. This type of person grows up subjecting all of his actions to a good and bad dimension and is often plagued or even paralyzed by guilt reactions. The obsessive preoccupation with good and bad interferes with the child's freedom and spontaneity. Furthermore, continually categorizing the child's behavior as bad clearly supports a negative concept of self that lasts throughout adult life. Moreover, the child who is continually told, "You're always slouching," or "You're lazy," or "You're so inconsiderate," eventually comes to believe his parents' definitions and subsequently behaves in ways that confirm these labels.

Sensitive parents refrain from analyzing or categorizing children or foisting a strict or fixed image on them. These parents strive to develop a flexible image of the child, not an image of *what he is.* They teach the child that he has the potential to become whatever he wants within the range of his abilities.

We suggest that parents not offer monetary rewards for good behavior, because this practice tends to place the child's behavior on a commercial basis rather than a personal one. Monetary rewards interfere with the child's natural generosity and desire to please and foster calculating attitudes. Often financial rewards or excessive gift-giving are compensation for a lack of real affection on the part of parents. Under these conditions, the presents serve to confuse the child's perception of reality; that is, the child feels rejected but the gifts indicate the opposite. Generally, the child creates a fantasy that he is loved to cover his real insecurity. The formation of this fantasy bond offers temporary relief from psychological pain but plays a restrictive, defensive role in the child's development.

Avoidance of Physical Punishment

It is important that parents never beat or physically abuse a child. If restraint is needed, parents can hold the child firmly and talk to him sternly or even move him physically to get him to go where they wish, without striking the child. Parents who are sure of their own power, who are assertive in their own lives and are not afraid of their own strength, can effectively stop their children's annoying behaviors as well as control their physically hurtful actions without hitting, spanking, or violently shaking them.

Harsh, cruel, or sadistic punishment can set up lifelong fears in the child as well as expectations of punishment from other people. These painful, primal feelings tend to persist into adult life. Often, these fears lead to serious anticipatory anxiety states and can intensify castration or mutilation anxiety. In general, it has been demonstrated that the child who was physically mistreated tends to provoke bad treatment from others in order to relieve powerful feelings of anticipatory anxiety and to mistreat his own children in the same manner.

Parents can learn to accept anger and ambivalent feelings in themselves. Individuals who feel comfortable with their anger are better able to control its expression and are therefore more capable of taking a strong stand in enforcing rules. These mothers and fathers are much more direct, forthright, and, consequently, more effective in disciplining their children. In addition, disciplinary action needs to be consistent rather than reflective of parents' mood swings. Considerable damage is caused by parents who act out hostility on their children that is based on their own mood swings. These angry reactions are generally disconnected from the child's actions.

The use of idle threats of future punishment to enforce rules and standards is not recommended. How many times have you overheard mothers and fathers routinely warning their children, "If you don't behave yourself, you're not going to get a present, or get to go to the park or to the restaurant," and so forth; yet most parents invariably fail to back up their threats with action. It is clear that threats of physical punishment or other negative consequences, which are *not* carried out, are counterproductive and undermine parents' authority. Similarly, the use of frightening ultimatums is damaging to a child. The parent who sadistically warns his child "If you're not good, I'm sending you to reform school, military school, or jail," inflicts an untold amount of misery on his child. In contrast, compassionate parents exercise restraint when they are tempted to use these threats as leverage in disciplining their children.

Parents who carry their threats out to a point, then change their minds at the last moment, succeed in terrifying their children and set up fears of abandonment that can last for years afterward. Also, these threats lead to feelings of insecurity, a melodramatic view of life, and a general state of discomfort. Adults who have suffered from these threats as children tend to dramatize their lives, making urgent, life-and-death situations out of normal everyday events.

Avoidance of Judgmental Attitudes

The frustrations, the despair, the wreckage of his [the adult patient's] life are ultimately traceable to his deficiency of self-esteem and to the policies that led to that deficiency. (Branden, 1969/1971, p. 253)

Much as physical punishment damages the child's psyche, parents' harsh, judgmental attitudes act to destroy his self-esteem. Most children grow up feeling that they are "bad." There is a deep-seated feeling that they are unworthy, unlovable, illegitimate, unacceptable, or inferior. They ascribe many reasons to why they feel that way. They believe they are bad because they cry or feel sad, because they have wants or desires, or because they feel angry or resentful. They view themselves as unworthy because they feel hatred at being judged bad and have learned to hate those who abused them. They feel they are bad because they feel sexual. The boy feels that he is bad because he is a boy; the girl, because she is a girl. Each may wish to be the other. Unhappy children often wish or actually fantasize about being the opposite sex.

The negative identity that is formed in the family and integrated into the child's self-concept will become a functional part of the child's and later the adult's personality dynamics. In many ways the identity remains irrefutable in spite of evidence to the contrary. The negative identity is implanted on a deep level and forms the substructure of a person's attitude toward self and others.

Many people attempt to compensate and deny their hidden self-attacks. As a result, their attempts to cope with inner feelings of being unlovable through compensation tend to alienate others, and no matter how much they are loved as an adult, they still cling to the "truth" of childhood. This is why so many people have difficulty in intimate relationships and are unable to accept love and closeness. They reject the new reality and hang onto the old view of themselves as an unconscious self-protective strategy, that is, to avoid disappointment and being hurt again.

Moralistic training procedures, where children are seen as sinful or bad, have a negative effect. Children are *not* inherently evil or born bad. Many parents, although not stating the belief out loud, implicitly believe that children are bad and tend to treat them accordingly. A child who is fortunate in having decent, moral parents does not need to be taught moralistic prohibitions or principles; he will learn ethical behavior and decency through observing and imitating his parents. Lectures and object lessons about goodness and righteousness are often counter-productive and can be destructive, especially when parents do not live up to their principles or personify their beliefs.

Another fundamental precept of effective child-rearing involves not teaching children that they are bad or selfish for wanting. Children's desires and wants are an important part of their personal identity. Individuals who progressively turn their backs on their wants and priorities are sacrificing themselves and surrendering a basic part of their identity. All that a person has are his feelings, perceptions, thoughts, wants, and unique ways of coping with his environment and pursuing his priorities. If children are implicitly taught to deny their wants and inhibit their desires, they will be progressively debilitated. Therefore, teaching children to be selfless, in the sense of being self-denying and unnecessarily deferring of their own wants, can be very damaging and later may seriously interfere with their pursuing goal-directed behavior.

Teaching a child to be self-denying need not be conscious or deliberate on the part of parents. Modeling has a powerful effect on children who grow up in families where parents are self-sacrificing. Individuals raised in families dominated by a self-denying parent find it difficult to surpass that parent personally or vocationally because of their guilt about leaving the parent behind. On the other hand, when parents lead a full life, they provide their children with a positive model that inspires active, goal-directed behavior, rather than creating a strong social pressure on them to renounce or give up important personal goals.

Reassuring the child that he is not bad after disciplining him helps him regain his self-esteem. Children need reassurance that they are *not* objectionable after they have been reprimanded or repeatedly punished. Responsive parents stress the fact that their child's behavior was irritating or offensive, not that he was a bad person, and that the unacceptable behavior can be changed. Many children, when severely punished, believe that their parents will be angry at them forever and despair of ever again being in their good graces. Indeed, some parents carry grudges from past incidents and continually remind the child of his previous misdeeds rather than treating each event separately. When angered, they pile up their attacks and overwhelm the child with a generalized feeling that he is not a good person. The child treated in this manner feels futile and despairs of ever being loved. With this negative image in mind, he behaves in a like manner, constantly getting into trouble at home and at school.

Comparisons are not useful or appropriate for motivating good behavior in children. It is important that parents avoid comparing their children negatively to siblings or to a neighbor's or a friend's children. These comparisons leave a strong impression of unworthiness.

Parents can also use humor to help their child get out of a bad mood and stop misbehaving. This is a valuable method for easing a child's guilt and shame, because humor can serve to reinforce the child's positive self-image while gently attacking the unpleasant behavior. Constructive playfulness and optimistic good humor about negative events or about the child's mistakes can often dispel the seriousness and drama of an otherwise painful or unpleasant situation. We are *not* talking here about the sarcasm or hurtful barbs that some parents use in order to control or degrade their children; on the contrary, we are referring to a style of humor that is respectful of the child. Not only is humor a useful adjunct to discipline, but children really enjoy their parents' being playful and spontaneously fun-loving. To illustrate, several 10-year-olds from an elementary school class commented on this trait in adults when they were asked to write down their answers to the question, "What's wrong with grown-ups?"

> Grown-ups almost never like to get silly. And when we have fun and get silly they always say "settle down." When they do get silly, it is the most fun we have. (Buscaglia, 1987, p. 10)

Controlling Children's Hostile, Manipulative Behavior

It is a good idea for parents to interrupt the behavior patterns in their child that are irritating or provoking before they find themselves starting to dislike or even beginning to hate the child. Obviously parents' covert hostility toward an annoying child creates tension and leads to more psychological damage than if parents were to intervene and firmly forbid the irritating behavior. In these instances, it is important for parents to express genuine anger in disciplining their child. Again, let us emphasize that it is essential that they be strong without physically acting out their aggression.

It is more constructive for parents to find out the cause of children's disruptive behavior than to continually punish its manifestations. Involved parents can take a sensitive interest in their child's arguments and expressions of sibling rivalry instead of allowing the hostility to continue for years. It is never advisable to allow a disruptive situation to persist within the family. It is so much more productive to get at the core problem by really talking things out.

Negative power on the part of children needs to be dealt with firmly. Negative power can be defined as an attempt to control and manipulate through weakness; for example, continually crying, "falling apart," behaving in a self-destructive manner, playing the victim, trying to make others feel guilty, having temper tantrums, showing selfishness, displaying intrusive behavior, or acting paranoid and mistreated. These destructive habit patterns are not in the child's best interests. They need to be controlled, or they will persist as adult character traits. It is important for parents to be aware that children do not typically outgrow these characteristics, but that they become lifelong habits that interfere with personal relationships.

Children can be taught that it is never appropriate to castigate or hate themselves for wrong-doing; rather, that it is much more functional and appropriate to change their behavior in the future. Self-attacks generally lead to more negative behavior. No matter how reprehensible one's behavior was, it serves no purpose to ruminate obsessively about the past. Parents can let the child know that everyone makes mistakes or acts badly at times, yet these behaviors are correctable. Children who feel guilty or have low self-esteem unconsciously seek punishment from external sources to relieve painful feelings of guilt or shame. Ideally, parents would try to avoid becoming the agent of the child's punishment when he is provoking a negative response in order to confirm his image of being bad. Again, it is more important to get at the root of the problem.

Battles of the will are best avoided. Such unnecessary power plays that degrade the child and force conformity and submission can be prevented. It is not advisable for parents to issue ultimatums or arbitrarily take a rigid stand. This stance or posture sets up situations that invariably lead to power struggles. Both parents and children suffer from this type of exchange. In fact, pervasive attitudes of defiance on the part of children will not be manifest when parents provide the necessary ingredients of love and strength of character.

We are not suggesting, however, an overly permissive attitude that permits regressive behavior, destructive acting out, or parent abuse. There is an obvious balance that is required that depends primarily on parents' maturity and self-control. If circumstances do arise where parents find themselves in a battle of this sort, they can learn to assert their power over the child without causing him to lose face or to feel devastated by the interaction.

When parents do find themselves in a power struggle, they can refrain from exploding in anger at their child, although this is a strong temptation once the child stubbornly refuses to behave. Irrational expressions of rage frighten the child, and he tends to perceive that his father or mother is out of control and therefore ineffective and weak. On the other hand, the parent who has access to his anger and feels comfortable expressing it in a controlled manner is neither feared by his child nor seen as incompetent.

Specific Situations

The Crying Infant

It is valuable for parents to recognize painful feelings in themselves that are aroused by their infant's cries of distress.

> If we could only put ourselves in the infant's place, we could understand these traumas better. Infants cannot rationalize. They cannot think in terms of hourly spans. Being starved and being alone in the dark in Pain means death. They have no conception when Pain will end, so they cannot defend against it in a cerebral way. (Janov, 1973, pp. 107-108)

Soon after their baby is born, new mothers and fathers find that their infant has a powerful impact on their lives. Besides readjusting their schedules, routines, and activities to fit the baby's needs, they are disconcerted to discover that they are intensely affected by the baby's crying. They may find themselves feeling anxious, tormented, and completely preoccupied by a baby who is uncomfortable and whose distress is of unknown origins.

It is important for parents to be aware that a small baby has tremendous leverage over parental responses and is able to affect his parents' behavior by the sounds he makes (Demos, 1986). A crying baby arouses painful primal emotions in his parents, bringing to the surface suppressed feelings from their own childhoods. For this reason, mothers and fathers will do almost anything to shut off these anxiety-provoking cries.

Understanding why their baby's cries have such a profound impact on their emotions and behaviors helps parents to separate their own primal pain from the pain their child is experiencing. This insight can reduce parents' anxiety and nervousness and, in turn, has a positive effect on their infant's emotional state.

Despite much advice to the contrary, it is impossible to spoil the infant by picking him up when he is crying; in fact, a baby should be held and soothed before he reaches an uncontrollably agitated stage, at which point it is much more difficult to comfort him. It is vital for parents to develop confidence in their instincts to provide affection and emotional support. There is no harm in offering maximum security and comfort for the infant, because the early years provide the basis of an infant's security in later life.

However, chronic whining or crying can become a manipulative tool as the child gets older. Submitting to the child's request, thereby rewarding him for crying uncontrollably or having a tantrum, only teaches him that he need not attempt to control emotional outbursts because they can be successfully used to manipulate. In addition, overly sympathetic responses to whining and crying reinforce the child's tendency to feel sorry for himself and support a victimized posture. *Ideally, parents would help their children learn that it is appropriate to cry when they are sad, not when they are angry.* This instruction can best be accomplished by explaining to the child that he is angry at those crucial times. Rather than becoming overly indulgent, the parent verbalizes "You must be pretty mad now," and other responses of that nature.

Handling Temper Tantrums

Parents need to develop an understanding of the many elements that go into a child's temper tantrum: anger, fear of disintegration, death wishes toward his parents, and the shock of feeling completely out of control of his body. Most people have witnessed a child in a tantrum at one time or another. He may throw himself violently about the room, hit the wall, kick the floor, and/or scream uncontrollably. Bruno Bettelheim (1987) has provided us with a good description of the child in the midst of a tantrum and the reasons it is so frightening to both parent and child:

> A temper tantrum is the expression of the child's despair of not having a self that works for him.... Once his despair has thrown him into a temper tantrum—the child is usually overwhelmed to the degree that everything else is blotted out, including recollection of what he wanted and failed

to get. The temper tantrum is his reaction to his inability to gain what he desires, but it also demonstrates to him the deficiency of his self. He experiences it as a total collapse. Incapacitated by his rage, he needs the help of others more than ever. (p. 153)

Appropriate parental responses to the child's tantrums are the subject of controversy. Many experts advise parents to remove the child who is throwing a tantrum from the situation and to isolate him in another room until he is calm. I strongly disagree with this technique, which is referred to by professionals as "time out," because being left alone to "cry out" his rage only encourages the child's hostile fantasies and acts to intensify his frustrated anger. Being left alone also contributes to the child's fear of his anger. It increases his anxiety about the disastrous effect he imagines his rage has on his parents. This type of treatment ultimately teaches the child to seek isolation whenever he is angry or frustrated, to feel guilty for his murderous fantasies, and to become increasingly inward and secretive.

Finally, isolating an angry child does not teach him anything about how to handle his anger; the only positive effect may be that the crying is eventually extinguished because it is not being reinforced by getting the parents' attention. However, the negative effects of time out far outweigh the benefits.

In most cases, it is helpful to try to stop the child's crying before it escalates into a full-blown tantrum. Parents who *really* know their child's idiosyncracies, habit patterns, and likes and dislikes can respond sensitively to the kinds of circumstances that might trigger a temper tantrum in their child. In many instances, the tantrums can be avoided entirely. Sensitive parents are often able to determine when they need to make a concerted effort to stop the tantrum and when it would be more helpful to allow the child to "cry it out."

Very often, a young child who is beginning to get into a very upset emotional state can be distracted by other activities, and this technique can be very rewarding. At a certain point, a parent can divert the child with a favorite toy, a new game, or simply by offering him a drink of water. As soon as the child is distracted in this way, the tantrum is over. Parents usually know when to offer this assistance, because there is typically a point when the quality or intensity of the child's crying shifts, and the parent senses that the child no longer seems to "have his heart" in the tantrum.

In some instances, it is better to contain the child; that is, to hold him gently but firmly and allow him to vent his rage. This technique, when handled sensitively, can be very useful as the child discovers that he can survive the painful emotions without disintegration and gradually learns to bring anger under sufficient control. This process is exceedingly painful for parents to go through privately, much less in public situations. The parent is plagued by self-attacks that he is destroying the child and causing extreme emotional pain; whereas actually, the reverse is true. When children are handled effectively in this manner and the process is "sweated through" with tenderness and concern on the part of parents, the child appears to be unusually relaxed for a considerable time afterward. Needless to say, it takes a very mature and loving parent to appropriately handle the tantrum situation in this manner.

Children need proper controls in order to learn self-control. Furthermore, parents need to set limits in order for their offspring to develop a healthy self-esteem. All children require love, regulation, and control in order to become self-regulating, self-directed adults. When they fail to receive this type of regulation, children necessarily grow up feeling unloved.

TEACHING CHILDREN DISCIPLINED ATTITUDES TOWARD WORK

Parents can help their children develop positive attitudes toward work and discourage attitudes of victimization. Parents generally underestimate their children's potentialities in relation to being useful and allow them to grow up with a good deal of time on their hands. Many youngsters spend much of their spare time besides play in useless activities that serve neither to educate them nor to develop their potentialities. To the contrary, children should be, and are capable of, entering into productive work in the home environment at an early age and, as they get older, they can expand their participation into more and more important functions. Indeed, children develop a sense of worthlessness from being allowed to stagnate in the home atmosphere. This is particularly true of teenagers, who are virtually as capable as adults to perform important work functions in life. Many adolescents are left to their own devices with endless amounts of time on their hands. Very often, they get into drugs or other negative pursuits. In any case, they tend to develop attitudes that are negative or refractory to constructive work habits.

Providing the youngster with a series of jobs serves as a useful discipline that is accepted matter-of-factly by a child who is viewed as a potentially productive member of the family. Here again, it is important for parents to recognize that *their* attitudes toward work are paramount. Parents who complain about their jobs or bosses and who feel paranoid and victimized will project this image in the minds of their youngsters. On the other hand, mothers and fathers who take pride in their vocational efforts and approach their work with energy and dedication will reinforce positive attitudes toward work in their children.

CONCLUSION

Just as an effective teacher maintains control in the classroom without nagging or angry outbursts, parents, too, can learn to maintain discipline without the type of recrimination and anger that so damages a child's psyche. They can become aware of and avoid acting out sadistic, angry attitudes in disciplining their child. They can develop a spirit of investigation as they try to uncover the causes of their child's distress or undesirable behavior. Discipline is best practiced with firmness, not cruelty; with understanding, not condemnation; and from an underlying motive of helping the child become not only the kind of person who likes himself, but also the kind of person whom other people like, respect, and enjoy being with. Indeed, the ideas for discipline and socialization described here are based on a philosophy that allows the gradual unfolding of the child's unique personality, his vitality, and his enthusiasm for life.

CHAPTER 11

A New Model for Family Interactions

> What strikes me as a ludicrous fact is that the marriage and family institutions to which such primacy of loyalty and devotion is being taught show anything but optimal health in contemporary society. That most marriages are not deeply satisfying relationships hardly needs documentation. A lot of praise and sanctification floats about us, however, on the matter of families. I think we engage in a lot of repression and denial. Put more simply, we double-pretend: we pretend families are mostly wonderful and then we pretend we are not pretending.
>
> Robert Harper (1981), "Limitations of Marriage and Family Therapy"
> (p. 5)

We must challenge the false idealization of the family and the destructive fantasy bonds that make unfeeling connections between people without regard for human concerns. The family, as a sacred institution that is exempt from critical or realistic appraisal, must come under constructive scrutiny.

Families could nurture children and help them grow and develop their full potential, but all too frequently this is not the case. In spite of evidence to the contrary, people strongly believe that present-day families are the backbone of a stable society and rigidly adhere to the notion that they contribute to the health and security of their members. In our extensive clinical experience, we have often found the opposite to be true. For example, it is interesting to note that in the reference population (described in Chapter 1) where people talked openly about their relationships and maintained an extended friendship circle, friendships worked very well, while the most intimate relationships—couple and family relationships—did not fare nearly as well. The most hurtful behaviors, dissatisfactions, and painful conflicts were observed within couples and between family members. The problematic nature of people's most intimate relationships was the most difficult issue to contend with and the most resistant to change and positive movement. Problems evident within the couple relationships were *not* manifested in the friendships. Indeed, friendships endured with much more consistency, integrity, and affection.

This finding is not unusual or restricted to this small population. In fact, intimate personal relationships within the reference population were significantly better than those in the larger society, and members of couples and families treated each other more kindly than the population at large. They were more aware of and sensitive to each other's needs and more tolerant of the personal freedom of their spouses and children. Their *worst* acting-out behavior, bickering, and episodic outbursts were comparable to the *routine* mistreatment within "normal" families. Nevertheless, family relationships in the group also exhibited patterns of *dysfunctional* interaction that were not substantially different from what outside family studies have demonstrated. Namely, individuals in the majority of marriages in our society are dissatisfied with their relationships, and the quality of life in most families has suffered accordingly (Beavers, 1977; Srole, Langner, Michael, & Opler, 1962). The effort of men and women to preserve an illusion of the love that once existed between them while rejecting loving operations is a serious problem. Indeed, *it is the most powerful counterforce to well-intentioned efforts to raise healthy, happy children.* This fantasy bond within the couple and family, projected onto a social system, supports a myth about family life that contradicts reality.

THE TRUTH ABOUT THE CURRENT STATUS OF FAMILY RELATIONS

Couples rarely sustain genuine loving feelings after making a commitment. In our society, we profess strong support for close, enduring relationships between men and women. Yet, the reality is that very often men and women are *not* friends and are not loving toward each other. People place a high value on a happy marriage, yet for most couples the marriage ceremony signals the end of romance.

Family members connect to each other in order to find security. Yet, precisely *because* of this connection, they treat each other with very little regard for their respective feelings or sensibilities, less even than they typically extend to friends or acquaintances.

Parents do not necessarily love their children. Parents are *supposed* to love their children and raise them to be happy, fulfilled adults. Yet most parents are not emotionally free enough to love their children, and most children end up resenting their parents.

Why are many young people so desperate to "get away" from their families, if, indeed, they feel loved and accepted? Why are they driven to leave home by motives that go beyond a natural desire to establish their own families? What has happened during the formative years to transform the infant's trusting look into the sullen, resentful expression of the teenager? It is clear that, despite their best intentions, most parents cannot sustain loving relationships with their children.

Freedom of speech is not tolerated in the majority of families. In most families, children are afraid to speak their minds because of fear of retaliation, fear of causing pain in their parents, fear of losing their parents' love. In an effective psychotherapy, dispelling myths, illusions, destructive ties, and self-deception helps to develop more honesty and integrity. These benefits open up the possibility for parents to relate to each other and their children on a more realistic basis. If individual members of a family expose the illusions and lies that they live with through candid and open communication, a new style of family interaction would be possible that could more successfully meet the basic needs of its members.

Families emphasize family ties over friendship with "outsiders" and promise eternal love and care. Parents claim that no other person or institution offers what they do. Yet, often family life is not only oppressive and controlling but also fails to satisfy the basic needs of family members. Friendships entered into by adolescents are especially suspect in the minds of those parents who wish to remain symbiotically merged with their children. Sometimes the struggling young person, torn between parental injunctions to be independent, to "stand on his own two feet," and covert commands from parents to remain passive and submissive to family policy, becomes overtly self-destructive, delinquent, or even suicidal (Richman, 1986). Boszormenyi-Nagy and Spark (1973/1984) attributed the extreme blind loyalty and social isolation manifested in many families to the pseudo "child-centered" nature of contemporary American life:

> Whether this is an accurate characterization or not, there is a widespread tendency toward *overloading the life of nuclear families with expectations for excessive commitment and satisfaction* [italics added]. (p. 162)

Families feel superior to other families. The propensity of parents to teach family superiority fosters class consciousness, status-seeking, and prejudice in young people. Many parents teach that *their* way is the right way and that other life-styles are wrong or inferior. There is a false sense of being special in these families. Family members are critical of others, placing themselves above neighbors and friends alike. Often they act friendly in social situations but criticize and depreciate other people afterward.

Typical family life is characterized by a cult-like submission to authority. This statement does not rule out defiant behavior or rebellious activity within the family. Both defiance and submission lack independence, are outer-directed rather than inner-directed, and are immature ways of connecting to parents and provoking parental responses.

There is a difference between what most people claim to value and how they actually conduct their lives. Freedom and a democratic form of government are highly valued by all of us, yet most people do not choose to live free, spontaneous lives that reflect their own point of view. Free from the obvious external authorities, people still prefer to set up others as authorities to rule their lives in more subtle ways. Many families are authoritarian systems in that they control their members through guilt and obligation and both indirectly and directly punish free choice, free speech, and independence on the part of individual family members.[1]

In light of this critical view of family practices, it is important to note that I am not implying that *all* families, or *all* mothers and fathers, are destructive to their offspring; *nor* am I implying that any other institution or agency of society should replace the operations of family in the arena of child-rearing. Indeed, I find my greatest satisfaction in my personal relationship with my wife and children.

The family system in itself is not the problem; it is the individual defenses and psychopathological tendencies of the individuals involved. Our energy is best directed toward *improving* those relations within the family that damage children, yet we must remain open to alternative life-styles, extended family relationships, and other means for improving children's lives. Finally, *it is imperative to state that, in my opinion, there is no organization or institution of any kind, including current family practices, that can substitute for personal, feelingful, and consistent, close relating to children.*

ISSUES AFFECTING THE NEW FAMILY

Bearing in mind that powerful resistances operate to perpetuate actions within the family that militate against the psychological development of its members, it is still valuable to conceptualize a new model for family interactions. Parents who are deeply concerned with developing themselves and improving their relationships with their children may benefit from the following guidelines.

Honesty and Openness

Parents can try to be more honest and open with their children. As emphasized throughout my work and in the work of many theorists, notably R. D. Laing (1969/1972) and Gregory Bateson (1972), lies and illusions can indeed fracture the child's sense of reality. In my opinion, the truth must be upheld in family life or else there are serious consequences. Parents have a natural desire to be protective and sparing of the child's feelings, but often their attempts to protect the child cause considerably more damage than facing issues squarely. Children who are aware of the realities of life as well as the shortcomings of the adults around them have a better basis to cope with adult stresses.

There are a number of topics that parents ⸻ difficult ⸻ ⸻ ing frankly and truthfully with their childre⸻ these subjects are strictly taboo. For example⸻ honestly admitting their fears and personal inadequacies. They tend to deny negative feelings toward their children and offer them a false build-up to cover up their disappointment in their offspring. In general, parents attempt to keep "family secrets" well hidden, avoid open discussion of family members, and are particularly secretive about the subject of sexuality. Lastly, they are reluctant to communicate the truth about death and illness to their offspring.

1. *Parents can try to admit their fears.* In an effort to validate their child's confidence in them, many parents deny their fears, acting self-assured or putting on a calm facade in anxiety-provoking situations. Other parents tend to punish their children for being afraid, rather than admitting that they are anxious themselves. Most mothers and fathers are ashamed that they still have fears or phobias that tormented them as children and are understandably reluctant to admit this perceived weakness to their offspring. Children, however, can sense the undercurrent of anxiety in their parents and often take on their parents' fears as their own. Therefore, sensitive parents would talk with their children about their anxieties and fears in specific situations. For example, a father who was concerned that his children *not* be limited by his own fear of heights asked a close friend to accompany his children on hikes to the mountains. In addition, he openly admitted his long-standing fear to the youngsters. Because of their association with an individual who was not frightened rather than with a father who attempted to cover up his anxiety in the situation, the youngsters did not take on the fear. Instead, they identified with their father's friend and were able to go beyond the limitations of their father in this problem area.

It is valuable for parents to become aware of the detrimental effects of playing the role of "super-parent" or pretending to be on top of all situations, when in reality they are uncomfortable or afraid. Rather than attacking a child for being shy or uncomfortable with people, a parent might admit, "I'm afraid too," "I have a hard time being around people I don't know," or "I really feel awkward myself in social situations." We cannot stress too much the overwhelmingly positive effect on children when parents approach these matters honestly and forthrightly, as compared with the extensive damaging effects when they attempt to deny or hide their fears.

2. *Parents can try to maintain honest communications with children about parents' negative and positive feelings toward them.* When parents are frank, yet sensitive, in telling their children about their negative feelings toward them, the results are constructive rather than harmful. Usually, parents conceal their feelings and perceptions because they are afraid to hurt their child's feelings. Again, children are sensitized to parents' *real* feelings, and the lack of honest disclosure merely confuses them, thereby compounding the problem.

Parents can stop talking to their child in a dishonest and phony style that covers up their disappointment, disgust, or anger. Many adults speak to children in blatantly sweet, artificial tones in order to disguise their covert hostility. But sometimes parents are more subtle and appear to fool their offspring with their professions of love. The child, nevertheless, senses his mother's or father's underlying rejection or hostility, yet tries to believe the words. The resulting mystification can have profound effects on the developing child's sense of reality and mental health. Indeed, the greater the discrepancy between the manifest content of a parent's communication and its underlying or latent meaning (the parent's real feelings and attitudes), the greater the potential for mental illness.

Mothers and fathers can try to answer their children's questions about parental feelings candidly and sensitively, as this would help their children develop a strong sense of reality. Being honest and forthright with children about negative feelings toward them does *not* imply brutal frankness or insensitivity to children. For example, if a child seeks reassurance of a parent's unconditional love with a question like "Do you love me all the time?" the honest parent could reply, "No, sometimes I don't feel as close to you as I do at other times," or "No, I feel loving toward you at times and hateful at others," or "No, I have a hard time loving anyone all the time. Love isn't exactly like that; it comes and goes like any other feeling." If the child asks, "Do you love my brother and me the same?" a parent could answer, "No, I like you in different ways, for different reasons. Sometimes I like you more, and sometimes I like you less than your brother." It clearly serves no useful purpose to offer false reassurances to children.

In much the same spirit, parents could confirm their child's negative emotional responses to other family members without becoming cynical or gossipy. For example, if a child expresses an honest but negative opinion about visiting relatives and his father had similar feelings, the father could say, "I hate going to Grandma's for dinner, too," or "I agree with you that most of those relatives are boring," or "Grandpa really is grumpy and mean; I don't blame you for not liking him."

Sensitive parents would also follow up these candid appraisals with an appeal to the child's emerging capacity to empathize with others. The father in the example above might say, "Even though I agree that Grandpa is mean, we don't need to be mean back or hurt his feelings. Grandpa is in a lot of physical pain." "Even though our relatives are boring, they have their reasons and their problems." Although parents would help children to understand the cause of other people's foibles, they would not use this understanding to negate or rationalize the child's feelings. In this way, a child learns to be understanding about the weaknesses and shortcomings of others without compromising his own integrity in relation to his perception of family members.

3. *Breaking the idealization of parents and family through open discussion.*

> There is concerted family *resistance* to discovering what is going on, and there are complicated stratagems to keep everyone in the dark, and in the dark they are in the dark. We would know more of what is going on if we were not forbidden to do so, and forbidden to realize that we are forbidden to do so. (Laing, 1969/1972, p. 77)

Parents can try to represent themselves honestly and break the process of idealizing the family. It is not necessary to disguise their limitations in the child's eyes. Furthermore, it worsens matters for a child who has grown up in a less-than-ideal emotional climate to be told by relatives and acquaintances how wonderful and special his/her family is. This build-up serves no purpose and distorts the child's reality.

On the other hand, helping a child from his earliest years onward to develop an objective, realistic picture of his parents would contribute to the child's developing a realistic, nondefensive view of himself as well. When children are *not* protected from seeing their parents' weaknesses and inadequacies, they will not be as threatened in later years when they discover flaws in the personality makeup of their parents.

One advantage that the children of participants in our parenting groups have is that their parents have *not* sought protection from having their weaknesses or faults exposed. Parents are honest about their own limitations in open discussions with their offspring, thereby minimizing the tendency *most* children have to idealize parents and family to their own detriment. Hardly any of these children have had to listen to rationalizations such as "Your father really loves you, he just has a hard time expressing it," or "Your mother only has your best interests at heart," when, in fact, the father is indifferent and the mother controlling.

Parents can learn to communicate an objective view of their strengths and their weaknesses to their children; however, most fathers and mothers do not admit personal truths, even to themselves.

Hypothetically, if parents were *really* aware and open-minded about their ambivalent feelings, the things they would actually tell their children would sound startling and unnerving to the conventional person. In view of present-day cultural traditions and the level of "honest communication," these statements would seem to come from outer space. Yet they are fairly typical of the unspoken truths in family situations:

- We find it very difficult to be close to each other or to you. We often pretend to love each other. Actually, we confuse a strong bond based on desperation and insecurity with real love.
- We often make sacrifices for you, but not necessarily the ones you want or need.
- We have both a positive and negative stake in your success. We want you to succeed and do well, partly because we wish you well, and partly because your successes or failures reflect on us.
- To some extent we are phony and try to disguise our fears rather than admitting them openly to you. As a result of damage sustained in our own growing up, we are often helpless, dependent, hostile, or anxious, and sometimes lack personal integrity.
- At times we have angry feelings toward you which we are not proud of and try to hide. Sometimes we feel sexual toward you and are deeply ashamed.
- We demand respect from you, but often don't deserve it. We pass on our wisdom or lack of it.
- Although we may act superior or righteous, we are not really better than others, but fall somewhere in the middle of a continuum, morally and emotionally, in terms of integrity and strength of character.
- We are disturbed by differences between you and us and are especially threatened by your independence or unconventionality because it disrupts powerful defenses that are a basic part of our adjustment.
- At times we can be incompetent, unthinking, and dazed to varying degrees because of our defenses. At those times, we are indifferent and inadequate in meeting your needs. Unfortunately, in a showdown, we most often place our defenses above your well-being.

Of course, these truths are rarely, if ever, spoken, yet children sense their underlying reality. Nonetheless, they distort their basic perceptions of the truth in order to protect and idolize their parents. Children who experience this type of honest communication would undoubtedly feel some pain. Yet there would be a sense of relief. Their parents' verbalizations would confirm their own perceptions. This point was emphasized by a 38-year-old male patient while terminating therapy:

PATIENT: Before I met you, Dr. F., I lived with total mental confusion, not feeling or knowing who I was or what had happened to me to make me so mixed up. I don't know how to say it, but now I still feel pain and sometimes I still fuck up, but I can deal with it. I'm not lost any more.

Breaking into the basic defense of family idealization is a major goal of effective psychotherapy. Parents who want their children to grow up with a healthy self-esteem, without deep-seated feelings of being bad, could keep this principle in mind.

Ideally, children would not be deceived about important family matters or the personal lives of their parents. Secrecy and "white lies" about a family member's undesirable personality traits, physical or mental illness, financial loss, business failure, addiction, suicide, criminal activity, or death can have a lasting detrimental impact on a child. It is immoral to mislead a child about important family issues and about their own personal lives because of the resulting confusion. For example, to tell a child that his father is ill with the flu or that he has an ulcer when, in fact, he is an alcoholic does *not* protect the child from his alcoholism.

It is very harmful to disturb a child's capacity for reality-testing. To mislead children is comparable to bookburning, thought-control, or to the brainwashings of prisoners of war. Parents should try to overcome their trepidation about revealing "family secrets" to their children that their children can *see* already. The truth can be imparted in a manner best suited to the child's capacity to take in and comprehend the meaning of the information.

4. *Vanity. Fathers and mothers can refrain from building up their children's vanity.* Parents who are consciously or unconsciously disappointed with their children and sense their children's inadequacies tend to respond to their disappointment by trying to build them up. This phony build-up teaches children to compensate for real or imagined weaknesses with illusion. If a mother is dissatisfied with the

looks of her daughter, she may constantly reassure the child that she is beautiful. Or, on the other hand, she may exaggerate and overly praise other traits or talents in her daughter. If a child is not bright, his/her parents may tell him/her that he/she is "really" intelligent, implying untapped potential, or they may build up ordinary athletic prowess to compensate.

The process of offering false praise and reassurances leads to increased efforts on the part of the child to compensate for perceived inadequacies or weaknesses. The effects of substituting a build-up for real acknowledgment and appreciation are extremely debilitating. In addition to the damaging impact on self-image, building up a child's vanity is a manipulation to maintain control and to limit independence. The child comes to need this false support, learns to respond to it, and gravitates toward people who flatter him or her. As an adult, he or she cannot accept *real* acknowledgment or genuine appreciation or trust people's honest appraisal of his accomplishments. Furthermore, parents' exaggerated build-up of their child reflects their underlying desire or need to live vicariously through the child's accomplishments. Vanity is thus manufactured, and becomes a strong connection of the fantasy bond between parent and child.

The interests of children are best served by not asking them to perform for their parents and others. This is an important and fundamental prescription; staging children is very different from supporting them in their self expression. Exhibiting a child or showing him/her off often leads to feelings of shyness, shame, inadequacy, and fears of being exploited. Many adults who were forced to perform as children still experience paralyzing feelings of stage fright and are extremely anxious in formal or public situations. Still others become phony, always act as if they are on stage, and are deeply involved in preserving a facade.

5. *Existential issues. Parents could try to be more open with their children about death and dying.* Most parents avoid these subjects with their children. Instead, they teach children to deny their separateness, their individual identity, and their essential aloneness in the world. Because they feel protective and want to spare the child anxiety, parents teach their offspring to rely on destructive fantasy bonds that offer a false sense of security.

Many fathers and mothers try to reassure their children with platitudes that block out the painful feelings accompanying the child's growing awareness of death's inevitability. Statements such as "You're still young; you don't have to think about that yet," "Only old people die," "I would never let anything happen to you," or "People don't die, they go to heaven," that avoid unpleasant realities are damaging rather than reassuring to the child. When beliefs about an afterlife, whether true or false, are used as a means of discouraging the child's growing awareness of, and reaction to, a personal death, or end to life as he knows it, they function to suppress the pain and sadness associated with this subject. Rationalizations about death or dying have a repressive effect on the child's feelings that leads to negative consequences.

Parents can learn to communicate with their children about death at a level appropriate to their age and ability to understand the concept. It is generally accepted that a child before the ages of 2 or 3 has little comprehension of death (Anthony, 1971/1973; Jackson, 1965). From ages 3 to 7, the child progresses through a number of stages in his conceptualization of death (Hoffman & Strauss, 1985; Speece & Brent, 1984). During this phase, many children express the desire to never grow up (or grow old) because "only old people die" (Anthony, 1971/1973). From ages 3 to 5, negation plays an important part in the thinking of many children about their own death. They become aware that their parents will eventually die, yet they still feel exempt from this fate. This form of thinking is characteristic of this stage in the child's development.

Children come to realize that they are mortal, and they lose their illusions of omnipotence and self-sufficiency, sometimes more thoroughly than many adults. Sylvia Anthony (1971/1973) cited cases where parents' denial or a "modified negation" of death played a part in the subsequent development of neuroses in the children. Further analysis of these cases revealed that *allowing* children to go through the stage in their development (ages 3 to 7) where they become progressively more knowledgeable about death arouses considerable anxiety and feelings of anticipatory grief in *parents* (Dugan, 1977). However, fathers and mothers who are genuinely concerned about their children could share this sadness with them without offering false protection. They would not attempt to soothe or cover over the truth. There is no real "need" to. Paradoxically, by facing up to existential issues of life and death personally and telling the truth to their children, parents offer greater security.

When children approach their parents with questions about death, asking, for example, "What happened to Mr. Jones?" they should be answered honestly and directly according to the parents' own system of beliefs. Parents might say, "Mr. Jones died, and he is no longer with us." If a child is reassured with myths and beliefs that are contrary to the parents' beliefs by well-meaning relatives or teachers, a parent could tell the child, "No, we don't believe that Mr. Jones just went away or 'passed on' or went to heaven. As far as we know, he's gone forever, and we won't see him anymore." Parents can honestly communicate the fact that the process of dying and death is somewhat of a mystery. They could indicate that they do not have all the answers, without making the child feel insecure or fearful. For example, if the child asked if everybody dies, a parent could say, "Yes, we're all going to die, but I don't really know when or how it will happen or what death actually is. Some people believe there is an afterlife, but no one really knows."

Being honest with children about death puts parents in touch with sad feelings about their own mortality. This was demonstrated recently by a father's remarks after a painful group discussion about helping children cope with death anxiety.

FATHER: When I thought about *really* looking at my kids, looking into their eyes, I found I had a lot of feelings in relation to myself. It's really painful to look at Bobby, because I feel what it would mean to him to lose me. It's a really painful feeling. I feel that same thing with Jenny, too, especially when I feel close to her. That brings out the feeling. (*sad*) When I really feel like I love them, or like I make them feel good, I feel like I can't stand the thought of them losing me.

If parents are willing to endure the sadness and pain of acknowledging their child's mortality as well as their own limitation in time, they can develop a true sense of empathy with their children rather than becoming alienated.

In summary, in each of the areas described above, parents need integrity in order not to give children mixed messages. To preserve self-esteem, a child must maintain curiosity about reality. If his sense of reality is systematically undermined by his parents' duplicity, the child will probably give up on his perceptions and accept parental distortions. Nathaniel Branden (1969/1971) has pointed out the devastating effects of parental dishonesty in discussing the child's "will to understand" and its relationship to a healthy self-esteem:

A child may find the world around him, the world of his parents and other adults, incomprehensible and threatening; many of the actions, emotions, ideas, expectations and demands of the adults appear senseless, contradictory, oppressive and bewilderingly inimical to him. After a number of unsuccessful attempts to understand their policies and behavior, the child gives up *and takes the blame for his feeling of helplessness.* (p. 115)

Independence and Individuation

Families often promote a false sense of togetherness and an image of merged identity that is detrimental to the child's sense of independence. Parents should refrain from using phrases and colloquialisms that support an image of phony "oneness" with the child, as it detracts from his/her individuality. "Now *we're* going to have *our* bath," "Now *we* feel tired and sleepy," "Don't *we* feel happy this morning?" or other "we" statements. In this manner, they could avoid overidentifying with the child's pain and discomfort. Instead, they could see him/her as another human being who must face his/her own distress and hurt. Within this framework, genuine empathy for the child's inevitable sadness and pain emerges, and parents are better able to comfort the child without blending their own experiences with those of the child. For example, they would treat their child as they would treat a friend, with respect and regard for his/her individuality.

Enlightened parents can teach children that friendships are as important as family. Family relationships are often characterized by obligation rather than free choice. Many times, friendship is more rewarding than family relationships, because friends are chosen on the basis of positive, likeable qualities, mutual respect, compatibility, and similar interests. In many cases, family members spend their lives together in an unpleasant, disrespectful atmosphere that injures all parties. It is important for parents *not* to underestimate the therapeutic value of friendship and to encourage their children to pursue close relationships outside the family circle. Such attitudes as "You can only trust your family" or "Your friends will let you down but your family *never* will" are misleading and should be discouraged. Fathers and mothers can help their children maintain friendship by providing a receptive, warm home atmosphere in which the children's friends are welcomed.

Parents could choose to "let their children go." They can foster independence in their children and discourage unnecessary or prolonged dependency. Sensitive parents provide the appropriate amount of care necessary at each successive stage of the child's development, but not a surplus. They are generally aware of the functioning level of their children at different developmental phases and encourage age-appropriate activities and behaviors.[2] For example, parents who understand that a 2-year-old toddler's negativism is typical for that particular developmental stage will be less likely to punish this behavior. Instead, they will interpret these manifestations as a normal progression toward self-assertion and treat them accordingly.

Parents can encourage their children's initiative and support them in taking steps that lead to individuation. Overprotective attitudes are very destructive and restrictive and act to conceal hostile or malicious attitudes toward children. A number of clinicians have suggested that anxious parents who overprotect their child are often hostile toward him on an unconscious level (Levy, 1943; Parker, 1983; Rheingold, 1964, 1967).

Parents show respect for their child's growing maturity by allowing him to progressively take over his own life according to the level of his capability. Hopefully, they would not make the mistake of *underestimating* their child's capability and readiness to accept responsibility. At appropriate stages of development, youngsters can take responsibility for doing their own homework; choosing their own friends; solving their social problems, complaints, and arguments; selecting the foods *they* enjoy; handling their allowance; picking out their clothes; taking care of pets; carrying out their share of household chores; constructively and creatively using their free time; and eventually choosing their own career and life-style.

Ideally, parents would not foist their interests on their children; rather, they would expose them to a wealth of experiences and let them discover their own interests. They should not attempt to force or manipulate them into career decisions. Instead, they would educate them and review the different alternatives. It is valuable to assist adolescents in job selection by helping them to match their interests and aptitudes. Although most mothers and fathers suffer a certain amount of anxiety and pain as their children grow up, break bonds, and find interests outside the family unit, these feelings are usually counterbalanced by feelings of satisfaction and pride as each child moves toward greater independence. It is crucial for parents to "let go," or the child learns to equate independence with defiance and feels unnecessary guilt. Ginott (1965) succinctly expressed this basic principle in his book, *Between Parent and Child*:

> A good parent, like a good teacher, is one who makes himself increasingly *dispensable* to children. He finds satisfaction in relationships that lead children to make their own choices and to use their own powers. (p. 89)

In this regard, parents can reward children for speaking up, for saying what they see, for asking questions about so-called forbidden subjects. As noted earlier, it is of particular importance that parents refrain from reacting defensively to the child's perception of them and other family members. In general, good parenting practice would minimize intrusive behavior as well as diminish the placing of unnecessary prohibitions, surplus authority, and excessive rules and regulations that influence children to shut down or stifle their curiosity. In allowing the child the maximum freedom possible at each age level, parents are implicitly expressing a belief in the child's inherent potential for making healthy choices and his capacity for self-regulation.

Prejudice

Parents can try to avoid teaching children suspicious or paranoid attitudes toward others, either by example or by words. It is destructive to transmit critical or cynical attitudes, including prejudices and stereotypes, toward people outside the family circle. Prejudices toward people who are different from one's social, ethnic, or religious group imprison the child and lead to a feeling of distrust toward "outsiders." They create fear and suspicion that foster insecurity and interfere with the child's feeling at ease with people of different backgrounds. These negative attitudes, whether racist, ethnic, or sexist, cause distrust among people and support an isolated self-protective posture that is undesirable for the child's future relationships.

DISCUSSION

In addition to the basic ideas outlined in the chapter, I wish to describe the type of positive personal relationship or friendship that parents could choose to build with their child. It is difficult to concisely define the subtle dimensions of a "simple," nondramatic style of relating that we believe best facilitates a child's healthy development. One must begin by delineating the characteristics of a respectful, affectionate style of coexistence that *ideally* would be maintained by parents, between themselves, because their relationship is at the core of family interaction. Couple relationships are at their best when they are uncomplicated and nonrestrictive, and both parties are self-motivated, independent, and productive in their respective lives. In a "good" relationship, interactions are imaginative, not imaginary, with a sharing and concern for each other's individuality.

Each feels free to communicate his/her wants and needs directly, without expending energy in unnecessary power struggles or petty disagreements. Each is supportive of the goals of the other, separate from his or her own needs. In other words, a nonhostile, nonintrusive atmosphere exists in which each individual is "left alone," in the best sense, to develop his/her interests, talents, and identity. Parents would accept responsibility for their children without making them feel indebted and bound to them.

In light of all the problems we have reported in couple and family relationships, *is it possible* for couples to relate personally with mutual respect and affection in long-term associations once they have been damaged in their upbringing? Can they improve their contact with their children and influence them in a positive direction, when they (parents) themselves have learned to be defended? Our clinical experience shows that most couples and families have great difficulty pursuing this type of life together. Living a simple life makes most people painfully aware of their limitations in time, whereas melodrama serves as a powerful, all-consuming preoccupation and distraction from the real issues of life and death. In general, people conduct their lives in a style that is the antithesis of the "simple" existence described here. In their coming together, they continually react to present-day events and to each other with dramatic, primal feelings from the past (Firestone, 1985). Murray Bowen (1976) has suggested that when the partners fail to win the love they missed in their respective childhoods, "much [of their] energy goes into seeking love and approval and keeping the relationship in some kind of harmony; there is no energy for life-directed goals" (p. 70). The child born to their union is also expected to meet his parents' unfulfilled needs from the past.

With respect to child-rearing, Bowen (1978) further contends that

> the two person relationship is unstable in that it has a low tolerance for anxiety.... When anxiety increases, the emotional flow in a twosome intensifies and the relationship becomes uncomfortable. When the intensity reaches a certain level the twosome *predictably and automatically involves a vulnerable third person in the emotional issue* [italics added]. (p. 400)

In the resulting dysfunctional family, this "vulnerable third person" is typically the innocent child; at times, he/she is systematically excluded from his/her parents' relationship, while at other times, he/she is drawn into their destructive bond and becomes "fused" with one or the other parent.

Nevertheless, returning to our original question, can people make fundamental changes in their lives and their child-rearing practices despite the damage they themselves incurred in childhood? In spite of every obstacle, the answer is affirmative. A person *can* choose to expose and challenge his/her defenses, recover the capacity to feel, increase personal competence, and mature emotionally, therein becoming a very different type of parent. This must be understood as an ongoing project of serious magnitude, requiring extensive and powerful personal commitment. Indeed, people *can* improve the quality of their own lives and the lives of their children.

NOTES

1. Boszormenyi-Nagy and Spark (1973/1984) have pointed out the profound effects of guilt reactions experienced by young people attempting to free themselves from family ties:

   A simple physical separation and escape from the overpowering force [the oppressive ruler in the family system] does not really liberate the escapee. Much less can one solve the tyranny of one's own obligations by simply shunning the creditor to the obligations. A mass escape for fear of responsibility of filial obligations can infuse all human relations with unbearable chaos. The individual can become paralyzed by amorphous, undefinable, existential guilt. (p. 12)

2. For a comprehensive treatment of physical and emotional development of children from birth through adulthood, see *The Developing Person* by Kathleen Stassen Berger (1980). Other informative books include: *Social Development: Psychological Growth and the Parent-Child Relationship* by Eleanor E. Maccoby (1980); T. Berry Brazelton's books, *Infants and Mothers: Differences in Development* (1983), and *Toddlers and Parents: A Declaration of Independence* (1974); *Babyhood* by Penelope Leach (1987); and *The Growing Years: A Guide to Your Child's Emotional Development from Birth to Adolescence* by Mark Rubenstein (1987).

CHAPTER 12

Fostering Positive Parental Attitudes toward Sex

> To an individual filled with persistent fears, sexual activity is not a promise but a threat; he is predisposed not to sexual fulfillment but to sexual failure and frustration which in turn strengthen his fears.
> Joseph C. Rheingold (1964), *The Fear of Being a Woman* (p. 255)

Psychologists and psychiatrists are aware that a good deal of human misery centers around sexuality and the difficulties most people encounter in attempting to achieve and sustain sexual satisfaction, especially in close interpersonal relationships. This fact is not surprising, as people's feelings about their bodies, the acceptance of their sexual identities as men and women, and their experiences in sex are fundamental to their sense of well-being and self-esteem. A healthy orientation to sex is reflected in an individual's level of vitality, overall appearance, and capacity for tenderness and compassion. By the same token, disturbances in sexual functioning have serious consequences, affecting every aspect of a person's overall adjustment, including activities and pursuits far removed from sexual functions. It is important, therefore, that we focus our attention on this aspect of human experience as it relates to child development.

TRADITIONAL ATTITUDES TOWARD SEXUALITY

In socializing children, parents are operating under enormous pressure from society to teach restrictive values and narrow, even distorted, views of sexuality. Despite the advances achieved by the "sexual revolution," conventional views of sex still reflect an underlying attitude that perceives sex as somehow "dirty" or as a function that should be hidden or compartmentalized (Berke, 1988; Calderone, 1974/1977). Distorted views of sex promulgated by society's codes and mores operate in conjunction with the specific defenses and limitations of parents to damage most children very early in their formative years.

The majority of adults in our society grew up in families where they incorporated distorted views about sex. Consequently, as parents, they pass on these same biases and feelings to their offspring. In addition, many children—far more than one would think—suffer sexual abuses at the hands of immature adults who themselves were the victims of destructive sexual attitudes and upbringing. Furthermore, most children assimilate negative stereotypic views of men and women that they retain throughout their adult lives. These hostile and sexist attitudes cause dissension in intimate personal relationships and complicate couple interactions.

Religious beliefs that traditionally emphasize the concept of original sin often contribute to people's tendencies to renounce sensual pleasure and their physical nature in return for the hope of eternal life. This type of religious interpretation influences them to sacrifice their present-day life in order to insure an afterlife. In turning against the body and giving it a negative connotation, many people have paid an exorbitant price, because their actions have had a disastrous impact on their sexuality and on their personal relationships.

Unfortunately, in recent years, there has been a good deal of anxiety attached to sexual functions because of the threat of sexually transmitted diseases. The rapid spread of herpes and the incredibly destructive effects of the AIDS epidemic, a disease that is life-threatening, certainly intensify the anxiety surrounding sexuality. These diseases can be used to support traditional moral views of sex as being sinful and, indeed, as appearing almost as a plague visited upon the human race for being sexual.

On an intellectual level, most people recognize that "unhealthy" attitudes toward sex are functions of social learning. Yet these views continue to be passed on to children, often on an unconscious level, and continue to exert a powerful influence on the developing child and his sexual identity. It would be valuable to examine first the ways in which even somewhat enlightened parents damage their offspring in this important function, and then to outline an approach to sexuality that could ameliorate and prevent a good deal of unnecessary suffering.

In my work with patients and in observing people in their everyday lives, I have become more and more impressed with the universality of sexually related pathology in our culture. I began to develop a set of guidelines and basic principles related to human sexuality that applied to the issues involved in child-rearing. By considering the harmful effects of unhealthy attitudes on children's sexual development, a more constructive approach emerged that was self-evident in many instances.

DESTRUCTIVE ATTITUDES TOWARD BODILY FUNCTIONS AND NUDITY

The negative views held by many parents in relation to nudity and the human body cause the majority of children to develop a deep sense of shame about their bodies. The formation of a negative body image, in turn, significantly affects sexual attitudes and sexual performance. Indeed, how an individual feels about his body and his sexuality is central to his self-concept. Most clinicians stress this point in their discussions of the child's developing sexual identity. For example, in his book, *Human Aggression*, Anthony Storr (1968) suggests that a person's self-esteem is "chiefly rooted in sexuality" and goes on to state that "we cannot escape our physical natures; ...a proper pride in oneself as a human being is rooted in the body through which love is given and taken" (p. 69).

Clearly, infants and young children enjoy a sense of freedom and a lack of self-consciousness about being naked. By the time they are 5 or 6, however, most children are deeply embarrassed or mortified to be seen without clothes. We must question the wisdom of the basic attitudes imparted to children in the intervening years that make them feel so ashamed and self-conscious.

Negative Connotations with Respect to the Physical Body

If parents dislike themselves, have a negative view of their bodies, and are ashamed of their productions, they will inadvertently pass on the disgust and shame that they feel about themselves and their physical nature to their children. It is natural for a person to extend his subjective views about himself onto his creations. Therefore, only if a person feels positive about himself and unashamed of his body and its products can he project positive feelings and attitudes toward his child. In addition, there is the tendency in a person to disown negative attitudes about his body and to project them onto his offspring. This dynamic is graphically illustrated in the story one of my patients told me about his father:

As a teenager, the patient played on the high-school basketball team. One night, his father came to the game late in the second quarter. At halftime, the boy was changing into a fresh shirt when his father strode onto the basketball court and, in front of the youth's teammates and the entire audience, loudly berated his son for "undressing in public." He referred to the teenager's body as "skinny" and told him that he should be ashamed of letting people see him without his shirt on.

The boy was horrified and humiliated by his father's bizarre and irrational attack. His hostility toward his father was reinforced by this traumatic event. The incident had powerful effects and led to generalized feelings about his physical appearance and sexuality. After telling the story, the patient had many insights into other events in which his father had projected his own feelings of self-doubt and disgust onto his son and had punished him.

The effects of early training can be seen in the critical feelings many adults have about their body image. In our own clinical work, we found that most men and women have critical thoughts or "voices" about various parts of their bodies. Their internal dialogue during sex impairs their ability to feel and enjoy satisfaction. The impact of these negative biases can be seen in many other areas of dysfunction. For example, recent studies have shown that many young women suffering from eating disorders are seriously damaged in their attitudes, feelings, and perceptions of their bodies and their sexuality. Overeating and the resulting disfiguring of the body act to inhibit sexual responses. By *making* herself unattractive, the young woman wards off sexual desire and avoids relationships with the opposite sex (Weiss, 1986). This process is accompanied by feelings of self-hatred that can reach very serious proportions.

Anorexia nervosa is a particularly destructive eating disorder that can actually lead to starvation and serious medical complications. Most experts agree that the dominant aspects of the anorexia syndrome, so prevalent among adolescent girls, are related to "the girl's distorted perception of her body and bodily functions" (L. J. Kaplan, 1984, p. 257). Unfortunately, diagnosable cases of both overeating and restrictive food intake are on the increase and represent a cause for alarm.

Views of Sex as "Dirty"

In my clinical experience, I have found that virtually every individual has developed a negative point of view about the body, especially the sexual region. The genital area is frequently given a dirty connotation, exemplified by "dirty jokes." It is interesting to note that dirty jokes relate to either sexual or anal material and that the two are often confused. This distorted attitude often has its origins in early childhood. Youngsters readily pick up or assimilate their parents' feelings of discomfort and, perhaps, even disgust about children's body and bodily functions while being diapered and, later, during toilet-training experiences. Older children associate functions of the genital area with those of the anal area, which by now has a dirty connotation, and tend to develop a vocabulary of "bad" words to describe both functions.

Parents often reinforce the dirty meaning of certain words by washing out the child's mouth with soap when he repeats words they consider nasty. Bruno Bettelheim (1987) clearly spelled out the underlying message that parents succeed in giving the child when they use this form of punishment:

> Unconsciously, the child responds to the obvious message, that he said something unacceptable, and also to the implicit one, that his parent views his insides—symbolized by his mouth—as dirty and bad; not only did he use vile language, but he himself is vile. (pp. 111-112)

In more serious cases, the effects of having one's products and one's body viewed with revulsion, as well as having been exposed to severe toilet training methods as a child, can lead to a sense of being dirty, contaminating and self-loathing when one becomes an adult.

A 34-year-old woman, recently divorced, entered therapy complaining of intense anxiety states aroused whenever she contemplated becoming involved in a new sexual relationship. Her presenting symptoms included a deep, unshakable feeling that her physical nature, her touch, and her body were in some way repulsive and contaminating to men. She reported that during her marriage she had been non-orgasmic and had frequently refused sexual relations with her husband because she was superstitious that her touch was destructive to him. She said that she firmly believed that having intimate contact with her made her husband feel bad. As a result of this somewhat bizarre idea, the patient held herself responsible for her husband's alcoholism.

In talking of her childhood, the patient remembered that her mother had held extremely strict views about cleanliness and had bragged to her friends that the patient had been successfully toilet-trained by the time she was a year old. Later she recalled that her mother had also routinely administered enemas to her from the time she was a toddler until early puberty.

Long-term therapy was required to get at the roots of the patient's neurosis and the trauma that contributed to her belief that she was unclean and contaminating in the physical sense.

"Dirty" connotations about sex not only arise from the confusion between genital and anal functions, but also originate in the fear and dread that surround the awareness of our physical mortality. Human beings recognize that their lives, as experienced through the sensations, feelings, thoughts, and movements of their *bodies*, are limited in time. They are aware, on some level, that it is the body that grows old, gets sick, becomes feeble, and eventually dies. Unconsciously, they come to despise the body in which they are trapped and see it as a prison. Thus, a good deal of people's self-hatred and resentment of their physical nature and of their revulsion toward bodily functions is related to the anxiety they feel in relation to death (Becker, 1973).

Views of Sex as "Bad"

In our culture, many parents imply that sex is bad or nasty. At the least, they demonstrate implicitly to their children the fact that sex should be secretive and confined to a separate sphere of life. Men's and women's negative attitudes about sex come into play very early in the lives of their children. It has been suggested that parents' views and feelings about sex may be transmitted through physical touch and other patterns of response to the infant in the first months of its life (Stern, 1985).

Nancy Friday (1977) emphasized this point in relation to female infants in her book, *My Mother/My Self*:

> We have no models of a mother who encourages her daughter's sexuality. To ensure our little girl does not get any funny ideas, we present her with the right one: a *nonsexual image of ourselves* [italics added]. (p. 390)

Further documentation for this hypothesis can be found in Rene Spitz's (1965) book, *The First Year of Life*. Spitz contended that both verbal and nonverbal forms of avoidance, prohibition, and overprotection are used in "the battle waged against thumb sucking and...[later reach a] high point in the extraordinary variety of sanctions imposed on masturbation" (p. 126).

Within many families, parents rarely display signs of sexuality or indicate in any way to their offspring that they enjoy an active sexual relationship. Several patients remembered their parents' sleeping in separate beds or bedrooms; others recalled searching with curiosity through parents' belongings, looking for any sign that their parents had sexual relations. In the extreme, some parents are even reluctant to express physical affection in front of their children. Others, while subscribing to the view that sex is simply another function of the human body like eating or sleeping, nevertheless make off-color jokes about sex or sneer at couples who express affection in public.

Many parents state that children *should* learn healthy attitudes about sex, but very few discuss sex openly and personally with their own children. Some mothers and fathers refuse to allow their teenage children to attend sex education classes, for fear they will be wrongly influenced.

On a societal level, there is support for the mistaken notion that sex is inherently bad, and this concept still exerts a powerful influence on conventional secular thinking. In some traditional religious beliefs, sex is perceived as an expression of the baser nature of human beings. The damage perpetuated by this notion is incalculable, because such strict views of morality have acted in a repressive manner to stifle children's natural curiosity and aliveness in their sexuality and to increase their guilt about sex (M. P. Gunderson & McCary, 1979). Distorted notions of human sexuality have functioned for generations to alienate individuals from their bodily sensations and feelings (Pagels, 1988; Vergote, 1978/1988).

Efforts to restrict natural sexual expression usually backfire and ironically lead to an increase in human aggression and in immoral acting-out behavior. Judeo-Christian doctrine and other philosophies of self-denial that equate thoughts with actions serve to suppress sexuality and place unnecessary limitations on important aspects of human life. The process of inhibition acts to increase hostility (Fromm, 1941). The corresponding increase and intensification in human destructiveness has reached serious proportions. It is therefore pragmatic that normal, natural sexual feelings and impulses should be understood and accepted rather than be limited or distorted.

Restrictions on Masturbation

Although societal attitudes toward masturbation appear to have changed from negative to positive over the past five decades (Calderone, 1974/1977), many mothers and fathers still react severely when they discover their child masturbating. They believe that this practice is unhealthy, physically or emotionally, for their child, despite reliable information to the contrary (Morris, 1971; Planned Parenthood, 1986). Parental overreactions to masturbation can make the child feel guilty; consequently, the child learns to be secretive and inward in carrying out this activity. Enlightened parents usually make concerted efforts to avoid being critical or judgmental. Nevertheless, if they have unconscious guilt or anxiety in this area, their covert attitudes will still impact on the child, leaving him confused and self-doubting about this form of pleasurable exploration. Latent guilt and negative attitudes toward masturbation have a direct carry-over to adult sexuality. Some patients reported feeling that they were permanently damaged by masturbation and perceived themselves as being inadequate sexually.

Overreactions to Incestuous Feelings

Most parents tend to react overdramatically to incestuous feelings they have toward their children. For example, some mothers feel frightened of sexual sensations they experience when their baby is sucking at the breast. Paula Caplan (1981) commented on women's fears in relation to their infant daughters:

> A rigid mother who feels that any sign of sensuality is dangerously sexual
> is likely to put physical and emotional distance between herself and her
> daughter early in the child's life. (p.60)

Some fathers and mothers avoid expressing physical affection to an older child of the opposite sex because they are confused or alarmed at their feelings of sexual attraction. Many children are punished as though they are to blame for arousing these "forbidden" emotions in parents. Some fathers experience so much guilt in relation to the attraction they feel toward their daughters that they punish them for any evidence of sexuality. One father insisted that his teenage daughter pass inspection before leaving for school each morning; he verbally abused her, forcing her to change clothes whenever he judged her dress too short or revealing. This type of reaction is not an isolated example.

The fear of incest contaminates father-daughter and mother-son relationships far more than one would think. It is puzzling why there is such a strong focus and overconcern about incest in our culture. It is vital that parents realize that *feelings* of attraction are natural between males and females living in close quarters. Indeed, these are among the most natural feelings in human relationships. Although parents' acting out direct sexual impulses with their children would generally be harmful and destructive to the child's development (Biller & Solomon, 1986; Hambidge, 1988; R. S. Kempe & C. H. Kempe, 1984; O'Brien, 1987), unnecessary suppression of sexual feelings is also damaging. It is important that parents become more aware that fears associated with taboos against physical closeness between family members can effectively limit them in their ability to accept the child's expressions of love. The child internalizes a feeling that there is something unacceptable or unlovable about him or her and comes to withhold love and positive feelings.

We need not wonder why sex is a taboo subject for individuals who have grown up incorporating the distorted views described above. The unfortunate consequences of these learned attitudes and dramatic overreactions should not be underestimated. An especially tragic case history that exemplifies the pathological effects on a young boy of his parents' belief in the evils of sex and their threats of castration may be found in Flora Schreiber's (1983/1984) book, *The Shoemaker: The Anatomy of a Psychotic*. The book describes how a traumatic "lesson" about the "demon in his penis" set up a delusional system in a 5-year-old boy that later developed into a full-blown psychosis. Following routine surgery to correct a hernia, Joe Kallinger was told by his adoptive parents that, prior to the operation, "a demon, an evil spirit" had "lived inside" his penis.

Joe put his hand on his crotch, but Anna [his mother] slapped it away.

"The demon makes your bird [the Kallinger's euphemism for penis] get hard," Stephen [his father] explained. "It makes it get hard and stick out so you got to do bad things with it. Then your soul goes to the Devil when you die."

"Dr. Daly drove out the demon, Joseph," Anna said. "He fixed your bird so it will *never* grow big. Demons can't live in birds that don't grow big, so your bird ain't going to get hard, understand?" (pp. 27-28)

Often talking to Joe during his puberty and adolescence about the demon and about soft, small penises and goodness, the senior Kallingers continued to warp his sexual instinct....

It is rare to be able to pinpoint a single episode from which a psychosis springs. But in the case of Joe Kallinger that episode is clearly his symbolic castration...[at age 5], strengthened by the process of destruction that had preceded it and followed it. (p. 31)

Joseph Kallinger was convicted of killing several women after sexually abusing them. He related his story and childhood memories to Flora Schreiber, while being interviewed in prison over a period of several months.

A patient of mine who was a hairdresser related a similar incident. When he was 7 years old, his father ordered him to lie on the kitchen table, held a knife over him, and threatened to cut off the boy's penis if he ever touched himself. The patient expressed fear of becoming an overt homosexual, and was extremely mild-mannered, frightened of women, and fearful of competing with other men. Although these are extreme examples of damage caused by parents' pathological attitudes toward sex, the point can be extended to cases that are less obvious. In general, restrictions on children's emerging sexuality, resulting from either unconscious imitation of immature parental responses or the distortions introduced by conventional morality and prevailing social attitudes, severely limit them as adults.

SEXUAL ABUSE

Freud's Interpretations of Childhood Sexual Trauma

Incidents of physical sexual abuse and child molestation are far more widespread than previously recognized. Until recent years, however, a person could read through many books on sexuality without finding reference to incestuous acting out. For example, the authors of the book *Betrayal of Innocence* (Forward & Buck, 1978), in researching current books on sex, found no mention of incestuous behavior. Yet statistics show that each year more than 336,000 Americans are involved in incestuous sexual relationships (Sarafino, 1979). Alice Miller (1981/1984), in *Thou Shalt Not Be Aware*, has emphasized the conspiracy of secrecy that surrounds the topic of incestuous relationships and the painful sexual experiences that children undergo in their families. She repudiated Freud's concept of infantile sexuality and his utilization of "drive theory" to explain away patients' reports of being seduced by family members. Initially, Freud (1896/1962) acknowledged the validity of his patients' revelations. Later, he interpreted the frequency of these reports as fantasy processes that originated in the patient's own sexual desires (Freud, 1925/1959).

The most relevant point in this evolution of psychoanalytic theory lies in the fact that Freud's retreat from his earlier position has had a significant impact on the professional community. Many psychoanalysts have continued to advocate this point of view, denying the validity of their patients' revelations of childhood sexual trauma. In their denial, they perpetuate the harmful effects stemming from the repression and secrecy surrounding these all-too-common incidents (Coons, 1986, Masson, 1984).

Author's Views of Sexual Abuse

Adult sexual contact with children almost always has destructive consequences (Cavaiola & Schiff, 1988; Friedrich & Reams, 1987; Livingston, 1987; Tong, Oates, & McDowell, 1987). Yet this problem is complicated by the immaturity and psychopathology of people who themselves suffered from suppression and inhibition of their sexuality. In other words, the population of sexual abusers or molesters is made up of those who were sexually damaged as children and wounded in their self-esteem. Therefore, we must look for the sources of this social problem in both individual psychological trauma and in a generally sexually suppressive cultural climate (Conte, 1984). Furthermore, although acts of a sexual nature and especially instances of physically aggressive sexual behavior are tremendously damaging to the child, the consequences of these acts are further contaminated in a social structure where sexuality is distorted and where dishonesty and secrecy take precedence over genuine concern for the child (Conte, 1988; Haller & Alter-Reid, 1986; Newberger & DeVos, 1988).

I am familiar with two incidents of sexual abuse to children where the problem was treated with unusual sensitivity, rationality, and understanding by family members. Both of these examples were characterized by overt sexual overtures toward female children by adult males. However, because the two little girls were treated with kindness by adults who understood mental health issues, without alarm, secrecy, shame, and condemnation, the effects of the incidents were not as damaging at the time as they might have been otherwise, nor, in later analysis, was there evidence of lasting scars.

Sexual abuse that is physically hurtful is obviously destructive psychologically. However, even in cases where the sexual contact was gentle, psychic trauma may have been experienced by the victim, compounded by the secrecy and suppression surrounding this subject.

Certain forms of seductiveness on the part of parents can also be very detrimental to children. Parents who act out their emotional hunger place an excessive sexual demand on the child. Mothers who are seductive in attitude, as well as behaviorally, have an especially damaging effect on their sons. In these instances, the youngster feels inadequate and weak because he senses that he is unable to meet the sexual needs of a grown woman. Indeed, these experiences threaten his sexual identity, emphasize the feeling that his penis is small, and can become an important causative factor in certain forms of sexual dysfunction.

In one case, a woman patient's parents attempted to involve her in their sexual relationship. During the course of her therapy, as she explored the sources of her aversion to making love, the patient, Irene, recalled the underlying tension that was always present in her childhood home:

IRENE: After my last session, I began to remember something strange that happened to me as a child. It was a particular time when my parents had me alone with them, in some kind of a confined area, and they were teasing and taunting me about touching my father. He was sitting on a bed in the nude, and my mother was insisting that I touch his penis. I kept saying, "No, no!" and they both laughed uproariously. I think I was about 5 years old, because we were still living in Texas. Every time I think back on that scene, I know there was something sick about it, the way they were using me to try to have some kind of sexuality between them.

It was so strange, because I never saw any touching or any affection between them in front of us kids, and my father never held me on his lap or hugged me. I got a strong message that I was not supposed to say anything about this to my sisters or to *anybody*. It was like a family secret. I don't know if they tried this game with my sisters, because I was too afraid to ask.

After expressing her outrage and grief at being exploited, Irene experienced less anxiety in being intimate with her husband. It was apparent that her parents' use of her as a sexual object for their own gratification had contributed directly to her fear of physical closeness.

The recent hysteria concerning sexual abuse, including the mandatory reporting of suspected offenders by mental health specialists, while drawing attention to the problem and preventing further abuse in many instances, nevertheless has also had negative consequences. For example, in cases in which the offender is removed from the home by court order, the family may be deprived of its only wage earner and may face financial hardship in addition to its other problems. Also, it is unlikely that sex offenders will be motivated to seek psychiatric treatment for their disorder if they are aware that psychotherapists and mental health specialists must report them to the authorities.

Another problem exacerbated by the focus on sexual child abuse is an intensification of the general misconception that men are mean and bestial. Many adult women who were molested as children unfortunately carry a man-hating, victimized orientation into their adult lives. Sometimes women use these early traumatic incidents as a rationalization for their present-day problems and failures, a problem which in reality may be due to factors other than the sexual abuses they suffered as children.

In some cases, where the sexual contact was nonaggressive, the abused child may have been deprived of the only affectionate contact that was available in the family. Often the child attempts to cover up and disown his pleasure in and attraction to the sexual activity, and there is considerable repressed guilt. Furthermore, in revealing the abuse, the victim suffers the additional torment of feeling responsible for the breakup of the family. In these cases, the damage incurred by the child as a result of revealing the abuse may be even greater than the actual sexual contact. Indeed, a perspective often overlooked in the extensive literature on sexual abuse is the fact that contact with the abuser may have partially fulfilled a deep need for affection. Many patients, both men and women, admitted that they found some aspects of the sexual contact with relatives pleasurable and gratifying.

One woman recalled that she looked forward to Sunday afternoon visits with her father and the sexual play he initiated. Her parents were divorced, and the girl lived with a cold, hypercritical mother. The warmth and affection she received from her father felt good to her despite the fact that she felt considerable shame in relation to keeping the activity hidden from her mother. In retrospect, this woman felt that her sexual experiences with her father had a detrimental effect on her primarily because of the secrecy that surrounded them.

It is obvious that while sexual abuse of children is in itself a serious social issue, cultural views of sex contribute to and complicate this psychological problem. In fact, sexual abuse is partially *induced* by societal distortions and the restrictions placed on people's natural sexual development.

VOICES THAT SUPPORT SEXUAL WITHHOLDING

The ongoing effects of problems in the area of sexuality that we have discussed thus far are evident in the types of "voices" or self-critical thoughts that men and women have about sex and their sexual partners. This thought process influences people to hold back natural expressions of affection, sexual responses, and even physical attractiveness as a self-protective defense.

A form of implicit social pressure exists in our culture against being "too romantic" or affectionate after men and women marry, make a home, and produce children. Although romantic love and long-lasting, close relationships are a professed belief, the majority of marriages do not reflect this posture. This reality tends to exert an indirect social pressure on the new couple to move away from intimacy or sexual activity as the partners "mature."

At every phase of lovemaking, both men and women may have self-critical thoughts about their bodies, their performance, their perceived lack of feeling, and their fear of personal closeness. Women patients have reported voices, such as, "You're too fat. He's not going to be attracted to you. He won't be excited. You're not going to be able to have an orgasm. You're moving too much. He doesn't like touching your breasts; they're too small (or too large)." Men have revealed voices that criticized them with such thoughts as, "You're not going to be able to satisfy her. You're not a real man. Your penis is too small. You're insensitive to her; you don't know how to touch a woman." These kinds of negative thoughts about the self *and* about one's partner lead to nervousness and tentative or hesitant behavior that disrupts the free flow of expression between the partners (Firestone, 1987a).

WITHHOLDING AS A BASIC DEFENSE

An even more primitive form of withholding arises early in the child's developmental sequence. The child "learns," at a deep level, to hold back his positive emotional responses and expressions of affection because these responses are not acceptable to the parent. This form of withholding generally evolves into deeply ingrained unconscious character defenses. This process was evident in the case of a young mother who sought professional help because of depression and recurring anxiety attacks. She reported that she often experienced feelings of claustrophobia during lovemaking. In anticipating these unpleasant feelings, she had gradually lost all desire for sex. When she became a mother, she also began to retreat from her infant son and felt self-conscious in showing affection for him. When she was drawn to him, she would become frightened that there were "sexual overtones" and would pull back sharply, cutting off all feeling for him.

The patient had grown up in a home where affection was virtually absent, even unacceptable. She was unable to recall if her parents expressed any affection to each other, to her, or to her brothers and sisters. As a small child, she learned to hold back her own affectionate responses. Later, as a young adult, she retreated from her sexuality. In one session, she described the progressive deterioration in her marriage:

PATIENT: I think that when I got pregnant, I lost any feeling for being sexual. I started to give it up, way before he was born.

THERAPIST: You think it had something to do with having the baby?

PATIENT: Yes, definitely. I know after I got pregnant, I felt happy maybe for a couple of weeks, but then my sexuality changed. I wasn't as interested or as happy. It was harder for me to make love and enjoy it.

I just had a thought that I don't remember any time that my parents were affectionate or loving—they didn't seem to want each other.

[Later]: I was thinking that in relation to my own son, I don't have a lot of those kinds of feelings. I don't feel like rushing home from work to see him.

I know I don't have that special feeling toward him. I don't let myself feel touched to see him. When I hear other mothers talking about how they feel toward their babies, I know I feel like cringing, embarrassed, like saying, "No, no, that's not the way to feel."

THERAPIST: You're uncomfortable with that—

PATIENT: Really uncomfortable with that thought, and it would be especially uncomfortable for him to feel that way toward *me*.

THERAPIST: It causes you pain to think that? Why does it cause you pain, do you think?

PATIENT: Because I feel like I'm afraid to be loved, you know, I feel a fear to be loved—(*cries*)—for him to look at me and love me. I feel afraid of that, like a real fear to be admired. Because I know his feelings would be so sweet toward me. They'd be so genuine, and it really does scare me to feel that.

THERAPIST: Why do you think it scares you?

PATIENT: I never felt it as a child. I never felt it toward my parents, toward my mother. I never felt that way. It almost felt unacceptable to me to feel that way.

It was apparent that this woman's sexual adjustment and ability to express tenderness to her child had been seriously impaired by growing up in a cold and isolated home atmosphere characterized by lack of physical affection.

In most of the families I have treated, one or both members of the couple had become sexually withholding to some degree prior to the birth of their children. They had pulled back to more familiar and defended patterns of relating, warding off closeness and increasing their dependency and sense of being fused.

We have noted the phenomenon of sexual withholding throughout the experimental community described previously and have observed its destructive effects. The majority of women revealed that over the years they tended to suppress their sexual desires in relation to their husbands. According to other, well-documented sources (Gelman, 1987; H. S. Kaplan, 1979), patterns of withholding appear to be typical of many marriages.

In suppressing their feeling responses in general, both men and women specifically block expressions of their sexuality, because this is perhaps the most vital, alive, and spontaneous form of relating. Therefore, an individual who has cut off feeling for himself, who has withdrawn from investing in his life and retreated into an inward, self-protective posture, will tend, in many cases, to avoid or shy away from fulfilling sexual experiences.

Passive Aggression

One dimension of withholding is passive aggression. Children who have been mistreated or deprived tend to develop angry responses that they act out later in their adult relationships. Men and women who are angry at each other often become withholding with their partners as a form of retaliation (Justice & Justice, 1976, p. 32). They tend to hold back what the other person desires or needs as an unconscious act of aggression. It is a problem of some complexity in the analysis of couple relationships, because people are unusually defensive about these passively aggressive withholding patterns.

A NATURAL OR "CLEAN" VIEW OF SEX

In helping children develop a healthy orientation toward their bodies and toward sexuality, parents face complicated issues in light of society's restrictive views and sanctions. Despite somewhat more liberal attitudes toward sexuality in contemporary times, Freud's (1910/1957) commentary on Victorian society's repressive mores is still applicable today:

> Our civilized standards make life too difficult for the majority of human organizations. Those standards consequently encourage the retreat from reality and the generating of neuroses, without achieving any surplus of cultural gain by this excess of sexual repression. (p. 54)

It is very difficult to deviate from the social mores and values in bringing up a child. However, if parents learn to view sex as a natural and simple activity, they become better equipped to teach their children that their feelings about sex are acceptable, even though others think differently.

Children can learn to conform to societal rules without turning against themselves. For example, parents can feel an obligation to socialize their children, and still assure their children that there is nothing shameful, ugly, or inherently bad about the naked body. They can inform their children that there are many misconceptions and unnecessary prohibitions regarding nudity, and that, very often, restrictions were instituted by individuals who were uneducated or misguided about sexuality and the human body.

Parents can adopt a pragmatic approach to these contradictory sets of values. They can teach their child that, even though not necessarily agreeing with the values, a person must abide by social standards. In adopting this strategy, they are also implicitly teaching their children a nonconforming, independent point of view, while helping them to adjust their behavior to the laws and restrictions of society. Parents who wish to promote a wholesome attitude toward sex in their children and foster a healthy sexual adjustment in them, must examine their own attitudes and work through their own anxieties in the sexual area.

In contrast to widely held societal beliefs and attitudes that perceive sex as dirty or obscene, sex is a natural, pleasurable human activity. Genital contact and the erogenous zones are sources of pleasurable sensations, and almost anything that comes into contact with these sensitive areas of the body can be a source of simple pleasure. Sex is also a strong motivating force in life and has the potential for creating a deep sense of well-being and fulfillment. Making love is one of the most enjoyable forms of communication. The sexual act can be playful, sensuous, emotional, affectionate, serious, carefree, or a combination of these, depending on the mood of the participants. On the other hand, when a person is damaged emotionally or sexually in the course of growing up, sexual contact may contain sadistic or masochistic components and elements of hostility toward self and others (Stoller, 1975). Sexual experiences appear to be the most fulfilling when they are the outgrowth of affectionate feelings. Loving, sexual contact combined with genuine friendship in a long-lasting relationship is conducive to good feelings in life and good mental health as well.

CONCLUSION

With respect to child-rearing, most experts agree that children are by nature curious about sex, bodily functions, and the anatomical differences between the sexes. Parents who were raised in an atmosphere in which they assimilated a distorted view of sex can be reeducated about the sexual nature of children and the various stages in children's sexual development. It is important for parents to maintain personal communication with their children about sexuality and to answer their questions as forthrightly as they would about other subjects. Developing more openness and a constructive perspective on sexuality is the only way that parents can prevent their children from forming a negative view of sexuality that can have serious consequences when they become adults.

CHAPTER 13

Establishing a Pragmatic Approach to the Sexual Development of Children

Sex education starts with the parents' attitudes toward their own sensuality.... Whatever the parents' unspoken feelings are, they will be conveyed to the children, even if their spoken words tell about birds, bees, and daffodils.

Haim G. Ginott (1965), *Between Parent and Child* (p. 147)

In light of their own limitations, how can parents communicate constructive attitudes about sex to their offspring in a forthright manner? Ideally, parents can be educated to view the emerging sexuality of their children as a natural human function. They can learn to respond to the child's sexuality and questions about sex in a manner that is calm and nondramatic. In this chapter, we will discuss guidelines that are applicable to the issues that arise in the course of a child's sexual development.

INFANCY AND EARLY CHILDHOOD

Premature Sexual Stimulation

Parents' overt sexual contact with their children is generally understood to have negative consequences, yet other forms of indirect sexual contact with children can also be damaging.

Early in a child's life, many parents develop a habit of taking their baby into their bed to comfort him when he cries, and this response appears to have a soothing effect. In general, this routine is not damaging to a young infant. Before he is much older, however, it is important for parents to respond to their infant's crying, to comfort him, and then to return him to his own bed. Initially, the infant may remain in a crib in his parents' room, but later can be moved to a separate room. Parents can be cautioned about making a regular habit of allowing their child to remain in their bed for extended periods of time or for the entire night. This practice is more destructive as the child gets older.

As noted earlier, premature sexual stimulation resulting from hungry or excessive physical contact with parents can be detrimental to a young child, especially if either parent is using the child as a primary source of comfort or affection. According to many analysts (Kohut, 1977; Masterson, 1985; Miller 1979/1981), children of both sexes who are "used" or exploited in this manner feel compelled to gratify their parents' unconscious primal needs at their own expense. In her book, *Thou Shalt Not Be Aware*, Alice Miller (1981/1984) has discussed the effects of premature sexual stimulation on children:

> Sexually stimulated children cannot develop this essential feeling of trust; their center is located outside themselves, and they are always ready to comply when something is expected of them. (p. 129)

Many women make excessive demands on their sons for intimate companionship as a function of their emotional hunger. When a mother allows her son to sleep with her in her husband's absence and then shifts him back to his own bed upon her husband's return, this seductive approach has a damaging effect on the boy's development. This is particularly true when her husband is out of town. The attempt to use a child in this manner is experienced as a sexual demand by the son and intensifies the Oedipal conflict. Besides feeling inadequate, many boys develop intense castration anxiety and guilt reactions when they are substituted for the father during these interludes.

Similarly, many young women who have difficulty finding satisfaction in their own marriages revealed that, as children, they were the special focus of their mother's attention, to the exclusion of other family members. Often their mothers had poor sexual relationships with their husbands and sought the affection and companionship of their daughters to alleviate the disappointment and feeling of emptiness in their own lives. In general, the implicit demands of immature parents of either sex exert a pull on the child that depletes the child's emotional resources.

It is important that children not be exposed to their parents' direct sexual activity other than to expressions of affection or playful gestures that point to the existence of a sexual relationship. Directly observing the sex act or hearing sounds coming from the parents' room causes many children to misinterpret sexual intercourse as an aggressive or hostile act and may therefore be alarming to them. They typically misconstrue the circumstances and imagine that their father is hurting their mother. Thus, this kind of direct observation is best avoided. On the other hand, if the child accidentally walks in on his parents while they are making love, rather than registering shock, dismay, or anger at the child's interruption, parents could simply greet the child warmly, ask him what he wants, and then resume their sexual activity after the child leaves the room.

If children express curiosity about the origins of the sounds they hear coming from their parents' room, they can be told that the sounds are indications of pleasure. The couple can tell their child that they enjoy being close and affectionate, not merely during the day, but also when they are together at night in the privacy of their bedroom. Perhaps the only "trauma" that a happy, well-cared-for child would suffer in relation to his parents' sexual relationship would be a somewhat primal feeling of being left out of their private life or "locked out" of their bedroom.

Toilet Training

Parents can learn to start toilet training procedures at the appropriate time, that is, when their children are ready to exert physical control over their own bodily functions. In addition to proper timing, toilet training procedures should be handled sensitively to avoid injuring the child's emerging feelings about his body. Excessive control or domination, as well as an overconcern with cleanliness and orderliness, damage the sense of autonomy and sexuality of many children. This effect is compounded by the fact that during this crucial stage of their development, children tend to confuse anal functions and sexual functions. Therefore, a relaxed attitude toward toilet training is essential for the child to develop a healthy body image.

Several studies have shown that severe, harsh, or intrusive toilet training is correlated with later emotional disturbance. As S. Fisher and R. L. Fisher (1986) reported in their research:

> We have consulted with numerous parents who were concerned because their children seemed unable to meet normal standards of bowel or urinary control. *Without exception* we have found that such parents treat their children intrusively. They act as if the child's body belongs to them and they have the right to manipulate and schedule it in any way they think proper. (p. 76)

The age at which children learn to control their bowel and bladder functions will tend to vary according to the individual child's personality, his physical development, his parents' training procedures, and the quality of the parent-child relationship. Parents can wait until their toddler indicates an interest in going to the toilet himself (usually around 18 months) before proceeding with training.

As soon as children acquire the language skills sufficient to indicate their desire to use the toilet, parents can capitalize on their offspring's enthusiasm about their newly developed verbal ability as well as the pride they take in their productions. Praise and affection following success increase the child's motivation to ask to be taken to the bathroom at the appropriate times. Developmentally, bowel control is usually accomplished before the child becomes adept at controlling the sphincter muscles of the urinary tract, which generally occurs between the second and third year (Spock, 1976). Parents who are sensitive and alert to their child's verbal signals and other behavioral cues are generally more relaxed *and* more successful at toilet training than are parents who tend to be tense, controlling, or intrusive.

Children's Questions about Sex

In our opinion, it is best for parents to answer their children's questions about sexuality directly and matter-of-factly. Answers to questions from preschoolers (as well as older children) about sexual matters can be given simply, factually, and in terms appropriate to the child's age and level of understanding and sensitivity. Most 3-year-olds, for example, have already noticed the anatomical differences between the sexes. They openly verbalize their observations and frequently ask their parents for explanations.

It is most important that parents use the correct terms for body parts in talking with children, even with 2- and 3-year-olds. Medical terminology, slang expressions, "cutsey" idiosyncratic phrases, or inaccurate folktales, for example, about where babies come from, are best avoided. Children need not be given long, elaborate explanations, that is, more information than they asked for at the time. Parents who feel relaxed about their own sexuality generally try to satisfy their offspring's curiosity about sex as honestly and nondramatically as they communicate information about any other topic or aspect of their lives. Why, for example, would a mother feel embarrassed to answer her child's question, "What are you and Dad doing at night in bed?" any more than, "What do you and Dad do when you go out on Saturday night?" Both inquiries express a child's curiosity about the parent's personal life and activities.

According to a study cited by Planned Parenthood (1986), children and adolescents want information about the following subjects: menstruation, wet dreams, masturbation, intercourse and pregnancy, birth control, sexually transmitted diseases, and homosexuality. These authors suggest that many parents avoid discussing these topics because they are afraid they will be unable to answer their questions adequately. Other parents may simply feel uncomfortable with certain subjects. In both cases, parents can admit these feelings of inadequacy and discomfort to their children.

Nudity

A relaxed attitude toward nudity on the part of parents is more constructive than a restrictive view. Many new fathers and mothers wonder whether their children should be exposed to nudity in the privacy of their homes. Some experts contend that the sight of parents' naked bodies "may stimulate genital excitement and sexual desire that can never be fulfilled" (Ginott, 1965, p. 157). I tend to disagree that there are negative effects from a child's exposure to nudity in the absence of parental seductiveness. This fact has also been noted by observers in nudist colonies, nude beaches, and topless beaches, where the human body is accepted quite naturally. Nudity in these situations does not typically lead to unusual sexual frustration or sexual anarchy.

Other researchers feel that, at least prior to puberty, "relaxed attitudes toward nudity in the home are a much healthier way of educating our children sexually" (Dodson, 1970, p. 187). Parents can determine *their own values* and feelings about nudity and honestly communicate them to their children. However, in recognizing that their attitudes about the human body and nudity will have a significant impact on their children's self-esteem and later relationships, parents would strive to overcome any deep-seated negative views they still might hold.

In applying the pragmatic approach described earlier, a sense of humor helps dispel the mystique and secrecy surrounding nudity and can place the subject in perspective. For example, parents might talk with their older children about the ridiculous attitudes held by some people toward the human body. These views *do* appear ludicrous when one considers that the same people who admire nude statues as beautiful works of art find *real*, live bodies so offensive that they make laws against public nudity. Interestingly enough, there is significant variation in the tolerance of nudity in Western civilization. For example, a woman exposing her breasts on the beach in the United States would be stopped by the police or arrested, yet women throughout most of Europe enjoy this freedom with no ill effect or social reprisal.

By the time they reach school age, most children become somewhat modest about their bodies and express a desire for privacy when undressing or bathing, even in families where the parents have always held relaxed attitudes toward nudity. Therefore, it is helpful for parents to respect each child's request or need for privacy and not be insensitive, intrusive, or overstep the personal boundaries of the child. At the same time, they would discourage a sneaky or "dirty" view of nudity, bodily functions, and sexuality in their offspring.

Masturbation

Parents need to understand, on an emotional level, that there is nothing "bad" or psychologically damaging about masturbation and that, to the contrary, it is a natural and simple function. At the same time, parents can teach their children to refrain from masturbating in public, because the activity is generally disturbing or offensive to others.

Early in their development, children discover that very pleasant body sensations occur when they touch their genitals. When a little boy proudly shows off his erect penis at bathtime or a small girl confides to her mother that touching her clitoris "feels good," it is unwise to react with warnings about "not touching." For parents who still feel some degree of discomfort with this natural sexual exploration yet who do not want to teach their child to be ashamed or secretive about masturbation, it may indeed require tact and composure to respond appropriately and sensitively. Parents of older children have found it helpful to admit to their children that they may still have some old-fashioned notions about masturbation because of the way *their* parents reacted to them as children.

With respect to parents' reactions to children's sexual activities, Ellen Galinsky (1981), in summarizing interviews with a large number of parents in her book, *Between Generations*, has made an important point: "Questions of sexuality do touch a central nerve. Parents, in watching their own reactions, can, if they are willing, learn much about themselves" (pp. 170-171).

Sometimes adults discover that they have adverse reactions to masturbation in spite of thinking progressively about the subject. For example, one 5-year-old boy who absent-mindedly pulled at the crotch of his jeans was asked by his aunt if he needed to use the toilet. His reply, "No," failed to satisfy his aunt. Pursuing her line of attack and grilling, she then asked him why he needed to tug at his pants if he really did not need to go to the bathroom. The boy's honest response—"because it feels good"—caused his aunt consternation. In retrospect, this insightful woman wondered why she had such a strong reaction and questioned the motives behind her intrusive behavior. She realized that because of her own strict upbringing, she had become very uncomfortable when she noticed her nephew's casual autoerotic sex play.

As is evident in the case of this woman, parents' reexamination of their own attitudes toward masturbation can lead to a reduction in interfering responses. Parents do not need to place strict controls on children's masturbatory activities, because children develop feelings of modesty on their own. Usually, they learn to confine this activity to the privacy of their bedroom as they approach school age—without exaggerated pressure or commentary.

The fact that masturbation in itself does not present a problem does not negate the fact that *excessive* masturbation is frequently a symptom of emotional deprivation; that is, that important needs of the child are not being met (Lief & Reed, 1971). Again, it is not the strict focus on masturbation that is the issue. This symptom generally indicates that the child is attempting to assuage emotional hunger by gratifying himself as a compensation. In the case of these maladjusted children, compulsive masturbation serves the same purpose as excessive thumb-sucking and other self-nourishing behaviors.

Sex Play

Just as young children like to explore their own bodies, they also enjoy exploring and touching each other. Their curiosity about anatomical differences between the sexes leads them to initiate sex play with siblings and playmates. When parents discover children involved in sexual play or such games as "Doctor and Nurse," it is much better not to rush in with accusations or send the neighbor's child home and then commiserate with the neighbor about this "alarming problem." It is better to respond nondramatically to children's sexual involvement with other children the same age.

Parents can tell their children in simple terms that it is natural for them to be curious about each other's bodies. However, it is necessary to point out that acting on these impulses in public will generally be frowned upon by others and can cause trouble. A calm, nonjudgmental attitude on the part of parents will support a child's healthy sexuality, love, and friendship with the opposite sex.

Sexual contact between children who are peers is part of normal growing up. However, the case of an adolescent's involvement with younger children sexually can be the precursor of real sexual abuse. This type of situation must be looked at and understood in a broader context in terms of both its effect on the adolescent and the younger child.

Sex Play between Children of the Same Sex

Informed parents treat incidents of same-sex play calmly, as they do masturbation and other types of sex play. During the latency period, many children exhibit their genitals with peers of the same sex and engage in mutual masturbation. Most parents are more disturbed by same-sex explorations than by heterosexual activities because of their fears of the child's developing a homosexual orientation when he becomes an adult. Many older children and adolescents exhibit these same fears and doubts about their sexual identity. These youngsters need to be reassured that sexual play with a friend of one's own gender is not an uncommon phenomenon or an indication of future, adult homosexuality. Regardless of one's attitude toward homosexuality, interest in same-sex relationships or infatuation within the same sex is not an abnormal expression during the latency phase; therefore, parents need not be unduly concerned about these practices.

Homosexuality

The present controversy over homosexuality, whether it is a symptom of an underlying malady or a choice of life-style, has called parents' attention to the fact that a certain percentage of young men and women prefer sexual relations with members of the same sex. There are contradictory viewpoints as to whether the tendency toward homosexuality is biologically innate or whether psychological factors are involved in the etiology of same-sex preferences. Regardless of cause, negative and punitive attitudes toward homosexuality cause considerable misery and grief for persons engaged in this life-style. Parents can become more aware of the complicated issues and cultural biases concerning homosexual preferences and can avoid compounding the problem with prejudicial and rejecting attitudes.

In regard to conflicting views as to whether homosexuality is a choice of life-style or a symptom pattern, I have found that in the majority of cases that I have treated, homosexuality appeared to be a symptom of an abnormal, immature, or confused sexual identity or orientation. It did not appear to be a "free choice" or life-style. Basically, the majority of these men and women did *not* have a choice. Generally speaking, there were serious problems in relating heterosexually and an inability to perform. There were intense fears and considerable hostility toward the opposite sex. These patients manifested fears of being devoured by women (men), fears of penetration (women), hostility and unresolved rage toward the mother (men and women), extreme dependence on a symbiotic tie (men and women), and many other deep-seated problems that prevented them from engaging and finding satisfaction in heterosexual intercourse. Many of these problems were directly related to dynamics in the family that injured these individuals in their self-esteem and confused them about their sexual identity.

Although personality assessment tests have shown that homosexuals do not constitute an "abnormal" population in other areas of personality functioning (Dean & Richardson, 1964; Hooker, 1969), this evidence does not sufficiently confirm the viewpoint that homosexuality is merely a choice of life-style. Many homosexual and lesbian patients that I have treated have complained of a deep feeling that something was wrong with them and experienced a sense of unfulfilled destiny that went beyond cultural norms. Perhaps these emotions have to do with their obvious inability to procreate, because the significance of this biological propensity cannot be negated.

The prejudice and persecution directed toward these individuals by heterosexuals who criticize or condemn homosexual tendencies contribute to the homosexual's sense of being different or "freakish." Although this form of social prejudice is most reprehensible, unfortunately, it has been intensified recently by the AIDS epidemic. Further discussion of the issues related to the etiology and symptomatology of homosexuality are complex and beyond the scope of this book.

Sexual Molestation

Protecting the child from sexual exploitation is currently a growing concern of parents. There are many damaged individuals other than psychopathic child molesters who act out sexually with children. Parents need to be cognizant of the adults with whom their child comes in contact and to observe their interactions with the child. If, for example, Uncle Harry is seductively playful or excessively physical with his 12-year-old niece, her parents would not allow him opportunity to be alone with her.

Parents have the authority and the responsibility to limit their child's contact with relatives, sitters, and other adults where behavior is suspect, and, as far as possible, can try to prevent situations that might be overtly sexual from ever arising. Unfortunately, some fathers and mothers, afraid of hurting a relative's or a friend's feelings, fail to confront this issue, even after noticing subtle or not-so-subtle advances on the part of that person. In these cases, the parents could calmly but firmly discuss this type of behavior with the offending relative or friend and/or forbid the contact. This intervention is just as important to the child's welfare as informing him of the actions to take in avoiding and protecting himself against "strangers" who might molest him.

I feel at risk in emphasizing this point because I do not want to discourage adults from being warm and affectionate to children in a physical way. But there is a distinction between that type of attention and a sexualized attention, which is usually apparent to a discerning parent. Moreover, the hysteria surrounding sexual abuse has had a very damaging effect on child therapists and other people who work closely with children. Hyson, Whitehead, and Prudhoe (1988) stated that "even if their [therapists'] way of relating to children has not changed, their sense of ease about it has" (p. 73). Acting on this fear and self-consciousness may be very detrimental to psychotherapy with children. The situation poses a similar problem for teachers, day-care providers, psychiatric social workers, and other professionals who have close contact with young people (Hyson *et al.*, 1988).

LATE CHILDHOOD AND ADOLESCENCE

Sex Education and Adolescent Relationships

By the time they reach puberty (12-13 years), children need to have information about the human reproductive process as well as methods to prevent pregnancy. Contrary to the beliefs of many, sex education, including information about contraception, does *not* increase the likelihood of premarital sex and unwanted pregnancy (T. D. Fisher, 1986a). Indeed, T. D. Fisher (1986b) found that "children who can talk to their parents about sex are less likely to engage in sexual activity, and are more responsible in their approach to sexuality" (p. 525).

Most adolescents have received very little factual information about sexual matters from their parents. One survey (Planned Parenthood, 1986) of 625 boys and girls, aged 15 to 18, found that 65% reported that they could not talk to their parents about sex. They asserted that their parents often had angry reactions to sexual questions, teased them about being interested in the subject, or tried to postpone the discussion.

What do parents say or do when their adolescent boy or girl expresses the desire to begin a sexual relationship? Obviously, each individual case is different in terms of the teenager's respective age and emotional maturity. Ideally, parents would openly discuss with the adolescent the pros and cons of his becoming involved sexually, as well as advising him of effective methods of birth control.

A report by the Alan Guttmacher Institute (Dryfoos & Bourque-Scholl, 1981) estimated that there are more than one million teenage pregnancies in the United States each year, most of them involving unmarried teens. There are significant social problems associated with many of these unwanted teenage pregnancies in a complex society such as ours. The problems are serious because the majority of adolescents, for the most part, are not mature or responsible enough to properly care for a child. Furthermore, there are insufficient facilities and social welfare services to provide substitute child care for babies born to "children" or immature adults (Schorr, 1988). Thus, it is imperative that young people be given accurate information about birth control and constructive guidance about their sexual relationships in general. Indeed, parents may find this an opportune time to confide in their children some of their own experiences as teenagers, such as falling in love and facing crucial decisions about starting a sexual relationship. They also can offer guidance by helping them explore their reasons for initiating a sexual relationship.

Menstruation and Nocturnal Emissions

Parental attitudes about and reactions to menstruation have caused much unnecessary damage to women, beginning in puberty and lasting throughout their lives. Perhaps in no other area of sexual functioning are myths and old wives tales so prevalent. For generations, young girls have been advised by their mothers about the "curse" and have been told that it involves considerable physical discomfort, erratic mood swings, embarrassment, and inconvenience. Because of ignorance and lack of proper sex education, the menses are viewed by many as somehow dirty or contaminating. In many primitive cultures, a menstruating woman is taboo, and sexual relations with her during this time are strictly prohibited. This prohibition exists in modified form in Western civilization, as many women find the thought of having intercourse during their period undesirable, unpleasant, or, at the least, problematic. In addition, misconceptions about the emotional upheaval women suffer before and during menstruation have resulted in hypochondriacal fears and an overconcern with the changes associated with this normal function.

Recognizing the widespread harmful effects that incorrect information and distorted attitudes toward menstruation have caused, parents would feel motivated to impart to children of both sexes the knowledge that menstruation is a natural female function, a sign of the girl's approaching maturity and potential for bearing children. It is important for mothers to communicate to their daughters that menstruation is not something to dread, that there is nothing bad or dirty about it, and that it is quite natural for women to engage in lovemaking during this time. Indeed, many women are more relaxed and experience more pleasure during this time because they are less worried about conceiving.

Adolescent boys are sometimes disturbed by nocturnal seminal emissions when they first occur. Lack of proper education leaves many adolescents with feelings that wet dreams are signs of abnormality or somehow equated with bedwetting. In addition, many youngsters are embarrassed and humiliated when they have an erection and fear someone will notice and call attention to them. Parents need to prepare their sons for these events and discuss them with sensitivity and understanding. They can explain to the prepubescent boy that both of these involuntary functions are signs that they are maturing normally into young men. It is important to keep in mind that negative attitudes toward the body and sexual inhibition in the family have a negative effect on the developing adolescent, causing him to feel abnormally ashamed of these natural functions. In addition, many adolescent boys develop doubts about their masculinity and fears based on wrong assumptions about the size of their penis. These youngsters can benefit from talking with an understanding adult, as these worries are common. It is also helpful to impart information that (1) the size of the penis in the dormant phase is not necessarily related to its size in erection, and that (2), indeed, penis size is not so important in actual sexual experience.

Dating Patterns

Adolescent relationships need to be taken seriously by parents. In talking with young people about their friendships and first sexual experiences, understanding parents would be careful about depreciating the emotional investment their teenagers have made in these relationships. For example, referring to a friendship between two 13-year-olds as "puppy love" or as a "crush" is humiliating and degrading. Even preadolescent children develop deep friendships with their peers and are capable of strong loyalties and powerful feelings in these relationships. Relations with members of the opposite sex are quite serious and precious to them, and they have a stake in preserving these friendships which, during adolescence, become more important to them than their relationships with siblings and parents.

Adolescents learn to love, both emotionally and physically, almost in the same manner as they learn any other skill. This learning can be best accomplished in close relationships with real relating. Therefore, it is generally advantageous for a young person to be involved in relationships that are increasingly sensitive and close as he matures. On the other hand, parents obviously would be concerned about a youngster who forms a destructive dependency bond to the exclusion of all other peer relationships and activities. Adolescents need to be reassured that they are not sexually inadequate or frigid if they are concerned about performance or if their first sexual experience is not completely satisfying or fulfilling. They can be informed that, for many people, sexual enjoyment develops with experience, and that society is responsible for propagating views of sex as a competition or a performance.

It is important for teenagers to get to know a variety of people; on the other hand, it is also valuable for an adolescent to learn to relate personally on a deeper level emotionally. Becoming involved in one superficial relationship after another can be interpreted as a defensive maneuver or a signal that intimacy is not tolerated. There is no danger in learning to care for another person and no threat in being vulnerable. Many mothers and fathers are afraid of their youngster's vulnerability to hurt and fail to realize how important it is for them to learn to take risks in a relationship and to contend with the vicissitudes of being close to another person. This type of experience is an important factor in achieving success later on in a long-term relationship.

Adolescent sexual training emphasizes combining sexual feelings with other important feelings, namely, affection, empathy, and a sense of responsibility and respect. In my counseling experience with parents, I typically suggest that they encourage their offspring to have meaningful and sensitive contact with members of the opposite sex. In general, parents would support their youngster's sexual freedom, realizing that his sexual development cannot be separated from other areas of maturation, independence, and concern for self and others. Their adolescent's emerging sexuality would not take on a falsely dramatic quality but would be harmonious with other parts of his personality growth and development.

Discouraging Stereotypic Views about Men and Women

Sensitive parents make every effort to challenge sex-related prejudice and stereotypic thinking in children and in adolescents. They try to correct prejudicial views and stereotypes of men and women that are based on ignorance and habit. In our culture, girls typically have been taught that sex must be linked to love in order to be meaningful, whereas most boys have been conditioned to believe that sexual conquests are more important. Socialization with respect to these gender-role differences has contributed in part to the perpetuation of sexual stereotypes.

Enlightened parents would point out popular misconceptions, including the view that men are mean, harsh, unfeeling, and not as committed to marriage and family as are women; that they possess a stronger sex drive than women; and that, once aroused, they cannot control their sexual impulses. These parents would also counteract sexist views of women as intellectually inferior, childish, and unreliable, views that define and characterize women as being less interested in sex than men and as craving stability and security at the expense of self-assertion and independence (Frieze, Parsons, Johnson, Ruble, & Zellman, 1978; Gordon & Shankweiler, 1971; Sherfey, 1966). Indeed, we must question the point of view that women are more emotionally in tune with children and inherently more feeling in personal relationships. Men and women are very similar in their sexual feelings, natural makeup, competence, desires, and physical attraction to the opposite sex (Oakley, 1972). Minimizing these prejudices has a positive ameliorating effect on hostility and "the battle of the sexes." In addition, challenging sexist views has a long-range positive effect on couple and marital relations.

Research has shown that parents of older adolescents are still capable of influencing their children's attitudes toward sex (T. D. Fisher, 1986a). Therefore, it is important that parents not only communicate healthy feelings and attitudes regarding men, women, and sex to their offspring but also serve as positive role models throughout childhood *and* adolescence.

CONCLUSION

A large majority of sexual problems would never arise if there were not other, more basic disturbances in the parent-child relationship. Children who grow up in an emotional climate where they feel loved and accepted, especially in relation to their physical nature and bodily functions, would not develop sexual dysfunctions as adults or feel confused about their sexual identity.

If, for example, a youngster is fortunate enough to have a feeling of acceptance about his body and a healthy self-esteem, it is highly unlikely that as an adolescent or adult he would become promiscuous in relations with the opposite sex. Promiscuity is symptomatic of a basic feeling of self-hatred and a sense of "badness" and worthlessness. Similarly, if a small child is lucky enough to have parents who are neither withholding of their affection nor hungrily seeking him out as a companion to compensate for an unhappy marriage, we would not expect to find this youngster engaging in compulsive masturbation or habitual sex play. In other words, when mothers and fathers are emotionally mature themselves, they naturally provide the necessary ingredients for their offspring's developing sexuality. They implicitly impart healthy attitudes toward sex through a myriad of behaviors and communications not directly associated with sexuality.

Finally, deep-seated defensive patterns, including withholding, emotional hunger, covert hostility, and the intolerance of being loved that are prevalent in many family constellations, are determining factors in a child's developing sexual problems. Parents who become increasingly aware of the basic defenses and prejudicial attitudes that play a destructive role in their child's sexual development can begin to counteract the damage. Proper attention to these issues is a significant aspect of preventive mental hygiene.

PART III

THERAPEUTIC INTERVENTIONS

CHAPTER 14

Historical Development of Our Approach to Child-Rearing

My understanding of parent-child relations has spanned 30 years of involvement in the field of clinical psychology. My investigations have focused on the problem of resistance in psychotherapy. Data gathered in the course of this exploration utilized the retrospective reports of patients and volunteer subjects, as well as ongoing observational studies.

The most valuable and reliable source of information related to child-rearing has been obtained through the longitudinal studies of infants, children, adolescents, and adults in the reference population described in Chapter 1. The observation and interaction with the people in this setting have led to the evolution of important hypotheses relating to child development and preventive mental health.

SYMPTOMS RELATED TO CHILDHOOD EXPERIENCES

My initial work with schizophrenic patients has had a profound effect on my theoretical orientation and approach to psychological maladies. Early in my career I developed a specific interest in and focus on the psychological factors involved in mental illness. I came to two important conclusions that affected my future as a psychotherapist. One, I fully believed that painful events in childhood accounted for the majority of the symptom patterns in these people, and that their symptoms were an honest attempt, albeit peculiar, ineffective, or inappropriate, to cope with disturbed environmental conditions that *did* exist for the individual involved; that is, painful emotions and memories were fact rather than fantasy.

Two, no matter how terrible the personal impact of negative childhood conditions, there were strong tendencies to defend and idealize parents and families, particularly the mother. Close personal interest and involvement on the part of the therapist that challenged this idealized view, together with specialized techniques and direct symbolic interpretation, had a positive effect on these psychotic patients. These interventions led to partial relief of symptoms, gradual recovery of genuine emotional responses, and noticeable improvement in patients previously thought to be untreatable with psychotherapy.

SELECTED TREATMENT MILIEU FOR SCHIZOPHRENIC PATIENTS

As a graduate student, I was offered an opportunity to work as a psychotherapist under the auspices of John N. Rosen, a well-known psychiatrist who had achieved fame for his contribution to the treatment of schizophrenia. Rosen's method of treating disturbed individuals in a noninstitutional setting, where therapists actually lived in the same interpersonal environment with their patients, left a lasting impression on me. As noted earlier, the wealth of information gleaned from this situation was extremely valuable in developing and expanding my own ideas. My current work, which involves observing and interacting with a unique group of people in a social environment as contrasted with office or laboratory conditions, is analogous in certain respects to Rosen's residential treatment center and has reconfirmed the importance of this type of comprehensive psychological laboratory.

PSYCHOTHERAPY WITH PSYCHOTIC PATIENTS

The aim of psychotherapy with psychotic patients is to influence the patient to return to the "real world," to recover genuine feeling for self and others, and to replace the process of withdrawal into fantasy with personal goal-directed activity. Individuals who rely on fantasy become progressively debilitated in their capacity to cope with environmental conditions. They feel guilty for rejecting significant others while choosing an inward, self-protective life. In my dissertation, *A Concept of the Schizophrenic Process* (Firestone, 1957), I suggested that the level of psychotic regression was related to the degree to which an individual depended upon fantasy for "nourishment" and psychological survival, which was, in turn, a function of the degree of early deprivation and parental rejection.

> The schizophrenic process is an attempt to withdraw from socialization and preserve some integrity. It is a solution in the sense that the psychotic delusions, hallucinations, and fantasies seem to alleviate the intense anxiety and panic, and in the patient's eyes, act to protect and preserve his life. (p. 132)

The patient, in effect, "mothers" himself in his fantasies; that is, in his imagination, he is joined or connected to the mother. In this "self-mothering" or self-nourishing process, the patient is at once the "good," powerful mother and the "bad," weak child (see Chapter 8).

In our treatment of schizophrenic patients, my colleagues and I provided a substitute form of mothering that helped to compensate for the earlier emotional deprivation. On the one hand, we directly challenged and exposed the patients' fantasy and symbolic defenses, while, on the other hand, we gave emotional support to our patients that enabled them to progress through early stages of development where they had previously been fixated. The therapy approach involved a full-scale environmental treatment program in which every aspect of the patient's surroundings was mobilized to effect a cure.[1]

From this clinical experience, I learned a great deal about the split in schizophrenic patients that parallels a similar function in people at large; namely, a division in the personality between a strong, idealized, superior parental aspect that expressed punitive attitudes toward the weak, helpless child aspect. The division between the parental and child manifestations was discrete and clearly distinguishable. Each part had a functional integrity within the personality. It was clearly expressed in the psychoses in the form of hallucinated voices of a parental quality that continually ordered about, attacked, and maligned the patient.

PSYCHOTHERAPY WITH NEUROTIC AND NORMAL PATIENTS IN PRIVATE PRACTICE

Later, in private practice, I was able to trace the thread that established the link between painful experiences in early life, present-day unhappiness, and problems in interpersonal relationships or careers. This process of discovery was initially more complicated. I found that unconscious material was not as accessible, and internal conflicts were masked in these normal or neurotic individuals. The defenses of neurotic patients obscured the core issues, whereas schizophrenic patients expressed their conflicts more symbolically in symptoms and productions that we were able to decode.

INTENSE FEELING THERAPY

With the advent of a special investigation of over 200 patients in a therapy that focused on and stimulated the free flow of feelings, we refreshed our contact with the unconscious material that we had observed and analyzed symbolically in cases of schizophrenia. Our techniques to elicit feelings were based on the work of Arthur Janov's (1970) primal therapy. We utilized such methods as a period of isolation, discontinuation of painkillers (cigarettes, alcohol, etc.), and requests for patients to keep a diary about their personal life. Our primary method was to encourage feeling expressions in patients through deep breathing and letting out sounds.

Our new experiences directly confirmed our original hypotheses. As we worked with this novel technique, we were very excited as individuals experienced deep feelings followed by a flood of insights into their childhoods that led them to understand and interpret their own material. They were able to make clear-cut connections between very painful events in their families and their problems in later life.

A major goal of the feeling release therapy was to assist patients in recovering and reexperiencing painful memories and feelings. Prior to this experience, the people who took part in this therapy had succeeded to some degree in shutting off painful feelings of anger, rage, anxiety, sadness, or grief when they were young. In protecting themselves from experiencing emotional reactions that they found too threatening at the time, they had become disengaged from their real selves as the center of feeling, perception, cognition, and behavior. In disowning their genuine reactions to early frustration, rejection, and deprivation, they projected their anger onto others and tended to feel victimized and passive. In trying to numb themselves against their pain, these individuals had repressed their memories of traumatic incidents that caused them to suffer as children.

Method of Intense Feeling Therapy

Techniques to help patients get in touch with their deeper feelings were as follows: lying on a mat on the floor, patients learned to breathe deeply and to permit sounds to escape as they exhaled. They were encouraged to let out all feelings and verbalize any thoughts that came to mind.[2]

To varying degrees, all patients who participated in this psychotherapy were able to learn this technique. Some began sobbing immediately, while others moaned or yelled out angry expletives. In the following series of journal entries, Laura, a 39-year-old mother, describes the subjective experience of her sessions during the intensive phase of treatment. Her purpose in taking part in the therapy program was to gain a greater sense of self and to develop more equality in her relationship with her husband. She revealed that she usually deferred to her husband and denied her own capabilities and accomplishments.

This entry in Laura's journal discloses experiences and insights from her sixth session:

August 31—Session 6. I saw a hovering figure—my father—he has something in his hand that I can't see. He is menacing. The scene shifts from my bedroom to the bathroom and I am standing behind him. I am *very* small. I watch him shaving with a straight razor. He wipes the shaving soap and whiskers on a strip of toilet paper. I can see him clearly from the back. He is wearing his riding pants.

I ask him to notice me, I beg. He pays no attention. I realize that he never paid any attention to me—no one did. I was not sure I was real. I wondered sometimes if I had ever really been born. Or if I had died and was just imagining that I was alive. How could I know I was real? By making noise?—I had to be quiet. By pinching myself?

I still get a feeling of unreality. Also, if a situation is very painful, like a fight with my husband, I pretend that it isn't really happening and I don't react to it.

This session clarified some of the reasons why Laura hid from painful issues and events in her present life and took a secondary status. For the first time, she understood how she projected the rejection by her father onto her husband. This gave her a measure of control over behaviors that had previously provoked anger and rejection.

September 5—Session 10. I cried for an hour—it seemed like days. It was the deepest crying I ever had. I thought over and over: no one loves me. Then I thought: I will die. When finally I quieted, I saw my father bending down to look me in the eyes. He looked very sad. We were in my bedroom. He said (or I said) "I wish you were dead." *He* said it.

Then I was in his office in the main office building. I could see it very clearly—his desk, piles of dusty books, dusty saddles, a box—a small mahogany coffin for a child. Something moved across the floor. Then I remembered that my mother had lost a baby. (I thought it had been before my sister Jan was born.) But it was after I was born. They wanted a boy again and lost it. I felt guilty, as though I had killed it because I did *not* want it. I still feel guilty and like no one loves me, a lot.

In this session, Laura became aware of the guilt she felt in simply being alive, a feeling of shame and remorse she had originally experienced when her parents had lost an infant son. She was able to connect this guilt with her habitual pattern of deferring to others, especially to her husband. She realized that she felt her opinions were not important because she saw herself as undeserving and unlovable.

Still later in her therapy, Laura touched on themes related to the frustration of her basic needs as an infant—anger and frustration aroused by her mother's inadequacies and immaturity.

September 17—Session 20. I felt terrible loneliness and cried and cried. I saw my mother's white breast again, as in the previous session. I realized why I could see only one breast last time—only one was out of her bra—like a nursing bra. The breast sagged; it was wrinkled and empty. My mother wanted to be taken care of, rather than taking care of me. This made me feel sad and lonely.

Direct oral material of this nature is usually present only at a deep unconscious level and is not typically accessible through traditional psychotherapy with a "normal" individual possessing the ego strength of this patient. As in the earlier sessions, Laura interpreted her own material and was able to integrate the powerful insights she gained.

The material uncovered by patients and participants in intense feeling therapy sessions provided them with a more objective view of their childhoods and of their families. At the same time, these people developed a renewed sense of compassion for themselves from realizing how they had been damaged in their early lives. It was evident to the therapists who were involved in these sessions that something remarkable was occurring; virtually every person appeared to be genuinely reliving, with intense emotional reactions, incidents and feelings from childhood. We conjectured that at critical points in their pasts, these individuals had chosen *not* to feel the extreme psychic pain that they now allowed themselves to endure in the session. The majority developed intellectual insights that explained their current behavior.

We observed, as did Arthur Janov with primal therapy, that the personal knowledge gained through the therapeutic release of feeling was unusually pure and direct. People were able to recall childhood situations and could clearly connect the early trauma to their present-day problems rather than intellectually analyzing the memories. Unlike Janov, who felt that the release would eventually drain the "primal pool" of pain and lead to total cure, we valued this procedure as an important, but incomplete, part of the therapeutic process. In our selective use of this method, we felt that the regressive aspects of therapeutic release of feelings must be dealt with as in other therapies, as a significant by-product that must be successfully integrated for a favorable outcome.

PRELIMINARY INVESTIGATIONS INTO VOICE THERAPY

Our clinical findings were again validated by our work with a specialized technique termed *voice therapy*. In 1973, my associates and I became interested in studying the reasons why people overreacted to verbal feedback or criticism. We had observed that individuals felt deeply hurt when external criticisms, correct or incorrect, matched the negative views they already held about themselves. From these observations, we discovered that most people judged themselves in ways that were very depreciating. Consequently, their reactions to external criticism were usually more extreme than were warranted.

We thought that it would be valuable for people to become aware of the areas in which they were the most sensitive, so we began to investigate these overreactions in patients and in our professional associates. We formed a specialized therapy group, which was composed of a number of psychotherapists, to study this problem. This particular group became the vehicle for eliciting and identifying the

contents of negative thought patterns that were associated with maladaptive behaviors.

The participants in this group concerned themselves with identifying critical thoughts they had about themselves, as well as describing their reactions to criticism. Their discussions tended to validate
my earlier ideas about a well-integrated pattern of hostile thoughts
that I felt was present in every individual.

The therapists discovered that when they expressed their self-
critical thoughts in the second person as attacks against themselves,
they had strong feelings of compassion for themselves and empathy
for their fellow participants. These preliminary explorations excited
us and led to further investigations into the mechanism of self-attack.

In my office practice, patients in voice therapy began to uncover
similar thoughts, at times displaying considerable animosity toward
themselves. At first, we were shocked by the malicious tone in which
both the patients and the therapists attacked themselves. We became
painfully aware of how divided people were and how much they
sabotaged their own efforts to cope in their everyday lives. As various
dimensions of the voice process were brought to the foreground in
both groups of individuals, my thinking about this destructive force
in people's lives gradually evolved. Subsequently, I expanded my
study to examine more systematically various procedures that could
be used to elicit the voice.

A number of volunteer "subjects"—friends and professional associates—began meeting on a regular basis to examine negative attitudes toward themselves and others. As the participants in this new
group began to express their self-attacks in the accepting atmosphere
of the group setting, they often launched into angry diatribes against
themselves that were reminiscent of specific experiences within the
family. They uncovered core defenses and well-established habit patterns that clearly originated in traumatic circumstances. As noted earlier, the participants themselves established the connection between
painful experiences in growing up and unpleasant residuals within
their personalities.

These group meetings had a very important impact on these
individuals. As they became familiar with the process of identifying
their negative thought patterns, they were better able to control
the maladaptive behaviors that were strongly influenced by the
voice.

UNIQUE PSYCHOLOGICAL LABORATORY

Early in this work, we described an unusual group of people who became close friends because of their common concern with their personal development and their desire to build genuinely loving relationships within their families. A remarkable fact about this group of friends was that its emergence and expansion was completely unintentional. No person or group of persons started out with the purpose of establishing it; it arose naturally as an extension of long-standing friendship between members of seven families.

From this original group of friends, which even then, some 12 years ago, was made up of about 30 individuals, an extended friendship circle of approximately 100 individuals has evolved. The following quote from "The Psychotherapeutic Community" in *The Fantasy Bond* (Firestone, 1985) provides a description of this group:

> The story of this extended friendship circle has many diverse roots. Its beginnings may be traced to a fantasy that is probably common to all people, that is, a dream to share a better world with close friends. This fantasy was particularly strong in the people from this environment, though they never fancied themselves as pioneers of a new order. They saw themselves as ordinary people with a natural desire to find an atmosphere where they could be themselves, and where they could be generous and caring toward others....
>
> The people in the original families had, for a long time, shared in travel and vacations and helped each other out in crises.... The individuals came from varying backgrounds and had different vocations, including engineering, teaching, business, and psychology. Yet, they had certain common characteristics. Most were highly individualistic, independent, and had a lively interest in people. In general, they were sensitive, intelligent people with a good sense of humor, who enjoyed discussing philosophical and psychological issues. They were questioning of life and concerned with child-rearing and humanistic pursuits. They were not "joiners" in the conventional sense; in fact, they tended to stay away from structured social organizations and groups. Paradoxically, it was this group of individuals who formed the core of what was to later become a much larger aggregation of people. (pp. 345-346)

One important phase in the development of this unique "laboratory" was the formation of a discussion group made up of my personal friends and associates. When I had told them about some of the results achieved in my early therapy groups, they were enthusiastic about starting a group themselves. They had been talking together on an informal basis for many years, but the idea of meeting together on a regular basis was appealing. These men and women were interested in the concepts I was developing at that time and anticipated that this new group would fulfill an educational purpose as well as a therapeutic one.

Style of Communication

The individuals in this social milieu represent a remarkable reference population that has acted as an important source of our hypotheses. They have combined their intelligence and experience and have played an important part in our theoretical formulations. To give the reader a sense of the atmosphere and style of communication of these people in their group discussions, we believe it would be valuable to quote from an unpublished commentary by Stuart Boyd (1982), a psychologist and professor at St. John's College in Santa Fe, New Mexico, who visited this psychosocial milieu and observed the activities and participants for a 3-month period. His findings and observations are summarized in his *Analysis of a Unique Psychological Laboratory*. In the following excerpt, Boyd comments on a group discussion he attended:

> For approximately two hours there was talk such as I have never heard, in an atmosphere I have never experienced, with consequences beyond usual expectation. I have spent many years conducting group therapy with just about all kinds of patients. Every possible topic has been discussed in some way, at some time. The differences on this occasion are worth reiterating. ...
>
> 1. These are not patients—they are friends meeting together.
>
> 2. This is not therapy—people are not here because of significant breakdown in the ability to work, to love, to play, to communicate. There are problems, and some members are problems to some others, but all within normal limits. The effects of the meetings are clearly therapeutic, whatever happens, and there are occasions when a neurotic problem is dealt with by direct methods, but the intention is not that of group therapy as commonly understood. ...
>
> 3. [These individuals] come to the meeting as friends, they conduct and interact in the meeting as friends, they leave the meeting (presumably) (still) as friends, and continue to live in common contact. They *don't* bring problems *from* somewhere else, *from* other relationships known only by hearsay or report to the others, nor do they go back *to* those *other* relationships with their supply of insights and painkillers and correctives from the therapy centre.... The life they bring is the life they are, with those they live it with. ... (pp. 179-180)

[The next day I played the tape of the evening talk.] The turn-about in my thinking occasioned by the theoretical shift in the meaning and understanding of "love" and the effect it has on the beloved has caused great turbulence in my thinking. As always the relationship to the child, the eventual bearer of social meaning, and to the parents, the transmitters of that meaning, catches my attention.... I am...excited at the prospect of re-working my thinking and professional skills in the light of what I have learned. (pp. 214-215)

People's participation in the group discussions and informal talks has enabled them to work together in a remarkably harmonious way. The everyday arguments and bickering that routinely disrupt relationships have been diminished to a considerable degree. Each person's right to speak his mind freely is carefully preserved and cherished, so that an open forum for the exchange of perceptions and feelings (without fear of retaliation for what one has said) has been maintained without interruption for over 12 years.

Within these groups, an individual might choose to talk about any number of subjects: practical issues, dreams, fantasies, anger, fears, or perceptions of another person that would be relevant to that person's development. The participants have confidence in the process of change and seek from their friends realistic perceptions and feedback that they use as information to develop themselves. Their exchange of perceptions over the years has been of a nonconfrontational nature. Therefore, these men and women have developed an unusual depth of compassion for each other and a far less defensive approach to life than is usual.

Couple Groups

In our observational study of this reference population and in our ongoing participation with these people in their group discussions, my associates and I discovered that individuals experience the greatest difficulties and problems in their closest, most intimate relationships—in their couple relationships and with their children.

We observed that the majority of men and women appeared to flourish as individuals with a stronger sense of self and point of view during temporary separations from their marriage partners. Although they missed each other in the interim, they found that they regained a sense of themselves as independent entities and recaptured feelings of attraction for the other person; however, upon reuniting, they found they quickly lost their individuality and sense of independence.

We also noted that married couples related in a manner far different than friends do, and different also from men and women whom we had seen in our private practice who were involved in "love affairs." Married partners talked differently; they often disregarded each other's personal boundaries, were closed, defensive, and no longer friends or companions. They felt obligated, guilty, and responsible for each other's happiness. Many felt trapped and so were resentful and angry.

These men and women were deeply concerned about these habitual patterns of interacting with their spouses. Consequently, over the last several years, they have devoted themselves to facing these issues honestly and have attempted to work through problematic aspects of their relationships. In the couples' groups, which occur on a weekly basis, they are involved in the process of learning how to remain friends with their spouses on a deep emotional level. The impact that these group discussions have had on the overall lives of people in this friendship circle was also described in Boyd's (1982) *Analysis*:

> It seems that what is now stimulating, re-energizing, and moving the community is the insight into the nature of relationships as they constitute connections and dependencies and manipulations, versus equalities, freedoms, and responsibilities. (p. 135)

> These people I speak of look different, certainly, but it is a difference in the positive direction of the cultural norm—health, posture, attractiveness of presence and clothing, happiness, adventure, striking generosity and friendliness, success in most of the ways of life. (p. 126)

Boyd goes on to conclude:

> How the community lives raises some very interesting issues for moral and ethical philosophy...but as far as "conventional" morality is concerned, it's no contest—truth versus hypocrisy; manifest improvement in happiness and stability versus anxiety and broken, hating relationships. (pp. 127-128)

Family Interactions

We observed destructive behavior patterns, similar to those observed in couples, in the family interactions of people living in the social milieu. Family members were often insensitive and disrespectful to each other in their expressions and communications; they talked *for* each other, they interrupted, they avoided really listening, they tended to blame, mislead, and manipulate through guilt. We noted these same characteristics in the majority of the families we treated in our private practice. In their interactions with their children, most parents were removed, unaware, or indifferent, while others seemed tense, overprotective, and nervously focused on their offspring. In studying the effect of these parental behaviors on children, we noted serious symptoms of disturbance occasionally appearing in the first few months of an infant's life.

In their ongoing group discussions, parents began to speak about these issues. Their talks were accompanied by painful feelings of deep concern for the well-being of their children. Their concern led to the formation of parenting groups where they talked openly, in an atmosphere of acceptance, about their difficulties.

Within the forum of the ongoing parenting groups, we gradually learned more about covert parental aggression. The participants openly exposed and challenged destructive elements in their relationships with their children. They realized that they had extended their habitual, routine style of relating within their marriages to their children and that they often felt "connected" and possessive in a proprietary sense.

Adolescent Groups

In other group discussions, the children spoke openly about their feelings and perceptions of their parents. In the years prior to the formation of our parenting groups, a discussion group was formed for the older children and adolescents who had become alienated from their parents and who were experimenting with drugs. When these teenagers first met with their parents and talked openly about the emotional pain that they were experiencing in their families, the parents felt deep sadness. One mother still recalls the profound impact of that first group meeting:

MOTHER: At first, I found it almost impossible to look at my three children as the other teenagers spoke. One 13-year-old girl, Kay, told her father, a psychologist, that she wished he loved her the way he seemed to love her brother; she said that he would hug her brother but walk right past her without even noticing her.

It was many minutes before Kay's father could respond, but when he did, almost everyone in the room was in tears. He said that he had similar feelings when he was a boy; that he had longed for his father to show him some small sign of affection, but that he had never had the courage to speak up the way Kay had talked to him.

I thought of my own daughter, Jane, of the anxiety I had felt when she was a baby and remembered how I had believed I was a bad mother. Then I recalled my own mother and the emptiness I felt in her presence. I wondered if my daughter felt that same empty feeling with me. Later in the meeting, Jane talked of the lack of affection in our family and how it hurt her. It was one of the most painful moments of my life to listen to her and to the other children trying so hard to say what they really felt.

Over a period of several years, the talks with the adolescents have had a powerful effect on both parents and children. The democratic exchange of perceptions and the sincere expression of feelings that occur during these meetings gradually dissolved the boundary between the generations. Parental and child roles began to be discarded, and the adolescents related to their parents on a more equal basis. Because the group situation put incidental pressure on parents not to talk their children out of their feelings and perceptions but to listen and respond honestly, we learned a great deal about the types of treatment that were hurtful to these adolescents.

Considerable effort was directed toward educating the children about feelings. The adolescents and preteen-agers have used the weekly group discussions to talk about a wide range of topics, including their concerns with peer relationships and their emerging sexual feelings. In one group session, the subject turned to feelings of rivalry and competitiveness. In the following excerpt from this session, Kristy, aged 14, talks about feeling jealous of her friend Erica:

KRISTY (to Erica): I hate it whenever anybody says anything about your hair. Like how neat and how nice your hair is, how they always wish they had hair like yours.

ERICA: I know I feel a lot the same way. I feel jealous of your face. I feel like you have a really pretty face. And I like to think that you're *not* pretty. But I know it's not true. I wish I looked the same. I'm also jealous that you're tall and blonde.

Gavin, aged 13, continues the discussion by talking about his competitiveness with Jim, aged 14.

GAVIN: I'd like to say to you, Jim, with girls being attracted to you, I just feel real angry at you a lot. Just for things that you do better than me or stuff that I don't do as good as you do. Why are girls attracted to you? You don't do anything for them. I'm always trying to be nice to them.

AARON (aged 10): I have competitive feelings toward all the boys. I know that I feel kind of left out. (To Jim) Sometimes I say things and you go "ha, ha, ha," you laugh at me. (sad) That makes me feel really bad. It really pisses me off toward you. (softly)

DISCUSSION LEADER: Try to speak up.

AARON: I feel—I feel angry at you.

DISCUSSION LEADER: Let it out.

AARON: (*Louder voice*) I feel like you try to overrule us. And I feel bad because—like I say something and you make fun of me. You make me feel like a fool. I feel like hitting you, because it really embarrasses me.

Later, after expressing anger back, Jim talks about his underlying disappointment and hurt related to Aaron's rejection of his friendship:

JIM: I have more feelings about this. With you, Aaron, whenever I try to be your friend, you don't express any interest in being my friend. You always *want* to feel left out. I start to feel good toward you and I start acting nice toward you, and you just totally reject me.

[Later] DISCUSSION LEADER: How did you feel after saying these angry feelings toward one another?

ERICA: I feel relieved, a lot. Especially toward you, Kristy, because I felt a lot like it's hopeless—we'll never be friends. And I feel more relaxed too, but I *do* feel like we could be friends. I don't feel angry now.

GAVIN (to Jim): I didn't want this to hurt our friendship or anything. But I did feel relieved with what I said, and I don't want this to end our friendship, you know, I want it to enhance it. I'd really like to be your friend.

AARON: I felt better. I felt good to get that off my mind about Jim making fun of me.

DISCUSSION LEADER: If a person feels angry at you, it's not the end of the relationship. People sometimes think, "well, that's the end of it—somebody is angry at me or doesn't understand me. If somebody feels that way about me, then it's the end of everything." But it really isn't. Talking about these angry feelings, coming to understand them, can help you to really feel better friends after you exchange these feelings.

It's important to listen when people are angry at you. Sometimes they're angry about real things about you. Sometimes they're actually distorting you. They're not seeing you the way you really are. But in either case, if there *is* real information that's negative about you, it may even touch on something that you don't like about yourself. So it's a good opportunity to learn something. In some way negative feedback is better than positive feedback because it touches on things that you could change about yourself that could make your life a lot nicer.

These young people have assimilated knowledge about interpersonal relationships that many adults lack. They have learned how to accept and deal with "difficult" feelings that patients entering psychotherapy are made aware of by their therapists.

Beginning with the early talks among the teenagers and continuing to the current discussion groups, a forum has been maintained for the free expression of views, which has led to a more realistic, objective view of parents. Challenging the idealization of parents and families in this sympathetic atmosphere has had a profound effect on the new generation. Relationships between family members have moved in the direction of genuine friendship with mutual respect and equality.

CONCLUSION

It was good to see young ones present during the discussion. There seem to be no inhibitions or taboos of content or language among them, and they are learning the tales and anecdotes. The process of transmission through generations is preserved. The young ones are respected as children but are not encouraged to be falsely childish—and of course there is a considerable difference in the two conditions, a difference that the community is sensitively aware of. (Boyd, 1982, p. 75)

They are never given token recognition of their presence, and then ignored.... [They] have their rights for recognition and audience and serious attention respected too, and they are never brushed aside or cut off in what they are saying, or trying to say. The youngsters are such fun to be with and are the bright hope of the community. (Boyd, 1982, p. 70)

Tracing the relationship between the discoveries in the different treatment milieus as they evolved has revealed the common thread of our experience. We have noted such trends as parents' covert aggression and its effects; the wide range of emotional abuses suffered in childhood and the resultant symptom manifestations in adults; the connection between people's self-limiting and self-destructive attitudes and prior experiences in the family; and the negative effects of each person's defense system on his close relationships, most particularly the negative effect on children.

The sequence of ideas and therapeutic procedures that evolved *were a direct result* of people allowing themselves, and others, to *freely* express their innermost feelings, thoughts, and perceptions. The group continually emphasized and significantly valued growth and independence and tried to emancipate themselves from constricting bonds. The uniqueness of this population as a living psychological laboratory lies in the fact that the people here have attempted, often against strong resistance, to alter basic defenses and to provide their children with a better atmosphere for growth than they experienced as children. The friendships have endured and, consequently, the depth of feeling and breadth of subject matter discussed in their talks now exceed the level of interaction and range of topics in most psychotherapy groups.

Within this close circle of friends, over a long period of time and under a wide range of conditions, we have been able to observe each individual's life-style and personal relationships. In these unusual circumstances, we have learned about important areas of personal interaction, matters usually hidden or open only to speculation for therapists who are working with patients in the office setting. I feel fortunate to have had the opportunity to be involved with these people and their endeavors. Their overall willingness to remain open in spite of guilt and fear has contributed to the growing pool of knowledge about the defensive process and about methods to ameliorate its effects on future generations.

NOTES

1. Psychotherapy with schizophrenic patients at John N. Rosen's residential treatment center is described in the Appendix of my dissertation, *A Concept of the Schizophrenic Process* (Firestone, 1957). The dissertation represents an extension of the work of Rosen in applying dynamic theories and formulations to the treatment and understanding of schizophrenia. In the Appendix, I presented case material and notes regarding the treatment of schizophrenics using direct analytic technique. Other clinicians who have written extensively about psychotherapy with schizophrenic patients include Arieti (1974); Sullivan (1931, 1953, 1962); Fromm-Reichmann (1960); Laing and Esterson (1964); Sechehaye (1951); Lidz (1973); Hill (1955); Schulz and Kilgalen (1969); and Karon and Vandenbos (1981), among many others. J. G. Gunderson and Mosher (1975) and Strauss, Bowers, Downey, Fleck, Jackson, and Levine (1980) offer comprehensive summaries of current trends in the treatment of these patients.
2. The concentrated therapy consisted of daily, 5 times a week, 1-1/2-hour sessions that took place over a period of 5 weeks, followed by several months of once- or twice-a-week sessions.

CHAPTER 15

Therapeutic Approach to Parenting Groups: Preventive Psychotherapy

Working with and for parents in structured support programs has demonstrated to me that parents want to and will develop trust and are willing to modify their behavior when dealing with their children. My experiences have only served to strengthen and confirm my belief that children can be helped through helping their parents. What we do for today's parents has a great bearing on how today's children will live out their lives.

Vincent J. Fontana (1983), *Somewhere a Child Is Crying* (p. xiv)

The procedures of voice therapy permitted us to uncover the core of each person's negative thoughts and elicit the associated affect, which led to an integrated approach. Participants in the voice therapy groups became increasingly aware that the parental hostility and anger they had internalized under stressful conditions in early family interactions continued to have a profound impact on their sense of well-being and seriously interfered with their goal-directed behavior. Later, in our ongoing investigation of the voice, these individuals became concerned with the perpetuation of the destructive thought process in their children. They applied their new understanding to the problems

A modified version of this chapter was published in *Psychotherapy*, Vol. 26, No. 4, Winter 1989.

they encountered in child-rearing. In this sense, the parenting groups described in this chapter were a logical step in the progression of our studies and reflected parents' interest in initiating preventive measures to break the repetitive cycle. Their purpose in forming these groups was twofold: (1) to expand their investigations of the specific circumstances in their childhoods when they had incorporated negative attitudes toward themselves; and (2) to uncover behaviors, attitudes, and feelings in themselves that they believed were detrimental to their offspring.

In addition to utilizing insight to modify attitudes and behaviors, as in traditional psychotherapy, the participants in our groups are continually shifting from a retrospective examination of the sources of their limitations and negative attitudes toward self, to an exploration of the ways in which they extend these hostile views of themselves to their offspring. In other words, two processes are occurring concomitantly as parents investigate the links between their past and present on a deep feeling level. Their primary purpose is to interrupt the intergenerational transmission of defensive attitudes and low self-esteem.

PARENTING GROUPS

As noted earlier, people's interests naturally turned to primary concerns about child-rearing, as there were many births in the reference population. In the parenting groups that were subsequently formed, the participants (26 men and 23 women) became increasingly willing to admit their underlying attitudes toward themselves and the ambivalent feelings that they experienced in relation to children. This setting also has provided an extraordinary situation for a longitudinal study of family relationships.

THERAPEUTIC PROCESS

Our parenting groups were formed in an attempt to prevent the compulsive repetition of emotional and physical abuses by increasing participants' awareness of the damage they had sustained in their upbringing and its effect on present-day relationships with their offspring. A related goal was to help these parents develop a sense of compassion toward themselves and their children.

In this section, we will describe the procedures utilized in these groups to initiate the process of change and delineate the methods whereby parents increased their self-awareness and sensitivity to children. We will demonstrate how they changed basic attitudes toward themselves and their children and developed more constructive styles of relating.

Our preliminary studies of voice therapy procedures applied to parenting groups suggest its suitability and value as an effective form of preventive psychotherapy (Goldston, 1977). The format consists of parents' (1) opening up and working through ambivalent feelings and attitudes toward themselves and their children; (2) recalling painful events from their own childhoods; (3) releasing the repressed affect associated with negative experiences in growing up; (4) understanding the connection between their present-day limitations and the defensive patterns set up to cope with early trauma; (5) exposing deficiencies in their families, thereby breaking the idealization of *their* parents; and (6) developing more compassionate child-rearing practices based on constructive attitude change.

Expression of Ambivalent Feelings and Attitudes

Initially, parents presented problems that disturbed them about their children, particularly complaints relating to specific aspects of their children's lives that caused them worry or distress. Because they were relatively knowledgeable about the developmental phases of childhood and the age-appropriate behavior seen at each stage, the parents were alert to potential problems and symptoms of disturbance.

After our initial discussion of the presenting problem regarding their child, our next step was to bring out the negative attitudes that parents held toward themselves utilizing voice therapy techniques. We asked parents to state their self-attacks in the second person— "You're such a fool," or "You never do things right"—as though they were being addressed or spoken to by another person. When negative attitudes are expressed in this fashion, considerable affect is released, malevolent attitudes are separated out, and there is generally significant insight into their source. Parents found it relatively easy to relate to the concept of destructive voices and thought processes and were able to identify these thoughts in themselves. Spontaneous insights were formed concerning parents' own childhoods, and they became cognizant of how they projected their negative qualities onto their children. For example, in a group discussion, Jerry revealed his negative attitudes toward himself:

JERRY: The main attack I make on myself is: (VOICE) *What kind of man do you think you are?* You can't do anything. *You are worse than a kid!* A kid can do more than you. You have never grown up. Yeah, you had a son, so it just happened (*sarcastic, snide tone*). Big thing! It was by mistake. You're still a kid. *Don't you realize that a kid can't have sexuality?*

In a later family session, Bill, Jerry's 25-year-old son, brought out *his* voice attacks, which were very similar to those of his father:

BILL: (VOICE) You are so disgusting. *What makes you think a woman could be attracted to you?* (*sarcastic, baiting tone*) You have no features that could be attractive to a woman. You're ugly. *You're short. You're small.*

Jerry recognized that he had projected his own derisive view of himself as a man onto his son and was able to see how this attitude had affected the young man's adjustment. Bill developed insight and understanding of the source of his insecurity with women.

After the parents expressed their self-attacks, we encouraged them to reveal their ambivalent reactions toward their children and to identify the specific circumstances, situations, and types of behavior in their children that aroused hostile or aggressive feelings. The participants then made connections between their self-attacks and the hostile attitudes manifested toward their children.

Gary, who was raised by a harsh, authoritarian father, spoke about the intense emotional reactions he had toward his son Doug, whenever he sensed the youngster was frightened of trying something new.

GARY: With Doug, it would be any situation where I would want him to do something and he wouldn't want to do it. He would say either that he didn't want to do it, or that he didn't know how; he was awkward about it—whatever it was. But I thought that he *could* and *should* do it. When he wouldn't do it, I would get so angry, because—(*pause*).

I know that I have this feeling in myself that if I feel like I'm supposed to be able to do something, then I've *got to do it!* (*angry tone*) And if I can't do it or even don't want to do it, I feel so critical of myself for not doing it. I would be exactly the same way with him. I would feel furious because he wouldn't do it, and then I felt like it was some basic failure in his life and failure in my parenting him—that I had to make him really do it.

It became crucial. Those were the most fierce times, things like "cut your meat the right way" or "you just climb that ladder, you can climb it." (*Yelling*) *"Climb the ladder!"* And he would be afraid...(*sad*) Thinking about it like this, I know I have exactly the same set of feelings toward myself.

While describing the turbulent feelings aroused in him by the boy's timidity, Gary recalled feeling terrified as a child by his own father in similar situations. However, not until he talked about the specific characteristics and behaviors in his son that had triggered his fury did he develop insight into both himself and their relationship. Connecting his own self-critical attitudes with the harsh feelings he had toward his son led to a sense of kinship with the boy.

In talking about the tendency to project negative feelings onto their children, several parents revealed the origins of their own self-depreciating attitudes. For example, Sonya talks here about feelings she has in relation to her younger son.

SONYA: I see him as odd. There's something wrong with him. It's a deep feeling, like I would say to him "There is something wrong with you." A strong attack on him—"Look right, straighten up." "Sit up, look right, change that face." (*cries*) (*deep sobs*) When I said that, I felt it switch from him to myself. You know, "Change your face." I know that was done to me. (*cries*)

   It was "Don't let it show." But really angry, "Just don't let anything show, don't let your feelings show." I have an image of him that he's sort of miserable, cut off and a misfit. I really see him as a misfit.

The following transcribed material is part of an actual parenting group session. This segment illustrates the kind of issues typically discussed and exemplifies the procedures at this stage in the therapeutic process.

R.Z. (father of two children): I was thinking about a specific situation where *I feel really uncomfortable with Danny.* If he's doing something that I don't like, if he's making a big mess or something like that, I'll try to get him to stop doing it, sort of disciplining him, like saying (loudly) *"Don't do that!"* But I come away from the situation regardless of the outcome feeling bad and questioning myself. I think partly it's because *I'm afraid I'm giving him a feeling like I felt when I was a kid, that he's bad.*

DR. F.: Passing on the same kind of feeling that you had toward yourself.

R.Z.: Exactly. The way that I felt about myself as a kid. I felt that I had to have good manners and that I had to really behave myself in order to be liked at all. That I was basically bad and I had to compensate for that, in order to get love.

C.M. (mother of two sons): I know that when you said that, the first feeling I had was for myself. It was *a really painful feeling of being defined like that and feeling I was bad. And it was easy to see in my feelings, particularly toward Johnny—he was bad, and everything he did was bad.* I know I put that on him strongly and it has hampered his life. It really has.

DR. F.: He's still the bad boy, and he thinks of himself that way.

R.Z.: It's very different than I would usually act. With someone else's kids, I'd say "Hey, come here," and the kid turns around and laughs or turns the other way, it doesn't matter. I wouldn't tend to make a big deal of it. But with my own kids, I do feel an obligation to stop it at all costs. It's a strong feeling that if I don't stop this, no one will. He'd *better* listen!

DR. F.: This type of showdown often brings out the very worst in the parents, behavior that they saw in *their* parents—crazy, angry, almost violent, sometimes physical beatings. It happens probably in most families at one time or another. It's so prevalent, it seems. Yet it's the very thing that we would say contradicts our values. Let's say we want our child to be independent, to have his own point of view, to have a strong sense of self, and here in the most primitive showdown with him, we give him "the business" or make him submit. We act very much out of character from the way we normally act.

J.S. (35-year-old woman with no children): I've learned much more recently about being with children from my friends. The first time you [husband] suggested we take one of the little kids to the movies, I was horrified. My parents were always shutting me up in public, so I was afraid the kids would disturb the movie or something. I was already acting under the premise that they're going to be bad. Like what R.Z. was saying, at different times I'd have a rage that would pop up in me, and then I'd notice somebody handling it differently than I would. So I've learned to do it that way. I don't have the rage anymore. But I thought that my parents had that rage towards me. Anything that I had an independent view on or if I might make somebody notice me in a crowd, they just were constantly irritated at me. The subject made me sad.

DR. F.: People are getting a perspective by watching others and getting some sense of what a child is, and they're beginning to relate more consciously to the fact that these things hurt them so much, these experiences, and to try not to get caught up in the automatic repetition of that, which is the key problem.

The participants reported experiencing a sense of relief from the guilt and remorse they had felt about their behavior toward their children after disclosing their negative attitudes and actions in the accepting, nonjudgmental atmosphere of the group. They observed that others revealed similar feelings of hostility and anger toward *their* children and therefore did not feel peculiar or different. Guilt feelings were further ameliorated by parents adopting new, more progressive attitudes and positive courses of action rather than feeling depressed and defeated about the state of their child's maladjustment.

Recall of Painful Events

We then asked parents to remember and refer to experiences in their families that had caused them pain and stress. They were encouraged to recall the specific incidents of abuse, both verbal and physical, to which they had been exposed as children and to share their emotions. The specific forms of psychological maltreatment that they reported included: indifference and coldness on the part of their parents, punitive attitudes and cruelty under the guise of discipline and socialization, threats of abandonment and loss of their parents' love, ridicule, name-calling, condescending ways of being spoken to, and misleading distortions of reality.

Many of the men and women who revealed the everyday, typical abuses they endured in their families emphasized the fact that the contradictory messages, the pretense, and the deception of their parents were often more hurtful and confusing than their parents' overt hostility or rejection. For example, one young woman described the humiliation she felt when she discovered her parents had deceived her about her placement in a "special" class for educationally handicapped children at school.

ELAINE: I must have spent hours and hours with my parents at parent-teacher conferences. I was failing in school, but nobody talked to me about it. They would say, "She doesn't read well." "Her attention span is bad." I felt like I knew what was wrong but no one ever asked me.

  It got to the point where my parents lied. One time, I thought I was doing better and I was really excited. I was in a class that I thought was normal, just a regular class and I was doing really well. Then they had this open house and I helped host it. That night I found out from someone at the open house that it was a "special" class for slow children. I never did well after that. I was shot down; they had acted as though they had put me in a regular class and had never talked the true situation over with me.

In another instance, Mrs. J. remembered being deceived about the death of her pet, and then being cruelly teased for believing the lies her parents told her:

MRS. J.: I remember I had a boxer, Sam, that I got when I was in the sixth grade. I got the flu, and my parents told me that Sam had gone to the vet's while I was sick. I kept asking every day, "Where's Sam?" And they kept saying, "He's at the vet's." And then one day I confronted my father and I said, "Look, where's Sam?" And he started laughing. He said, "Well, he died, you idiot! Couldn't you have guessed?" But it was such a shock, because I really believed them—that he was at the vet's. It was so painful. I really loved that dog.

As the participants revealed traumatic incidents from their childhoods, they became aware of almost uncanny parallels between the specific abuses they had suffered in their development and their own faulty patterns of child-rearing. For example, one woman, Mrs. C., described being abandoned by her mother when she was 2 years old. (This case study is documented in Chapter 6.) In a repetition of the mother's desertion, Mrs. C. had left her own son when he was a toddler, after she became frightened of the strong aggressive impulses that she felt toward him. At the time, however, she failed to connect the two events in her mind. Later, in sharing her experiences with others in the parenting group, she recognized the full impact of her mother's desertion and realized that she had unconsciously and compulsively repeated her mother's pattern. She also recognized that she had somehow blamed herself for her mother's desertion and had experienced intense feelings of anger toward herself. When she became a mother, this repressed rage emerged and was extended to her small son, causing extreme anxiety.

It is important to note that Mrs. C.'s feelings of rage were divided into two components: (1) the anger and sadistic feelings her mother felt *toward* her as a child were directly incorporated or internalized; and (2) the suppressed frustration, hurt, and outrage that Mrs. C. felt back toward her mother were redirected or turned against herself in the form of self-hatred. This reaction is often the case. At the time the child suffers abuse, the anger felt by the child *toward* the punitive parent is not expressed because of the child's fear of annihilation or retaliation. In addition, rage reactions are associated with a fear of total ego disintegration and a dread of losing the parent. The child equates death wishes with actual destruction and subsequent loss of a dependency object.

In another group meeting, a father talked about his inability to "be himself" or "be natural" in interactions with his 3-year-old son. As he explored the reasons behind his awkwardness, he began to remember details of his own childhood and how he had felt at that age:

J.B.: I noticed that I can actually have more closeness with adults than I can with Scott. I have a superstition that when Scott is older that I'll be able to get closer to him. So I've been searching to find out why I have those thoughts.

I thought that I was avoiding Scott in the same way that I was avoided, and that I wouldn't give to him something that I didn't get for myself. Then I started to remember that my father wasn't there from the time that I was one until I was about four. He was away during the war and then when he finally came home, he got so busy at work, he was hardly ever home.

It's very rare that I ever have any real relations with Scott. Mostly it's the relation of not being there even when I'm there.

DR. F.: And even when you're in close quarters, you tend to be insulated, you're saying—

J.B.: Right. I was really surprised to see that I'm actually better adapted at having feelings toward adults than toward Scott.

DR. F.: Why do you think that is?

J.B.: Because I'm doing it, in this instance. Because I won't give to him what I didn't get myself.

DR. F.: And that makes you feel sad.

J.B.: It's a combination of shame and a wasted sadness. He's there wanting, just like I was there wanting, and there's no real reason. I don't even believe that I'm incapable but I believe I'm acting irrationally. (*sad, crying*)
      [Later in the discussion]

DR. F.: The point you made about feelings, that painful feelings are aroused in you when you would treat Scott in a way that was different from the way you were treated—this would lead to a lot of pain for you, just to feel that way. It somehow emphasized the pain that *you* went through as a child yourself.
      Your father's absence tormented you; you've spoken about it before this, how he avoided the family. And long after he came back from the war, he still used work to avoid any contact, the way you've described it. And in some way, you developed the same pattern in relation to your own family.

Release of Repressed Affect

From our previous clinical work, we learned that most individuals tend to deny the validity of early trauma as well as minimize the emotional impact these incidents had on them as children. Therefore, we usually encouraged participants to express the feelings associated with the painful events they recall from their childhoods. We felt that it was important for parents to experience these feelings in order to develop compassion for themselves and their children. We focused on methods that led to a catharsis and found that the catharsis was usually followed by deep insight and new knowledge of self. The expression of emotion was facilitated by giving verbal support; that is, if an individual began to indicate affect, we would say, "Let it out" or "Don't hold back" or "Try to really feel that," or other supportive statements.

At first, most of the participants failed to recognize the importance of painful childhood experiences; some even looked back on them matter-of-factly or with humor, even though, upon later examination, the incidents had left deep psychological scars. In their talks together, however, these parents were able to reexperience the depth of feeling associated with the original trauma and to gain perspective. In addition, they became increasingly sensitive to the painful emotions expressed by others in the group and developed greater empathy for their children.

One woman, C.S., while investigating her feelings of irritability with children, recalled an incident involving her father that had occurred when she was about 9 years old. In recounting the story in the accepting atmosphere of the group, she was overcome with feelings of sadness about the humiliation she had suffered at the time. She was struck by the fact that she had looked at the incident as humorous prior to talking about it in the group.

C.S.: I remember one time I was drinking milk, and I got milk on my top lip. And my father just reached over across the table, and I remember that he was like a monster. He reached over and grabbed me. He held me tight and started yelling at me for getting milk on my top lip. Then he just started beating me and I, I wet on him, I was so scared. (*sad*)

[Later]: That particular incident was something people told in my family and laughed about. It was a funny story—when I wet on my father—it was a real funny thing to them. And it was funny to me until now, when I really thought about it.

Because of the commonality of experiences that had occurred during people's formative years, one person's revelations had the effect of stimulating the recovery of memories in others; that is, parents strongly identified with the stories related by their fellow participants. In some cases, individuals who had been very defended against remembering events of their childhood or experiencing the deep emotions associated with them were able to recall incidents in detail after listening to others tell of their experiences. This was a very powerful and moving part of the therapy process. Other clinicians (Rocklin & Lavett, 1987; Steele, 1986) have emphasized the importance of recalling and reexperiencing early trauma as part of the therapeutic process.

Recognition of the Connection between Current Limitations and Early Defenses

Although, for the most part, the parents in our parenting groups were well-adjusted individuals, through talking more openly about themselves, they became cognizant of many areas of endeavor in their lives where they still felt limited.[1] They brought up material relating to patterns of inwardness, passivity, paralyzing forms of withholding, and passive-aggressive responses that they had found difficult to overcome. They were able to link these habit patterns and behaviors to specific events in childhood or to the emotional climate that originally had caused them to construct nonfunctional defensive patterns. Consider these statements of Carl, a father, who tended to isolate himself because of extreme social awkwardness, recalling his relationship with his mother:

CARL: My mother was always concerned about appearances. She only cared about what other people thought. I don't think she had the slightest real interest in anything I was doing.

    I think I still relate to people a lot that way. If I'm sitting in a room with people, I wonder "What are they thinking about me?" And if I'm with my daughter, my only focus is what other people are thinking about her. If there's a group of kids, I don't think about what other people are thinking about the other kids, but I worry about what they are thinking about my daughter. The sole standard I was raised under is what other people thought of me.

Following this insight and the working through of related feelings, this man felt considerably relieved of the pressure to maintain a facade and found himself more at ease in social situations. Similarly, at this stage in the process of change, other participants developed *more* sensitivity to themselves in relation to their limitations and became *less* guilty, ashamed, and self-punishing. Our original methodological design was not intentionally retrospective or historical; rather, the parents *spontaneously* adopted a style of recalling past hurts and derived considerable benefit from their insights concerning the sources of their self-defeating habit patterns.

In learning how they had been limited in their early lives, these people could not help but recognize that they had also been implicitly taught to blame themselves for their inadequacies. As they came to a deeper understanding of the sources of their weaknesses, they began to adopt a more compassionate attitude toward themselves and their children. In effect, they began to perceive themselves as *having been damaged* rather than thinking of themselves as "bad" or to blame for their limitations and mistakes. These insights were also applied to child-rearing situations. In other words, in realizing how they were damaged, they began to forgive themselves. Concomitantly, parents changed their focus from attacking and criticizing themselves for the damage to their children to altering their attitudes and behavior in a positive direction.

Parents' Exposure of Inadequacies in Their Families

As the men and women developed more compassion toward themselves, it was inevitable that they would challenge the idealized images they held of their parents. Because they observed the destructive effects of psychological trauma in their friends and felt empathy for other people and their limitations, they gradually developed more clarity in relation to their own parents. They became progressively aware of the fact that *they*, too, had built a false image of their parents. Virtually all the participants noted strong tendencies in themselves to protect and excuse their own parents and to rationalize the abuses they had suffered as children. As they dealt with these issues at a deeper level, they began to experience the full brunt of the outrage and grief they felt in being limited by these early experiences. Their basic attitude was *not* one of blaming, but more one of accounting for what happened in their childhoods and of reacting emotionally to the discoveries. Moreover, we have consistently found that individuals who persist in hating or blaming their parents, in effect, are holding onto the bond with their families and fail to progress in therapy.

Although it is vital that the participants experience and express the full range of their emotional responses to the abuses that now limit them, it is important to remember that expressing these affects can lead to negative therapeutic reactions in many people. Unless they have high ego-strength, individuals can suffer serious regressions after uncovering the powerful feelings of repressed rage. In *Voice Therapy* (Firestone, 1988), I elucidated the complicated aspects of this problem.

> In general, the problem of voicing aggression toward parents and parental introjects is a serious issue in any therapeutic endeavor. When patients become aware of the damage they sustained in their early development, they experience a good deal of pain and sadness. These memories and insights give rise to primitive feelings of anger and outrage. Feeling their murderous rage is symbolically equivalent to actually killing, or expressing death wishes towards the parents themselves. Therefore, patients often experience intense guilt reactions and anxiety when they mobilize these emotions. To compound matters, the symbolic destruction of parental figures leaves the patient fearful of object loss. (p. 243)

Therefore, careful attention must be paid to the possibility of setbacks at this crucial stage in the therapeutic process. Therapists need to be especially sensitive to patients' tendencies to turn their rediscovered rage against themselves *as they did originally*. They must allow their patients ample time to work through each resurgence of repressed affect, as deeper levels of damage and deprivation are revealed.

Parents disrupted their idealization of the family through sensitive treatment of their children. As the parents changed, they began to develop a new perspective on child-rearing; that is, they saw that they could be different from their own parents. Becoming sensitive to their children in ways their parents had *not* been sensitive tended to further break into the idealization of their families. People developed a new point of view concerning their parents, perceiving them more objectively as real people with strengths and weaknesses. Further, as they observed other parents treating their children differently, they developed a different view of themselves, realizing that they *could* gain control and were not compelled to repeat destructive patterns. As they altered their responses to their offspring, they were forced, in a sense, to recognize that their parents had abusive or undesirable qualities, and that the damage they had sustained as children had in some sense been unnecessary.

Being tender toward their children also tended to reawaken painful feelings in these parents. For example, a young mother talked of feeling uncomfortable and self-conscious when she expressed affection to her 6-year-old son:

K.R.: Bruce was sitting next to me in the movie, and I put my arm around his shoulder and, with affection, touched his face. He was asking me a couple of questions about the movie, and I was explaining it to him, and once in a while, I volunteered some information.

But I felt so much. I was confused by the power of what I was feeling. It was painful, and I started second-guessing myself and felt self-conscious. But mostly it was really strong affection, and it was so different to feel that. And I just acted on it without thinking. [Prior to that occasion, K.R.'s responses to her son were overprotective and somewhat cold and indifferent.]

I thought that I was more aware of my feelings from these talks and from listening to other people talking, and I think this incident really affected me, because for a couple of days after, I had a bad headache.

DR. F.: It seemed like you felt distrustful toward yourself and self-conscious after indicating strong positive feelings. I think most people have a good deal of embarrassment at seeing themselves as kind and loving and tender and letting that be seen, letting that be noticed.

K.R.: One thing I almost forgot was that I had a feeling of liking myself in that situation, and it was so painful to me. I couldn't show that, that I liked myself, because I felt like I was being really nice to Bruce.

DR. F.: You were pained to like yourself.

K.R.: That was the most painful part of it, to like myself. I forgot that I felt that. I'm much more comfortable thinking I'm terrible and irritable, and many times I act that out to prove it.

DR. F.: You can imagine how deep that embarrassment and self-consciousness about your loving impulses toward children really are. Your identity is that of a person who's hateful to children. But it's just the opposite. You're a person who loves children and can barely tolerate it. You somehow find that unbearable, to see yourself as tender or kind. You're so used to thinking of yourself as bad or destructive.

K.R.: It made me different from my mother. That's the clearest thing, I think.

DR. F.: So you think you should punish yourself for being different.

K.R.:Because it shows her up.

DR. F.: You're very frightened of exposing your mother. This is the protection of parents, actually. You feel like there will be retaliation if you expose them, if you tell the family secret.

In disrupting this basic defensive process of idealizing the family, many individuals encountered considerable resistance and sometimes suffered temporary setbacks in their progress. People often turn against themselves shortly after gaining a more realistic picture of their parents. This regression was evident in K.R.'s interaction with her son after the incident described above. Immediately after feeling closer to him, she felt self-conscious and pulled away for a period of time. She distrusted that her feelings for her son were real. However, discussing her feelings of embarrassment and pain had the effect of ameliorating or preventing a more serious adverse reaction.

In general, if individuals persevere and develop a more objective view of their families, as many of these parents have done, they will find themselves acting from an entirely different perspective in relation to child-rearing.

Development of More Compassionate Child-Rearing Practices Based on Constructive Attitude Change

In isolating the traumatic experiences that were harmful to them in their formative years, parents began to formulate positive attitudes and countermeasures that served as constructive guidelines to child-rearing practices which, in turn, minimized damage to their offspring. In becoming more compassionate toward themselves, they developed a sensitive interest in their children and initiated steps to prevent their children from incorporating an image of themselves as "bad." They learned the importance of not labeling children's wants as greedy or selfish; instead, they supported the positive strivings of their children that would give them a sense of worth. They were more successful in avoiding negative or destructive interactions with their children, as well as offering them experiences that would enhance their self-esteem.

To illustrate, one father's change in attitude is apparent in the following transcription:

FATHER: I've realized a number of things about the way I treat children and the way other people treat children since we've been talking. One of the things I realized was the frequency and the routineness of talking to children in terms of good and bad, that almost everything that a child is told is based on good and bad. Whether he obeys the parent or not, he's good or bad. "Are you going to be a good boy and do this?" or "You're bad when you do that." So I've made a real effort to talk to my daughter and other children in other ways.

Mrs. C., the mother described in Chapter 6, talked about the recent positive changes in her feelings toward children:

MRS. C.: Since we've had these talks, I feel that I've stopped avoiding a lot of areas of my life that had caused me pain. Talking like this has brought out a lot of things about myself and my childhood that had made me feel bad about myself. But now I know the reasons why I felt that way about myself, why I was afraid of children, and why I didn't do well with my children, especially when they were first born. I feel a lot more relaxed and that has a huge effect on my whole life.

DR. F.: You're not afraid in that way.

MRS. C.: Right. I like children. I get a lot of joy out of taking care of them. I had always thought of myself as a woman who was different because I was afraid of being with children. But I don't feel that's true about me anymore.

Another father, Donald, who had spoken often of feeling compelled to push away his children because their affection caused him pain, spoke here about feeling differently:

DONALD: I feel like I've been really affected by these talks. Just listening to different people talk about their feelings from their childhoods and also feelings that they have towards their kids, I feel that I can identify with everything that's said and everything that each person says about how they feel.

It makes me more aware of those feelings that I have towards my own kids, why I feel that way, and what happened to me. I feel hopeful that I can change that pattern and that I can break the chain from generation to generation.

CONCLUSION

The dimension of our parenting groups that differentiates them from other forms of group psychotherapy is their dual focus: (1) on parents' attitudes toward their children and (2) on the experiences parents went through in their own childhoods. This dual concentration helps parents have more compassion *for themselves* by developing feeling for what happened to them as children. Regaining feeling for themselves may well be the key element that enabled them to alter their child-rearing practices in a positive direction.

The purpose, therefore, is for parents to develop an empathic understanding of the sources of their limitations and to see their child from that same perspective—that is, to pass on this compassionate view to their offspring. In this sense, the format of the parenting groups may be the most effective psychotherapy for the parents themselves. Consideration for their children's well-being acts as a strong motivating force for parents. Taking advantage of the opportunity to modify their destructive responses to their child helps them in their own healing process. Indeed, it appears that only through understanding themselves can parents really change the attitudes and feelings they express covertly and overtly toward their children.

The procedure of identifying negative thoughts toward oneself and toward one's children was found to be very effective when applied in the parents' group setting. The group format is both economical and efficient for utilization as preventive mental hygiene. We have found that we can generalize from the knowledge and experience of the parents in the groups depicted here, despite the fact that many of the participants were quite knowledgeable about psychological issues, and that they had an unusual support system available to them.

On a preventive level, it is vital to recognize the issues that are involved in breaking the chain of emotional and physical child abuse perpetuated through the generations and to intervene, wherever possible, in cases where infants and children are experiencing emotional problems and maladjustment (Broussard, 1979; Fraiberg, Adelson, & Shapiro, 1980; Greenspan, 1981). The process of attitude change demonstrated in these parenting groups appears to be a powerful psychotherapy, both for parents and their offspring. More formal studies are needed to explore further the possibilities and potentialities of utilizing this specialized group therapy process in an overall mental health program.

NOTES

1. In the reference population, there was a relative absence of clinically classified disorders. Nevertheless, there was a high incidence of physical, sexual, and psychological abuse in childhood reported by the participants in the parenting groups. It is questionable, however, that they suffered more abuse than the general population.

CHAPTER 16

The Value of Selective Separation as a Psychotherapeutic Intervention

> It is amazing to me to observe how often an allegedly sick child or adolescent becomes relatively undisturbed when (1) treated by a therapist as a full-fledged person and (2) given the hope and the right of breaking away in the not too distant future from the confines of the family.
>
> Robert Harper (1981), "Limitations of Marriage and Family Therapy"
>
> (p. 6)

Most psychotherapists are aware that patients' sustained contact with a damaging home environment is very detrimental and can be interpreted as an indication of a negative prognosis. Children who are trapped within dysfunctional family systems represent a particularly difficult treatment problem. The child's neurosis is basically a defensive adaptation to his immediate surroundings; therefore, it is extremely difficult to change faulty behavior patterns when faced with the same general circumstances that originally led to the need for defensive reactions. Furthermore, psychiatrists, clinical psychologists, and other psychotherapists who work with *adult* patients have confirmed the observation that very often continued contact with toxic family members has negative consequences. They have been particularly cognizant of the deterioration in their patients' personalities and functioning levels surrounding holidays and family reunions with parents and siblings.

With respect to separation as a therapy procedure for children, in cases where the primary caretaker is chronically ill, severely depressed, grossly neglectful, abusive, or mentally ill, some form of separation as a preventive *or* ameliorative measure has found general acceptance. For example, in appraising the benefits of separation from a disruptive family situation, Michael Rutter (1981) stated that "a change for the better in family circumstances was associated with a marked reduction in psychiatric risk for the child" (p. 210). His findings were based on an extensive study of children who had been separated from their parents in early childhood as a result of family discord or family problems.

Clinicians have long been concerned with the damage that infants and young children might sustain in being separated from their mothers (Bowlby, 1953). Over the last two decades, research findings have begun to challenge the tendency to equate *maternal separation* with *maternal deprivation* (Robertson & Robertson, 1971; Rutter, 1981). In clarifying this important distinction, Rutter strongly suggests that it is the *quality* of relationships that matters, rather than the *presence or absence of separations* from the mother. In more recent writings, Bowlby (1979) has focused his attention on the "emotional problems of parents" in discriminating between dysfunctional patterns of parenting and the problems inherent in separation experiences.

A similar evolution has occurred in my own clinical work. Initially, I had the same views that Bowlby (1953) expressed in his original treatise about separation from the mother. I had to reeducate myself that it was the *quality* of care rather than the specific designation of a single person as the mothering figure that was most important. In addition, I had a strong predisposition toward keeping children and their biological parents together at virtually all costs, but I had to gradually relinquish that position as I observed destructive interactions and their effects in so many parent-child relationships.

POSITIVE EFFECTS OF SEPARATION EXPERIENCES

The treatment of young patients with severe intractable asthma at the Jewish National Home for Asthmatic Children in Denver was generally successful because of a radical and innovative approach to psychosomatic illness.[1] A major part of the treatment was to separate the children from their parents for a 2-year period. During this period, only two brief visits with the family were permitted. Most often, the separation had a positive effect, and symptoms were ameliorated. In the new circumstances, psychological stress was reduced, and many of the children improved immediately, despite the loneliness and homesickness of the "parentectomy" (a term relating to the lengthy separation from family).

The children ranged in age from 5 to 16 and, in order to qualify for admission, had to have been diagnosed as suffering from intractable asthma prior to the time of admission. The youngsters who qualified as intractable had spent significant portions of their lives in hospitals in their own cities and were not able to carry out a normal life program. When they arrived, they were sickly and many looked emaciated, like prisoners of war. One would naturally anticipate that the atmosphere at this asthma research center would be somewhat morbid and depressing, but the opposite was true. The mood was generally positive, and there was little evidence to indicate that this was a place for sick children. I was amazed by my first encounter with the children. Most of them appeared to be exuberant and healthy; asthmatic symptoms and breathing problems were minimal.

Reporting on this particular form of residential treatment, Seiden (1965) stated:

> During their two-year stay, their health improves so rapidly and significantly that hospitalization [referring to the above-mentioned treatment program] is often considered a life-saving experience.... Ruling out improvements in specific medical or psychological care, workers in this field have concluded that *separation itself is the key factor in improvement* [italics added]. (p. 27)

EARLY SEPARATION OF INFANT AND PARENTS

In assessing the work of Anna Freud and Dorothy Burlingham (1944) with groups of children separated from their mothers in wartime England, Seiden (1965) stated:

> These studies disclosed that there was a wealth of feeling and spontaneity and an absence of jealousy and rivalry unheard of in ordinary relations between young contemporaries. Of particular interest is the observation

that attachments to a sole mother figure disturbed these positive peer relations. (p. 27)

Throughout Freud and Burlingham's (1944) book, *Infants Without Families*, there are statements indicating that, in many instances, the children in the Hampstead Residential Nursery were *positively* affected by the lack of the mother-child bond or attachment.

Seiden (1965) also drew attention to the kibbutzim in Israel that provided a combination of nuclear and extended family practices. Formed in 1932, the kibbutz had a unique arrangement for raising children. Basically, the children lived from birth on (after they were 4 days old) with their age group, rather than at home with their families. Bruno Bettelheim (1969), after visiting several kibbutzim, recorded his impressions:

> My conclusion must be that despite published reports to the contrary the kibbutz system seems quite successful in raising children in groups by other than their mothers, and this from infancy on. (p. 52)

Sociologists, psychologists, and anthropologists (Kaffman, 1961; Neubauer, 1965; Rabin, 1958, 1965; Rabin & Beit-Hallahmi, 1982; among many others) have evaluated the long-term effects of this unusual extended family grouping on the first generation of children. They have concluded that generally there has been "no adverse psychological *sequelae* associated with [this form of] upbringing" (Rutter, 1981, p. 64).[2]

DELETERIOUS EFFECTS OF CONTACT WITH THE FAMILY

Theodore Lidz (1969/1972) has provided us with an especially clear illustration of the unfortunate outcome that can occur when the recovered schizophrenic patient returns home. He described the pathological elements in a patient's bond with her mother that had a devastating effect on the patient upon her reunion with her family.

> A college girl was admitted to the hospital after having been removed from a train bewildered and acutely delusional. I interviewed her parents when they arrived.... It was difficult to learn much about the patient for the mother told about herself, her Pilgrim ancestry, and her ambitions as a writer. When I finally interrupted and asked about the daughter's college career and her interests, I learned that the girl's whole life revolved about

becoming a novelist; she had a passion for Virginia Woolf. The mother became enthusiastic; she prayed that her daughter would become another Virginia Woolf. I hesitated, and then commented, "But Virginia Woolf had psychotic episodes and committed suicide." The mother did not hesitate when she replied, "It would be worth it."...

While making rounds some weeks later I noted several novels by Virginia Woolf in the patient's room and asked about them. She replied in a flat voice, "Mother sent them—she has a thing about Virginia Woolf." Over the next months the patient talked of her despair over her inadequacies as a writer, her desires for a marriage in which she could help a husband assert himself, and her resentments over her obligation to live out her mother's aspirations for her. I had some difficulty in believing that she was complying to the extent of becoming psychotic like Virginia Woolf, which proved a serious, a fatal error. When the patient emerged from her psychosis, her mother insisted she continue her treatment on the west coast where they lived. At home, caught up in her mother's control, she relapsed, and then followed the fate foisted upon her by committing suicide. (pp. 620-621)

In this extreme example, the mother's need or malevolent motivation toward her daughter and its relationship to mental illness were more clear and direct than usual. I am familiar with a multitude of cases in which parents' hostile wishes toward their offspring remained unconscious and could only be inferred from communication patterns or from subtle behavioral cues. However, the insidious effects of parents' aggressive impulses toward these seriously disturbed patients were readily observable following patients' home visits as well as during parents' visits to the treatment center.

When they have contact with family members, less disturbed or neurotic patients are similarly affected, although sometimes to a lesser degree. Very often their progress in psychotherapy is interrupted and symptoms of the original disturbance reappear. In some instances, the regression has been irreversible, and the patients have terminated therapy. Two cases which I described (Firestone, 1987b) in a paper, "The 'Voice': The Dual Nature of Guilt Reactions," revealed negative outcomes primarily because intense feelings of guilt were aroused in these patients during brief interactions with their families. The guilt reactions of these patients were directly associated with their progress in therapy as they compared their new lives with the self-destructive lives of family members. Even in so-called normal individuals, we have observed only occasional examples of positive results from interactions with original family members. These usually occurred in reunions with parents and siblings who had been involved in psycho-therapy or who had otherwise significantly altered their destructive behavior patterns and attitudes.

Regressive Behavior Observed in Children in Reunions with Parents

Temporary regressions have also been observed in normal chil-dren in reunions with their parents following a period of separation. For example, John Bowlby (1973) described behavior typical of 199 children between the ages of 2 and 8 who had been separated from their mothers for 1-day visits to a research center and reunited with them at the end of the day:

> At the sight of mother...[the child's] needs for autonomy and indepen-dence vanished, and he reverted to the degree of babyishness he had over-come early in the morning. (p. 35)

In subsequent writings, Bowlby (1979) has concluded:

> Children always behave in a more babyish way with their parents than with other people.... Inevitably the presence of mother or father evokes primitive or turbulent feelings not evoked by other people. (p. 15)

Anna Freud and Dorothy Burlingham (1944) also observed vary-ing degrees of emotional upset and regression in children following reunions with their families and upon their subsequent return to the Hampstead nursery.

THE VALUE OF AN EXTENDED FAMILY

An extended family may be defined as consisting of one or more adults in addition to the child's natural parents who maintain con-sistent contact with the child over a significant period of time. A close friend, a favorite relative, a godparent, a "Big Brother," or a psychol-ogist could be considered to belong to this category. One noteworthy and very important advantage of an extended family situation or sup-port system is that it allows parents to be selectively separate from their children when the parents are the most hurtful. At the same time, the circumstances are such that the needs of the child are still carefully and conscientiously attended to.

Parents who learn to differentiate between love and emotional hunger could avoid children if they would realize that their hunger or anxiety could be potentially destructive to the children. In the extended family situation, the parents can stay away from the child when they find themselves inward, unresponsive, and cut off from feeling. Children are better off separate from their parents when their parents are hostile or unable to relate personally. Sustained unfeeling contact, where the child is not seen or heard, can be more harmful than limited contact.

In addition, close association with people other than the child's parents or siblings acts to compensate for parents' fears and inadequacies. The extended family situation offers a variety of inputs, points of view different from the parents' views, that expand the child's world and give him an enlarged perspective and more realistic picture of life. This expanded view helps break into the dependency and idealization of parents and provides the child with a more comprehensive and secure base from which to operate. Furthermore, in the case of illness or emotional breakdown in the natural parent, there is a support system already available.

Interactions with a number of individuals within an extended family system can disrupt an inward, isolated, protective orientation and challenge the narrow, stereotypic attitudes toward others often held by the family. An extended family relationship offers the child an ally, a person in whom he can confide, an adult who is relatively unbiased and objective concerning the child's relationship with his parents. Children in an extended family setting are also provided with relationships that are generally free of the proprietary interest most parents have in their children. They tend to develop a sense of independence in their interactions with adults, rather than clinging to a toxic, overdependent relationship with one or both of their parents. Moreover, other adults are more objective and freer to be a positive influence in the child's life because they are not as prone to guilt reactions or anxieties as the natural parents.

In the experimental social milieu, all of the children know adults other than family members whom they consider as friends or confidants. Most of the children have benefited significantly from contact with empathic, sensitive adults outside of their families.

MISCONCEPTIONS ABOUT "BONDING"

Infants whose experiences have created pathology are likely to continue
to grow anomalously only if they remain in the same environment. (Kagan,
1984, p. 109)

A review of current literature on child development indicates that
many child psychiatrists, pediatricians, and other child-care workers
continue to endorse the view that the future health and psychological
well-being of the child depend on parents' "bonding" with their infants, preferably as soon as possible after birth (Carter, 1988; Helfer,
1982; Kennell *et al.*, 1974; Montagu, 1986).[3] By contrast, our own work
with families at large and specifically in this social milieu has caused
us to reconsider and reevaluate this type of attachment. We have
found that strong bonds and feelings of connection between parent
and child are very often based more on the unfulfilled needs of the
parent for love than on a genuine concern and affection for the child.
The desperation experienced by immature, emotionally hungry
parents in relation to forming and preserving bonds with their children, in the proprietary sense of the word, is characteristic and has
negative consequences for both parties to the contract.

On the basis of our observation and experience, we contend that
"instant bonding" between natural parents and children is not necessarily essential to successful parenting, but indeed may be profoundly
damaging to family life. Another significant finding concerns the relative absence of this destructive form of bonding between adults and
children who were not their own. In most cases of foster parenting,
there was less of a need to utilize the child in an exploitive or destructive manner.[4] The case studies and observations reported here have
demonstrated conclusively that many parents who had a detrimental
effect on their own children were capable of offering nurturance and
warmth to other children.

In an unusual situation in which parents cooperated in sharing
the responsibility for the physical care and emotional development
of their children (the experimental social milieu described earlier),
many benefits and positive effects were observed, although certain
problems were encountered. In the extended family constellations that
evolved over the years, we have had a rare opportunity to observe
the results of separation experiences and substitute parenting as part
of a longitudinal study. Our preliminary findings elucidate, perhaps
more clearly than has been previously demonstrated, the positive ef-

fects of separation and the powerful and potentially destructive nature of continued interaction with parents who were hostile, immature, or inadequate. What follows is a brief history of this experimental work and an analysis of the salutary effects, as well as the problems, as attempts were made to interrupt the *harmful aspects* of parent-child bonds.

SUBSTITUTE PARENTING

The children are not raised in some all-enveloping cocoon of love. They are treated naturally, within the naturalness of this setting—and, again, nothing seems to be hidden from them—including honest feelings of disapproval. There is, however, a sense of over-all responsibility for them, which nonetheless allows them choice of how they are going to be within the perceived limits of their understanding. (Boyd, 1982, p. 165)

In discussing long-term separations of parent and child, it is important to summarize briefly the stages that led up to this form of therapeutic intervention in the reference population. The idea of separation was not developed intentionally through a direct line of deductive reasoning; rather, the concept evolved through a number of events and circumstances. The depth of understanding achieved by many individuals into the genesis of their own limitations and problems in relating made them aware of the central issues in child-rearing. They were tuned in to the destructive processes in their original families that had injured them psychologically. They naturally turned their attentions to interventions that would minimize the repetition of these negative patterns of behavior with their children. One of the interventions considered and later adopted by many parents was temporary or even long-term use of foster parents in the group context. We were fortunate to be able to observe both long- and short-term results in an attempt to determine the advantages and disadvantages of this course of action.

The initial separation experiences took place within the framework of a long-standing tradition of sharing child-rearing functions with others in the community. Against this background, the first incidence of separation took place many years ago when one of the adolescent boys, Steve, decided that he wanted to break away from his family and become more independent. At age 15, Steve had participated in the young people's discussion group for 2 years and had been talking to one of the adults on a friendship basis for several months. The man who met with Steve and his family described the initial family meetings:

> The meetings with the family were invaluable in knowing the dynamics of what made Steve and his brother, Bobby, the way they were. It was a horror story—a snake pit. Their mother intruded into every part of their lives. They had nothing left of themselves. They had no independence. She destroyed any perceptions they had of what was going on. The most touching thing I felt toward Steve was that, somewhere inside himself, he wanted to be different. But he was overwhelmed by the frustration of getting that part outside, out from where it was completely locked. I knew he could be soft somewhere, but it was locked inside him—by his mother. After a time, I asked her not to come to the family meetings. One summer Steve came over to our house to spend his vacation, and he stayed. He never went back home again. It was the beginning of the long, slow change in him. It seems almost impossible that he is the way he is today. It's too much to talk about without being deeply touched.

Steve was the first of the young people to separate from his family. In his case, the impact on his life was tremendous. At that time, the colleagues and friends were not self-conscious about this turn of events and had no feelings of anxiety or guilt. They recognized that his home life had been an extreme situation and that his move toward independence was a logical corrective measure. No one felt that anything radical had been attempted. Later, a number of other teenagers became more independent in relation to their families. Following their participation in a 17-month voyage around the world (1976-1978), several of the young people who had served as crew on the schooner for the entire voyage returned home and chose to live with family friends rather than with their own families.

Evolution of Separation in Selected Cases with Young Children

With the younger children in the friendship circle, events proceeded at a much slower pace than the separation experiences with the teenagers. Historically, the first separation of a younger child from his parents occurred quite by accident on a family vacation. The youngster, 5-year-old Danny, was traveling with his parents and several family friends in Mexico during the Christmas holidays in 1974. On one leg of the journey, Danny's parents decided to fly home and asked one of the women if she would take Danny with her. This woman was a close family friend, a person with whom Danny was already familiar.

Prior to the separation, the relationship between Danny and his mother had been characterized by behavior on both their parts that was irritating to their traveling companions. The boy had become a real pest, whining and complaining the entire trip, clinging to his mother, whose overprotective stance and inadequate efforts to soothe the youngster only served to provoke him and consequently others. Danny's father, while authoritarian in his disciplinary style, was equally ineffectual.

After the separation and during the drive, Danny gradually relaxed and appeared much happier. When the caravan of cars stopped for lunch, the teenagers played catch with the youngster and discovered that he was a well-coordinated, strong, potentially athletic boy rather than the babyish sissy they were familiar with. During the 3-day drive, each evening as darkness fell, Danny began to inquire about his mother. The woman taking care of Danny became concerned and, in talking with him, discovered why he felt bad and withdrew each evening. With tears in his eyes, Danny confided that "My mommy said she would die if something happened to me. I want to see her so she can see that I'm not hurt, so she won't die." After revealing the source of his worries, he relaxed and fell asleep.

The most significant event of the trip occurred when Danny and his parents were reunited. The youngster rushed into his mother's arms and within a few minutes became his former whiny, complaining self. In spite of his happiness, strength, and companionship with his new friends, Danny seemed compelled to literally "run back" to the misery of the bond with his mother. This sequence of events and many other similar examples gave us additional insight into the relationships between parents and children and contributed to a growing pool of knowledge about destructive family bonds.

As ties of friendship grew stronger between these parents, they began gradually to share in many child-rearing functions beyond the scope of a simple exchange of babysitting duties. There was no formalization or systematic attempt to organize a child-rearing program; rather, parents and their close friends began to cooperate informally in helping each other in this area.

Soon after the incident that led to a temporary separation of Danny and his parents, several other young children began spending weekends with people other than their parents. Lengthier separations evolved quite slowly and with careful consideration of specific factors in each child's development. Parents were motivated primarily by their desire to extend to their children (and to their friends' children) the social atmosphere that *they* found so nourishing and nontoxic. Decisions about separations were made individually according to the degree of impairment observed in the child and the parents' requests for help in raising their child.

When Kathy's parents approached their close friends, a couple they had known for years, to ask for help with their 5-year-old daughter, their desperation and concern were apparent. The little girl seemed lost in a world of her own and was mostly oblivious to her surroundings. Her face was pale, her expression lifeless, and dark circles under her eyes accentuated her waiflike appearance. Kathy's parents thought she would benefit from being around their close friends, a couple who were lively and warm. They asked them to take care of Kathy for a while, until she showed improvement. Because the early effects of separation were so dramatic, the people involved took the subject more seriously and maintained their efforts.

Gradually, a number of men and women became substitute parental figures for their friends' children. This form of assistance was actively sought by parents, with the full realization of what their request implied. They were deeply appreciative for their friends' involvement in the well-being of their children.

Benefits in Substitute Parenting

We cannot always change the situation and we cannot often change it profoundly. We can seek to make it possible for the patient to escape from it into a different way of living rather than into irrationality and delusion. (Lidz, 1969/1972, p. 633)

In this section, we will discuss the benefits of long-term separation undertaken as a psychotherapeutic procedure in selected cases. In foster parenting, the child is either partially or totally cared for by substitute parenting figures. In this friendship circle, many parents have sought help in raising their children and have asked close friends to assume the role of foster parents. The individuals who became foster parents were known to the child prior to the separation and generally before the child's emotional problems were recognized. In each case, parental inadequacies were such that the parents themselves felt strongly that their offspring would have a better chance for developing if they were cared for by others. There was deep concern on the part of these parents because their children were already exhibiting symptoms of underlying psychological disturbances.

Although the children were living in the same general environment as their natural parents and continued to have contact with their families, friends acting as substitute parents were primarily responsible for the child's well-being and upbringing. Despite the fact that it appeared to be a very involved, time-consuming, and long-term process, the primary goal at the time was for the biological parents to eventually reestablish good relationships with their offspring after making fundamental changes. In the majority of cases, the children tended to improve significantly; often there were positive results immediately after separation from their parents.

Case Studies

Robert. At the age of 8 months, Robert had become increasingly agitated, usually throwing several violent tantrums each day. He would scream, arch his back, and attempt to throw himself from his mother's arms. After serious deliberation and much discussion with interested parties, Robert's parents asked their best friends to assume total care of him until the time they might feel it appropriate to become closely involved with him again.

While living with his foster parents, Robert improved rapidly, learned to accept physical affection, and has subsequently developed into a sweet, outgoing 9-year-old. The objectionable characteristics that had begun to develop in the first year and that made him appear unlovable gradually disappeared. In contrast, Robert developed positive traits and behavior patterns similar to those observed in the children of his foster parents. At first, because of the early onset of Robert's symptoms, we conjectured that his disturbance might have been caused by a constitutional weakness or a biological propensity toward hyperactivity. However, in this case, it was obvious that the parental environment had been the major contributing factor in the early symptom formation.

Mary. Mary, at 3 months, had developed signs of possible autism or Pervasive Developmental Disorder. At 4 months, the infant's parents sought the help of friends in raising their daughter. This couple subsequently developed a close, loving attachment to Mary. I remember my feelings at the time. I was amazed and impressed in observing these foster parents and their investment and devotion to Mary, who was a very unappealing child for many, many years. No natural parent could have offered her more. Eventually, when her major symptoms subsided, we found that she was an appealing little girl. She developed into a friendly, spirited youngster who now attends a regular first-grade class. I never would have believed that she could have developed to this extent because she originally seemed so lifeless and unpleasant. In this case, the foster parents succeeded in literally saving this small child's life, in the psychological and perhaps even in the physical sense of the word.

All of the people who knew Mary were shocked at the early onset of her symptoms in what at first seemed to be normal circumstances. However, in retrospect, her close friends who were unusually perceptive revealed that they felt uneasy observing Mary's mother interacting with her young infant, but found it difficult to pinpoint the source of their concern. One person, trained professionally as a child-care specialist, noted that the mother, a quiet, reserved, immaculately dressed woman, treated the little girl as if she were an appendage or part of her own body. She also tended to carry her small daughter as she would carry a purse, with seeming disregard for her as a real flesh-and-blood person. This mother was neither overtly hostile nor obviously anxious in her care of the child; however, "something" was happening in the mother-child relationship that disturbed everyone. Actually, there was a strong connection or maternal bond with very little real feeling or affection. The constant contact without emotional nurturance literally drained the life and vitality out of the child.

The insidious ramifications for Mary's development were progressively more apparent as she approached her third month. She failed to develop the smiling response typical for that age and had a pinched expression, reminiscent of babies in Rene Spitz's (1946) film of institutionalized infants. Other than intense rage reactions expressed in lengthy crying spells, she was lifeless and disinterested in outside stimuli.

As noted, Mary's foster parents provided a very favorable environment in that they offered consistent warmth and interest in this disturbed infant as a person rather than as an extension of themselves. The foster mother possessed an intuitive understanding of the little girl's desire to give up and cease functioning and consistently intruded into the infant's autistic withdrawal. Although untrained as a child psychologist, she was nonetheless able to successfully bring the child out of her original prepsychotic state through repeated interventions that required a great deal of energy, determination, and devotion on her part.

In the next phase of Mary's recovery, the substitute parents had to deal with serious perceptual problems, as well as her continual provoking behavior with both peers and adults. Her disruptive acting-out behaviors were controlled or limited, and, in contrast, her sociable responses were promptly reinforced with affection and tangible rewards. By the time she was 4 years old, Mary's "real" self began to emerge, and she manifested signs of outstanding intelligence. There were positive indications of affection and emotional investment.

As she approached the age where she was to enter kindergarten, new symptoms of disturbance surfaced in the form of paranoid ideation that other children and people were against her. However, because of the basic trust she had developed in her foster parents and myself, she was able to reveal that she was tortured by visual and auditory hallucinations, figures, or imaginary playmates that "told" her that she was bad and that her friends hated her. She was gradually able to learn to appropriately express anger and frustration, thereby halting the process of projection and paranoid thinking before it developed into a more well-established delusional system. As of this writing, she is a much happier person, both lively and curious. Her parents, who had originally despaired of their child's ever being normal, cannot adequately express their appreciation and gratitude to their friends, who effected a "miracle cure" for their very disturbed child.

Danny. When Danny, the youngster previously described, was 6 years old, his parents asked another couple to raise the boy. Their experience during the Christmas vacation convinced them that Danny was desperately in need of a home environment very different from the one they were able to provide. In addition, Danny's parents were going through a painful separation and divorce at the time.

For several years, it seemed that this youngster had "inherited" his father's perfectionistic standards, his deep cynicism, and his tendencies toward self-hatred and isolation. (Danny's efforts to separate himself from incorporated negative attitudes that were prevalent in his father are documented in Chapters 4 and 5.) However, the years spent being cared for by another couple have gradually had a positive effect, and Danny's self-hating, self-critical attitudes have been significantly reduced. At age 17, he is a very personable young man with definite career goals and aptitudes. He recently developed a serious relationship with a young woman for whom he cares a great deal. He appears to be affectionate and concerned and displays a maturity beyond his years.

Brian. When he was 8, Brian's mother suffered her first emotional breakdown and in succeeding years was committed to mental hospitals on several occasions. She was eventually diagnosed as a chronic schizophrenic. During the periods of her hospitalization, Brian stayed with friends and, upon his parents' divorce, chose to live with his father. As a child, Brian was miserable and depressed a good deal of the time. Later, as a young teenager, he spent the majority of his time living in the home of an associate and his wife. His mood generally improved, and he developed into a strong leader among his group of friends. Today, he is married and is the father of three children. His abilities and perceptiveness have made him one of the most active and well-respected individuals in the friendship circle. In contrast, his older brother, when offered the same choice and opportunity to separate from his mother, chose to remain in the maternal environment and maintained the symbiotic tie, with ultimate tragic results. Becoming increasingly disturbed himself as he entered adulthood, he killed his mother during a psychotic episode and is now incarcerated in a facility for the criminally insane.

Obviously, this example is unusual and extreme in emphasizing the benefits of separation and compassionate foster parenting. Yet, in most cases when surrogate parents in the social milieu became involved with a child, there was significant improvement, and results indicate that separation from the natural parents was an important determining factor in the child's movement toward health.

Problems of Separation in the Reference Community

Parents gradually became increasingly aware of communications and behaviors in themselves and their couple relationships that disturbed their offspring. Some of them were successful in altering disturbed behavior patterns, whereas others began to consider separation as a therapeutic intervention.

Despite parents' interest in help from others, there was serious resistance. The desperation with which many parents held onto their original toxic style of relating to their child frequently caused difficulties in the transition for the foster parents who were working with the child, for the actual parents, and, most important, for the child. The cases of Mary and Danny, cited above, proved less problematic in this regard than other parent-child separations largely because of two factors: (1) The parents possessed a painful awareness that their child's psychological health was contingent upon the separation. In the case of Mary, her parents made every effort to leave their child alone, thereby allowing the substitute parents to have complete supervision over each aspect of her life. Mary's illness was so serious that the couple avoided interfering with her because they were concerned that their contact with her might cause further damage. (2) The parents experienced a sense of relief in being freed of the everyday caretaking responsibilities for their children. Once the bond or connection was broken, these parents maintained their interest, but they had very little contact with their children on a day-to-day basis. Although they continued to have marital problems and disputes, they avoided extending this damage to their children because their interactions with them were minimal.

Other fathers and mothers, who had a strong proprietary interest in their children despite their desire for others to be involved, were intrusive in a manner that aroused guilt in the new parents. Frequently, parents' possessive attitudes were stimulated or reinforced by grandparents and other relatives who were unable to comprehend why the children were being raised by "outsiders." The social pressure toward conventional family life in general made parents continually question the steps they had taken on behalf of their offspring, and, in the majority of cases, caused them to feel guilty in spite of their intellectual understanding and the obvious positive results for their children. Both parents and the foster parents suffered from the resurgence of the natural parents' strong need to have their child "belong" to them.

In addition, most mothers and fathers exhibited a strong compulsion to repeat abusive or overprotective patterns with their children. Until they learned to master this tendency, they continued to act out these patterns with their offspring, even after separation. This compulsion has been noted in an exaggerated form by Rosen (1953), in a case in which the mother's overriding need to make the child mentally ill was an active part of her defense system. The case reported by Lidz (1969/1972) of the young woman whose mother wanted her to live out the life of Virginia Woolf exemplified this type of mother and graphically documented the irresistible pull exerted on such patients.

In the case of Barbara, her compelling need to make her young daughter ill was related to the fact that she had suffered from an acute schizophrenic episode herself when she was 16 years old. In protecting her own mother, she exerted a similar pull on her child. When Barbara's daughter was 5 years old, it was discovered that she was delusional and had occasional hallucinations. Subsequent involvement with foster parents significantly reduced or relieved these symptoms. In spite of Barbara's insight into her overprotectiveness, emotional immaturity, and rejecting attitudes toward her daughter, she could not resist an urge to intrude into and interfere with her daughter's life. Her involvement offended the foster parents and caused her child to regress. This pattern was acted out repeatedly with adverse results, despite Barbara's best intentions.

In many other cases, parents continued to act out hurtful patterns with their children after separation. Parental substitutes often became angry when the natural parents interfered with the therapy process to the detriment of the child's well-being. When this happened, the natural parents felt hurt or insulted, and both parties tended to feel at odds in relation to the child. This tension was obviously destructive to the child. This problem was crucial in the case of Barbara and her daughter.

At one point, the girl's foster parents became quite concerned and, in a family meeting, suggested to Barbara that she limit her contact with the child. Barbara felt deeply wounded; her friends' perception of her as being a detrimental influence on her daughter's life activated her own strong self-attacks that she was a "bad" mother and a "terrible person." Several months prior to this meeting, however, it had been Barbara herself who recognized the pervasive and insidious effect she was having on the little girl and who attempted to correct it.

However, her daughter's rapid improvement after the separation had been obvious to everyone, including herself. Indeed, it was probably this factor more than any other that triggered this mother's compulsion to repeatedly act out behavior patterns that were, in effect, antagonistic to her daughter's development. In a later parents' discussion group, Barbara's painful revelations confirmed this interpretation of her actions:

BARBARA: Recently I saw L. on the boat, very free and very happy, and the way she moved reminded me of me. It was a painful feeling to see that. (*sad*) But then immediately after that, I was ripping her apart in my mind. But I know that's what I do to myself. It was almost in a snide way, tearing apart her movements.

It's something about seeing her enjoying an activity that I love, and seeing *her* love it. I knew how she felt. I could identify with her, and then right afterward, I ripped her apart. But it made me realize that I do that with myself. Right after I'm really happy, I tear myself apart in that same way. So I know I extend that self-hatred to her.

After gaining this and other insights related to her overidentification with her daughter, Barbara found it easier to resist the strong inner pressure to have aversive contact with her. Very gradually, as a result of this deeper insight into the damaging effects of sustained contact, Barbara was better able to control her tendency to counteract the therapeutic separation she herself had initiated.

It is important to note that during the critical period of maternal interference, the substitute parents withdrew from relating to the child. They realized that Barbara's renewed interest in the child had dampened their own feelings of affection and interest. They became aware of the fact that they had generalized the anger they felt at Barbara's intrusion, and they experienced feelings of helplessness and futility in relation to having a favorable effect on the child. At a subsequent meeting with both sets of parents, these issues were openly addressed and partially overcome.

In general, we have found that the natural parents must remain completely supportive of the foster parents to the extent of *not* interfering with their child-rearing practices for positive results to be maintained. Another major problem for foster-home placement is the guilt reaction felt by both sets of parents and the child. Complete support and cooperation between the natural parents and the surrogate parents is virtually a necessity because of the incredible guilt on everyone's part. For example, many of the children felt especially guilty in showing preference for their parental substitutes. Often the children attempted to hide their happiness or enjoyment of their foster parents' company if their parents were in the vicinity. Their guilt took the form of regressive acting-out behavior that was very provocative to the new parents. Many children expressed feelings of having to "make my parents feel good," or having to "take care of my mother." These issues were paramount and have been addressed in the parenting groups. We found that the more happy, independent, and self-fulfilled the natural parents were in their own lives, the less guilty were the child's reactions.

REUNION

It is important to emphasize once again that the ultimate aim was to reunite the natural parents with their children. However, these reunions initially had a traumatic effect on both parties and aroused painful emotions. Parents who were functioning well prior to the reunion showed symptoms of regression in diverse areas, such as work and personal interactions; they displayed erratic mood swings and childlike manifestations in their personalities.[5] Needless to say, there were powerful side effects for the children as well.

The fact that attempts to reestablish the original parent-child relationship caused considerable stress tended once again to confirm our hypotheses that (1) malfunctions in parent-child relating were closely linked to the parents' defense system; (2) parents were still operating under a compulsion to repeat destructive patterns that had been enacted on them as children; and (3) most parents had difficulty making the transition from a childlike mode of existence to an adult mode of relating that accepted real responsibility for another person. There were countless examples of this type of regression in parents that adversely affected the well-being of their children at early stages of reunion. In spite of all we knew, we were surprised at the strength of these reactions and the complications involved in parents' trying to reestablish meaningful contact with their children.

These reactions reminded us of other regressive tendencies at critical junctures in people's lives as they moved toward self-actualization and fulfillment; for example, when they contemplated marriage or having children and first started making plans; during pregnancy and immediately following the birth of the child; and when they were actively involved in changing or attempting to improve their relationships with marital partners and/or children. It is obvious that the working through of these issues in regard to reunion was time-consuming and complex; success depended upon the resiliency of the natural parents and the flexibility of their defensive structure. Consequently, these reunions were accomplished with varying degrees of success.

CONCLUSION

The sacredness of the parent-infant bond may be one of the last unsullied beliefs. The barrage of books and magazine articles on attachment and the necessity of skin-to-skin bonding between mother and infant in the first postnatal hours is generated by strong emotion, suggesting that something more than scientific fact is monitoring the discussion. If the infant can be cared for by any concerned adult, and the biological mother is expendable (this is not yet proven), then one more moral imperative will have been destroyed. (Kagan, 1984, p. 57)

Although in some sense, the process of experimental separation is still in the rudimentary stages, an overall analysis of our 12-year experience with a number of parents who exchanged and shared child-rearing functions shows that this form of intervention has proven beneficial for the children *and* for their parents. Indeed, in a few cases in which the child showed only limited progress, it appeared that the separation was not a failure as such, but that it had not gone far enough. Often the child's natural parents continued to intrude and remained in relatively close contact within the group context, and therefore the children were not truly separated from the harmful influences that had caused their original problems. It is only a conjecture that a more complete separation would have had more salutary results. The whole issue remains a problem requiring further investigation. Even in cases in which the preventive measures undertaken failed to reverse the early damage to children, the foster care may have succeeded in arresting further damage.

In general, results have been very positive. Virtually none of the 18 children born into this social milieu have exhibited thumb-sucking, nor have they used pacifiers beyond the earliest months. They have not become overly involved with, or excessively dependent on, transitional objects, such as blankets, stuffed animals, or favorite dolls, as sources of comfort or stimulation. Most of the children were breast-fed for a brief period early in infancy and appear to be less orally deprived. They displayed much less self-stimulatory behavior than other children their age. For example, none of the children were "crib-rockers," nor did they habitually put objects or their fingers into their mouths. Toilet-training was accomplished easily through a simple, natural process and was clearly *not* the result of any formalized or strict training procedures. Overall, the results noted above were influenced by an implicit morality toward children and positive attitudes toward child-rearing, rather than adherence to calculated practices or techniques.

Observers have commented on the early age at which the children talk and relate to each other. Children of toddler age developed feelings of empathy for their playmates and were quick to comfort another youngster who was hurt or crying. The youngsters engaged in interactive play at an earlier age than normal; most chose activities that involved another child or children rather than engaging in isolated activities or "parallel" play. Teachers, doctors, and other interested individuals have noted the children's maturity, friendliness, and generally pleasant demeanor. The school-aged children rarely quarrel or act out meanness or hostility on their classmates, in contrast to the behaviors of many of the other students. According to one second-grade teacher, who instructs four of the youngsters, the children's friendliness and their consideration of their classmates are outstanding characteristics. In her comments to a parent she said:

These four children are the core of my class. It was easy to see that they were friends, and their overall effect on the atmosphere of my class is quite unusual. They are very helpful to the other children; their niceness and generosity have had such a positive effect on the other children. They are remarkable.

This type of response to the children has been typical. People are continually impressed with the children's behavior in public and their unusually equal relationships with adults.

We realize that the experimental psychosocial milieu described here is unique and atypical. The majority of members are intelligent, educated professionals and business executives with an abiding interest in psychology and an unusual support system. Yet we can generalize from their knowledge and experience when they parallel observations of parent-child relationships in the larger society and, when appropriate, can apply the concepts and procedures that were an outgrowth of the community experience. The approach can be modified to accommodate to new circumstances and can play a part in preventive mental hygiene programs.

On a preventive level, it is important to recognize the issues involved in the selective separation procedures discussed here and to begin applying these interventions carefully in cases in which infants and children appear to be at high risk for emotional problems and maladjustment. In addition, the concept of parents' exchanging child-rearing functions could be worked out, to varying degrees, among parents in the context of parenting groups networking in the community at large. Currently, this is an idealistic notion, but in the context of future developments and potential understanding of the destructive elements in parent-child relationships, progress could be made.

NOTES

1. This facility has been renamed the National Jewish Center for Immunology and Respiratory Medicine.
2. Emanuel Berman's (1988) essay, "Communal Upbringing in the Kibbutz: The Allure and Risks of Psychoanalytic Utopianism," provides a more recent analysis of kibbutz child-rearing that qualifies or is in disagreement with other, more positive findings.
3. Studies conducted by Macfarlane (1977), however, indicate that *immediate* mother-infant contact does not appear to make any lasting difference in the relationship for most experienced mothers with healthy babies. Macfarlane's studies suggest that "for many women the development of maternal love is a fairly gradual affair" (p. 117). Robert Hoekelman (1983) has stated: "It will take the public a long time to appreciate that instant bonding is not necessarily essential to successful parenting" (p. xv).
4. Obviously, this is not always the case, as youngsters have been misused by adults other than their parents in a manner that indicates the presence of destructive attitudes and feelings. Yet this fact does not negate the hypothesis that there is a greater tendency to form *negative* ties or bonds on the part of natural parents as contrasted with foster parents.
5. Parental distress in changing attitudes and behavior toward children reflected the strength of the neurotic reciprocity involved. It appeared to "make the parents sick (anxious) to not make the child sick," a phenomenon reported by many family therapists (Boszormenyi-Nagy & Spark, 1973/1984; Framo, 1970/1972; Kerr & Bowen, 1988; Minuchin, 1974; Palazzoli, Boscolo, Cecchin, & Prata, 1975/1978).

CHAPTER 17

A Summary Plea: Preserving the Humanness of the Child

What we call the child's character is a *modus vivendi* achieved after the most unequal struggle any animal has to go through; a struggle that the child can never really understand because he doesn't know what is happening to him, why he is responding as he does, or what is really at stake in the battle....

To grow up at all is to conceal the mass of internal scar tissue that throbs in our dreams.

Ernest Becker (1973), *The Denial of Death* (p. 29)

THE ESSENTIAL NATURE OF THE CHILD

The prolonged dependence of the human infant on his parents for physical and psychological survival provides the first condition for the development of neurosis. The infant's need for "reliable maternal support" is so absolute and failure to provide it so nearly universal that "varying degrees of neurotic instability... are the rule rather than the exception" (Guntrip, 1961, p. 385). Parents feel, and are very much aware of, the responsibility implied by their child's utter dependence on them. At the same time, they are awed by the unique capacity for human response in their baby. From the neonate's first smile of recognition, parents sense the potential for deep feeling.[1] Later, they become aware of the potential for creativity and philosophical thought in his undeveloped mind. These latent qualities make the child precious and special. They inspire unusually strong and tender feeling responses from parents. Nonetheless, because of their own limitations, most parents transform this extraordinary creature into an ordinary creature. They offer the gift of life and then unknowingly take it back. In attempting to socialize their children, they unwittingly deprive them of their humanity. Despite their best intentions, they stamp out the very qualities that distinguish them from animals—their unique abstract intelligence, their ability to use symbols creatively, and their capacity for deep feeling.

Regrettably, the socialization process in the nuclear family categorizes, standardizes, and puts the stamp of conformity on most children. It imposes a negative structure, a self-regulating system, that cuts deeply into the child's feeling reactions and conditions his thoughts and behaviors to meet certain accepted standards. Thereafter, the child continues to impose the same structure and programming on himself in the form of a restrictive, self-punishing voice. The results are double-edged. Once a human being is "processed" in this way and deprived of individuality, he is reduced to an animal level of existence. However, the individual child retains his capacity to suffer, and his condition is now worse than that of an animal; he has been deprived of his human qualities, yet still retains the propensity for experiencing emotional pain and misery.

THE EFFECT OF EXPERIENCES IN THE FAMILY

The infant at birth is unusually sensitive and vulnerable to sensory inputs (Stern, 1985; Stratton, 1982). From the beginning, a baby is very reactive to his immediate surroundings. The parental environment has a profound impact on him, and he responds with his whole body to painful intrusions from the outside world.

As we have shown throughout this book, if circumstances force the young child to deny his sensations, perceptions, and feelings in order to protect himself from painful events, he will progressively turn his back on life. In "processing" their child, well-meaning parents obliterate the child's curiosity and creativity, his awareness of the world around him, and his capacity to feel and care deeply for himself and other human beings.

For this reason, we appeal to all adults concerned with the well-being of children to consider this damaging aspect of family life. In order to *really* protect our children, we must try to overcome our prejudices and narrow views of the nuclear family and objectively examine dehumanizing child-rearing practices that characterize most family interactions.

Years of clinical experience with patients and their families have convinced me of certain unavoidable and painful truths about family life and its adverse effect on both children and on parents. Originally, I had no intention of investigating the structure of the nuclear family. My abiding interest was in tracing the pathology of my patients and in trying to understand the meaning of their symptoms and suffering.

In tracking down the mysteries of people's resistance to a better life and, in particular, in studying the voice process, I was forced to look at the destructive parental attitudes and responses that were so detrimental to the well-being of my patients. I discovered that the origins of people's self-defeating behavior and misery were directly traceable to the trauma and abuse they had suffered within the traditional family structure. Finally, I had to begin to question my earlier thinking about the family. Like most people, I had considerable resistance to closely examining this structure, because I had a defensive stake in the sanctity of the family. However, as I explored the lives of my patients, my own personal experiences, and the critical issues raised by parents in the reference population— individuals who openly revealed every aspect of their family life—I became increasingly aware that destructive bonds and the organization of psychological defenses around the fantasy bond within the family were important sources of human suffering and primary causative factors in psychopathology.

THE WIDESPREAD NATURE OF EMOTIONAL CHILD ABUSE IN OUR SOCIETY

Parents and professionals alike have difficulty facing the fact that the mistreatment of children is *not* an isolated phenomenon to be found in relatively few pathological family constellations. Within the average or statistically normal family, acts of psychological brutality and violence against the child's personality and spirit occur routinely. These abuses are far more widespread than previously thought. Reprehensible though physical child abuse and sexual abuse can be, focusing on this form of mistreatment may well serve to divert our attention from other, equally painful experiences routinely endured by children within most families. With respect to physical or to emotional child abuse, virtually *no* family can withstand close scrutiny. At the same time, to castigate or blame mothers and fathers, or to become moralistic or punitive about damaging parental responses, compounds the problem and causes additional suffering. There is a great deal of difference between accounting for and understanding the roots of psychopathology, as compared with focusing blame.

THE DISTINCTION BETWEEN ADULTS AND CHILDREN

Most people have a misconception about adults as distinguished from children; they perceive adults as more mature emotionally than children, based on the assumption that adults have somehow outgrown or transcended the fears, turmoil, and pain of their childhoods. This premise is generally false; people rarely leave behind the primitive longing, the fear, and the feelings of helplessness they experienced as children. Residuals of the hurt child exist in every person and are acted out in petty arguments, in expressions of intense jealousy and rivalry, and in desperate moves to preserve dependent, symbiotic relationships.

In an ongoing seminar and forum made up of a large number of professionals and intelligent lay people, we attempted to "define" the basic concept and nature of the child. In this forum, we were surprised to discover that there were very few distinctions between the emotions experienced by adults and those felt by the children. Most parents were functioning at approximately the same emotional level as their children; they had simply become more sophisticated at covering up unacceptable feelings. They had matured in their physical mastery of the world but not in their emotional development. In that regard, they were older, but not wiser.

We found that most adults had remnants of intense rage toward parents and parental substitutes, as well as unrequited longings to be taken care of, admired, and loved. They experienced the same dependency needs they had felt as children and were plagued by guilt reactions and feelings of worthlessness and powerlessness. From these revelations, we concluded that parental role-playing in relation to children was not authentic or appropriate. Much of what is passed on to the child, based on parents' experience and so-called emotional maturity, is dishonest and demeaning to the child. Parental lectures, admonitions, and warnings to children and, later, to adolescents about human relationships are based more on defensive ignorance than on real knowledge about life.

ARGUMENTS CONCERNING "THE INVULNERABLE CHILD"

Some experts argue that many adults *do* transcend traumatic childhoods. For example, a number of clinicians have demonstrated that certain resilient or "invulnerable" children have been capable of overcoming severe emotional deprivation and/or cruelty and have developed into competent, well-adjusted adults. This phenomenon has been used to support the argument that constitutional factors overshadow environmental influences in the etiology of mental disturbances. However, more recent studies found that the children who experienced severe abuse and neglect, yet who developed few symptoms as adults, generally had a significant other—a relative, family friend, or teacher—who took an interest in them and provided them with support (Cohler, 1987). This successful reliance on nonparental support coincides with our experience.

Other theorists view children as possessing innate aggression—a perspective reflecting Freud's concept of the "death instinct." For example, Melanie Klein (1948/1964) has deemphasized parents' role in the psychological disturbances of their children by stressing that the child projects his own rage onto his parents and then feels persecuted and paranoid. Thus, the child is perceived as creating much of his own misery and distress. This view, still held by many psychoanalysts, often serves as a cover-up for parental abuses and is damaging to parents and to children.

Furthermore, we contend that an individual's suicidal potential—his propensity for committing emotional suicide and, in extreme circumstances, actual suicide—does not reside in an innate "death instinct" as postulated by Klein (1948/1964), Freud (1925/1959), Menninger (1938), and others. Until a child becomes fully aware of the concept of death, his aggression is derived directly from the frustration of his wants and needs; it does *not* stem from an inborn instinct for aggression. The universal tendency toward self-destruction, assumed by these theorists to be derived from the death instinct, represents instead a powerful defense against the anxiety and dread of death. Although on a phenomenological level, we, too, are cognizant of a person's self-hatred and aggressive behavior toward other persons, we contend that this aggression is based on resentment and torment related to the human condition; that is, we hate ourselves for our frailty, weakness, vulnerability, and the impossibility of ensuring our survival in the ultimate sense.

A human being is *not* by nature suicidal, but in the face of death, he often chooses to give up his life as a defense. Basically, he divests himself of an emotional involvement in a life he must certainly lose. Self-destructive tendencies associated with aggression turned against the self are manifestations of people's attempts to accommodate to death by deadening themselves in advance (Firestone & Seiden,1987).

CULTURAL FACTORS THAT SUPPORT
DEHUMANIZATION OF THE CHILD

On a broader scale, all societies and complex social structures are generally restrictive of individuality and personal expression in the face of existential anxiety, and all cultural patterns or practices represent to some extent a form of adaptation to people's fear of death. Increased submission to the defensive process of conformity represents a generalized movement toward a suicidal process and destruction of all that is human (Berke, 1988; Lasch, 1984).

> Despite the fact that each family or group has its own unique life-style, there are many general attitudes, behaviors, roles, and routines in society that most of us accept uncritically. Many of these socially approved patterns of behavior and points of view reflect the individual defense patterns of each person. Thus, *society represents a pooling of individual defense systems.* (Firestone & Catlett, 1989, p. 29)

The child is first exposed to the idiosyncratic conditioning of the microculture of the family in which he is raised. As he expands his boundaries into the neighborhood, the school, and the larger society, he encounters new imprinting and socialization processes. In general, chronic and progressive self-denial has become a socially acceptable defense against death anxiety in our culture. For example, as people grow older, they come to feel or believe that it is increasingly inappropriate to fully participate in and continue life-affirming activities—including sports, social relationships with old friends, and the pursuit of newness, adventure, change, and personal development. There is a steady decline and an inclination toward passivity and inactivity. In rationing their pleasure and increasingly restricting their lives, they experience boredom, a sense of emptiness, and feelings of a life not fully lived. They rationalize their self-denial and progressively give up life in the face of impending death.

Modern society can be seen as moving toward more elaborate and more effective defenses and the cutting off of feeling. In that sense, the socialization process can be conceptualized as suicidal in nature, because its mores and conventions fit in with, and validate, each individual's self-limiting, self-destructive thought process or "voice." Its institutions reinforce the formation of bonds within the couple and the family, fostering an illusion of connection linked to immortality. Conventional views strongly support an individual's tendency to cut off feelings for himself and others, which, in turn, leaves him more susceptible to self-destructive behavior.

In addition, because of modern modes of transportation and increased communication through the media, societies are becoming more standardized. Cross-cultural studies show that previously diverse societies are becoming increasingly similar in practices and mores, and individuality is on the wane.

R. D. Laing (1988) commented on this state of affairs in a recent interview:

> Until it was decided by dictate that you're not allowed to see things other people don't see, hear things other people don't hear, or smell things other people don't smell, we all didn't have to hear, smell, and see things the same way. This was never the case in the history of humanity. The ordinary human might, when depressed, see the sky become dark or the sun cloud over. The whole world was once part of man's psyche. But no longer. Everything now has got to be experienced all the time in the same way as everyone else. Experience has become homogenized. (p. 62)

Society is constantly evolving. Over the millennia, people have unknowingly created increasingly complex institutions, conventions, belief systems, and sanctions in their attempt to adapt to death anxiety by limiting life and dulling feeling and awareness. Each generation has been raised by people whose ancestors were themselves reared by parents who knew and feared death as a reality and defensively retreated from investing in their lives. Each succeeding generation has added its own incremental building blocks to the system of denial and accommodation, contributing to the increased rigidity and power of the defensive process.

Today, when a young person breaks away from family ties and struggles to be an individual within our social structure, not only does he have to overcome inner anxieties about being separate and helpless in the face of his inevitable fate, but he is also subject to the strong social pressure exerted by conventional thinking. Negative pressure has a powerful delimiting effect on personal freedom, sexuality, integrity, and the natural drive for affiliation with other people.

As a result of early training and acculturation within the context of the family, an individual cannot easily escape his own imprinting and self-programming, even in situations and subcultures where he is exposed to a freer atmosphere. Most adults remain prisoners of their own internal conditioning. They are trapped between neurotic guilt about moving toward personal goals and away from family ties, and existential guilt about retreating from life and moving toward self-defeating and self-destructive behavior. For example, if people achieve more than their parents did, if they seek gratification of wants denied them in their families, they experience painful feelings of recrimination. If, however, they submit to this guilt and retreat, thereby regressing to an inward posture of passivity and fantasy, they become progressively more demoralized and self-hating. In a certain sense, each individual is suspended between these polarities of guilt, and they form the boundaries of his experience (Firestone, 1987b).

THE DILEMMA OF DEFENSES

The same defenses that once helped protect us from painful emotions when we were young, now handicap us and restrict our responses to the people closest to us, especially our children. Defended parents, as we have seen, inadvertently deprive their children of their basic human qualities—their feelings and their intellectual capacity—while attempting to spare them the pain that they themselves have suffered. In this sense, a person's self-protective defenses are generally destructive to others. Yet it serves no purpose for parents to punish themselves. This process of self-attack in parents is demoralizing; it leads to painful guilt reactions and to an even more alienated attitude toward their children. It is better for parents to change their behavior than to blame and castigate themselves.

It is often difficult for clinicians to interrupt this cycle of guilt and self-castigation in parents, and, at the same time, help them see *why* they act out abusive, intrusive, or suppressive behavior on their children. The crux of the therapeutic process involves parents' developing insight into the origins of their defenses and limitations without increasing their guilt. Therapists must be able to help parents understand the sources of their self-hatred and aggression so that they can recover feeling for themselves, thereby gaining control over actions they disapprove of.

In becoming aware of, and sensitized to, the important issues involved in sensitive child-rearing, parents could devote their efforts to "letting their child be" in the sense of allowing his real personality and unique qualities to emerge. They could provide experiences that help him access his inner world, while striving to avoid interactions and child-rearing practices that cause him to close up. An analogy to psychotherapy is appropriate here. Overinterpreting, diagnosing, categorizing, and analyzing patients usually has the same dehumanizing effect on them as an insensitive socialization process.

It is very important for parents not to distort or fracture the experiences of their children by provoking them unnecessarily and causing them to feel unduly angry or hostile. By far, the most damaging interactions between parents and children are those that arouse the child's anger, causing him to hate his parents. Somehow, in his rage, the child loses his humanness and specialness and turns his aggression against himself.

In destroying the child's capacity for loving, parents are in effect destroying the uniqueness of their child. On the other hand, allowing the child to love them is perhaps the most difficult task faced by parents. Many adults find it unbearably painful to break through well-established defenses in order to accept love and to live in harmony with another human being. Indeed, when parents feel a deep love for their children, they feel so much at times that it actually hurts; it may be emotionally or even physically painful. If they would choose to bear with these feelings and suffer through this poignant pain along with their children, they could develop a true sense of empathy. Parents who are able to relate to their children closely in a non-alienated posture open up the possibility for *their* children to live and to feel for *themselves*.

CONCLUSION

An awareness of the finite existence of all human beings makes life and living all the more precious. There is not a hidden significance or formula to life that may be discovered; rather, it is each individual's investment of himself, his feelings, his creativity, his interests, and his personal choice of people and activities that imbues life with its special meaning.

There *is* hope in understanding the psychodynamics involved in the formation of debilitating family bonds and the mechanisms that people use in an attempt to protect themselves against painful separation anxiety and the fear of death (the ultimate separation). In a sense, all human beings must mourn the anticipated loss of themselves and their loved ones in order to retain their capacity for genuine feelings. Sadness is therefore an inescapable part of a feelingful existence, not in the sense of having a morbid preoccupation with dying, but in a consciousness of limitation in time. Recognizing and living with these existential truths enhance those precious and irretrievable moments we spend with our children. This awareness can serve to remind us how vital it is *not* to damage a child's feelings, self-respect, special qualities and desires, and the spirit in which he approaches life and invests it with his own personal meaning.

My optimism in writing this book stems from my feeling that some people, by not surrendering to their internal processing and their parents' fears and anxieties, can break the chain of pain and neurosis that is passed from generation to generation. Parents learning to value their own lives, can better allow their child to preserve his human heritage rather than taking back the life they gave. Perhaps over many generations there could be movement toward a better environmental picture in relation to child-rearing. Perhaps, in future generations, parents will no longer be "the lost children."

Lastly, I want to thank so much the people who offered me their insights and personal experiences in our films and written material. I would like to express my indebtedness to them for their honesty, integrity, and courage, because they have been a continual source of support and inspiration to me in this endeavor. In reading these pages and coming to the conclusion of this work, I find myself at times overcome with feelings of sadness, and tears fill my eyes. The source of this sadness is difficult for me to ascertain—whether it comes from a feeling for children and the damage they experience at the hands of insensitive adults, or from personal limitations caused by painful events in my own childhood, or from the human suffering I have observed over the years, or simply from the fact that one is inevitably touched by feeling deeply for others.

I want to close with a personal plea to professionals and parents alike to consider their own humanity and the humanity of children, to give value to their own lives and their experiences in spite of painful existential issues. I hope that we can move beyond our limitations and reach out to children in a way that will spare them so much unnecessary suffering.

NOTES

1. Daniel N. Stern (1985), in *The Interpersonal World of the Infant*, calls attention to the 2- to 3-month-old infant's ability to elicit strong, positive social responses in its parents:

   The period roughly from two to six months is perhaps the most exclusively social period of life. By two or three months the social smile is in place, vocalizations directed at others have come in, mutual gaze is sought more avidly, predesigned preferences for the human face and voice are operating fully, and the infant undergoes that biobehavioral transformation resulting in a highly social partner. (p. 72)

APPENDIXES

APPENDICES

Documentary Videotapes on Interpersonal Relationships and Psychotherapy

The Glendon Association has assisted me in the production of a series of 18 videotapes about human relationships. Excerpts from these documentaries, produced and directed by Geoff Parr, appear throughout this work.

Closeness without Bonds: A Study of Destructive Ties in Couple Relationships (Parr, 1985a).*
The Inner Voice in Suicide (Parr, 1985b).*
Micro-Suicide: A Case Study (Parr, 1985c).*
Parent-Child Relations Series:
    Hunger vs. Love: A Perspective on Parent-Child Relations (Parr, 1987a).
    The Implicit Pain of Sensitive Child-Rearing (Parr, 1988b).
    The Inner Voice in Child Abuse (Parr, 1986).*
    Parental Ambivalence (Parr, 1987b).
    Therapeutic Child-Rearing: An In-Depth Approach to Compassionate Parenting (Parr, 1987c).
Sex and Pregnancy (Parr, 1985d).
Teaching Our Children About Feelings (Parr, 1985e).
Teenagers Talk About Suicide (Parr, 1988a).*
Voice Therapy with Dr. Robert Firestone (Parr, 1984).*

*With supplementary discussion videotape.

APPENDIX B

Continuum of Negative Thought Patterns

Any combination of the voice attacks listed on the following pages can lead to serious suicidal intent, particularly those thoughts that promote isolation, ideation about removing oneself from people's lives, and beliefs that one has a destructive effect on others. Voices urging one to give up special activities, vicious self-abusive thoughts accompanied by strong anger, and, of course, voices urging self-injury and a suicide attempt are indications of high suicide potential or risk, especially when combined with thoughts influencing isolation.

Levels of increasing suicidal intention	Content of voice statements*
Low self-esteem	1. Self-critical thoughts of everyday life, self-depreciation.	*You're incompetent, stupid. You're not very attractive. You're going to make a fool of yourself.*
	2. Voices rationalizing self-denial. Thoughts praising and approving selflessness and asceticism.	*You're too inexperienced to apply for this job. You're too shy to make any new friends. Why go on this trip? It'll be such a hassle. You'll save money by staying home.*
	3. Cynical attitudes toward others combined with self-attacks leading to alienation and distancing.	*Why go out with her (him)? She's cold, unreliable; she'll reject you. She wouldn't go out with you anyway. You can't trust men (women).*
A tendency toward isolation	4. Thoughts influencing isolation. Rationalizations for time alone, but using time to attack oneself.	*Just be by yourself. You're miserable company anyway; who'd want to be with you? Just stay in the background, out of view.*
Psychological pain	5. Vicious self-abusive thoughts and self-accusations (accompanied by intense angry affect).	*You idiot! You bitch! You creep! You stupid shit! You don't deserve anything; you're worthless.*

Category	Thought Pattern	Voice Statement*
Substance abuse	6. Thoughts urging excessive use of substances followed by self-accusations (weakens inhibitions against self-destructive actions, while increasing guilt and self-recrimination).	*It's okay to use drugs, you'll be more relaxed. Go ahead and have a drink, you deserve it.... You weak-willed jerk! You're nothing but a drugged-out, drunken bum.*
Sense of hopelessness	7. Thoughts urging withdrawal or removal of oneself completely from the lives of people closest. (Rational, moral justification for immoral acts, e.g., one's children would be better off if one left or committed suicide.)	*See how bad you make your family (friends) feel. They'd be better off without you. It's the only decent thing to do—just stay away and stop bothering them.*
Progressive withdrawal from favored activities	8. Voices influencing person to give up priorities and favored activities.	*What's the use? Work doesn't matter any more. Why bother even trying? Nothing matters anyway.*
Perturbation (intense agitation)	9. Injunctions to inflict injury on self at an action level (intense rage against self). (Basis of self-mutilation sometimes observed in seriously disturbed patients.)	*Why don't you just drive across the center divider? Just shove your hand under that power saw!*
	10. Thoughts planning details of suicide (calm, rational, often obsessive, indicating complete loss of feeling for self).	*You have to get hold of some pills, then go to a hotel, etc.*
	11. Injunctions to carry out suicide plans (extreme thought constriction).	*You've thought about this long enough. Just get it over with. It's the only way out!*

*Specific voice statements that can be identified as typical at each level of increasing suicidal intention.

References

Ainsworth, M. D. S. (1982). Early caregiving and later patterns of attachment. In M. H. Klaus & M. O. Robertson (Eds.), *Birth, interaction and attachment* (pp. 35-42). Skillman, NJ: Johnson & Johnson Baby Products.

Ainsworth, M. D. S., Blehar, M. C., Waters, E., & Wall, S. (1978). *Patterns of attachment: A psychological study of the Strange situation.* Hillsdale, NJ: Lawrence Erlbaum.

Anthony, E. J. (1972). The contagious subculture of psychosis. In C. J. Sager & H. S. Kaplan (Eds.), *Progress in group and family therapy* (pp. 636-658). New York: Brunner/Mazel.

Anthony, E. J. (1987). Children at high risk for psychosis growing up successfully. In E. J. Anthony & B. J. Cohler (Eds.), *The invulnerable child* (pp. 147-184). New York: Guilford Press.

Anthony, S. (1973). *The discovery of death in childhood and after.* Harmondsworth, England: Penguin Education. (Originally published, 1971.)

Arieti, S. (1974). *Interpretation of schizophrenia* (2nd ed.). New York: Basic Books.

Badinter, E. (1981). *Mother love: Myth and reality: Motherhood in modern history.* New York: Macmillan. (Originally published, 1980.)

Baer, D. M., & Sherman, J. A. (1964). Reinforcement control of generalized imitation in young children. *Journal of Experimental Child Psychology, 1,* 37-49.

Baer, D. M., Peterson, R. F., & Sherman, J. A. (1967). The development of imitation by reinforcing behavioral similarity to a model. *Journal of the Experimental Analysis of Behavior, 10,* 405-416.

Bandura, A. (1969). *Principles of behavior modification.* New York: Holt, Rinehart & Winston.

Bandura, A. (Ed.). (1971). *Psychological modeling: Conflicting theories.* Chicago: Aldine-Atherton.

Bandura, A. (1986). *Social foundations of thought and action: A social cognitive theory.* Englewood Cliffs, NJ: Prentice-Hall.

Bandura, A., & Walters, R. H. (1963). *Social learning and personality development.* New York: Holt, Rinehart & Winston.

Barnes, M. & Berke, J. (1971). *Mary Barnes: Two accounts of a journey through madness.* New York: Ballantine Books.

Bateson, G. (1972). *Steps to an ecology of mind.* New York: Ballantine Books.

Bateson, G., Jackson, D. D., Haley, J., & Weakland, J. H. (1972). Toward a theory of schizophrenia. In G. Bateson, *Steps to an ecology of mind* (pp. 201-227). New York: Ballantine Books. (Originally published, 1956.)

Beavers, W. R. (1977). *Psychotherapy and growth: A family systems perspective.* New York: Brunner/Mazel.

Beck, A. T. (1976). *Cognitive therapy and the emotional disorders.* New York: New American Library.

Beck, A. T., Rush, A. J., Shaw, B. F., & Emery, G. (1979). *Cognitive therapy of depression.* New York: Guilford Press.

Becker, E. (1973). *The denial of death.* New York: Free Press.

Bellack, A. S., & Hersen, M. (1977). *Behavior modification: An introductory textbook.* Baltimore: Williams &Wilkins.

Beres, D. (1966). Superego and depression. In R. M. Loewenstein, L. M. Newman, M. Schur, & A. J. Solnit (Eds.), *Psychoanalysis—A general psychology: Essays in honor of Heinz Hartmann* (pp. 479-498). New York: International Universities Press.

Berger, K. S. (1980). *The developing person.* New York: Worth Publishers.

Berke, J. H. (1988). *The tyranny of malice: Exploring the dark side of character and culture.* New York: Summit Books.

Berman, E. (1988). Communal upbringing in the kibbutz: The allure and risks of psychoanalytic utopianism. In A. J. Solnit, P. B. Neubauer, S. Abrams, & A. S. Dowling (Eds.), *The psychoanalytic study of the child, Vol. 43* (pp. 319-335). New Haven: Yale University Press.

Bettelheim, B. (1969). *The children of the dream.* New York: Macmillan.

Bettelheim, B. (1971). *Dialogues with mothers.* New York: Avon Books. (Originally published, 1962.)

Bettelheim, B. (1979). Individual and mass behavior in extreme situations. In *Surviving and other essays* (pp. 48-83). New York: Alfred A. Knopf. (Originally published, 1943.)

Bettelheim, B. (1985). Punishment versus discipline. *Atlantic Monthly, 256*(5), 51-59.

Bettelheim, B. (1987). *A good enough parent.* New York: Alfred A. Knopf.

Biller, H. B., & Solomon, R. S. (1986). *Child maltreatment and paternal deprivation: A manifesto for research, prevention, and treatment.* Lexington, MA: Lexington Books.

Black, C. (1981). *It will never happen to me!* Denver: M.A.C. Printing and Publications Division.

Blanck, G., & Blanck, R. (1974). *Ego psychology: Theory and practice.* New York: Columbia University Press.

Bloch, D. (1985). The child's fear of infanticide and the primary motive force of defense. *Psychoanalytic Review, 72*(4), 573-588.

Boszormenyi-Nagy, I., & Spark, G. M. (1984). *Invisible loyalties: Reciprocity in intergenerational family therapy.* New York: Brunner/Mazel. (Originally published, 1973.)

Bowen, M. (1961). The family as the unit of study and treatment: (1) Family psychotherapy. *American Journal of Orthopsychiatry, 31*(1), 40-60.

Bowen, M. (1965). Family psychotherapy with schizophrenia in the hospital and in private practice. In I. Boszormenyi-Nagy & J. L. Framo (Eds.), *Intensive family therapy: Theoretical and practical aspects* (pp. 213-243). New York: Harper & Row.

Bowen, M. (1976). Theory in the practice of psychotherapy. In P. J. Guerin, Jr. (Ed.), *Family therapy: Theory and practice,* (pp. 42-90). New York: Gardner Press.

Bowen, M. (1978). *Family therapy in clinical practice*. New York: Jason Aronson.

Bowlby, J. (1953). *Child care and the growth of love*. Harmondsworth, England: Penguin Books.

Bowlby, J. (1973). *Attachment and loss, Vol. II, Separation: Anxiety and anger*. New York: Basic Books.

Bowlby, J. (1979). *The making and breaking of affectional bonds*. London: Tavistock Publications.

Boyd, S. (1982). *Analysis of a unique psychological laboratory*. Unpublished manuscript.

Branden, N. (1971). *The psychology of self-esteem: A new concept of man's psychological nature*. New York: Bantam Books. (Originally published, 1969.)

Brazelton, T. B. (1973). Effect of maternal expectations on early infant behavior. *Early Child Development and Care, 2*, 259-273.

Brazelton, T. B. (1974). *Toddlers and parents: A declaration of independence*. New York: Delacorte Press.

Brazelton, T. B. (1983). *Infants and mothers: Differences in development* (rev. ed.). New York: Delta/Seymour Lawrence.

Brody, S. (1956). *Patterns of mothering: Maternal influence during infancy*. New York: International Universities Press.

Bromberg, N. (1955). Maternal influences in the development of moral masochism. *American Journal of Orthopsychiatry, 25*, 802-812.

Broussard, E. R. (1979). Assessment of the adaptive potential of the mother-infant system: The neonatal perception inventories. *Seminars in Perinatology, 3*(1), 91-100.

Broussard, E. R. (1984). Maternal empathy: Its relation to emerging self-representations and empathy in infants. In J. Lichtenberg, M. Bornstein, & D. Silver (Eds.), *Empathy II* (Vol. 2). Hillsdale, NJ: Analytic Press.

Buscaglia, L. F. (1987, November 22). Living & loving: Out of the mouths of 10-year-olds.... *Los Angeles Times*, Part VI, p. 10.

Butler, P. E. (1981). *Talking to yourself*. New York: Stein & Day.

Calderone, M. S. (1977). Eroticism as a norm. In E. S. Morrison & V. Borosage (Eds.), *Human sexuality: Contemporary perspectives* (2nd ed., pp. 39-48). Palo Alto, CA: Mayfield Publishing. (Originally published, 1974.)

California School of Professional Psychology. (1987). The treatment and prevention of child abuse: A training workshop sponsored by the California School of Professional Psychology, Berkeley, California State Psychological Association, San Francisco Psychological Association. Berkeley, CA: Author.

Caplan, P. J. (1981). *Between women: Lowering the barriers*. Toronto: Personal Library.

Carter, C. S. (1988). Patterns of infant feeding, the mother-infant interaction and stress management. In T. M. Field, P. M. McCabe, & N. Schneiderman (Eds.), *Stress and coping across development* (pp. 27-46). Hillsdale, NJ: Lawrence Erlbaum.

Cavaiola, A. A., & Schiff, M. (1988). Behavioral sequelae of physical and/or sexual abuse in adolescents. *Child Abuse and Neglect, 12*, 181-188.

Chernin, K. (1985). *The hungry self: Women, eating, and identity*. New York: Times Books.

Chess, S., & Thomas, A. (1987). *Know your child: An authoritative guide for today's parents*. New York: Basic Books.

Clyman, R. B., Emde, R. N., Kempe, J. E., & Harmon, R. J. (1986). Social referencing and social looking among twelve-month-old infants. In T. B. Brazelton & M. W. Yogman (Eds.), *Affective development in infancy* (pp. 75-94). Norwood, NJ: Ablex Publishing.

Cohler, B. J. (1987). Adversity, resilience, and the study of lives. In E. J. Anthony & B. J. Cohler (Eds.), *The invulnerable child* (pp. 363-424). New York: Guilford Press.

Conroy, P. (1986). *The prince of tides*. Boston: Houghton Mifflin.

Conte, J. R. (1984). Progress in treating the sexual abuse of children. *Social Work, 29*, 258-263.

Conte, J. R. (1988). The effects of sexual abuse on children: Results of a research project. *Human sexual aggression: Current perspectives. Annals of the New York Academy of Sciences, 528*, 310-326.

Coons, P. M. (1986). Child abuse and multiple personality disorder: Review of the literature and suggestions for treatment. *Child Abuse and Neglect, 10*, 455-462.

Cooper, D. (1971). *The death of the family*. New York: Vintage Books. (Originally published, 1970.)

Dean, R. B., & Richardson, H. (1964). Analysis of MMPI profiles of forty college-educated overt male homosexuals. *Journal of Consulting Psychology, 28*(6), 483-486.

Demos, V. (1986). Crying in early infancy: An illustration of the motivational function of affect. In T. B. Brazelton & M. W. Yogman (Eds.), *Affective development in infancy* (pp. 39-73). Norwood, NJ: Ablex Publishing.

Deutsch, H. (1944). *The psychology of women: A psychoanalytic interpretation* (Vol. 1). New York: Grune & Stratton.

Deutsch, H. (1945). *The psychology of women: A psychoanalytic interpretation: Vol. 2, Motherhood*. New York: Grune & Stratton.

Dodson, F. (1970). *How to parent*. New York: New American Library.

Dryfoos, J. G., & Bourque-Scholl, N. (1981). *Factbook on teenage pregnancy: Tables and references for teenage pregnancy: The problem that hasn't gone away*. New York: Alan Guttmacher Institute.

Dugan, M. N. (1977). Fear of death: The effect of parental behavior and personality upon the behavior and personality of their children. *Dissertation Abstracts International, 38*(3), 1318-A.

Earls, F., Beardslee, W., & Garrison, W. (1987). Correlates and predictors of competence in young children. In E. J. Anthony & B. J. Cohler (Eds.), *The invulnerable child* (pp. 70-83). New York: Guilford Press.

Ellis, A., & Harper, R. A. (1975). *A new guide to rational living*. North Hollywood, CA: Wilshire Book Co.

Ellison, R. (1947). *Invisible man*. New York: Random House.

Elmer, E. (1967). *Children in jeopardy: A study of abused minors and their families*. Pittsburgh: University of Pittsburgh Press.

Elmer, E. (1975). A social worker's assessment of medico-social stress in child abuse cases. In *Fourth National Symposium on Child Abuse* (pp. 86-91). Denver: American Humane Association.

Emerson, S., & McBride, M. C. (1986). *A model for group treatment of adults molested as children*. Las Vegas, NV: University of Nevada. (ERIC Document Reproduction Service No. ED 272 814).

Epstein, A. W. (1987). Observations on maternal protective behavior derived from unconscious phenomena. *Journal of the American Academy of Psychoanalysis, 15*(3), 407-414.

Fairbairn, W. R. D. (1952). *Psychoanalytic studies of the personality*. London: Routledge & Kegan Paul.

Farber, E. A., & Egeland, B. (1987). Invulnerability among abused and neglected children. In E. J. Anthony & B. J. Cohler (Eds.), *The invulnerable child* (pp. 253-288). New York: Guilford Press.

Faulkner, W. (1987). *As I lay dying*. New York: Vintage Books. (Originally published, 1930.)

Ferenczi, S. (1929). The unwelcome child and his death-instinct. *International Journal of Psycho-Analysis, 10,* 125-129.

Feshbach, N. D. (1980). Corporal punishment in the schools: Some paradoxes, some facts, some possible directions. In G. Gerbner, C. J. Ross, & E. Zigler (Eds.), *Child abuse: An agenda for action* (pp. 204-221). New York: Oxford University Press.

Fierman, L. B. (Ed.). (1965). *Effective psychotherapy: The contribution of Hellmuth Kaiser.* New York: Free Press.

Finkel, K. C. (1987). Sexual abuse of children: An update. *Canadian Medical Association Journal, 136,* 245-252.

Firestone, R. W. (1957). *A concept of the schizophrenic process.* Unpublished doctoral dissertation, University of Denver.

Firestone, R. W. (1984). A concept of the primary fantasy bond: A developmental perspective. *Psychotherapy, 21,* 218-225.

Firestone, R. W. (1985). *The fantasy bond: Structure of psychological defenses.* New York: Human Sciences Press.

Firestone, R. W. (1987a). Destructive effects of the fantasy bond in couple and family relationships. *Psychotherapy, 24,* 233-239.

Firestone, R. W. (1987b). The "voice": The dual nature of guilt reactions. *American Journal of Psychoanalysis, 47,* 210-229.

Firestone, R. W. (1988). *Voice therapy: A psychotherapeutic approach to self-destructive behavior.* New York: Human Sciences Press.

Firestone, R. W., & Catlett, J. (1989). *Psychological defenses in everyday life.* New York: Human Sciences Press.

Firestone, R. W., & Seiden, R. H. (1987). Microsuicide and suicidal threats of everyday life. *Psychotherapy, 24,* 31-39.

Fisher, S., & Fisher, R. L. (1986). *What we really know about child rearing: Science in support of effective parenting.* Northvale, NJ: Jason Aronson.

Fisher, T. D. (1986a). An exploratory study of parent-child communication about sex and the sexual attitudes of early, middle, and late adolescents. *Journal of Genetic Psychology, 147,* 543-557.

Fisher, T. D. (1986b). Parent-child communication about sex and young adolescents' sexual knowledge and attitudes. *Adolescence, 21(83),* 517-527.

Fontana, V. J. (1983). *Somewhere a child is crying: Maltreatment—causes and prevention* (rev. ed.). New York: New American Library.

Forward, S., & Buck, C. (1978). *Betrayal of innocence: Incest and its devastation.* Los Angeles: J. P. Tarcher.

Fraiberg, S., Adelson, E., & Shapiro, V. (1980). Ghosts in the nursery: A psychoanalytic approach to the problems of impaired infant-mother relationships. In S. Fraiberg (Ed.), *Clinical studies in infant mental health: The first year of life* (pp. 164-196). New York: Basic Books.

Fraiberg, S. H. (1968). *The magic years: Understanding and handling the problems of early childhood.* London: Methuen. (Originally published, 1959.)

Framo, J. L. (1972). Symptoms from a family transactional viewpoint. In C. J. Sager & H. S. Kaplan (Eds.), *Progress in group and family therapy* (pp. 271-308). New York: Brunner/Mazel. (Originally published, 1970.)

Freedman, D. A. (1975). The battering parent and his child: A study in early object relations. *International Review of Psycho-Analysis, 2,* 189-198.

Freud, A. (1946). *The ego and the mechanisms of defence* (C. Baines, Trans.). New York: International Universities Press.

Freud, A., & Burlingham, D. (1944). *Infants without families: The case for and against residential nurseries.* New York: International Universities Press.

Freud, S. (1957). Five lectures on psycho-analysis. In J. Strachey (Ed. and Trans.), *The standard edition of the complete psychological works of Sigmund Freud* (Vol. 11, pp. 9-55). London: Hogarth Press. (Originally published, 1910.)

Freud, S. (1957). Mourning and melancholia. In J. Strachey (Ed. and Trans.), *The standard edition of the complete psychological works of Sigmund Freud* (Vol. 14, pp. 243-258). London: Hogarth Press. (Originally published, 1917.)

Freud, S. (1957). On narcissism: An introduction. In J. Strachey (Ed. and Trans.), *The standard edition of the complete psychological works of Sigmund Freud* (Vol. 14, pp. 73-102). London: Hogarth Press. (Originally published, 1914.)

Freud, S. (1959). An autobiographical study. In J. Strachey (Ed. and Trans.), *The standard edition of the complete psychological works of Sigmund Freud* (Vol. 20, pp. 7-70). London: Hogarth Press. (Originally published, 1925.)

Freud, S. (1961). Civilization and its discontents. In J. Strachey (Ed. and Trans.), *The standard edition of the complete psychological works of Sigmund Freud* (Vol. 21, pp. 64-145). London: Hogarth Press. (Originally published, 1930.)

Freud, S. (1961). The ego and the id. In J. Strachey (Ed. and Trans.), *The standard edition of the complete psychological works of Sigmund Freud* (Vol. 19, pp. 12-66). London: Hogarth Press. (Originally published, 1923.)

Freud, S. (1962). The aetiology of hysteria. In J. Strachey (Ed. and Trans.), *The standard edition of the complete psychological works of Sigmund Freud* (Vol. 3, pp. 191-221). London: Hogarth Press. (Originally published, 1896.)

Freud, S. (1964). An outline of psycho-analysis. In J. Strachey (Ed. and Trans.), *The standard edition of the complete psychological works of Sigmund Freud* (Vol. 23, pp. 144-207). London: Hogarth Press. (Originally published, 1940.)

Friday, N. (1977). *My mother/my self: The daughter's search for identity.* New York: Delacorte Press.

Friedrich, W. N., & Reams, R. A. (1987). Course of psychological symptoms in sexually abused young children. *Psychotherapy, 24,* 160-170.

Frieze, I. H., Parsons, J. E., Johnson, P. B., Ruble, D. N., & Zellman, G. L. (1978). *Women and sex roles: A social psychological perspective.* New York: W. W. Norton.

Fromm, E. (1941). *Escape from freedom.* New York: Avon Books.

Fromm-Reichmann, F. (1960). *Principles of intensive psychotherapy.* Chicago: University of Chicago Press.

Galinsky, E. (1981). *Between generations.* New York: Times Books.

Garbarino, J. (1976). A preliminary study of some ecological correlates of child abuse: The impact of socioeconomic stress on mothers. *Child Development, 47,* 178-185.

Garbarino, J., & Gilliam, G. (1980). *Understanding abusive families.* Lexington, MA: Lexington Books.

Garbarino, J., Guttmann, E., & Seeley, J. W. (1986). *The psychologically battered child.* San Francisco: Jossey-Bass.

Garmezy, N. (1971). Vulnerability research and the issue of primary prevention. *American Journal of Orthopsychiatry, 41*(1), 101-116.

Gelman, D. (1987, October 26). Not tonight, dear. *Newsweek,* pp. 64-66.

Genevie, L., & Margolies, E. (1987). *The motherhood report: How women feel about being mothers.* New York: Macmillan.

Gibran, K. (1923). *The prophet.* New York: Alfred A. Knopf.

Gilbert, C. (1973). *An American family* [TV documentary]. New York: WNET, PBS.

Ginott, H. G. (1965). *Between parent and child: New solutions to old problems*. New York: Macmillan.

Goldberg, A. (1972). On the incapacity to love: A psychotherapeutic approach to the problem in adolescence. *Archives of General Psychiatry, 26,* 3-7.

Goldston, S. E. (1977). An overview of primary prevention programming. In D. C. Kline & S. E. Goldston (Eds.), *Primary prevention: An idea whose time has come* (Proceedings of the Pilot Conference on Primary Prevention, April 2-4, 1976) (pp. 23-40). DHEW Publication No. (ADM)77-447. Washington, DC: Government Printing Office.

Goleman, D. (1985). *Vital lies, simple truths: The psychology of self-deception*. New York: Simon & Schuster.

Gordon, M., & Shankweiler, P. J. (1971). Different equals less: Female sexuality in recent marriage manuals. *Journal of Marriage and the Family, 33,* 459-466.

Gove, W. R., & Hughes, M. (1980). Reexamining the ecological fallacy: A study in which aggregate data are critical in investigating the pathological effects of living alone. *Social Forces, 58*(4), 1157-1177.

Greenberg, J. R., & Mitchell, S. A. (1983). *Object relations in psychoanalytic theory*. Cambridge: Harvard University Press.

Greenspan, S. I. (1981). *Psychopathology and adaptation in infancy and early childhood: Principles of clinical diagnosis and preventive intervention*. Madison, CT: International Universities Press.

Greenwald, J. (1973). *Be the person you were meant to be (antidotes to toxic living)*. New York: Dell Publishing.

Greer, G. (1971). *The female eunuch*. New York: McGraw-Hill. (Originally published, 1970.)

Greer, G. (1984). *Sex and destiny: The politics of human fertility*. New York: Harper & Row.

Grotstein, J. S. (1981). *Splitting and projective identification*. Northvale, NJ: Jason Aronson.

Gunderson, J. G., & Mosher, L. R. (Eds.). (1975). *Psychotherapy of schizophrenia*. New York: Jason Aronson.

Gunderson, M. P., & McCary, J. L. (1979). Sexual guilt and religion. *Family Coordinator, 28,* 353-357.

Guntrip, H. (1961). *Personality structure and human interaction*. New York: International Universities Press.

Guntrip, H. (1969). *Schizoid phenomena object-relations and the self*. New York: International Universities Press.

Haller, O. L., & Alter-Reid, K. (1986). Secretiveness and guardedness: A comparison of two incest-survivor samples. *American Journal of Psychotherapy, 40,* 554-563.

Hambidge, D. M. (1988). Incest and anorexia nervosa: What is the link? *British Journal of Psychiatry, 152,* 145-146.

Harper, R. A. (1981). Limitations of marriage and family therapy. *Rational Living, 16*(2), 3-6.

Helfer, R. (1982). The relationship between lack of bonding and child abuse and neglect. In M. H. Klaus, T. Leger, & M. A. Trause (Eds.), *Maternal attachment and mothering disorders* (2nd ed., pp. 15-21). Skillman, NJ: Johnson & Johnson Baby Products.

Hill, L. B. (1955). *Psychotherapeutic intervention in schizophrenia*. Chicago: University of Chicago Press.

Hinde, R. A. (1974). *Biological bases of human social behaviour*. New York: McGraw-Hill.

Hoekelman, R. A. (1983). Introduction. In V. J. Sasserath (Ed.), *Minimizing high-risk parenting: A review of what is known and consideration of appropriate preventive information* (pp. xiii-xvi). Skillman, NJ: Johnson & Johnson Baby Products.

Hoffman, S. I., & Straus, S. (1985). The development of children's concepts of death. *Death Studies, 9,* 469-482.

Hooker, E. (1969). Parental relations and male homosexuality in patient and nonpatient samples. *Journal of Consulting and Clinical Psychology, 33*(2), 140-142.

Hyson, M. C., Whitehead, L. C., & Prudhoe, C. M. (1988). Influences on attitudes toward physical affection between adults and children. *Early Childhood Research Quarterly, 3,* 55-75.

Jackson, E. N. (1965). *Telling a child about death.* New York: Hawthorn Books.

Jacobson, E. (1964). *The self and the object world.* London: Hogarth Press and The Institute of Psycho-Analysis.

Janov, A. (1970). *The primal scream.* New York: G. P. Putnam's Sons.

Janov, A. (1973). *The feeling child.* New York: Simon & Schuster.

Johnson, A. M. (1951). Some etiological aspects of repression, guilt and hostility. *Psychoanalytic Quarterly, 20*(4), 511-527.

Jones, J. G. (1982). Sexual abuse of children: Current concepts. *American Journal of Diseases of Children, 136,* 142-146.

Justice, B., & Justice, R. (1976). *The abusing family.* New York: Human Sciences Press.

Kaffman, M. (1961). Evaluation of emotional disturbance in 403 Israeli kibbutz children. *American Journal of Psychiatry, 117,* 732-738.

Kagan, J. (1984). *The nature of the child.* New York: Basic Books.

Kaplan, H. S. (1979). *Disorders of sexual desire and other new concepts and techniques in sex therapy.* New York: Brunner/Mazel.

Kaplan, L. J. (1978). *Oneness and separateness: From infant to individual.* New York: Simon & Schuster.

Kaplan, L. J. (1984). *Adolescence: The farewell to childhood.* New York: Simon & Schuster.

Karon, B. P., & Vandenbos, G. R. (1981). *Psychotherapy of schizophrenia: The treatment of choice.* New York: Jason Aronson.

Karpel, M. (1976). Individuation: From fusion to dialogue. *Family Process, 15*(1), 65-82.

Kaufman, G. (1980). *Shame: The power of caring.* Cambridge, MA: Schenkman Publishing.

Kaufman, J., & Zigler, E. (1987). Do abused children become abusive parents? *American Journal of Orthopsychiatry, 57*(2), 186-192.

Kempe, R. S., & Kempe, C. H. (1984). *The common secret: Sexual abuse of children and adolescents.* New York: W. H. Freeman.

Kennell, J. H., Jerauld, R., Wolfe, H., Chesler, D., Kreger, N. C., McAlpine, W., Steffa, M., & Klaus, M. H. (1974). Maternal behavior one year after early and extended post-partum contact. *Developmental Medicine and Child Neurology, 16,* 172-179.

Kernberg, O. F. (1975). *Borderline conditions and pathological narcissism.* New York: Jason Aronson.

Kerr, M. E., & Bowen, M. (1988). *Family evaluation: An approach based on Bowen theory.* New York: W. W. Norton.

Klaus, M. H., & Kennell, J. H. (1976). *Maternal-infant bonding.* St. Louis: C. V. Mosby.

Klein, M. (1946). Notes on some schizoid mechanisms. *International Journal of Psycho-Analysis, 27,* 99-110.

Klein, M. (1964). *Contributions to psycho-analysis 1921-1945.* New York: McGraw-Hill. (Originally published, 1948.)

Kohut, H. (1977). *The restoration of the self.* New York:International Universities Press.

Korbin, J. E. (1981). "Very few cases": Child abuse and neglect in the People's Republic of China. In J. E. Korbin (Ed.), *Child abuse and neglect: Cross-cultural perspectives* (pp. 166-185). Berkeley: University of California Press.

Laing, R. D. (1967). *The politics of experience.* New York: Ballantine Books.

Laing, R. D. (1971). *Self and others*. Harmondsworth, England: Penguin Books. (Originally published, 1961.)

Laing, R. D. (1972). *The politics of the family and other essays*. New York: Vintage Books. (Originally published, 1969.)

Laing, R. D. (1988). [Interview with Anthony Liversidge.] *Omni, 10*(7), 56-63, 74-76.

Laing, R. D., & Esterson, A. (1964). *Sanity, madness, and the family: Vol. I. Families of schizophrenics*. New York: Basic Books.

Langs, R. (1982). *Psychotherapy: A basic text*. New York: Jason Aronson.

Lasch, C. (1979). *The culture of narcissism: American life in an age of diminishing expectations*. New York: W. W. Norton.

Lasch, C. (1984). *The minimal self: Psychic survival in troubled times*. New York: W. W. Norton.

Leach, P. (1987). *Babyhood* (2nd ed.). New York: Alfred A. Knopf.

LeMasters, E. E. (1963). Parenthood as crisis. In M. B. Sussman (Ed.), *Sourcebook in marriage and the family* (2nd ed., pp. 194-198). Boston: Houghton Mifflin. (Originally published, 1957.)

Lerner, H. G. (1988). *Women in therapy*. Northvale, NJ: Jason Aronson.

Levy, D. M. (1943). *Maternal overprotection*. New York: Columbia University Press.

Lidz, T. (1972). The influence of family studies on the treatment of schizophrenia. In C. J. Sager & H. S. Kaplan (Eds.), *Progress in group and family therapy* (pp. 616-635). New York: Brunner/Mazel. (Originally published, 1969.)

Lidz, T. (1973). *The origin and treatment of schizophrenic disorders*. New York: Basic Books.

Lidz, T. (1983). *The person: His and her development throughout the life cycle* (rev. ed.). New York: Basic Books.

Lidz, T., Cornelison, A., Carlson, D. T., & Fleck, S. (1972). Intrafamilial environment of the schizophrenic patient: The transmission of irrationality. In G. Handel (Ed.), *The psychosocial interior of the family* (2nd ed., pp. 276-291). Chicago: Aldine Publishing. (Originally published, 1958.)

Lief, H. I., & Reed, D. M. (1971). Normal psychosexual functioning. In A. M. Freedman & H. I. Kaplan (Eds.), *Human behavior: Biological, psychological, and sociological* (pp. 505-518). New York: Atheneum.

Livingston, R. (1987). Sexually and physically abused children. *Journal of the American Academy of Child and Adolescent Psychiatry, 26*(3), 413-415.

Loewenstein, R. M. (1966). On the theory of the superego: A discussion. In R. M. Loewenstein, L. M. Newman, M. Schur, & A. J. Solnit (Eds.), *Psychoanalysis—A general psychology: Essays in honor of Heinz Hartmann* (pp. 298-314). New York: International Universities Press.

Maccoby, E. E. (1980). *Social development: Psychological growth and the parent-child relationship*. New York: Harcourt Brace Jovanovich.

Macfarlane, A. (1977). *The psychology of childbirth*. Cambridge: Harvard University Press.

Mahler, M. S., Pine, F., & Bergman, A. (1975). *The psychological birth of the human infant: Symbiosis and individuation*. New York: Basic Books.

Main, M., Kaplan, N., & Cassidy, J. (1985). Security in infancy, childhood, and adulthood: A move to the level of representation. *Monographs of the Society for Research in Child Development, 50*(1-2, Serial No. 209), 66-104.

Maslow, A. H. (1954). *Motivation and personality*. New York: Harper & Brothers.

Massie, H. N., Bronstein, A., Afterman, J., & Campbell, B. K. (1988). Inner themes and outer behaviors in early childhood development: A longitudinal study. In A. J. Solnit, P. B. Neubauer, S. Abrams, & A. S. Dowling (Eds.), *The psychoanalytic study of the child* (Vol. 43, pp. 213-242). New Haven: Yale University Press.

Masson, J. M. (1984). *Assault on truth: Freud's suppression of the seduction theory.* New York: Farrar, Straus & Giroux.

Masterson, J. F. (1985). *The real self: A developmental, self, and object relations approach.* New York: Brunner/Mazel.

Menninger, K. (1938). *Man against himself.* New York: Harcourt, Brace & World.

Miller, A. (1981). *Prisoners of childhood: The drama of the gifted child and the search for the true self* (R. Ward, Trans.). New York: Basic Books. (Originally published, 1979.)

Miller, A. (1984). *For your own good: Hidden cruelty in child-rearing and the roots of violence* (2nd ed.) (H. Hannum & H. Hannum, Trans.). New York: Farrar, Straus & Giroux. (Originally published, 1980.)

Miller, A. (1984). *Thou shalt not be aware: Society's betrayal of the child* (H. Hannum & H. Hannum, Trans.). New York: Farrar, Straus & Giroux. (Originally published, 1981.)

Miller, A. (1987). The 12 points. *Mothering, 44,* 24-25.

Minuchin, S. (1974). *Families & family therapy.* Cambridge: Harvard University Press.

Minuchin, S., Rosman, B. L., & Baker, L. (1978). *Psychosomatic families: Anorexia nervosa in context.* Cambridge: Harvard University Press.

Montagu, A. (1986). *Touching: The human significance of the skin* (3rd ed.). New York: Harper & Row.

Morris, D. (1971). *Intimate behaviour.* New York: Random House.

Neubauer, P. B. (Ed.). (1965). *Children in collectives: Child-rearing aims and practices in the kibbutz.* Springfield, IL: Charles C Thomas.

Newberger, C. N., & DeVos, E. (1988). Abuse and victimization: A life-span developmental perspective. *American Journal of Orthopsychiatry, 58,* 505-511.

Ney, P. G., Moore, C., McPhee, J., & Trought, P. (1986). Child abuse: A study of the child's perspective. *Child Abuse and Neglect, 10,* 511-518.

Novey, S. (1955). The role of the superego and ego-ideal in character formation. *International Journal of Psycho-Analysis, 36,* 254-259.

Oaklander, V. (1978). *Windows to our children.* Moab, UT: Real People Press.

Oakley, A. (1972). *Sex, gender, and society.* New York: Harper & Row.

O'Brien, J. D. (1987). The effects of incest on female adolescent development. *Journal of the American Academy of Psychoanalysis, 15*(1), 83-92.

Ogden, T. H. (1982). *Projective identification and psychotherapeutic technique.* New York: Jason Aronson.

Oliver, J. E., & Cox, J. (1973). A family kindred with ill-used children: The burden on the community. *British Journal of Psychiatry, 123,* 81-90.

Oliver, J. E., & Taylor, A. (1971). Five generations of ill-treated children in one family pedigree. *British Journal of Psychiatry, 119,* 473-480.

Pagels, E. (1988). *Adam, Eve, and the serpent.* New York: Random House.

Palazzoli, M. S., Boscolo, L., Cecchin, G., & Prata, G. (1978). *Paradox and counterparadox: A new model in the therapy of the family in schizophrenic transaction* (E. V. Burt, Trans.). New York: Jason Aronson. (Originally published, 1975.)

Parker, G. (1983). *Parental overprotection: A risk factor in psychosocial development.* New York: Grune & Stratton.

Parr, G. (Producer and director). (1984). *Voice therapy with Dr. Robert Firestone* [Video]. Los Angeles: Glendon Association.

Parr, G. (Producer and director). (1985a). *Closeness without bonds: A study of destructive ties in couple relationships* [Video]. Los Angeles: Glendon Association.

Parr, G. (Producer and director). (1985b). *The inner voice in suicide* [Video]. Los Angeles: Glendon Association.

Parr, G. (Producer and director). (1985c). *Microsuicide: A case study* [Video]. Los Angeles: Glendon Association.

Parr, G. (Producer and director). (1985d). *Sex and pregnancy* [Video]. Los Angeles: Glendon Association.

Parr, G. (Producer and director). (1985e). *Teaching our children about feelings* [Video]. Los Angeles: Glendon Association.

Parr, G. (Producer and director). (1986). *The inner voice in child abuse* [Video]. Los Angeles: Glendon Association.

Parr, G. (Producer and director). (1987a). *Hunger vs. love: A perspective on parent-child relations* [Video]. Los Angeles: Glendon Association.

Parr, G. (Producer and director). (1987b). *Parental ambivalence* [Video]. Los Angeles: Glendon Association.

Parr, G. (Producer and director). (1987c). *Therapeutic child-rearing: An in-depth approach to compassionate parenting* [Video]. Los Angeles: Glendon Association.

Parr, G. (Producer and director). (1988a). *Teenagers talk about suicide* [Video]. Los Angeles: Glendon Association.

Parr, G. (Producer and director). (1988b). *The implicit pain of sensitive child-rearing* [Video]. Los Angeles: Glendon Association.

Partridge, S. E. (1988). The parental self-concept: A theoretical exploration and practical application. *American Journal of Orthopsychiatry, 58*(2), 281-287.

Pfeffer, C. R. (1986). *The suicidal child.* New York: Guilford Press.

Planned Parenthood. (1986). *How to talk with your child about sexuality.* New York: Doubleday.

Rabin, A. I. (1958). Infants and children under conditions of "intermittent" mothering in the kibbutz. *American Journal of Orthopsychiatry, 28*, 577-586.

Rabin, A. I. (1965). *Growing up in the kibbutz.* New York: Springer Publishing.

Rabin, A. I., & Beit-Hallahmi, B. (1982). *Twenty years later: Kibbutz children grown up.* New York: Springer Publishing.

Rapaport, D. (1951). Toward a theory of thinking. In *Organization and pathology of thought* (D. Rapaport, Trans.) (pp. 689-730). New York: Columbia University Press.

Reik, T. (1941). *Masochism in modern man* (M. H. Beigel & G. M. Kurth, Trans.). New York: Farrar, Straus & Co.

Rheingold, J. C. (1964). *The fear of being a woman: A theory of maternal destructiveness.* New York: Grune & Stratton.

Rheingold, J. C. (1967). *The mother, anxiety, and death: The catastrophic death complex.* Boston: Little, Brown.

Rich, A. (1976). *Of woman born: Motherhood as experience and institution.* New York: W. W. Norton.

Richman, J. (1986). *Family therapy for suicidal people.* New York: Springer Publishing.

Ricks, M. H. (1985). The social transmission of parental behavior: Attachment across generations. *Monographs of the Society for Research in Child Development, 50*(1-2, Serial No. 209), 211-227.

Robertson, J., & Robertson, J. (1971). Young children in brief separation: A fresh look. In *The Psychoanalytic Study of the Child*, Vol. 26, pp. 264-315). New York: Quadrangle Books.

Rocklin, R., & Lavett, D. K. (1987). Those who broke the cycle: Therapy with non-abusive adults who were physically abused as children. *Psychotherapy, 24*(4), 769-778.

Rohner, R. P. (1986). *The warmth dimension: Foundations of parental acceptance-rejection theory.* Beverly Hills, CA: Sage Publications.

Rosberg, J., & Karon, B. P. (1959). A direct analytic contribution to the understanding of postpartum psychosis. *The Psychiatric Quarterly, 33*(2), 296-304.

Rosen, J. N. (1953). *Direct analysis: Selected papers.* New York: Grune & Stratton.

Rosenbaum, M., & Richman, J. (1970). Suicide: The role of hostility and death wishes from the family and significant others. *American Journal of Psychiatry, 126*(11), 128-131.

Rosenfeld, A. (1978, April 1). The "elastic mind" movement: Rationalizing child neglect? *Saturday Review,* pp. 26-28.

Rubenstein, M. (1987). *The growing years: A guide to your child's emotional development from birth to adolescence.* New York: Atheneum.

Rutter, M. (1981). *Maternal deprivation reassessed* (2nd ed.). Harmondsworth, England: Penguin Books.

Sabbath, J. C. (1969). The suicidal adolescent: The expendable child. *Journal of the American Academy of Child Psychiatry, 8,* 272-289.

Sager, C. J., & Hunt, B. (1979). *Intimate partners: Hidden patterns in love relationships.* New York: McGraw-Hill.

Sandler, J. (1985). *The analysis of defense: The ego and the mechanisms of defense revisited.* New York: International Universities Press.

Sandler, J. (1987). The concept of superego. In J. Sandler (Ed.), *From safety to superego: Selected papers of Joseph Sandler* (pp. 17-44). London: Karnac Books. (Originally published, 1960.)

Sarafino, E. P. (1979). An estimate of nationwide incidence of sexual offenses against children. *Child Welfare, 58*(2), 127-134.

Satir, V. (1983). *Conjoint family therapy* (3rd ed.). Palo Alto, CA: Science and Behavior Books.

Schorr, L. B. (1988). *Within our reach: Breaking the cycle of disadvantage.* New York: Anchor Press.

Schreiber, F. R. (1984). *The shoemaker: The anatomy of a psychotic.* Harmondsworth, England: Penguin Books. (Originally published, 1983.)

Schulz, C. G., & Kilgalen, R. K. (1969). *Case studies in schizophrenia.* New York: Basic Books.

Sechehaye, M. A. (1951). *Symbolic realization: A new method of psychotherapy applied to a case of schizophrenia* (Monograph Series on Schizophrenia No. 2) (B. Wursten & H. Wursten, Trans.). New York: International Universities Press.

Seiden, R. H. (1965). Salutary effects of maternal separation. *Social Work, 10*(4), 25-29.

Seiden, R. H. (1984). Death in the West: A regional analysis of the youthful suicide rate. *Western Journal of Medicine, 140*(6), 969-973.

Shearer, S. L., & Herbert, C. A. (1987). Long-term effects of unresolved sexual trauma. *American Family Physician, 36*(4), 169-175.

Sherfey, M. J. (1966). *The nature and evolution of female sexuality.* New York: Random House.

Silver, L. B., Dublin, C. C., & Lourie, R. S. (1969). Does violence breed violence? Contributions from a study of the child abuse syndrome. *American Journal of Psychiatry, 126,* 404-407.

Silverberg, W. V. (1952). *Childhood experience and personal destiny: A psychoanalytic theory of neurosis.* New York: Springer Publishing.

Skinner, B. F. (1938). *The behavior of organisms: An experimental analysis.* New York: Appleton-Century-Crofts.

Skinner, B. F. (1953). *Science and human behavior.* New York: Macmillan.

Speece, M. W., & Brent, S. B. (1984). Children's understanding of death: A review of three components of a death concept. *Child Development, 55,* 1671-1686.

Spitz, R. A. (1946). *Grief: A peril in infancy* [Film]. New York: New York University Film Library.

Spitz, R. A. (1950). Anxiety in infancy: A study of its manifestations in the first year of life. *International Journal of Psycho-Analysis, 31,* 138-143.

Spitz, R. A. (1965). *The first year of life: A psychoanalytic study of normal and deviant development of object relations.* New York: International Universities Press.

Spock, B. (1976). *Baby and child care* (rev. ed.). New York: Pocket Books.

Srole, L., Langner, T. S., Michael, S. T., & Opler, M. K. (1962). *Mental health in the metropolis: The midtown Manhattan study.* New York: McGraw-Hill.

Sroufe, L. A., & Ward, M. J. (1980). Seductive behavior of mothers of toddlers: Occurrence, correlates, and family origins. *Child Development, 51,* 1222-1229.

Steele, B. F. (1986). Child abuse. In A. Rothstein (Ed.), *The reconstruction of trauma: Its significance in clinical work* (pp. 59-72) (Workshop Series of the American Psychoanalytic Association, Monograph 2). Madison, CT: International Universities Press.

Steele, B. F., & Pollock, C. B. (1974). A psychiatric study of parents who abuse infants and small children. In R. E. Helfer & C. H. Kempe (Eds.), *The battered child* (2nd ed., pp. 89-133). Chicago: University of Chicago Press.

Stern, D. N. (1985). *The interpersonal world of the infant: A view from psychoanalysis and developmental psychology.* New York: Basic Books.

Stewart, A. (1953). Excessive crying in infants: A family disease. In M. J. E. Senn (Ed.), *Problems of infancy and childhood: Transactions of the Sixth Conference, March 17 and 18, 1952, New York, N. Y.* (pp. 138-160). New York: Josiah Macy, Jr. Foundation.

Stoller, R. J. (1975). *Perversion: The erotic form of hatred.* New York: Dell Publishing.

Storr, A. (1968). *Human aggression.* London: Allen Lane/The Penguin Press.

Stratton, P. (Ed.). (1982). *Psychobiology of the human newborn.* Chichester, England: John Wiley & Sons Ltd.

Strauss, J. S., Bowers, M., Downey, T. W., Fleck, S., Jackson, S., & Levine, I. (Eds.). (1980). *The psychotherapy of schizophrenia.* New York: Plenum Medical.

Suitor, J. J. (1987). Mother-daughter relations when married daughters return to school: Effects of status similarity. *Journal of Marriage and the Family, 49,* 435-444.

Sullivan, H. S. (1931). The modified psychoanalytic treatment of schizophrenia. *American Journal of Psychiatry, 11,* 519-540.

Sullivan, H. S. (1940). *Conceptions of modern psychiatry.* New York: W. W. Norton.

Sullivan, H. S. (1953). *The interpersonal theory of psychiatry.* New York: W. W. Norton.

Sullivan, H. S. (1962). *Schizophrenia as a human process.* New York: W. W. Norton.

Szalai, A. (Ed.). (1972). *The use of time: Daily activities of urban and suburban populations in twelve countries.* The Hague, Netherlands: Mouton.

Tansey, M. H., & Burke, W. F. (1985). Projective identification and the empathic process. *Contemporary Psychoanalysis, 21*(1), 42-69.

Tong, L., Oates, K., & McDowell, M. (1987). Personality development following sexual abuse. *Child Abuse and Neglect, 11,* 371-383.

Tronick, E. Z., Cohn, J., & Shea, E. (1986). The transfer of affect between mothers and infants. In T. B. Brazelton & M. W. Yogman (Eds.), *Affective development in infancy* (pp. 11-25). Norwood, NJ: Ablex Publishing.

Vergote, A. (1988). *Guilt and desire: Religious attitudes and their pathological derivatives* (M. H. Wood, Trans.). New Haven: Yale University Press. (Originally published, 1978.)

Wallis, C. (1987, October 12). Back off, buddy. *Time*, pp. 68-73.

Watzlawick, P., Beavin, J. H., & Jackson, D. D. (1967). *Pragmatics of human communication: A study of interactional patterns, pathologies, and paradoxes.* New York: W. W. Norton.

Wegscheider, S. (1981). *Another chance: Hope and health for the alcoholic family.* Palo Alto, CA: Science and Behavior Books.

Weigert, E. (1970). *The courage to love: Selected papers of Edith Weigert, M.D.* New Haven: Yale University Press.

Weiss, F. (1986). Body-image disturbances among obese adults: Evaluation and treatment. *American Journal of Psychotherapy, 40*(4), 521-542.

Westen, D. (1986). The superego: A revised developmental model. *Journal of the American Academy of Psychoanalysis, 14*(2), 181-202.

Wexler, J., & Steidl, J. (1978). Marriage and the capacity to be alone. *Psychiatry, 41*, 72-82.

Whitaker, C. A., & Malone, T. P. (1953). *The roots of psychotherapy.* New York: Brunner/Mazel.

Wilkie, C. F., & Ames, E. W. (1986). The relationship of infant crying to parental stress in the transition to parenthood. *Journal of Marriage and the Family, 48*, 545-550.

Willi, J. (1982). *Couples in collusion: The unconscious dimension in partner relationships* (W. Inayat-Khan & M. Tchorek, Trans.). Claremont, CA: Hunter House. (Originally published, 1975.)

Wilson, J. Q. & Herrnstein, R. J. (1985). *Crime and human nature.* New York: Simon & Schuster.

Winnicott, D. W. (1958). *Collected papers: Through paediatrics to psycho-analysis.* London: Tavistock Publications.

Winnicott, D. W. (1986). *Home is where we start from: Essays by a psychoanalyst.* New York: W. W. Norton.

Wynne, L. C. (1972). Communication disorders and the quest for relatedness in families of schizophrenics. In C. J. Sager & H. S. Kaplan (Eds.), *Progress in group and family therapy* (pp. 595-615). New York: Brunner/Mazel. (Originally published, 1970.)

Zigler, E. (1980). Controlling child abuse: Do we have the knowledge and/or the will? In G. Gerbner, C. J. Ross, & E. Zigler (Eds.), *Child abuse: An agenda for action* (pp. 3-32). New York: Oxford University Press.

Zilboorg, G. (1931). Depressive reactions related to parenthood. *American Journal of Psychiatry, 10*(6), 927-962.

Zilboorg, G. (1932). Sidelights on parent-child antagonism. *American Journal of Orthopsychiatry, 2*(1), 35-43.

Index